LEADERSHIP
Multidisciplinary
Perspectives

D1507683

edited by
Barbara Kellerman
Fairleigh Dickinson University

with a foreword by
James MacGregor Burns

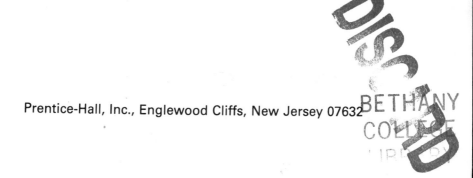

Prentice-Hall, Inc., Englewood Cliffs, New Jersey 07632

Library of Congress Cataloging in Publication Data
Main entry under title:

Leadership : multidisciplinary perspectives.

   Includes bibliographical references and index.
      1. Leadership—Addresses, essays, lectures.
I. Kellerman, Barbara.
HM141.L396   1984   303.3'4   83-13899
ISBN 0-13-527671-3

Editorial/production supervision and
   interior design: Virginia M. Livsey
Cover design: Ben Santora
Manufacturing buyer: Ronald Chapman

To my mother, Ellen Kellerman

Doch da bist du entgegen gekommen,
Und ach, was da in deinem Aug geschwommen,
Das war die susse, lang gesuchte Liebe.

                              Heinrich Heine

Printed in the United States of America

10 9 8 7 6 5 4 3 2 1

ISBN 0-13-527671-3

Prentice-Hall International, Inc., *London*
Prentice-Hall of Australia Pty. Limited, *Sydney*
Editora Prentice-Hall do Brasil, Ltda., *Rio de Janeiro*
Prentice-Hall Canada Inc., *Toronto*
Prentice-Hall of India Private Limited, *New Delhi*
Prentice-Hall of Japan, Inc., *Tokyo*
Prentice Hall of Southeast Asia Pte. Ltd., *Singapore*
Whitehall Books Limited, *Wellington, New Zealand*

CONTENTS

FOREWORD

James MacGregor Burns

To turn these pages is to be reminded again of the continuing impact of the classic work of the Greek philosophers, of Weber and Simmel, of Lasswell and Erikson, and of others who have made the study of leadership such a rich and creative area. To peruse the chapter bibliographies is to recognize again the important work of more recent analysts—scholars such as McFarland and Janda and Bass, Jennings and Hollander, Paige and Tucker, and a host of others, along with authors of contributions to this volume.

Much of the recent work on leadership, as reflected in this collection, consists of clarification of earlier concepts and discarding of inadequate ones. Thus we are no longer constrained by the man-on-horseback theory of leadership (the hero seemed linked only to his horse), by the old "traits approach" to leadership, by the "gee whiz" aspects of the theory of charisma. We recognize, I believe, that leadership is interpersonal, that leaders cannot be seen in isolation from followers, that the linkage between the two embraces the dynamics of wants and needs and other motivations, that leadership is largely a teaching process beginning with the parental nurturing of children, that creative leadership is closely related to conflict and crisis or at least to debate and dialogue, and that—above all—transforming leadership carries grave but not always recognized moral implications.

I am, perhaps, a bit more optimistic than editor Kellerman as to the state of the discipline. I believe an enormous mass of data has been accumulated in both the large-scale studies that have been conducted and in a vast array of specialized investigations, though this mass may not yet be a "critical" one. Glenn Paige's comprehensive and penetrating bibliographical study of leadership attests to this. Nor have we been lacking in concepts and definitions to any greater degree than many other fields of study, though here again we still lack a widely accepted parsimonious and rigorous (if not elegant) "general theory" of leadership. I agree in any case with Professor Kellerman that progress has been impeded by dissimilar frames of reference, and indeed one of the great values of this volume is its effort to transcend individual disciplines.

The problem is that no field of study calls for a more difficult and daring crossing of disciplinary borders than does the study of leadership, and no field suffers more from narrow specialization. Thus the long absorption of social psychologists in small-group leadership studies produced a vast accumulation of data that were both a stimulus to further analysis and a burden on it. In my own work as a practicing historian, I have found difficulty in applying psychological, including psychoanalytical, concepts to explanations of the personality and behavior of major figures, especially in broad historical studies that cover many leaders in many eras, but I am heartened by Bruce Mazlish's lucid treatment of the problem below, and especially by his conclusion that historians can supply depth of context and a sense of development and change.

Markedly lacking in work on leadership, in my view, is both empirical and theoretical follow-up that would explicate, expand, validate, or perhaps invalidate major work that has already been published in the field. Perhaps I may offer my own study of leadership as an example. I have advanced a concept that stresses the interrelationship of leadership initiatives and the raising of followers' consciousness and of followers' responsiveness in terms of hierarchies of wants, needs, hopes, expectations and demands, as well as values; the human and moral implications of helping followers rise to higher levels of moral development and the consequences in turn for their leaders; the role in all this of the processes of confrontation and conflict; and the consequences for better understanding of the nature of social change and historical causation. Yet much of this had to be conceptualized rather than fully analyzed or, certainly, proved. I, and I presume many of my co-workers in this particular vineyard, must hope that younger scholars are coming forward to conduct the empirical analysis, and even pick up the work of the Lasswells and the Maslows and to carry on the pioneering studies of the Kohlbergs and the Eriksons—and such hopes are lifted by the impressive studies offered in this work.

But the problem of the "general theory" of leadership remains. The vast and diverse empirical work in leadership will continue here and abroad, but it may swell rather than flower in the absence of continued central theoretical work of broad proportions and yet rigorous quality. A summons here to more and better "grand theory" would be mere rhetoric. What we need is not only more and better general theorists of leadership in the various disciplines but also a place for them to study, to interact, to think, and to write. What we need is an Institute for the Advanced Study of Leadership, and let us hope that some person who has been preaching and exemplifying leadership through life—or the friends or heirs of such a person—will establish such an institution in this country or abroad, as an act of *intellectual* leadership in the face of the dire challenges to moral and political leadership in the coming decade and the next century.

INTRODUCTORY REMARKS

Barbara Kellerman

Leadership has been a subject of contemplation and debate at least since the Golden Age of Greece. Yet in his book *Leadership,* James MacGregor Burns was able to write that "leadership is one of the most observed and least understood phenomena on earth." And indeed, although there is a small body of literature that addresses what leadership ought and ought not to be, there is surprisingly little on what leadership *is.* The work that exists in this area tends to be prescriptive rather than descriptive.

Exactly why leadership has been so inadequately explored is not clear. But there is little doubt that it has always been outside the academic mainstream. My own discipline, political science, which would seem to have as a central concern issues of direction, power, and authority, has remained curiously aloof from what most people think of when they hear the word *leadership: political* leadership. With some notable exceptions to be sure, political scientists have been reluctant to investigate what motivates the interactions between leaders and led, what accounts for the variations among them, or even to describe precisely the different types of leaders and leadership processes.

It should be noted that within the last decades social psychologists and organization theorists have done some excellent empirical work in the area. In particular they have studied leadership in small groups and leadership in large organizations. Nevertheless, as this relatively narrow range of investigators would seem to suggest, there has never been a broadly based, sustained effort to fully describe and explain this complex phenomenon. Even among those interested in some of the same questions, there has been little or nothing in the way of collaborative work. In short there is, as yet, no critical mass of materials on leadership. And we are not even close to the construction of a metatheory of leadership that would span time, cultures, and circumstances.

Why is it that that which is so manifestly important has been so little studied? With regard to contemporary scholarship, perhaps the most obvious problem is the widespread confusion about definitions of terms. Quite simply, there is no agreement on what the key words mean.

Consider the following:

1) What is leadership? Getting people to follow. How many people? All the people all the time? By what means and to which ends? Is force a legitimate leadership tool?

2) Where is leadership exercised? In politics. But of course not all leadership takes place in the public sector, nor is the state the only unit with a leader at the head. Corporate (economic) leadership then? Religious (moral) leadership? Interpersonal leadership?

3) Who is the leader? The leader is the one who holds the highest office. Or is the leader the one with the most personal power or influence? Is the leader at the forefront? Or does the true leader in fact take cues from the led?
4) And who are the led? The led are most of us, at least some of the time. When? Under what circumstances?

Clearly, at this point, terms such as *leader* and *leadership* mean different things to different people. They also mean different things to different fields. In the administrative sciences, for example, the word *leader,* and the more pedestrian word *manager,* are often used interchangeably. But in psychoanalytic theory the *leader,* by definition, is someone of considerable drama: a powerful father figure who watches over us, and whom we need and want to look up to. To social psychologists the leader is typically the one with the most personal influence, while to political scientists the leader is the one who occupies the position or fills the role that allows him or her to wield the greatest power.

I am simplifying somewhat, but in fact the point can be stretched still further. For not only can the key words in Leadership Studies mean something quite different, depending on who uses them, but the frames of reference are also dissimilar. Cases in point: Anthropologists analyze leadership by taking a cross-cultural perspective; political scientists are interested in how constituted leaders function within particular nations or states; social psychologists consider leadership as an interpersonal process that can take place between as few as two people; and organization theorists are interested in how those few who are high on the bureaucratic ladder do, can, and ought to manage the many who are further down. Moreover, the frame of reference is not necessarily a traditional academic discipline. It can be a particular group or setting—for example, patterns of leadership among adolescent boys, or in American universities.

Because the terms and contexts lack consistency, and because different disciplines encourage us to ask different questions, it follows that, with regard to leadership, the major concern of one scholar may be of little or even no import to the work of another. The philosopher is interested in ethics: What makes good leadership—for the led as well as for the leader? But ethical questions are of no practical significance to the sociologist whose primary task is to describe how collectives function in the real world, or to the political scientist who inquires exactly how those in charge conduct the public business. Consider the question of the leader as an agent of sociopolitical change. To some of the authors in this book it is crucial. To others it simply does not apply.

I would argue that this lack of a common language tells us much about why leadership has been so little explored. The problem is actually twofold. First, the major terms have never been defined so that they are clear to all who would employ them. Second and more important, the individual dis-

ciplines, because they inevitably focus on their own questions and conceptualizations, are simply too narrowly based to undertake a broad enough
investigation. As much as anything else that comes to mind, leadership is
a subject that demands an interdisciplinary approach. It has been our
inability to recognize the need for a multidisciplinary and even cross-cultural effort that has fostered our persistent ignorance in this truly critical
area.

This book is a first requisite step toward cooperative work in Leadership Studies. It is the first to provide interested students as well as practitioners with a comprehensive range of perspectives on the interactions
between those labeled leaders and those labeled followers. As such it serves
as both an introduction to the subject and as a forum for related ideas that
may be expected to stimulate more advanced discussion and study.

Despite all the above-mentioned differences in language and approach, there is profound agreement among the diverse contributors to
this volume on at least three key points:

1) Leadership has to do with no less significant a matter than with how people
   in groups organize themselves.
2) Leadership is concerned with issues of dominance and deference that are
   endemic to virtually all living things.
3) Knowing more about leadership will enable us to better understand our past
   and present and, hopefully, to better manage the future.

This volume consists of a series of original essays by scholars from
different disciplines, and with different areas of expertise, each of whom
has thought a good deal about the ways in which his or her field considers
leadership issues. It is a self-contained work that presents an overarching
view of leadership from those disciplinary perspectives that particularly
apply.

Part One—Overviews—consists of eight chapters that contain broad
discussions of the ways in which particular fields consider leadership issues,
as well as original analyses and commentary. Each of the authors was asked
to address some of the following questions in light of their area of expertise:
What is leadership? What does that imply about followership? How does
your particular discipline think about leadership questions? Does it address
the issue of causation? Is the moral dimension an imperative? What does
your field have to say about leadership and the nature of man? Does your
discipline offer any particular theoretical and/or methodological approaches to leadership questions?

The discussion begins with an investigation of how leadership has
been understood by those whose task may be described as keeping us from
being condemned to repeat our past: historians. It moves on to a psychoanalytic consideration of why it is that leadership phenomena have

undergirded group life everywhere and, from what we know, always. This is followed by an anthropological exploration of leadership across time and place, an uncovering of the various leadership systems as they have emerged in different world cultures. The next three chapters look at the ways in which three fields that would seem to have leadership questions at the core—political science, social psychology, and organizational behavior—have done their best work and organized their most important ideas. Part One concludes with a chapter in which the field itself imposes at least an implicit judgment about what constitutes good leadership. The feminist perspective—which is, incidentally, increasingly regarded as an important corrective to past work in Leadership Studies—suggests that leadership ought to imply authority on *behalf* of, rather than power or authority *over*.

Part Two—Viewpoints—differs from Part One in the balance each of the authors strikes between an overview of the field, and a personal response to a particular question. The authors in this section, while grounding their work in their discipline, have chosen to focus either on a narrower problem, or they have taken a bold stance with regard to the way in which their discipline might most fruitfully consider leadership issues. The discussion in Part Two begins with the assertion—rooted in both sociological and psychological materials—that in many cases, "The power and authority in relation to social control customarily attributed to 'leaders' is largely illusory. . . ." It moves on to a piece that takes the opposite tack: it illustrates how as few as two people can play key roles in doing no less than transforming the cultural sensibilities of an age. This is followed by an essay which explores how different people make meaning of leadership, or the exercise of authority. Another political scientist has a say in the next chapter; the problem considered here is the mental health of constituted leaders who have increasing responsibility for public decisions, and growing control over weapons of mass destruction. The philosopher has the last word: he outlines what some would label an ideal of leadership, although it is presented here as a model to be emulated by ordinary people functioning in the routine circumstances of daily life.

The eclectic quality of this book represents the coming together of isolated ideas that are, in fact, related, and that must be brought to bear on each other if we are to attain an increased understanding of leadership phenomena. Specifically, the intention is to encourage a body of work in Leadership Studies that:

—demonstrates a heightened awareness of differences in the relevant terms, contexts, levels of analysis, values, and hidden agendas;

—is deep in that it spans the various levels of analysis including individual, group, organization, and society;

—is broad in that it integrates at least the historical, anthropological, psychological, political, and sociological perspectives as they are represented in this book;

—attends to the need—in this area perhaps above all—to break down the boundary between theory and practice.

I said earlier that leadership—as manifested in all aspects of the human condition—has been inadequately explored. The evidence suggests, however, that this neglect is starting to give way. Perhaps it is a sense of peril, fragility or uncertainty that impels us; whatever the cause, leadership is increasingly recognized as a subject that demands the most careful attention. This book is for the rapidly growing number of students of the subject—from the academy and the professions, from the public and private sectors—in the hope that on this topic at least, what is learned can be applied for the individual and collective benefit of us all.

CONTRIBUTORS

BARBARA KELLERMAN is Associate Professor at the Institute for Leadership Studies at Fairleigh Dickinson University. She received her Ph.D. in Political Science from Yale University. Kellerman is the author of numerous articles on leadership, the presidency, and decision making. She coauthored *Making Decisions*, and authored *All the President's Kin*. She is also the author of the forthcoming book, *The Political Presidency: A Theory of Leadership*.

JAMES MACGREGOR BURNS is Woodrow Wilson Professor of Political Science at Williams College. He received his Ph.D. in Political Science from Harvard University. Among Burns's many books are *Roosevelt: The Soldier of Freedom*, *Leadership*, and, most recently, *The Vineyard of Liberty*.

SUSAN J. CARROLL is Assistant Professor of Political Science at Rutgers University and Senior Research Associate at the Center for the American Woman and Politics at the Eagleton Institute of Politics. Carroll received her Ph.D. in Political Science from Indiana University. She has participated in a wide range of activities concerned with women and politics and she is the author of a forthcoming book on women candidates.

MARTIN M. CHEMERS is Professor and Chairman of the Department of Psychology at the University of Utah. He received his Ph.D. in Psychology from the University of Illinois. Chemers is the author of numerous articles and chapters, especially on small-group leadership. He is coauthor of several books, among them *Leadership and Effective Management* and *Improving Leadership Effectiveness: The Leader Match Concept*.

MELVYN A. HILL is Associate Professor at the Institute for Leadership Studies of Fairleigh Dickinson University. He has a doctoral degree from the Committee on Social Thought of the University of Chicago as well as a Ph.D. in Clinical Psychology from York University in Toronto. Hill is editor of *Hannah Arendt: The Recovery of the Public World* and the coauthor of *Working through Narcissism* and *The Concept of the Ego in Psychoanalysis*. He has a private practice in psychoanalysis.

JAMES G. HUNT is Professor and Area Coordinator of Management, College of Business Administration, Texas Tech University. He received his Ph.D. in Business and Psychology from the University of Illinois. He has coauthored many books, including *Managing Organizational Behavior*, *Organization Theory: An Integrated Approach* and *A Multiple Influence Model of Leadership*. He established the Leadership Symposia Series and has coedited the volumes in the series, currently seven in number.

SONJA M. HUNT is Associate Professor at the Institute for Leadership Studies of Fairleigh Dickinson University. She received her Ph.D. in Psychology from Manchester University, England. She has written widely, especially on the psychological and sociological aspects of health care, and she is coauthor of *Individual Development and Social Experience*.

LEONARD GROB is Associate Professor at the Institute for Leadership Studies of Fairleigh Dickinson University. He received his Ph.D. in Philosophy from Pennsylvania State University. His areas of special interest and expertise include Phenomenology and Existentialism. He is currently writing on the relevance of Martin Buber's ideas on dialogue to educational leadership.

ROBERT KEGAN is Lecturer in Education at the Harvard Graduate School of Education, a member of the Core Faculty of the Massachusetts School of Professional Psychology, and Co-director of the Clinical Developmental Institute. He received an interdisciplinary Ph.D. from the Harvard Graduate School of Arts and Sciences. Kegan has published numerous articles and chapters on life span psychology and he is the author of, most recently, *The Evolving Self: Problems and Process in Human Development.*

LISA LASKOW LAHEY is a doctoral candidate in Human Development at the Harvard Graduate School of Education.

BRUCE MAZLISH is Professor in the Department of the Humanities at the Massachusetts Institute of Technology. He received his Ph.D. in History from Columbia University. Among Mazlish's many books are *In Search of Nixon, James and John Stuart Mill,* and *The Revolutionary Ascetic.*

STANLEY A. RENSHON is Associate Professor at the City University of New York, Herbert Lehman College and The Graduate School and University Center. He received his Ph.D. in Political Science from the University of Pennsylvania. He has written numerous articles in political psychology, and he is the author of *Psychological Needs and Political Behavior* and the editor of *Handbook of Political Socialization: Theory and Research.*

DAVID M. ROSEN is Assistant Professor at the Institute for Leadership Studies of Fairleigh Dickinson University. He received his Ph.D. in Anthropology from the University of Illinois. He has published several articles on social control, stratification, and education and social reproduction. He is the editor of *Readings in Anthropology.*

MONICA STRAUSS is an Art Historian in New York City. She received her Ph.D. in Art History from the Institute of Fine Arts, New York University. She has published several articles on twentieth-century German art and three exhibition catalogs, most recently *The Bauhaus: Weimar, Dessau, Berlin.*

1

HISTORY, PSYCHOLOGY, AND LEADERSHIP

Bruce Mazlish

Historians, generally, are nontheoretical in inclination. It is not that they don't use theories but, a bit like Molière's gentleman who spoke prose all his life without recognizing the fact, they profess astonishment or pretend to do otherwise. Thus, it is probably preferable to say that, at least until recently, historians have tended to be nonanalytical, that is, they used general theories, but without analyzing them or being explicit about their usage. In this mode, historians have claimed that "telling the story," "wie es eigentlich gewesen [as it actually happened]," is all the theory they need. Narration, not analysis, is the method of choice.

Until recently, then, historians dealing with leadership in their narratives have neither conceptualized it nor thought much about the theories that might underlie an account of it. A new wind, however, has been sweeping through the forest of history, and quantitative and psychological theories, along with sociological ones, are blowing over the traditional narratives. One can now consider with some confidence the subject of leadership in history from a theoretical point of view.

How do historians deal with leadership in their work? What work has been done? How good is it? Do historians pass moral judgments on leaders? These are some of the initial questions to be examined.

The first thing to be said is that historians have always been attracted to the "great man in history" theory. Biography is a major adjunct of history, as is the "cult of personality." What I am calling traditional history, generally devoid of causal analysis other than the account itself, frequently "explained" a whole period or a major event in terms of some leading personality: the Napoleonic period; or World War I (or II) as the result of decisions taken or not taken by individual statesmen.

The "great man in history" approach was often accompanied by a moral judgment. Some historians, it is true, embraced historicism and, immersing themselves in the values of their hero's time, passed no external judgment. Others, conceiving of history as "science," believed it inappropriate to deal at all with moral concerns. Most historians, however, certainly in the eighteenth and probably in the nineteenth century, believed that one task of an historian was to bring the great figures of the past to the bar of historical judgment. History was to "instruct"; it was "philosophy teaching by examples."

Thus, while in general, in the "great man" perspective leaders often took on mythical proportions, they could also turn into villains, as in Lord Acton's work. By the end of the nineteenth and into the early twentieth century, a muckraking tradition also arose, which tilted toward the denigration of the hero in history. Modern efforts at studying leaders psychologically are frequently perceived as being in this tradition. They are seen as "reducing" the leader to his psychic hang-ups, although avoiding an explicit moral judgment; that is, psychology is substituted for morality.

Such an accusation is true to a certain extent. It is said that "no man is a hero to his valet"—and, we can add, to his psychohistorian, in the sense that his weaknesses as well as strengths will be brought alive in an analytic study. As with a child discovering his parent has clay feet, so the reader of psychohistory discovers the frailties of his larger-than-life subject. The full reality is presented to him, and he must integrate the two images, the mixture of good and bad, in the "hero." In short, a kind of "moral" judgment adheres to the psychohistorical study of the leader, the "great man in history," willy-nilly, although, it must be emphasized, in a *very special form.*

In any case, the traditional "great man in history" approach, moral or amoral in intent, is out of favor among historians today. In its place stands the study of masses of people: social history. Such history tends to base itself on explicit theory. It does not attempt to tell a story so much as to analyze demographic, or climatic, or economic, and so forth, factors operating on great numbers of people. It seeks to give a voice to the "dark masses"—the peasants, the workers, the minorities—whose individual names have not emerged from the pages of history.

In principle, then, quantitative and new social history oppose an emphasis on the "great man in history." The mass, not the leader, is the new hero. In fact, however, even the social historians are in the ironic position of discovering that masses are not leaderless, and that it is the interaction of leaders and led that stands at the center of much of historical action. Such interaction is to be studied, admittedly, in new, analytic terms. It is in this guise, then, that the "great man in history" has returned, breathing with fresh vigor.

The next thing to be said is that any historical treatment of leadership must take into account the particular historical context. Leadership in Tsarist Russia cum Soviet Union is obviously different from leadership in a representative democracy, such as America. Periods of charismatic leadership are different from periods of bureaucratic leadership. Historians are especially well equipped to deal, even without much reflection, with the "given" background to their study of leaders, and are least susceptible to the siren call of generalities and typologies that ignore or play down local conditions.

One consequence is that an effort to show how historians deal with leadership in all areas and times—Europe, Asia, the Americas; ancient, medieval, and modern—would require a large book unto itself. I shall more modestly seek here to illuminate the general questions, sketching the main ways the subject has and can be approached in the specific area of American history, which also has the virtue of being "modern" by self-definition.

A few more preliminary statements before we seek to ground our analysis in the actual workings of American historians. In the early twentieth century, two bodies of theory came into being concerned with leadership and leaders. The first was the work of the sociologists. A Robert Michels, a Gaetano Mosca argued that, whatever Marxist or democratic political philosophy might say about rule by the masses, an inexorable law of organizations would prevail: all large institutions quickly settle down to a situation in which power and leadership flow from the top rather than the bottom. This is supposed so for a variety of reasons; one is that the control of communications ends up as the control of organization—and the leaders control communications.

If accepted, and, of course, some scholars will disagree, their theories should have posed a problem for historians dealing with the question of leadership in a representative democracy such as America. It must be admitted, however, that the course of American historiography rolled on, untouched by such foreign, sociological notions. So, too, with the work of Max Weber. While American historians were far more familiar with his ideas about leadership, their applicability to America seemed peripheral, if not remote. We had no charismatic, Napoleonic leaders—Washington even turned down the chance to be a routinized king, let alone a charismatic hero—and our explanations of "organizational man" tended to be home-grown and anecdotal.

The second body of theory, the psychological, has had much more effect in recent times. Our "therapeutic society" seems particularly open to psychological explanations. We have been the most hospitable haven for psychoanalysis. One reason may be that our dominant motif of individualism lends itself to a concern with individual personality. Another may be our heritage of a Puritan concern with self-scrutiny. Either, by itself, might not suffice to account for our psychological absorption. Together, they make for a powerful secular urge: a psychological concern with the "spiritual" health and development of the single individual. Psychoanalytic theory, especially, has aroused the interest of historians in the nature of our leaders, and offered a possible means of understanding them in terms that are sympathetic to our national psyche.

Up to now, at least, such interest has been in leaders, not leadership. The reason has already been adumbrated: historians have tended not to generalize or theorize. This situation is changing; in studying the changed situation, we must ask whether it makes sense to keep talking about "leadership" in general. Or are we really talking about *political* leadership?

Leadership can take many forms—intellectual, artistic, religious, as well as political. When in the late 1960s The American Academy of Arts and Sciences held a conference, whose results were published as a *Daedulus* issue called "Philosophers and Kings,"[1] it tried to take account of this fact. Thus, there were articles on William James and even Charles Merriam, intellectual leaders, as well as one on James Mill, both an intellectual and political leader, along with others on Ataturk, de Gaulle, Bismarck, Nkrumah, and similar political figures. The exceptions merely proved that the study of leadership really centers on the study of political leadership.

Even Erikson's pioneering studies of two great religious figures, Luther and Gandhi, end up dealing with them as great political revolutionary figures. The reason for the above is simple: Literary scholars, for example, do not conceptualize leadership as a relationship between a great poet and his audience, though they may deal with the reality. It is mainly in political science that, at least as seen by historians, leadership appears to be a recognizable area, a subdiscipline with theoretical pretensions, underlined by the effort to accumulate empirical data. The historical wing of political science meets the political wing of historical studies, and historians for the reasons given at the beginning of this article explicitly or implicitly contribute to and draw upon leadership studies.

In what follows, as in what has preceded, therefore, we concentrate, as historians have done, on political leadership, where a structure of power relations—representative democracy with parties, in the American case—exists and can be analyzed. Corporate leadership is a comparable study, so recognized in leadership studies, but not central as is the political to historical studies. Thus, we will pass by such studies as Richard Lebeaux's *Young Man Thoreau*[2] or Anne Jardin's *The First Henry Ford*,[3] noting only that they do contain materials germane to the study of intellectual or corporate leadership. Our focus will be on the political leaders, especially presidents, whose terms of office often supply the periodization utilized by historians.

In sum, we shall strive to study the treatment of leadership, in the specific case of American history, in terms of our general themes, relating context and theory throughout. Our bibliographical survey of work on leaders from prerevolutionary to contemporary times, highly selective, will be undertaken, not for itself, but for heuristic purposes. We shall also look at psychoanalytic theory per se, and then its application to American figures, concentrating especially on Woodrow Wilson. At the end, we shall see if history itself has anything to contribute to the theory of leadership.

PREREVOLUTIONARY AND REVOLUTIONARY LEADERSHIP

Historically speaking, if democracy meant total equality, one might argue that leaders and leadership would be nonexistent subjects in a democratic society. History, however, does not follow logic. Even a Sparta had its Lycurgus. In fact, equality of condition does not preclude leadership, whether arrived at by rotation or election, in war or in peace. Sociologists such as Michels and Mosca appear correct in their assertion that all societies shake down into leader-led structures.

In America, the earliest settlers did not even aim at an equalitarian democracy. Far from it. John Winthrop, probably the first great leader in America, bluntly informed his fellow Puritans in 1630 that God had allotted each individual his unequal place in society; and each was to follow his calling in that place, fulfilling God's purpose, without insubordination. Winthrop, as God's agent, would supply the leadership.

Early colonial American leadership was theocratic: religious leaders were also political leaders (thus anticipating the situation created by the Iranian Revolution, as led by Khomeini). In the Puritan commonwealth, the franchise was restricted to church members, and church and state alike were conceived of as being one part of a single covenant: "We are entered into a covenant" with God, "for this worke," intoned Winthrop, meaning by "worke" the commonwealth. The pulpit was also the seat of political power; the printed sermon the means of exercising leadership, religious and secular.

The proliferation of sects undermined the asserted Erastianism. Puritan theocracy did not last, as we know. After a revolution in 1776 established an independent USA, the new nation settled into a form of representative government which, with relatively minor adjustments, has persisted to the present. This is the context in which leadership in America has been exerted.

At the beginning, in early revolutionary times, there was a widespread belief that in a democracy, even a representative one, unanimity should prevail. George Washington was typical in his distaste for political parties and his belief that leadership should be exercised directly in terms of a general public rather than through a party. Unanimity, he believed, was the sign of correct policy and correct leadership. James Madison and his fellow Federalists knew better. They realized that factions were a necessary part of the human condition in society and that, indeed, a plurality of parties was a necessary condition for freedom. Their view, and the reality of parties, prevailed.

But the myth of the "unanimous" leader continued to flourish. It drew strength from the first "father of his country," George Washington, and the increasingly hagiologic treatment of him, begun in the eighteenth century and immortalized by "Parson" Weems. Mythologized and made Godlike, Washington's leadership of his country was portrayed as patriarchical, uncontested, and self-evident, needing no further explanation. More sober histories followed—and some debunking—but even the best rarely looked at Washington as a *man* whose qualities somehow provided a special kind of leadership for other *men*. Washington was depicted, and often well depicted, but not analyzed in more theoretical terms. Only with James T. Flexner's *George Washington: The Forge of Experience*[4] and Marcus Cunliffe's *George Washington, Man and Monument*[5] do we recognize efforts at a more psychological understanding of the first father's personality and hints at its fit with the psyche and party affiliations of his fellow men.

It should not come as a surprise that historians confront seriously the issue of leadership initially in relation to revolutionary America. Here for the first time a national stage is being constructed. Leadership in colonial America, of course, existed: Divines, such as Cotton Mather, and governors, such as Thomas Hutchinson, exercised power, but on a limited, parochial scale. Revolution calls forth new, and at first, less institutionalized kinds of leadership, and new men to act on the widened stage. In America, these were the Founding Fathers, though even a Hutchinson takes on new importance as a counteractor in the revolutionary drama. (Bernard Bailyn's *The Ordeal of Thomas Hutchinson* addresses him in these terms.)[6]

The Library of Congress, celebrating the revolutionary bicentennial, held a conference on leadership in the American Revolution. The ensuing volume by that name deals with political, intellectual, military, and psychological dimensions of that leadership.[7] As befits historians, most of the pieces are directed to limited, specific subjects rather than to the construction of general theories. Still, the focus is clearly on "leadership." An earlier article, "The Founding Fathers: Young Men of the Revolution," by Stanley Elkins and Earl McKitrick, is more theoretical in intent.[8] The authors' thesis is that the Founding Fathers, that is, the Federalists, pushing for a new nation and a constitutional convention, were of a younger generation than the antirevolutionists and then the antifederalists. The "Fathers" were really rebellious "sons," formed in the crucible of revolution, continental in vision, and desirous of playing parts on a national stage. The particular explanation is inspired by and contributes to a general theory of revolutionary leadership which emphasizes generational and, implictly, psychological factors.

The psychological context in which that leadership was exercised is explored by Edwin G. Burrows and Michael Wallace in "The American Revolution: The Ideology and Psychology of National Liberation."[9] They call attention to the repetitive use of filial images by the future revolutionaries and the need to break the ties binding the colonies to the Mother-Father, Great Britain. Psychological needs cohere to the ideology, which offers a rational platform on which the revolutionary leaders can appeal. Only leaders who "fit" the psychological and ideological bills of the situation will suit the populace, a theme explored further by Bruce Mazlish in his contribution to the Library of Congress Symposium on Leadership.[10]

Historians have written other psychological studies of American revolutionary figures, but these are not overtly connected to an inquiry into the nature and dynamics of leadership. For example, Bernard Bailyn has given us brilliant "miniatures" of Thomas Jefferson and John Adams, generally undernoticed by students of the revolution and of leadership alike.[11] We have already mentioned studies of Washington; Jefferson has called forth even greater attention to his personality, as in the works of Winthrop Jordan *(White Over Black)*[12] and Fawn Brodie *(Thomas Jefferson)*.[13] In these accounts, however, personality is not explicitly connected to the study of leadership, though the essential materials are present.

PSYCHOLOGICAL THEORIES OF LEADERSHIP

Before turning specifically to work on postrevolutionary political leaders, it will be useful to sketch in another piece of background, vital for leadership studies. A brief look at the psychological theories available to and used by historians is in order, so that we may adequately evaluate the specific contributions.

By and large, until the advent of psychoanalysis, the psychology used by historians in dealing with leaders was intuition, or seat-of-the-pants psychology. No explicit theory intruded on the historian's use of empathy (or lack of it). Because psychoanalysis was an historical, developmental psychology, which had the added dimension of dealing with mental life in its unconscious as well as conscious dynamics, it offered an appealing alternative. Freud, of course, was the founder of psychoanalysis. His original theory used a drive model: libidinal and aggressive energy, in a closed system, seeking satisfaction and, if denied direct satisfaction, manifesting itself in repressed, sublimated, symptomatic, and other such forms. It is this Freudian model that historians have been prone to use in their work.

Since the 1940s, however, there has been an explosive development of theories and data within psychoanalysis itself, and the challenge to historians has been to master this recent work and to apply it to their studies of leaders. After all, if historians in significant numbers are finally resorting to theory, they must be familiar with the latest efforts.

The first thing to note is that historians have tended to stick closer to orthodox Freudian notions than have political scientists. The latter have been inspired initially by Alfred Adler's ideas—the line leads from Harold Lasswell, through the Georges, to James David Barber—with their emphasis on power relations, and de-emphasis of sexual factors. Adler had spoken in terms of inferiority and superiority complexes. Political scientists developed these notions into a theory of "personality and politics." Lasswell, for example, devised a formula, p) d) r = P, in which private motives, such as feelings of low self-esteem (p), are displaced onto a public object (d), and rationalized (r) into the public interest (P = political man). Alexander George spoke of "Power as a Compensatory Value for Political Leaders," while Barber, in turn, tried to establish a typology of presidential leadership, the now famous active/passive, positive/negatives axes, building on their work.

Historians, though increasingly uneasy with Freud's id orientation, either because materials on the first five to six years of life are generally missing from the historical record or, more importantly, because the "social" component—the superego aspects—seems pushed aside or reduced in significance, have not been much impressed with Adler. They have looked to other, more faithful disciples of Freud. Foremost of these has been Erik H. Erikson, whose work is too well known to need detailing here. Briefly, Erikson's genius was to retain the Freudian emphasis, but to add the claims of ego and superego in historically relevant fashion, and to focus on an identity crisis whose dimensions were more available in the historical records, for example, through adolescent diaries, journals, accounts, acting out, and so forth.*

With Erikson in the 1950s and 1960s the new subdiscipline of psychohistory took root in the profession and blossomed. The paraphernalia of a recognized field appeared: formal academic courses; professional journals, such as *The Psychohistorical Review* and *The Journal of Psychohistory;* and

---

*For a discussion related to this and the preceding paragraph, *see also* Kellerman's chapter.

associations such as The Group for the Study of Psychology in History, affiliated to the AHA.

Erikson's own emphasis on the study of "second fathers" as well as "rebellious sons" merged directly with considerations of leadership, and he himself wrote specifically on followership, and disciples, as parts of the great man's mission. Further, Erikson's theory of psychosexual stages—his famous eight stages of the life cycle—gave historians a developmental scheme which accorded with their historical sense of the way in which a great man's leadership changed over time.

Meanwhile, within psychoanalysis itself, a new development—object relations theory—was taking its place alongside ego psychology. Starting a quarter of a century ago in the work of Melanie Klein and British analysts such as Winnicott and Balint, this model put the emphasis elsewhere than on drives. Object relations theory postulates that the nursing infant at first fuses the image of itself and its mother, and then separates the two at a later stage into an internal self-image and an object image of its mother. Pleasurable feelings in the parenting interaction lead to "good" object images and the opposite to "bad" images. The emphasis is on the formation of a stable and "good" self, as against the classical Freudian focus on psychosexual stages of drive satisfaction.

More recently, the "hot" subject, drawing on object relations theory, is narcissism. As a clinical concept narcissism has almost as many definitions as there are practitioners in the field. At its core, however, is the narcissist's feeling of an insecure self, which may split or fragment at any moment. Self-love tends to mask self-hate. We have noted that Erikson popularized the concept of identity, where the identity question is "Who am I?" Now the self-question is "Am I?" In the individual, presumably as well as in the culture, it is asserted that there is a pervasive sense of emptiness and lack of cohesion. (One effort to explore the cultural context for the presumed increase in narcissistic disorders is Christopher Lasch's *The Culture of Narcissism;*[14] but *see* Bruce Mazlish's "American Narcissism"[15] for a critical evaluation.)

Closely aligned with narcissistic psychology per se are two related developments: borderline conditions, as studied especially by Otto Kernberg, and self-psychology, as elaborated by Heinz Kohut. Both may be seen as different versions of a central concern with narcissism.

Now the effect of these different developments in psychoanalytic theory is still very much in process, with historians just beginning to react to the more recent theories. Barely able to take in the theories of Freud and Erikson, the craft is now being asked to cope with the very demanding elaborations of a Winnicott, a Kernberg, or a Kohut. One of the few historians who, along with his collaborator, the sociologist Gerald Platt, has tried to deal with the theoretical consequences of the new work, has been

Fred Weinstein. In the joint work *Psychoanalytic Sociology*,[16] and in his own exemplification of it, *The Dynamics of Nazism*,[17] Weinstein has argued that pre-object relations theory has been unable to deal adequately with what is most vital to the historian's concerns: group phenomena rather than individual life histories. Only the use, Weinstein contends, of some form of object relations theory allows the historian to understand the psychological dynamics of movements drawing on heterogeneous followers.

Weinstein's and Platt's theoretical challenge can be expected to have increasing effect on the work of future psychohistorians. Kohut's work is already having such effect, as we shall show shortly. As we move now to a consideration of specific work in which political leadership is a central issue, we shall bear in mind the spectrum of psychoanalytical theories that play over the historian's exercise of his art cum science in this new subdiscipline.

A CASE STUDY:
WOODROW WILSON

American presidential leadership is a central part of general leadership studies. By accident or design, more sustained work on the psychological dimensions of Woodrow Wilson has been done than on any other president; and he serves us well as a case study in the various psychological approaches available for use, the lineaments of which we have just briefly tried to discern.

The first entry in this literature is the sketch penned by the economist John Maynard Keynes, in *The Economic Consequences of the Peace*.[18] Keynes, in his chapter "The Conference," gave a penetrating portrait of the American president at Versailles. As he remarked, the question as to Wilson's behavior there "is difficult and depends on elements of character and psychology." He concludes "In the language of medical psychology, to suggest to the President that the Treaty was an abandonment of his professions was to touch on the raw a Freudian complex." Though well aware of Freud's work, Keynes did not use it in any technical sense, but depended on his own intuition and a keen eye, along with firsthand, though short, acquaintance. It is a superb piece of work.

In the 1930s another work on Wilson was commenced. Its authors, Sigmund Freud and William Bullitt, like Keynes, had been disillusioned in their idealistic regard for the American president who at Versailles was to save the world for democracy. The hero, it turned out, had clay feet. A negative transference ran riot with the orthodox Freudian approach, especially in Bullitt, who became the prime author of the eventually published book *Thomas Woodrow Wilson*.[19] In it, Wilson was reduced to a messiah complex, a boy who, fearful of his father, never grew up to be a mature man. Unchecked by a real historical sense, reductionist in approach, the book was a disaster for psychological studies of political leaders when it finally appeared in 1966 (though drafted in 1932, the publication was held back by the authors' disagreements, and then by an agreement not to publish while the second Mrs. Wilson lived).

Fortunately, before then, Alexander and Juliette George had published their *Woodrow Wilson and Colonel House* (1956)[20] Here was a study solidly grounded in the minutiae of historical data, steadily guided by Adlerian theory which, however, did not obtrude on the presentation, and guided by a conscious awareness of leadership problems. The only thing remotely resembling it previously was the chapter on Wilson in Richard Hofstadter's *The American Political Tradition*.[21] A fairly traditional intellectual historian, Hofstadter had moved increasingly to a nonanalytic, but informed, use of psychology. His book as a whole was a study of leadership, though again not with a profound generalizing intent.

That task was reserved for the Georges. Though political scientists, they acted as professional historians as well. The result was a most powerful and persuasive presentation of Wilson as a leader who turned his own struggles with aggression (against his father) into struggles between supposed moral "good" and practical "evil." Lasswell had spoken of the political actor who translates his own private problems into public goals, rationalized and idealized, and thus provides leadership for others. The Georges show Wilson, in specific detail, as such a "compensating" leader.

The Georges' book has provoked an enormous amount of controversy, lighting up the whole field of leadership studies. Authur Link, the eminent Princeton historian and custodian of the Wilson papers—and image—has stalwartly defended the traditional historical citadel against intrusion by alien psychology. He has challenged the Georges on an array of historical "facts"; and they have responded. More recently, Link has enlisted the assistance of a medical doctor, Edwin Weinstein. In collaboration, they have attacked the Georges' emphasis on a psychological etiology for Wilson's erratic leadership behavior.[22] Weinstein put forth data and theories claiming to show that Wilson's "symptoms" were grounded in organic causes—dyslexia and subsequent brain damage—rather than psychosomatics, though broadening his approach in his recent book *Woodrow Wilson: A Medical and Psychological Biography* to allow for some of the latter as well.[23]

The Georges, in turn, have responded, enlisting the aid of a medical doctor, Michael Marmor. Their review of the new manuscript material that has appeared since their book, as well as of the criticisms directed against them, has served to confirm their belief in the validity of their interpretation of Wilson. Marmor's report to them (his findings have also been published separately in *The New England Journal of Medicine*)[24] rejects Weinstein's "stroke" interpretation as simply not the most plausible one to fit the data. More importantly, Marmor cautions historians not to trust too much in the speculations of physicians working retrospectively, and points out how Weinstein has either left out material or distorted it to fit his diagnosis.

The Georges, for their part, have point by point refuted Link's criticisms, in the process showing *his* omissions and distortions of evidence. It is a classic rejoinder.[25]

Two useful points emerge from this controversy, making edifying what is unedifying. The first is that historians and psychiatrists who bridle at the notion that their "great man," their president, could possibly suffer from psychological problems, preferring instead to claim an organic basis for the erratic behavior of their hero, may be lured into doing what they accuse psychohistorians of doing: they distort the evidence. The second is that verification is occasionally possible in psychohistory after the publication of the original work: new evidence confirmed, rather than disconfirmed, the theses advanced by the Georges. Their analysis of Wilson's leadership is still, therefore, an illuminating and sustainable one, even if not necessarily the final word.

Another historian, John Mulder, has subsequently shifted the focus of the historical attack on the Georges' thesis in his book *Woodrow Wilson, the Years of Preparation.*[26] Mulder, paying more attention to Wilson's father, Joseph Ruggles Wilson, has tried to show that he was not the simple authoritarian and "perfect" figure depicted by the Georges, but a more or less "failed" father—he was ousted from his leadership of Columbia Theological Seminary (Columbia, South Carolina) in the midst of Wilson's adolescence—which effect on Wilson's psychological nature, while profound, was more complicated than that shown by the Georges. In short, additional historical "facts" must compel a change in psychological "interpretation."

From another direction, the political scientist Robert Tucker's article "The Georges' Wilson Re-examined: An Essay on Psychobiography," has come an interesting challenge to the Georges' chosen psychological theory.[27] Tucker questions the efficiency of Adlerian theory, the limitations of which he probes, and suggests that a form of self-psychology—that of Karen Horney—leads to a more comprehensive understanding of the data and better illuminates the nature of Wilson's leadership qualities. Horney's self-psychology is different from current narcissistic theory, or Kohut's self-psychology, and an interpretation in the latter terms per se is lacking. (It is doubtful if August Heckscher's forthcoming work on Wilson will offer such a reading, though hopefully it will take such theoretical approaches into account.)

This brief summary of the pertinent literature on Wilson allows us to make the following preliminary observations. For once, there has been sustained attention to the same figure, seeking to interpret, explicitly or implicitly, the sources of his leadership in terms of his personality. Historians have tended to be hesitant or dubious about the use of explicit psychological theory, and wish to call any theory back to the "facts." Political scientists have been more venturesome and more conscious about psychological theories and their bearing on style and substance of leadership. The odd economist or psychiatrist who wanders into the field seeks to use intuition, in one case, or organic medicine, in the other, to supplement or supplant more analytic approaches. In the end, pushed or pulled from different directions, the study of Woodrow Wilson, specifically, and of leadership studies, generally, has benefited greatly from the unusually sustained and "cumulative" attention paid to it.

One last observation is in order. The work on Wilson is still largely in terms of his individual leadership qualities, mainly conceived in isolation from the led. Brilliant as is the Georges' study, it stands only on the periphery of this problem.

To open up this problem, let me simply assert certain propositions. 1) *The* leader as such does not exist; there is no "leader" for all peoples and all seasons. 2) The leader does not exist, fully formed, before the encounter with the group he is to lead; he finds his style and identity in the course of interacting with the led. 3) The leader leads in part by tapping into a "psychic repository"—myths, symbols, fantasies, and so forth—or culture, prevailing among the led; he appeals by activating a selected part of these "collective representations." 4) The leader creates his own image, in the process becoming it, while giving direction by it to the aspirations of his followers. 5) The leader embodies his personal leadership in an ideology, and also an organization.[28]

Now, if we agree that these are suggestive focuses for analyzing the relations of leader and led, how can we apply them in a specific case, such as that of Woodrow Wilson? The existing Wilson literature leaves us with the question and no sustained effort at an answer, even in this most sustained of psychohistorical inquiries into one man's leadership qualities.

OTHER PRESIDENTS

Other presidents, alas, have not benefited from such consistent attention. The Wilson literature offered us a "linear" development; the other presidents, taken together, offer us a "synoptic" comparison. We shall see what a brief survey of such work reveals. The fact that our survey will read like a series of one-minute book reviews says something about the episodic nature of the historian's attention to presidential leadership as such. It also illustrates the erratic use of psychological theory in such studies, and the dramatic lack of cumulative scholarship, defined as scholarship which takes sustained heed of previous efforts in the field.

In any event, studies of postrevolutionary presidential leadership benefit from the fact that the setting was clearly in evidence by the time of Tocqueville and his classic *Democracy in America:* political parties in a representative democracy. Tocqueville emphasized individualism and equality of conditions in America. He recognized, however, that equality could subvert individualism by means of a social tyranny of the majority. A mass "leadership," amorphous and undirected, could assert itself. For Tocqueville, this meant that organized political parties counted for little; he also badly underestimated the power of the president and seemed to view individual leadership as more or less nonexistent.

Tocqueville did recognize one of the paradoxes of American life: the coexistence of intense conformity and of intense individualism. He was writing at the time of Jackson's presidency, when the Transcendental Movement was also at its height. Jackson, implicitly calling for a kind of conformity, pitched his appeal to the common man, implying that, all being equal, all could equally lead the country. Emerson extolled the self-reliant individual, and proclaimed that "the root and seed of democracy is the doctrine, judge for yourself. Reverence thyself."

Yet, the reality was that Jackson was a strong leader, reverenced by much of the American electorate. The nature of his leadership, with its deep roots in an appeal to the strain of violence running through American history, and now embodied in Jackson's personality, has been dramatically—perhaps overdramatically—limed by Michael Paul Rogow in his book *Fathers and Children: Andrew Jackson and the Subjugation of the American Indian.*[29]

Jackson, as another scholar, Hugh Brogan, put it, "demonstrated a new sort of political leadership." In regard to the Indians, he used his powers to support the state of Georgia in its scheme to seize their tribal lands. He inaugurated the national spoils system, dismissing one out of every ten officials on his accession to the presidency. He extended the use of the veto power and dismissed his entire cabinet, with one exception, at one fell swoop (a coup unmatched to this day). By such actions, Jackson imposed the power of the presidency on his country and its party system in a manner that can be called "revolutionary," a development largely ignored by Tocqueville.[30]

After Jackson, the next "great" American leader is acknowledgeably Abraham Lincoln. Until the last few years, we had to be satisfied with the treatment of this admittedly depressive and complex man by the literary critic Edmund Wilson, in his chapter "Abraham Lincoln," in *Patriotic Gore,*[31] a subtle and penetrating sketch; and by Richard Hofstadter, in a chapter in *The American Political Tradition.*[32] Now we have George Forgie's *Patricide in the House Divided*[33] and, just published, Charles Strozier's *Lincoln's Quest for Union: Public and Private Meaning;*[34] both authors are historians. Forgie's book is a good illustration of what happens when an historian approaches his subject with a basically parlor-room Freudianism, ill-equipped to do justice as a result to either the historical or psychological dimension of his subject. The result is a lurid reduction of Lincoln, in a manner justifying the otherwise invalid attacks of critics such as Jacques Barzun or David

Stannard. Psychohistorians in such a case can well appeal to the old saying "God save us from our friends; our enemies we can take care of ourselves."

Of an altogether different order is Strozier's work. Thoroughly grounded in original historical inquiry, to which it has been guided by a fully informed psychological awareness, it demonstrates the way in which new theory can enlighten or rediscover old facts. Kohutian in inspiration, the work offers us a deepened and more intimate knowledge of both Lincoln the man and the politician. Though neither Forgie's nor Strozier's book explicitly deals with theories of leadership, the latter work is a rich contribution, implicitly, to the growing use of narcissistic theory in explaining the sources of a great man's turn to politics and his appeal to followers.

Concerning Theodore Roosevelt, our next "great" president, we have had two very readable and popular books recently. Edmund Morris's *The Rise of Theodore Roosevelt*[35] at best deals with Theodore Roosevelt's personality indirectly, and has been taken to task on this account in an important article by an analyst, Miles Shore.[36] David McCullough's *Mornings on Horseback*[37] shows more interest in the personality formation but is admittedly nonanalytic in the doing. A number of articles, especially Kathleen Dalton's "Why America Loved Theodore Roosevelt" (and especially her unpublished Ph.D. thesis on Theodore Roosevelt), carry us much further in this direction[38] Dalton's article is directly and importantly related, in fact, to general considerations of leadership, as she explores the ways, setting up a typology in the process, in which Theodore Roosevelt "tapped an emotional wellspring in the culture."

More recent presidents, great and small, are fairer game for psychological cum leadership studies, perhaps because of the greater availability of material, more likely because they, too, are natural members of our "therapeutic society." On the border of this new therapeutic society are Herbert Hoover and Franklin Delano Roosevelt. Thus the reviewer of a recent book on Hoover laments that the author "does give reason to suspect . . . that Hoover's psychological makeup had much to do with his failure of leadership. The Great Engineer may have also been a considerable neurotic, the Great Depression a personal depression as well."[39] No psychological study of Hoover, however, yet exists.

As for Franklin Delano Roosevelt, James McGregor Burns's fine *Roosevelt: The Lion and the Fox*[40] foreshadows Burns's later sustained interest in psychology and leadership studies, but is not yet imbued with the theoretical elements of that future interest. In his major work, *Leadership*, Burns, a political scientist more than an historian per se, offers a theoretical setting in which particular portraits are placed.[41] The psychological theory is more that of Maslow's humanistic psychology than Freud's classical analysis, but consistently applied in the interests of a generalizing aim. In the light of such work, one wonders how Burns would write his book on FDR today! (A "revisit" by him to his book, in the form of reflections on it, would be a major contribution to the field of leadership studies.) As of yet, Burns's "intuitive" approach to Franklin Delano Roosevelt has not been surpassed.

Truman has had no major psychological study. Eisenhower will receive such attention from Fred I. Greenstein in a soon to be published book; meanwhile, we have his paper "A Tory Theory of the Presidency: Eisenhower's Leadership Re-examined."[42] Lyndon Baines Johnson, of course, is the subject of Doris Kearns's *Lyndon Johnson and the American Dream;*[43] the psychology here is eclectic, but informed and gifted. John Fitzgerald Kennedy is, as many see it, the "victim" of Nancy Gager Clinch's *The Kennedy Neurosis;*[44] in this case, there is clear psychological acknowledgment to Karen Horney and Harry Stack Sullivan, but the result is too frequently reductionist, although light is shed in the process (along with a lot of heat). The historian Arthur Schlesinger, Jr., in *A Thousand Days,* gives a very personal and partisan picture of JFK, written in a traditionally narrative manner, the flavor of which can be gotten from the initial quote from Ernest Hemingway extolling the strong, brave men whom the world kills when it cannot break them; Schlesinger, of course, is well known for his contribution to the discussion of the growth of the "imperial president."[45] Garry Wills's *The Kennedy Imprisonment*[46] is a malicious portrait, not just of John F. Kennedy but of all the Kennedy males, which is nevertheless telling in its psychological portraiture; Wills opposes systematic use of psychological theories, however, and this shows in his one-sided treatment of the clan.

With Richard Nixon there is a burst of activity. His compulsion to put himself on the couch in public, his obviously "psychological" character, his heavily personalized policies, have convinced many otherwise skeptical people of the importance of personality in politics. Before Watergate, two scholars analyzed his character, with an eye to the effect on his leadership. James David Barber devoted a long chapter—practically a book within a book—to Nixon as an active-negative type. *The Presidential Character*[47] is an effort to establish a formal leadership typology, and Nixon is merely one example among many; but the portrait of Nixon is valuable in its own right, illuminated by Barber's Lasswellian/Adlerian inspirations. Bruce Mazlish's *In Search of Nixon*[48] offers a more dynamic portrait from a relatively orthodox Freudian and Eriksonian perspective; it relates the personality to the policies, but only offers rather disappointingly slim hints as to the interaction of Nixon and the American public.

After Watergate, a number of books appeared, mainly by psychiatrists, depicting him as if he were a patient. One of the better of the bad lot is David Abrahamsen's *Nixon vs. Nixon.*[49] One of the worst is E.S. Chesen's *President Nixon's Psychiatric Profile.*[50] None of them has much to offer leadership studies, and all of them demonstrate the danger of operating in an historical vacuum. The historian Fawn Brodie's *Richard Nixon*[51] might have been expected to fill that vacuum but, concentrating on the young Nixon, she offers little historical or leadership observations; instead we get a mixed array of psychological insights. It is not clear how the book builds on Barber and Mazlish's work, and one misses the kind of cumulative scholarship to be found in the literature on Woodrow Wilson.

With Jimmy Carter and Ronald Reagan, we come to the end of our presidential survey. Carter has had two books devoted to his personality: Betty Glad's *Jimmy Carter, in Search of the Great White House*[52] and Bruce Mazlish and Edwin Diamond's *Jimmy Carter*.[53] Both are psychologically informed and explicitly interested in the consequences of personality for leadership, but diverge in their approach and findings. Betty Glad is now also at work on a book on Reagan's personality, but what stands out most vividly at this writing is the way in which the current president has had a sort of "free ride," psychologically as well as politically, up to now. The reasons for this are worth investigating, though they would take us too far afield here. Suffice it to say that Reagan has shown unusual leadership abilities, of a special kind, and an analysis in these terms will be highly rewarding.

CONCLUSIONS

Our survey leads to a number of conclusions. For example, it is clear that women do not figure in the study of presidential leadership as we have outlined it—for the simple reason that there have been no women presidents in the USA. Women, then, are appendages to male presidents; and we could, in these terms, have cited work on Mary Todd Lincoln, Jacqueline Kennedy, and others. Only Eleanor Roosevelt could be considered to have become a political force—a leader, though not a president, in her own right.

It is less clear, though closer examination reveals it, that in nonmilitaristic America, military men have a leg up on becoming presidents. Washington, Jackson, Teddy Roosevelt, and Eisenhower all rode a white horse of sorts to the White House. Leadership on the battlefield seems to impress the American electorate as preparation for leadership in the political arena (examples not mentioned, such as Zachary Taylor and Ulysses S. Grant, suggest how unreliable is this expectation). JFK and Nixon both welcomed military service in WW II, knowing its value for their future nonmilitary campaigns. Why is the military mark so important in confirming someone as a leader in other fields? Are leadership qualities seen as general in form? Does the American love of "strong" leaders—a JFK, for example, would not allow himself to be photographed wearing glasses lest it "weaken" his appearance—find confirmation in the exercise of a willingness to use violence? Historians tend to pass over such general questions in a nonreflective manner.

The next conclusion evident from the list just given, in so far as it goes from Franklin Delano Roosevelt to the present, is that historians are not very busy engaging in contemporary leadership studies: Burns, Weinstein, Kearns, Barber, and Glad are all political scientists. Only Mazlish and Schlesinger and perhaps Wills are professional historians; the rest are psychologists of various sorts, and journalists (Wills is partly this, too). Two facts appear to offer a partial explanation: Historians, as we have noted, tend to be not much interested in theory construction, and many regard contemporary history as no history.

If, however, we go back before Franklin D. Roosevelt, we see historians taking a more prominent role. Dalton and Strozier are both historians; almost all the writers on Washington and Jefferson are, too. Only Wilson calls forth the political scientists as much as the historians. In short, political scientists concentrate on contemporary figures, historians on more dated ones; political scientists aim at a generalizing "science," historians at a more idiographic account. The moral: Each could benefit from the other's interests. Historians, to regard them alone for the moment, are engaged in a debate over how far to move toward theory and analysis, but are obviously moving in that direction—and should be so encouraged.

In so doing, historians can offer leadership studies a depth of context and a sense of development otherwise lacking. Without such a contribution, there is a thinness, a stasis, and a pseudoscientific air that tends to hang over the new subfield. The historian, used to interdisciplinary work, can bring the insights of sociology and psychology to bear on the rich, "real" data of politics, on man's existence over detailed time. So regarded, history is, indeed, an "experimental" science, helping in the construction of a theory of leadership.

The application of psychology to historical materials, with an eye to leadership, also allows for a "testing" of various theories of personality, that is, examining roughly the same materials with varied theories—Freudian, Adlerian, Sullivanian, Kohutian—and evaluating the possibly divergent interpretations, as well as weighing which theories deal with the data most exhaustively and illuminatingly.

Unfortunately, almost all existing psychological theories are better equipped to deal with individual life histories than with group phenomena. Among the latter must be counted leader-led relations. As the saying goes, it takes two to tango. Social scientists, among them historians, rather than psychologists, seem most likely to make significant contributions here, because of their professional immersion in social relations; as yet, however, there is little to cite of value, although one possible lead might be Richard Hofstadter's essay on "The Paranoid Style in American Politics."[54] Here an historian looks at the "led" in a way that raises the question of how a given leader could and should deal with them. Do leaders themselves share in the "paranoid style"? Stand outside it, but cynically exploit it? Fight against it? A moment's reflection on Truman's and Eisenhower's experiences with McCarthy suggests the reality behind these questions.

Let me express some personal preferences at this point, and somewhat arbitrarily list what I feel to be the most suggestive existing lines of inquiry. From the psychoanalytic side, I find the work of Heinz Kohut most stimulating in this regard. From the political scientist side, James McGregor Burns's monumental work on leadership;[55] and from the historical and sociological side (that is, as efforts at theory rather than practice per se), Bruce Mazlish's article "Leader and Led, Individual and Group"[56] and Fred Weinstein's and Gerald Platt's *Psychoanalytic Sociology*.[57] One does not have to agree with these authors; they are, however, in my view, raising the right sorts of questions.

"The future," some wit has remarked, "isn't what it used to be." Neither is the past. Historians are becoming increasingly aware of this fact. Facts themselves are meaningful in terms of theory; they derive meaning from theory and contribute to the testing and construction of theory. Theorizing in relation to social phenomena is the most subtle and complex of all such enterprises. Leadership Studies is one such enterprise, where we need all the insight and wisdom we can gain. In the future, historians, to pun a bit, must not only follow but also learn to lead in this field more than they have in the past.

NOTES

1. "Philosophers and Kings," *Daedulus* (Summer, 1968).
2. Richard Lebeaux, *Young Man Thoreau* (Amherst, Mass.: University of Massachusetts Press, 1977).
3. Anne Jardin, *The First Henry Ford* (Cambridge, Mass.: M.I.T. Press, 1970).
4. James T. Flexner, *George Washington: The Forge of Experience* (Boston: Little, Brown, 1965).
5. Marcus Cunliffe, *George Washington: Man and Monument* (Boston: Little, Brown, 1958).
6. Bernard Bailyn, *The Ordeal of Thomas Hutchinson* (Cambridge, Mass.: Belknap Press of Harvard University Press, 1974).
7. *Leadership in the American Revolution: The Psychological Dimension* (Washington, D.C.: Library of Congress, 1974).
8. Stanley Elkins and Earl McKitrick, "The Founding Fathers: Young Men of the Revolution," *The Political Science Quarterly*, LXXVI, 2 (June, 1961).
9. Edwin G. Burrows and Michael Wallace, "The American Revolution: The Ideology and Psychology of National Liberation," *Perspectives in American History*, 6 (1972).
10. *Leadership in the American Revolution: The Psychological Dimension*.
11. Bernard Bailyn, "Boyd's Jefferson: Notes for a Sketch," *New England Quarterly*, 33 (1960) and "Butterfield's Adams: Notes for a Sketch," *William and Mary Quarterly*, 3rd ser. 19 (1962).
12. Winthrop Jordan, *White Over Black* (Chapel Hill, N.C.: University of North Carolina Press, 1968).

13. Fawn Brodie, *Thomas Jefferson* (New York: W.W. Norton & Co., 1974).
14. Christopher Lasch, *The Culture of Narcissism* (New York: W.W. Norton & Co., 1978).
15. Bruce Mazlish, "American Narcissism," *The Psychohistory Review,* vol. 10, no. 3/ 4 (Spring/Summer 1982).
16. Fred Weinstein and Gerald Platt, *Psychoanalytic Sociology* (Baltimore, Md.: The Johns Hopkins University Press, 1973).
17. Fred Weinstein, *The Dynamics of Nazism* (New York: Academic Press, 1980).
18. John Maynard Keynes, *The Economic Consequences of Peace* (New York: Harcourt, Brace and Howe, 1920).
19. Sigmund Freud and William Bullitt, *Thomas Woodrow Wilson* (Boston: Houghton Mifflin Co., 1966).
20. Alexander George and Juliette L. George, *Woodrow Wilson and Colonel House* (New York: The John Day Co., 1956).
21. Richard Hofstadter, *The American Political Tradition* (New York: Knopf, 1948).
22. E. Weinstein, J.W. Anderson, and A. Link, "Woodrow Wilson's Political Personality: A Reappraisal," *The Political Science Quarterly* (Winter 1978–79). See the reply by Alexander L. George and Juliette L. George, "Woodrow Wilson and Colonel House: A Reply to Weinstein, Anderson and Link," a paper prepared for presentation at the fourth annual meeting of the International Society of Political Psychology, Mannheim, Germany, June 22–June 27, 1981.
23. Edwin A. Weinstein, *Woodrow Wilson: A Medical and Psychological Biography* (Princeton, N.J.: Princeton University Press, 1981); and "Woodrow Wilson's Neurological Illness," *Journal of American History,* LVII, 2 (September 1970).
24. Michael Marmor, *The New England Journal of Medicine,* 307, 528–535 (August 26, 1982).
25. A version of the Georges' Mannheim paper is published in the *Political Science Quarterly,* vol. 96, no. 4 (Winter 1981–82).
26. John Mulder, *Woodrow Wilson: The Years of Preparation* (Princeton, N.J.: Princeton University Press, 1978).
27. Robert Tucker, "The Georges' Wilson Re-examined: An Essay on Psychobiography," *The American Political Science Review,* LXXI, 2 (June, 1977).
28. For further development of these propositions, *see* my article, cited in footnote 56.
29. Michael Paul Rogow, Fathers and Children: *Andrew Jackson and the Subjugation of the American Indian* (New York: Random House, 1975).
30. Hugh Brogan, "Tocqueville and the American Presidency," *Journal of American Studies,* vol. 15, no. 3 (December 1981).
31. Edmund Wilson, *Patriotic Gore* (New York: Oxford University Press, 1962).
32. Hofstadter, *The American Political Tradition.*
33. George Forgie, *Patricide in the House Divided* (New York: W.W. Norton & Co., 1979).
34. Charles Strozier, *Lincoln's Quest for Union: Public and Private Meaning* (New York: Basic Books, Inc., 1982).
35. Edmund Morris, *The Rise of Theodore Roosevelt* (New York: Coward, McCann & Geoghegan, 1979).
36. Miles Shore, "On Action and Affect," *Journal of Interdisciplinary History,* XI, 2 (Autumn 1980).
37. David McCullough, *Mornings on Horseback* (New York: Simon & Schuster, 1981).
38. Kathleen Dalton, "Why America Loved Theodore Roosevelt," *The Psychohistory Review,* 8, no. 3 (Winter 1979).
39. Carl M. Brauer reviewing David Burner, *Herbert Hoover,* in *The Chronicle Review,* Feb. 20, 1979, p. R9.

40. James McGregor Burns, *Roosevelt: The Lion and the Fox* (New York: Harcourt, Brace & Co., 1956).
41. _____, *Leadership* (New York: Harper & Row, 1978).
42. Fred I. Greenstein, "A Tory Theory of the Presidency: Eisenhower's Leadership Re-examined," prepared for delivery at the 1979 Annual Meeting of the American Political Science Association. A published version of this paper is "Eisenhower as an Active President: A Look at New Evidence," *Political Science Quarterly*, vol. 94, no. 4 (Winter 1979–80). *Compare* Richard H. Immerman, "Eisenhower and Dulles: Who Made the Decisions," *Political Psychology*, vol. 1, no. 2 (Autumn 1979).
43. Doris Kearns, *Lyndon Johnson and the American Dream* (New York: Harper & Row, 1976).
44. Nancy Gager Clinch, *The Kennedy Neurosis* (New York: Grosset and Dunlap, 1973).
45. Arthur Schlesinger, Jr., *A Thousand Days* (Boston: Houghton Mifflin Co., 1965).
46. Garry Wills, *The Kennedy Imprisonment* (Boston: Little, Brown, 1982).
47. James David Barber, *The Presidential Character* (Englewood Cliffs, N.J.: Prentice-Hall, 1972).
48. Bruce Mazlish, *In Search of Nixon* (New York: Basic Books, 1972).
49. David Abrahamsen, *Nixon vs. Nixon* (New York: Farrar, Strauss and Giroux, 1977).
50. E.S. Chesen, *President Nixon's Psychiatric Profile* (New York: Peter Wyden Publishing Co., 1973).
51. Fawn Brodie, *Richard Nixon* (New York: W.W. Norton & Co., 1981).
52. Betty Glad, *Jimmy Carter: In Search of the Great White House* (New York: W.W. Norton & Co., 1980).
53. Bruce Mazlish and Edwin Diamond, *Jimmy Carter* (New York: Simon & Schuster, 1979).
54. Richard Hofstadter, *The Paranoid Style in American Politics and Other Essays* (New York: Vantage Books, Random House, 1964).
55. Burns, *Leadership*.
56. Bruce Mazlish, "Leader and Led: Individual and Group," *The Psychohistory Review*, vol. 9, no. 3 (Spring 1981).
57. Weinstein and Platt, *Psychoanalytic Sociology*.

THE LAW
OF THE FATHER
Leadership
and Symbolic Authority
in Psychoanalysis

2

Melvyn A. Hill

Psychoanalysis emerged at the end of the nineteenth century when the cumulative effect of industrialization, urbanization, and democracy led to increasing psychological pressure among those directly affected by these changes. Most of Freud's early patients were women who were caught in the conflict between their traditional role in the household and the desire for greater freedom to be educated, to work, and to make their own decisions in life.[1] His male patients were frequently torn between their loyalty to the traditions handed on by their fathers, and the perception that they no longer offered a guide to action in the changing world.[2]

The object of psychoanalytic investigation is the relationship between psychic structure and conscious patterns of thinking, feeling, and acting. Freud argued that the psyche is structured in the process of socialization through which the individual learns to recognize the possibilities and restrictions that confront desire from the side of social reality. And at the heart of that process lies the phenomenon of *authority*, mediating the relationship between the individual and society. A concern with authority turned out to be central to psychoanalysis, because it was central to the conflict between traditional roles and values and the changing realities of the world. When somebody experiences a conflict over essential aspects of his life that he can neither understand nor master, the process of socialization has failed.

As a science of society psychoanalysis exhibits two peculiarities. The first is that it grew out of practice. It was essentially a theory of psychotherapy. The second is that it gave central importance to the influence of the family as the agent of society in relation to the individual. If we lose sight of these facts, we turn psychoanalysis into an abstract theory of mind and society that belies its concern with the actual experience of becoming a member of society. And that amounts to the encounter between the individual and authority, not at the level of the state but at the immediate level of the child's emerging desire. Freud believed that this encounter determined the individual's relationship to authority in the broader spheres of life. It provided the unconscious psychological structure for authority, regardless of its specific content.

Whereas sociologists like Max Weber were concerned to proceed from a study of the different forms that authority takes, trying to discover a logic in their succession—such as the famous trilogy of charismatic, traditional, and rational authority—Freud looked for the underlying structural unity behind the phenomenon. As a psychoanalyst he had come to believe in the unifying simplicity of the hypothesis of a structure that remains unconscious but that nevertheless determines behavior. He defined the problem faced by his male and female patients not so much in terms of their experience of the conflict between tradition and modernity but rather in terms of the effect on them of an authority that contradicted itself, and consequently gave rise to a contradiction within the individual between the conscious and unconscious response to socialization.

In order to discuss authority as psychoanalysis sees it, I believe it is important to follow in Freud's footsteps by recounting the way he came to understand the role of authority in socialization. That, in turn, will prepare the way for understanding Freud's view of leadership, which followed.

THE ANALYST AS LEADER

If psychoanalysis developed in relation to the practice of psychotherapy, its first peculiarity as a social science, it seems logical that Freud first observed and wrestled with the question of authority in the context of his own role as a therapist. While this may seem to be a far remove from the question of leadership, it turns out to be the foundation of Freud's thinking about relationships where one person exerts influence over another.

When it turned out that hydrotherapy and electrotherapy did not help his patients recover from neurosis, Freud turned to hypnotherapy. This represented an attempt to exert direct power over the will of the patient: to have the patient act according to the hypnotist's suggestions to become well. But while he gained this healing power, Freud also found that it reduced his patients to utter dependence on him. And if that did not happen, he could not overcome their resistance to the hypnosis, especially since he was sympathetic to their refusal to submit to another's will. The structure of the hypnotic relationship demanded an authoritarian therapist who could overcome the patient's neurotic will in order to replace it with a will to health. But benevolent despotism did not fit well with Freud's hope that patients would recover on the strength of their own desire to be well. The question was how he could lead his patients to health without dominating them. He discovered that he had to remove direct power over the patient from his repertoire as a therapist. In its place he put analysis, and specifically, analysis of the transference, in order to liberate the patient's will to health.[3]

Analysis moved on two fronts at the same time. One was the attempt to trace back the patient's conflicts to their origin in early experience. The other was the attempt to show how the patient's expectations of Freud repeated that early experience. The first kind of interpretation reconstructed what happened and had been forgotten. The second deconstructed what was happening in the present transference of the past situation onto the analyst. Together they gave the patient conscious awareness of the memories stored up in his unconscious, and of the way they influenced his desire in the present. It meant that Freud had invented a new kind of authority for himself as a psychotherapist: the authority of the one who is supposed to know the unconscious. By sharing that knowledge with the patient, Freud gradually gave up his authority in the relationship. As a mode of influencing another we could call Freud's concept of psychoanalysis a means of transforming leadership. This is the kind of leadership that obtains in the relationship between parents and children, where the children are gradually educated to do for themselves what they once needed the parents to do for them. It is the model of socialization where the transformation of the child's feelings, thoughts, and modes of action proceeds in line with its internalization of the values of the culture. In other words, adults know what to do themselves, without the supervision of authority figures.

When a patient enters analysis he is essentially asking the analyst to take on the role of parent, and transfers onto him a childlike trust and love originally felt for mother and father. Freud overcame this transference by analyzing it, and at the same time analyzing the origin of the patient's problems in the family. The desire stirred up in the present by the transference provided the energy for the transformation Freud effected through the therapy.[4]

If we compare the two modes of power and influence Freud discovered in hypnosis and analysis, we arrive at the two extremes in a spectrum of possible modes of authority and leadership. Hypnosis requires an absolute surrender and an absolute domination, while transformation requires the gradual cancellation of authority as the partners gain an equal understanding of reality, and internalize the values and kinds of action that reconcile desire with its object. But perhaps more important than this concept of a spectrum is the fact that there is a common starting point for both positions, in the opposition of the absolute ruler to the completely dependent subject. The transformation begins only when that relation of ruler and ruled is consciously admitted and questioned. Consequently we can presume that as we move from the absolute to the transforming mode of leadership on this spectrum, knowledge, responsibility, and participation are more equally distributed. The process of analysis, therefore, is essentially "democratizing."

THE PARENT AS LEADER

So far I have taken as the point of departure the first peculiarity of psychoanalysis: that it proceeds from the specific nature of Freud's psychotherapeutic practice. The second peculiarity that I mentioned was the central importance Freud assigned to the family as the bearer of the authority of society in raising the child. Actually the first leads directly into the second: both the interpretations aimed at reconstructing the patient's significant past experiences, and those aimed at deconstructing the transference, lead to the question of the patient's relationship to authority in his family as a child. In other words, what kind of leaders were the parents, and what kind of follower was the child? Of course this will vary with each patient, but Freud succeeded in providing a general outline of the kinds of issues that are inherent in the experience and transformation of authority in the family.

The earliest authority in the family is absolute. The parents are entirely responsible for the infant and therefore omnipotent in relation to it. Without their good will, the infant cannot survive. It is utterly helpless and completely dependent. But there is a fundamental irony in this relationship: the more benevolent the parents are, the more solicitous they become of the infant, striving to cater to its every need. And, conversely, the more it is the center of the parents' concern, the more powerful the infant becomes. Thus Freud called it "his majesty the baby." And following the insight of Sandor Ferenczi, he attributed to the infant a fantasy of its own omnipotence, confirmed by the responsiveness of its nursery environment.[5] The benevolent despotism of the nursery proceeds on the basis of an inversion of the actual situation: the caretakers become enslaved to the infant, and it becomes their master. The leader obeys, and the follower commands.

The way out of this original condition of infantile omnipotence and parental servitude consists of a series of psychological reversals. The first brings both parents and child to recognize their real power relationship: the parent emerges as the all-powerful one, and the child as the helpless dependent. From that point the education of the child proceeds, giving it the knowledge, power, and skill that is required for subsistence and, as these are acquired, freeing the child from both dependence on the parent and the parent's authority. The child discovers that the parents are like itself: they master reality by their own effort. And the imaginary omnipotence once claimed by the infant, and then attributed to the parent, is deconstructed. In its place there is the transforming leadership of the child by the parent, with the acquisition of the capacity to master reality.

According to Freud this critical shift in the relation of child and parents occurs in two stages. The first consists of the break in the child's earliest total involvement with the mother. Initially, as Margaret Mahler pointed out, they constitute a symbiotic unity, with the mother completely devoted to the child, and the child loving the mother completely because she provides for all its needs and desires.[6] The child can only begin to develop independently when this unity is cut. The father carries that responsibility: he has to claim the child by insisting on their separation. This gives it the chance to come into the individual identity conferred on it by the culture, and specifically by its unique place in the family.

Lacan has insisted that this "law of the father" is a principle of the culture that can be introduced on the authority of either parent.[7] It is not patriarchal in the literal sense of inhering in the authority of the male, although that is how it occurred in Freud's time, when the father did in fact monopolize the position of the one who speaks for the culture. As the roles of male and female have become equalized, so have their responsibility for exercising that authority. But as the principle of separation comes between the symbiosis of mother and child, it is a "law of the father," since it requires a symbolic third term that has to be introduced between the two originals, and logically it falls to the father.

With this introduction of the "symbolic father," the child begins to acquire the language of its culture, since it now has to speak in order to negotiate its needs and desires in relationship with other speakers. But this is also the point where it tries to recapture the two-in-one it has lost by intruding into the relationship of its parents, which it conceives on the same lines, as a two-in-one, imagining them to enjoy the very satisfaction it has lost.[8] Freud called this struggle of the child to be included in its parents' relationship, the Oedipus complex. But even as it has been denied its mother, it is now denied the chance to replace either mother or father in their relation to each other. What is particularly painful for the child is to realize that it lacks the power to convince one of the others to satisfy its desire. The incest taboo imposed on the authority of the culture—certainly of modern Western culture—thus compels the child to repress its desire. And here the line between what is conscious and unconscious takes its origin. Too painful to endure consciously, the child forces itself to forget about its desire, and devotes itself to developing other interests and learning the lessons required by those in authority. It can enjoy its parents' love in the form of their affection, but cannot join in their intimacy, which it still understands in terms of its lost paradise.[9]

The authority of the culture that the parents are required to exercise in order to teach their child the taboo against incest is once more absolute. Freud described its effect on the child as an experience of a castration threat. But whereas the parents occupied an omnipotent position before, now their authority is limited: as long as the child obeys this taboo, it is free to be itself. Furthermore, the taboo is accompanied by a promise that when it achieves sufficient independence it will be allowed to find its own sexual partner. Freud called this the principle of postponed gratification.

The contradiction in oedipal authority is simply that the parents themselves indulge in precisely the kind of intimacy and pleasure that they deny the child. While they "have" each other, the child "has" only itself. In this formulation we find the main lines of the Oedipus complex, and the definition of the child's struggle to master its contradictory response to its parents, who essentially confront it with a no-win situation.

Looking more closely into the child's experience, it consists of a conflict between its love and hate for both parents. It loves the good parents who take care of its needs and desires, while it hates the bad parents who frustrate its desires at the same time as they satisfy their own.[10] This also colors its attitude toward the beliefs and values that the parents try to teach the child. Each of these involves a certain postponement of an immediate gratification by the parent, so that the child acquires the capacity to learn how to make its own way in the culture. But this frustration is affected by the much more powerful sexual frustration for which the parents are responsible. Consequently the oedipal conflict of loving and hating the parents provides the context for the internalization of the culture.

The more easily the child yields to the restraints on its desire, the less conflict it will experience between love and hate. But the more severe that conflict, the less it will be able to meet the requirements of the culture and fulfill the conditions for being loved within the family. The degree of ambivalence that the child experiences in the oedipal conflict limits the transformation of its relationship to the parents, and of its eventual ease in being a full member of the culture. What affects the child's ability to overcome its oedipal love? A major factor is the way the parents communicate the requirements of the culture: whether they do so as if they were an expression of their personal power, or rather as a requirement that they themselves have had to meet. If they insist that their authority is personal, then they exacerbate the contradiction between the rule they impose on the child and the rule they live by in their own relationship. Simply put, it is a question of whether they can indicate that the family is governed by a symbolic authority that links it to the world. Otherwise they invite the child's resistance and intensify its ambivalence.

A lucky child will have parents who conceive their role symbolically, so that it will be able to work through its ambivalence—its having both good and bad images of the parents—while still managing to learn to meet the conditions that they set for their love. The child's oedipal desire is renounced as it learns to act in ways that are rewarded in the culture and supported by the parents. An unlucky child is stuck with its anger. To protect the parents from it, the child has to find another object—either itself or another—to be angry with. Its ego can assume either a sadistic or a masochistic position, the severity of which will increase with the extent of the aggression it has to deflect.[11] These distortions in the formation of the ego become critical in the child's character. They do not necessarily take the form of an open rebellion against the parents' authority with the attendant risk of retaliation and punishment. In fact, the child can appear to leave its parents' authority unchallenged while nevertheless rebelling against it through the way it adopts of relating to others, and of the kind of life it goes on to lead.

Donald Winnicott, the distinguished British psychoanalyst, suggested yet a further possibility of pathology in the development of the child-follower's ego. He argued that a child may become perfectly good at meeting all of the parents' conditions for love, but only at the level of a pretense. This pretense at pleasing the parents puts the child in the position of developing a false self rather than an ego with which it is truly identified. That true self remains essentially untouched by the experience of authority, and therefore cut off from access to reality through action. Winnicott believed that this typical structure of the schizoid personality is in fact a common element in the "solution" to oedipal struggle.[12] Taking his analysis a step further, we can foresee the possibility of a child who saves itself from the fear of punishment, if it were to rebel openly, by a form of secret rebellion; while it appears to conform with the parents' expectations, it lives another life on the quiet. Child-followers of this kind are only concerned to appear to obey the rules but, like Gyges in Plato's *Republic,* the minute they are out of the leader's sight they pursue a course of action they invent for themselves that runs contrary to, while evading, the directions they have been given.

By emphasizing the role of the parent as the leader whom the child follows, I have tried to open the way to a psychoanalytic theory of leadership. For if psychoanalysis is peculiar in the central importance it gives to the family in the process of socialization, it regards the situation of authority in the family as the key to the structure of authority in society at large, and hence also as the key to leadership. The critical point is that the parent becomes a parent only as a member of the society and culture whose authority it exercises in relation to the child as follower. Thus the Oedipus complex is not simply a family matter but, on the contrary, represents the claim that society makes on the family and, in particular, on the child. The parent is obliged to enforce the taboo against incest on behalf of society, although there is considerable scope in the way this is done. But whatever the parent does or says in relation to the child carries a symbolic significance that derives from the authority of the culture and refers to the reality of the society.

THE LAW OF THE FATHER

Freud saw in the Oedipus complex the foundation of social relationships and of the continuity of a culture. By working its way through the Oedipus complex the child becomes a member of its society and learns to make its way in the world. Thus, in trying to explain the origins of society and culture, Freud actually wrote about the origin of the Oedipus complex.

Perhaps I can put this more simply. Freud began to study the child's socialization through the authority of the family in response to the problems he encountered with his patients. He constructed this model of the ontogenesis of the psychic structure to serve as a guideline for his work with patients. But this led to the question of the social origins of the Oedipus complex itself, which is transmitted down through the generations. Here he had to consider the phylogenesis of culture and, in particular, of its mode of authority. The question was how did the Oedipus complex become the typical experience of authority? This led him to consider that the transformation of human beings from a state of nature to the organization of culture and society was made possible by the formation of a psychic structure.

This second transformation—from nature to culture—mirrors the first—from infant to adult. Consequently, if we can conceive of the "symbolic father"—the third term in the oedipal triangle, which separates the original dyad of the two-in-one—as leading the child into its culture and social world, we can follow Freud's speculation in placing a "primal father," not yet symbolic but "real," as the original authority in the Darwinian horde of humanoid creatures in the state of nature. In fact he traced the origin of the "symbolic father" back to the loss of this "primal father" who was then symbolically replaced in the form of the third term of the Oedipus complex. How this came about is the theme of Freud's writings on authority and leadership in society.

The basic text for Freud's approach to this problem is *Totem and Taboo*,[13] but he took up this theme time and again. Thus we find it in *Group Psychology and the Analysis of the Ego*,[14] *The Future of an Illusion*,[15] as well as in the widely read *Civilization and Its Discontents*.[16] The central concern that connects these works is the idea that socialization not only imposes submission on the child but also provokes a tendency to resist authority in one way or another. The same alternation between submission and resistance arises in the world at large, and poses the problem of how to manage it. Mostly the solution takes the form of domination in its various guises, not the least of which, for Freud, is political leadership as such, with its alternating seductions and threats, infantilization and brutalization. Religion comes to the aid of politics by offering people a delusional wish fulfillment. In effect it stimulates their anxiety, providing the means to keep them in line. But much of this trend of thought was not original with Freud. His critical contribution consists in the way he traced the origin of authority in society and culture.

Totem and Taboo presents Freud at his most radical and original on the question of authority. It is here that he traces the emergence of the "symbolic father" as the source of authority in culture from the "primal father" in the state of nature. There are, in effect, three levels of significance in Freud's myth of the primal horde. They refer to the reign of the "primal father," the covenant of the sons, and the repetition of the Oedipus complex in relation to the "symbolic father."

On the first level, he posits a "primal father" who asserts his sexual possession of all the females in the horde, denying the sons access to them. For the sons, this father appears omnipotent and an ideal figure. Individually they believe that they lack the power to stand with him. But they overcome their inadequacy as individuals by coming together to plot his murder.

On the second level, the sons now find that each represents a potential threat to every other in a deadly struggle to be the one who replaces the murdered father. In order to survive they are compelled to renounce the place of the father collectively, and to arrange a set of relationships among themselves that will obviate the need to kill each other. This takes the form of a contract to share the women among themselves, and to provide for their allocation among subsequent generations. Hence the taboo against incest—whereby no father can claim possession of his daughters—and the rule of exogamy—whereby they essentially arrange to exchange their daughters so that their sons can mate exogamously. They seal this contract in the blood of the dead father, and they observe an annual totem feast, in which the animal stands in for—and thus symbolizes—the father, as a reminder of the nature of their contract.

The now dead and absent father who is symbolically invoked, provides the negative legitimacy and authority for the new order of equality based upon sexual exchange. To break the law would mean a return to the threat of communal war and the possibility of an absolute tyranny.

The third level of the myth shows the point of connection between this phylogenetic event embedded in the legitimating symbol of culture and the ontogenetic encounter of the child with the authority of this culture. The boy experiences the authority of his father, who enforces the incest taboo in the family. To a certain extent he is placed in the same position as one of the sons in the primal horde, since the father appears to claim monopoly over the women in the household. Hence his powerful hatred for the father. But now the father can come to his aid by indicating the symbolic source of his authority and his responsibility to the fundamental law of the culture. The boy can then learn to appreciate that he will be free to find a mate exogamously, and he can overcome his patricidal impulses by realizing that he is himself a potential bearer of the same symbolic authority and a beneficiary of the same social arrangement. This marks the resolution of the boy's Oedipus complex.

Unfortunately the outcome is seldom so clear-cut. At issue is the transformation of the boy's love for both mother and father, with the full force of the instinctual drive behind it. And while his parents may help him to understand the symbolic order under which everyone lives, all three are working against the inertia of the drive, or its powerful attachment to its original objects. Hence the residual conflict. For if we can posit a remaining level of conflict in the boy, the same would hold for his parents, and their parents, and so on. The parents themselves, therefore, are not the ideal custodians of symbolic authority but are influenced by their own unresolved conflict with authority.

Thus the actual father, and the "symbolic father" whom he represents, remains hateful, and the sons continue to rage against him. This rage may not be consciously acceptable, since the child's ego tries to preserve the image of itself as loving and dutiful and therefore loved by its father, but it finds an outlet in the unconscious representation of a hateful and persecutory authority, the superego, that constantly obstructs the ego with reproaches and ridicule and is in turn rebelled against ineffectually by the ego. Behaviorally this takes the form of the ego's striving against the norms of the culture and against authority, as well as having to suffer the punishment that follows.[17] Hence Freud's conviction of the reserve of hostility to civilization and the patterns whereby people destroy what they have built up themselves.

THE RISK OF PLURALITY

Freud wrote from the point of view of the male child, and within the context of a male-dominated society and culture. Certainly men at that time remained subject to paternal rule far longer than was the case with women; sons had to achieve economic independence before marrying, while daughters were married off young. Hence Freud's myth of the primal horde exemplified the origins of that kind of family and social structure. But the essential outlines of his argument can be applied regardless of the sex of the parent or child: the essential point is the transformation from the incestuous dyad to the exogamous couple through the authoritative enforcement of the incest taboo in the culture. The child-follower has to repress, renounce, or sublimate its impulses in response to the leadership of its parents, and here we find the psychological grounds for the analogy to the relationship between the leaders and the led in politics and society at large.

The achievement of power puts the leader in a position analogous to a parent in relation to the members of the group, who then become his children. That, at least, is the unconscious structure that influences their dynamic. But they can transform this situation by elevating their grasp of the power relationship to the level of symbolic understanding. Then it becomes clear that they are there together in order to take care of the requirements of the group in relation to society as a whole, or of the society in relation to its broader environment. In politics, the law of the father makes it possible for people to act collectively rather than to disintegrate as groups under the pressure or rival ambitions to dominate, exploit, or abuse by asserting tyrannical power. The other side of this law, however, requires that the group experience its responsibility in association with the leader, so that they are ready to act in support of his leadership. The point is that both leaders and followers are then powerful but at the same time respectful of each other's contribution.

It is important to remember that the structure Freud analyzed in terms of the Oedipus complex—or the struggle to achieve a culture and society that can survive through the generations—remains unconscious. But one can well ask, if we are dealing with adults and with members of a culture, what importance can Freud's theory have, other than to explain the process of initiation? The answer lies in the fact that integration into a culture is never fixed. Indeed, every time a new group or organization emerges, or an old group or organization declines, the Freudian structure may influence the sequence of events.

Let us take the problem at its simplest manifestation: even once the brothers have renounced their desire to replace the father, and have agreed to the principles of incest taboo and exogamy, they still have to confront any number of decisions concerning the life of their society. And these decisions have to be accepted and integrated into the ongoing transmission of their culture. In short, every new sphere that requires their pioneering influence will evoke the possibility of conflict on the old lines. For the fact of the matter is that in the life of groups, no matter how well founded, there is a constant need to achieve a common will in order to maintain the group's capacity to act in its own interests. And the prospect of a common will always evokes the earliest form it took, in the will of the "primal father," as well as the earliest rebellion against it, and so on.

The plurality that characterizes our life on earth, and the issue of collective power that it constantly begs, will always stir up the questions that we have presumed answered in our individual and collective past.[18]

Thus there is no finality to the authority the brothers establish with the totem, since it only speaks to the immediate sphere of their common concern. The contract they made has to be made over and again, whenever the need arises to define the common will out of the possibility of conflicting wills among the many.

Freud himself examined two forms of organization that typically rely upon a rigid hierarchical construction of authority, where the leader comes very close to occupying the position of the "primal father."[19] In the Catholic Church and the army he saw all decisions coming down from the top, and being followed because of the love and faith that the institutions induce in the believers and the men. Decision making in these organizations remains a virtual monopoly of the one on top, modified at best by the need for information from below. And in this situation Freud discovered not only the reward of grandiosity and omnipotence enjoyed by the leader but also the rewards of dependence and relief from responsibility enjoyed by the followers. Both, therefore, enjoy a kind of return to childhood as the child imagines it: a parent with unlimited powers who knows everything and takes care of the child, and the child with unlimited freedom to feel safe and provided for. But while this constitutes the unconscious meaning of this structure, its effect in the world is utterly different.

The Catholic Church enjoys vast worldly powers that it uses to benefit its followers, especially its workers, and at the same time is secure in those powers because of the anxieties it can manipulate in order to keep its believers in line. Similarly the army can use the loyalty of its soldiers to carry out orders, thereby giving its generals the assurance that their own wills carry weight in the determination of affairs, as well as the politicians who, in turn, rely on their service. The subordinates who live in the unconscious fantasy of being taken care of by the leaders who "love" them, thus become pawns in the hands of those who have climbed to the top of these organizations. Of course this registers among the believers and the soldiers, if only unconsciously.

Indeed, one of the techniques of autocratic leadership is to find a suitable scapegoat for this resentment among the subordinates, in order to maintain the line of authority free of the hostility it engenders. Thus the armed forces require their enemy, and the believers require their heretics and infidels. Without them it is unlikely that the church or the army would continue in their accustomed form.

What we witness in a system of hierarchical domination is that the regression to the original condition can only be approximated in so far as it is accompanied by a phenomenon of scapegoating, or negative authority, where the followers adhere partly by splitting off the hostility that they direct against the alien enemy, and in part out of fear of the very hostility that they have been taught to believe typical of the alien enemy. In the case of armed forces this is clear. And in the case of the Catholic Church which dominated Freud's Vienna, the Jews provided the alien target. Elsewhere, no doubt, it was the Protestants, and so on.

The advantage of a dominant hierarchy is that it gives the leaders a feeling of security in their power to make decisions. But it also stirs up their fear of losing that power, so that they have a profound distrust of their followers. Thus the relationship between leaders and followers in this situation is characterized unconsciously by the distrust of the leaders and the resentment of the followers. And if the followers are thrown an enemy as a sop to their hostility, the leaders depend on the extent of their omnipotence for a source of reassurance and protection from their fears.

Psychoanalysis had not really provided the guidelines for the constitution of a democratic organization. Rather, it has provided a set of negative guidelines, or cautions. First it enables us to see that the problem of the unconscious structure persists, and is never finally resolved. Unless it is taken into consideration, we end up with paranoid leaders and hysterical followers, and an organization, or state, that produces the temporary well-being of those at the top only at the risk of considerable turmoil and open conflict. Soon enough the situation becomes one of open repression and arbitrary punishment, in which the leaders try to maintain their position on the basis of terror. Collaspe of tyranny of this sort is built into the logic of its structure.

On the other hand, democratic leadership and organization cannot, in fact, accommodate every need, desire, or opinion of the many who belong and have a right to a place in the group. But the fact of this limitation is not a function of the kind of authority or power that the leadership exercises. And it is not a matter of regression to a primitive state. It is, on the contrary, a factor inherent in the nature of human plurality and in the limited means whereby a group can define a common objective, and achieve it. Consequently an effective democratic organization is one in which sufficient recognition of this limitation—on at least three levels—is given in the process of decision making.

First, the reality of the group process—the requirement of achieving a common will—has to be addressed openly and accepted by its members. Second, that process has to include a clear recognition of the pressures that the group faces from its environment. These have to be honestly assessed, and not converted into a threat of persecution that the leaders can then exploit in order to provide the followers with a scapegoat for their resentment against their subjugation. The environment, in other words, is a collective responsibility. Third, the process should include the recognition of the information, knowledge, and expertise that are contributed by the different members and units within the group. Thus the members are regarded and treated as adults, rather than as incompetent children. And as adults they enjoy confidence in their own sphere of competence (while accepting its limits) as well as in the competence of others. The division of labor, in other words, requires the open recognition of interdependence.

It may seem that with these three conditions I have somehow strayed from Freud and psychoanalysis. Actually I have not. These are simply the conditions that have to be met in the resolution of the Oedipus complex in the case of the child and its parents. And it is the same set of conditions that society has to keep in place if it is to avoid the regression of its organizational imperative back to the level of conflict and hostility in Freud's mythical—but all too real—horde.

Perhaps the negative conclusion that I have drawn will appear overly pessimistic. But the reality of political upheavals in this century, with the extent of their violence and brutality, suggest that the capacity to achieve a symbolic level of authority in society is tenuous. Those countries with a history of political stability are rare, perhaps even exceptions. And while the unconscious influence of the Freudian structure can hardly explain political instability on its own, it certainly helps us to understand the importance—and the difficulty—of establishing a fundamental law that embodies and protects the symbolic principal of authority being exercised for the good of the whole. There is always the danger that the followers have to obey the law while the leader acts as if he were exempt.

At the level of organizations, the same principal suggests that a leadership hoping to prove effective in relation to a changing environment and changing opinions among its members will also pay attention to the flow of communication and information. Participation in the decision-making process, and understanding the conclusions reached, remain essential characteristics of an organization that avoids domination and submission, with their accompanying unconscious and counterproductive tendencies to fear and resentment. The law of the father proves to be essential not only to limit the possibilities of corruption and tyranny but in order to realize the goals of organizations and the values of a democratic society.

NOTES

1. *See,* for example, the case histories of Anna I., Frau Emmy, Miss Lucy, and Fraulein Elizabeth Von R., in Josef Breuer and Sigmund Freud, *Studies on Hysteria, The Standard Edition of the Complete Psychological Works of Sigmund Freud,* eds. James Strachey, vol. II (London: The Hogarth Press, 1955).
2. *See* "The 'Rat Man' " in *The Standard Edition of the Complete Psychological Works of Sigmund Freud,* vol. X and "An Infantile Neurosis" in vol. XVII.
3. Sigmund Freud's Papers on Technique are included in *The Standard Edition of the Complete Psychological Works of Sigmund Freud,* Vol. XII.
4. In this connection the seminal work is James Strachey, "The Nature of the Therapeutic Action of Psychoanalysis," *International Journal of Psycho-Analysis,* 15 (1934), pp. 117–26.

5. *See* Freud, "On Narcissism," *The Standard Edition of the Complete Psychological Works of Sigmund Freud,* vol. XIV, and Sandor Ferenczi, "Stages in the Development of the Sense of Reality," chapter 8 of his *Sex and Psychoanalysis,* trans. Ernest Jones (New York: Dover Publications, 1956).

6. *See* Margaret Mahler, Fred Pine, and Anni Bergman, *The Psychological Birth of the Human Infant: Symbiosis and Individuation* (New York: Basic Books, 1975).

7. Jacques Lacan, "The Function and Field of Speech and Language in Psychoanalysis," and "On a Question Preliminary to Any Possible Treatment of Psychosis," in *Ecrits,* trans. Alan Sheridan (New York: W.W. Norton & Co., 1977).

8. *See* Melanie Klein's pioneering study "Early Stages of the Oedipus Conflict and the Super-Ego Formation," *The Psycho-Analysis of Children,* trans. Alix Strachey (New York: Delacorte Press, 1975).

9. *See* Freud, "Three Essays on the Theory of Sexuality," *The Standard Edition of the Complete Psychological Works of Sigmund Freud,* vol. VII.

10. In part IV of *Totem and Taboo* Freud traces the role of ambivalence toward the father in the formation of the totem, and he shows the analogy with the formation of the superego in childhood. Since Freud was writing about families in which authority was primarily invested in the role of the father, he does not show how this same transformation can take place in relation to the mother. Melanie Klein, however, complements his work in that respect, beginning with her paper cited in footnote 8. Her later work on the schizoid-paranoid position and the depressive position clarifies the problem of ambivalence in the child's object relations. Klein, however, tends to understand the parents' authority chiefly in terms of the child's experience of hostility and deprivation. The symbolic dimension of the family as the transmitter of cultural authority tends to be underemphasized in her work.

    See Sigmund Freud, *Totem and Taboo* (1913), *The Standard Edition of the Complete Psychological Works of Sigmund Freud,* vol. XIII, and M. Klein, "The Early Development of Conscience in the Child," (1933) in *Love, Guilt and Reparation & Other Works* (New York: Delacorte Press, 1975).

11. Along with my colleagues Maria Gear and Ernesto Liendo, I have attempted an exploration of character structure in relation to the assumption of a sadistic and masochistic orientation. Whereas Melanie Klein stressed the sadistic dimension in the formation of object relations, Edmund Bergler, who practiced in Vienna and New York, developed an elaborate theory of masochism. In our view sado-masochism is a bipolar structure of identification in relation to an object, and the conscious awareness of the structure is an inverted form of its representation in the unconscious and its realization in action. *See* Maria Gear, Melvyn Hill, and Ernesto Liendo, *Working Through Narcissism: Treating its Sadomasochistic Structure* (New York: Jason Aronson, 1981). *See also* Edmund Bergler, *The Basic Neurosis: Oral Regression and Psychic Masochism* (New York: Grune & Stratton, 1949).

12. *See* Donald Winnicott, *The Maturational Process and the Facilitating Environment* (London: Tavistock, 1965), and *Through Pediatrics to Psycho-Analysis* (London: The Hogarth Press, 1958).

13. Sigmund Freud, *Totem and Taboo* (1913), *The Standard Edition of the Complete Psychological Works of Sigmund Freud,* vol. XIII.

14._____ , *Group Psychology and the Analysis of the Ego* (1921), *The Standard Edition of the Complete Psychological Works of Sigmund Freud,* vol. XVIII.

15._____ , *The Future of an Illusion* (1927), *The Standard Edition of the Complete Psychological Works of Sigmund Freud,* vol. XXI.

16._____ , *Civilization and Its Discontents* (1930), *The Standard Edition of the Complete Psychological Works of Sigmund Freud*, vol. XXI.

17. Edmund Bergler presents a highly modified analysis of the formation of the superego as an internalized representation of a sadistic authority that disguises its destructive intent with pseudomoral injunctions. It is in this context that one could discuss the discrepancy between the traditional standards of one generation and the changed reality for the one that follows. Here the disjunction might not be a source of sadistic corruption so much as the lag between the psychic mechanisms for internalizing authority and the requirements for adaption to change in reality. *See* E. Bergler, *The Superego* (New York: Grune & Stratton, 1962).

18. Hannah Arendt provides the most illuminating discussion of the phenomenon of human plurality in relation to the realities of political power. For Arendt freedom consists precisely in the political right of groups to come together in order to create the power to act in the world. Authority derives from that power. It can also shore itself up by relying on violence. But in the end even the tyrant requires the support—and so the power—of those who wield the instruments of violence. For a general discussion, *see* Hannah Arendt, *The Human Condition* (Chicago: University of Chicago Press, 1958), and for a more simple analysis of the concepts of power, violence, and freedom, *see* her treatise *On Violence* (New York: Harcourt Brace Jovanovich, 1970).

19. Freud's discussion of the church and the army occurs in part V of *Group Psychology and the Analysis of the Ego*.

3

LEADERSHIP SYSTEMS IN WORLD CULTURES

David M. Rosen

Any survey of world cultures would reveal that in all sociocultural systems there are leaders. These are persons or groups of persons who can mobilize human, material, and symbolic resources of society toward specific social ends. At the same time, the near universal existence of leaders tends to gloss over differences of such magnitude among these persons that any universal parsimonious definition of leadership appears unlikely. Rather than searching for such a definition of leadership, this essay is designed to explore the differences in forms of society-wide leaders from a cross-cultural, historical, and evolutionary perspective. The main questions will be: what are the varying forms of leadership as they have emerged over time? How are these tied to the structure of the sociocultural systems from which they are derived? And what do they tell us about the possibilities for leadership in modern complex societies such as our own?

THE LEADERSHIP SYSTEM

Put simply, leadership is a role that is understood in terms of the social and cultural context within which it is embedded and which shapes the particular forms it takes in any society. Following Banton, I understand roles to be sets of rights and obligations that are tied to social positions. In this analytical sense the concept of role is a normative construct, distinct from the actual way in which rights and duties may be carried out in concrete social situations.[1] Both leadership roles as well as the specific institutional supports and constraints within which leadership roles function constitute what I term the *leadership system*.

In this essay, the focus is upon those factors that comprise the leadership system in any given society. These can be thought of as involving three broad sociocultural dimensions: 1) the formal numerical distribution of leadership roles in society, 2) the means by which individuals or groups gain access to such roles, and 3) the means available to leaders for carrying out their roles. These major dimensions can be respectively termed: 1) the mode of distribution, 2) the mode of allocation, and 3) the mode of mobilization. Each of these dimensions of the leadership system contain specific elements which help determine the overall structure of the leadership system in any given society.

The elements which serve to make up the three dimensions of leadership are presented in terms of "ideal types."[2] The concept of the ideal type, as used in anthropology and sociology, is that of an abstract representation of a particular phenomena in which the essentials of that phenomena are presented. Virtually any phenomena can be presented in terms of ideal types, and typically ideal types are contrasted to one another. Most important, ideal types do not exist in reality. That is to say, if we compare the ideal types of "state" versus "stateless" society, "democracy" versus "theocracy," it is unlikely that any real system will completely conform to the essence of the ideal type. In this essay both the elements which make up the dimensions of leadership systems, as well as leadership systems themselves, are presented in terms of ideal types. Such models of leadership systems and their components facilitate the comparison of differences and similarities between leadership systems both cross-culturally and historically.

The Mode of Distribution:
Open versus Closed Systems

Differences in the mode of distribution can be understood in terms of the distinction I make between open versus closed systems. This refers to variation in the actual number of societywide leadership roles available in society. Examples of differences in leadership roles are widely available in the ethnographic literature. My use of the distinction between open versus closed systems is adapted from Diamond's discussion of cross-cultural differences in the organization of valued roles. Diamond points out that organization of valued roles (such as leadership) can be seen as taking on three broad forms: situational, generalized, and restricted.[3] These can be understood as follows:

1. *Situational* leadership roles are those where the existence of the role itself is temporary and largely a matter of circumstance. Leadership roles in many small-scale societies fall into this category, and the emergence of the role usually depends upon individual ability in relation to a specific task. People essentially take on the leadership roles they wish within any specific set of circumstances. Leadership here seems such an ambiguously constructed phenomena that for some anthropologists it seems unclear whether or not the term *leadership* is even appropriate to such systems.[4]

2. *Generalized* leadership roles refer to roles which individuals obtain as a result of general progress through the life cycle. Among the Masai and other pastoral groups in Africa, for example, the male population is organized into named groups on the basis of age so that all members of an age group fall into the leadership category upon reaching maturity. What is crucial about both situational and generalized role-distribution systems is that they are relatively open; there are no specifically defined numbers of leadership roles in society. Individuals take up these roles as they wish or as they move through the phases of the life cycle.

3. *Restricted* role distribution exists where there are only a relatively small number of leadership positions available. In the most autocratic state societies there is typically one "head of state" in the person of a king, a pharaoh, a führer, and so on. Some other dictatorial regimes may be run by junta or committee. More democratic states provide a greater range of societywide leadership roles in the forms of senators or parliaments. Thus, although there is a vast distinction between Ramses II and Ronald Reagan, they both function in societies where the leadership-role system, in comparison to other societies, is relatively closed.

The Mode of Allocation: Achievement and Ascription

Until now I have considered, albeit in a brief way, the actual number of societywide leadership roles. Of equal importance is the question of how individuals or groups gain access to such positions. Here a useful distinction to employ is the classic dichotomy between achievement and ascription.[5] The distinction between these two concepts (as applied to leadership) turns on whether or not specific groups or persons are more or less autonomically assigned to leadership positions or whether such roles (despite their limited number) are potentially available to those who aspire to them. Like the distinction between open and closed systems, the distinction between achievement and ascription is best conceived of as an ideal type analytical distinction, for in no society is there a leadership role which is totally a function of achievement or ascription. Leadership systems are best understood in terms of the degree to which access to the role is achieved or ascribed.

In many simple societies age and sex form the basic ascriptive criteria which determine eligibility for specific roles, even though individual achievement within such roles may determine leadership. In more complex restrictive systems, access to leadership roles may be limited to royal houses, families, or kin groupings. But even here, some element of achievement may involve members of ascriptive categories in competition for leadership roles. The bloody history of dynastic and monarchical successions is illustrative of this process, even where access to the most coveted positions are based upon highly ascriptive criteria.

The problem of distinguishing between achievement and ascription also raises the problem of distinguishing between real versus ideal behavior, between what people actually do from what they may claim to do. In many societies ideological claims are often made that access to leadership positions is a matter of achievement. The formal requirements of the United States Constitution clearly spell out that the only requirement for president is that a person be a native-born US citizen at least thirty-five years of age. Yet it is clear that historically, various ascriptive criteria such as sex, religion, and race have placed severe restrictions on the actual ability of a person to run for high office.

Despite these problems of definition and description the distinction between achievement and ascription has wide currency to the degree that it serves to define the dominant modes by which access to leadership positions can be organized.

The Mode of Mobilization: Power and Influence

Leaders as defined earlier are those persons or groups who can mobilize human, material, and symbolic resources toward specific ends. Thus far I have dealt primarily with the structure of the leadership system in terms of role distribution and access. Here, I turn to the specific problem of the means utilized by leaders in the process of resource mobilization.

The mobilization of resources in any social system depends upon the ability of leaders to direct the behavior of others. Exactly how this direction is carried out seems to vary greatly from society to society. One common way of understanding these differences turns on the distinction between the use of coercion and the use of persuasion in implementing leadership goals. The former is termed *power* while the latter is termed *influence*.[6]

In many societies it seems that leadership and the use of power are inextricably woven together. Leaders seem to enjoy (although in some instances with severe limitations) the right to use direct or indirect coercion to achieve specific ends. In feudal England the king could make use of both the executioner's sword as well as the church to ensure compliance. Nowadays many leaders can mobilize the high legal and administrative bureaucracies of the state in massive displays of power.

As has long been pointed out by Weber and others, however, the effective use of power requires social legitimation.[7] Put simply, the power holder must be seen as the rightful wielder of such power. Power legitimized in this way is usually termed *authority* and it is difficult, if not impossible, for leaders to wield power without authority.

Certainly, there are everyday occurrences in society where power can be used without authority. The difference between a murder and an execution turns on the absence of legitimacy in the former act. In democratic societies the use of power by a leader is circumscribed so that the nonlegitimate use of power can also delegitimate the leader. Watergate and the subsequent downfall of the Nixon administration in the United States is an example of the delegitimation of the office holder in the face of the nonlegitimate use of power. Moreover, the growth of democratic societies has effectively curbed the arbitrary use of power and increased restrictions on the legitimate use of power on the part of leaders. Conversely, leaders, even in democratic societies, have usually sought to expand their base of power; that is, to expand those areas in which the use of power would be considered legitimate.

The struggles about power and legitimacy which often preoccupy modern democracy are, however, unknown in most primitive societies. For in such systems the legitimate use of power is almost completely unknown. Instead, they are characterized by the degree to which influence, the use of persuasion, is the one and only means by which leaders prevail. In such systems, leaders lead by example, in the hope that others may follow. In fact, these are societies with plenty of leaders but hardly any followers.

Leadership and the Historical Development of Society

The elements discussed and defined here provide, in a rather abstract way, some basic conceptual tools for analyzing leadership systems. At the same time, however, we are equally interested in discussing the conditions under which different elements within leadership systems will predominate. Here, both cross-cultural and historical data suggest that the elements of leadership systems are not only analytically distinct but temporally distinct as well. The historical record indicates that the development of society generally involves a movement from the small-scale societies anthropologists usually term *simple* or *primitive* to the complex nation-states of the modern world. Broadly speaking, *this movement has been characterized by increasing economic and social inequality in nearly every sphere of life.* Thus, the watershed of complex society has been the development systems of caste, class, bureaucratic, and sexual stratification unknown or muted in simple systems. Paralleling this the development of leadership systems is equally clear: leadership systems have tended to become increasingly closed, ascribed, and power based. Although there have been major reversals in this trend in some of the Western democracies, socioeconomic disparity, social complexity, and the overall truncation and centralization of leadership systems all seem fused to one another.

To be fully appreciated, developments in the history of leadership systems need to be linked to current knowledge concerning the relationship between leadership and the control of economic resources. Here the data indicate that leadership is closely correlated with varying levels of control over economic resources. Moreover, this relationship seems so strong that it has been suggested as a cultural universal. Put simply, leaders seem to largely be those persons drawn from groups and categories of persons who tend to control important economic resources of society. Not surprisingly, then, as society has become increasingly complex and economically stratified, so too have leadership systems come to reflect basic social and economic inequalities.

But of far greater significance is the considerable difference between primitive and complex society with respect to the degree and kind of linkages between leadership systems and the control of economic resources. In primitive societies, the leadership system seems to be involved in the distribution of prestige and ceremonial goods, with only limited involvement in the production of strategic, life-sustaining resources. In complex societies, however, the sphere of politics and the sphere of economics are highly intertwined. Moreover, it is only in modern social systems that economics and politics are so embedded in one another that the concept of political economy becomes a useful one for understanding society.

Leadership and the State

Another way of viewing the development of leadership systems turns on the distinction between "stateless" and "state level" societies. In discussing societywide leaders, in most modern societies we speak of "heads of state" as well as others who can affect the mobilization of resources on an enormous scale. In referring to the "state" in its most abstract sense (as opposed to the "state of New York") we are referring to an aggregate of institutions which link up the subsystems of a complex society. But the state did not always exist. In much the same way that economic stratification marks the transition from simple to complex society, so it also marks the transition from stateless to state-level societies. Moreover, there is considerable agreement that once state societies come into being they have at least two broad functions: 1) a coordinative function by which the basic resources of society are managed and integrated and 2) a hegemonic function by which the system of social stratification is supported and perpetuated over time.[8] Thus to the degree that the state functions in both these capacities, societywide leaders must adopt two broad perspectives: 1) a universalist perspective by which they represent themselves to be leaders, guardians, and representatives of society as a whole and 2) a particularistic perspective by which they help to protect the structure of inequality and privilege which appears to be tied to state formation. In sum, then, the emergence of state-level leadership systems is also linked to a movement from open, achieved, influence-based systems to one which is closed, ascribed, and power based.

Leadership and Sexual Bias

One of the most significant problems for discussion deals with the degree to which women have access to leadership positions. This is an extremely complicated issue which can only be dealt with briefly here. It is clear that even in simple societies there is some degree of role differentiation based upon age and sex. While age may be only a temporary obstacle to access to particular roles, sex seems to be a near universal barrier to some roles.

It is sometimes argued that a universal distinction has historically existed between the so-called public and private domains of society. This is between the set of social relations centered upon the family and household and those which extend into the wider spheres of social life.[9] Because of their involvement in child rearing and childbearing, women's activities seem to preclude their involvement in the kinds of societywide positions I have defined here as constituting leadership. There is some evidence to suggest that in the most primitive societies, the distinction between public and private domains is relatively meaningless and that in such systems there are no clearly developed household and family units which can be distinguished from the society at large. In such systems sex-role differentiation seems to involve parallel but rather coequal role systems, and sexual differences do not seem to imply sexual hierarchy. From this perspective leadership positions can be seen as open to all. Support for this position is often gleaned from observations made of simple societies prior to extensive European colonial expansion. Other evidence is derived from the examination of recently studied primitive societies which appear to be among the simplest in terms of social organization.[10]

Most of the contemporary ethnographic data from primitive and complex societies, however, suggest a clear male bias in leadership systems. This has sometimes been linked to the presence of warfare or extensive intervillage trade networks, where the physical mobility of men (that is, their lack of involvement in child care) tends to favor their involvement in leadership.

Others have argued that the emergence of the state also tends to favor the emergence of males in positions that would favor male leadership. The argument here is that because men were not involved in childbearing and child rearing they were more easily recruited into positions favoring personal mobility.[11] Thus for a variety of reasons, many of which are linked to the relative mobility of men and the relative immobility of women, leadership systems, except in the most primitive of societies, appear to be male biased and male based. Obviously, in more contemporary, complex societies there have been a variety of ways in which women have limited their involvement in child-rearing activities, thus opening up for themselves the possibility of attaining the kinds of societywide roles historically available to men.

LEADERSHIP SYSTEMS: A COMPARATIVE TYPOLOGY

In evaluating the dimensions of leadership I have suggested that the emergence of complex society and the development of the state with its attendant forms of economic stratification has tended to promote leadership systems of a nonegalitarian variety. With these observations in mind it may also be useful to develop a typology based upon the different ways in which the elements of leadership combine. This typology would largely be a deductive ordering of the formal elements defined earlier.

Nevertheless, the combinations are informed by our broad understanding of the development of leadership systems as defined above. Just as the basic elements of the dimensions of leadership were themselves presented in the form of ideal types, so any typology developed from these elements also constitutes an ideal type. Consequently, the leadership systems defined by the typology are quite abstract and gloss over much of the great social and cultural variation in human society. At the same time the typology does allow us to see how historical development has altered the basic composition of leadership systems.

The typology presented here (*see* Figure 3-1) distinguishes among four broad types of leadership systems: Egalitarian, Semiegalitarian, Rank, and Stratiform. Two subtypes of semiegalitarian leadership are also included (categorical and managerial) as are two types of stratiform leadership systems (authoritarian and democratic). Again, these types certainly do not exhaust the variety of leadership systems which have been described. What the typology does capture, however, are the major principles which underlie the cross-cultural and historical variations in leadership system. Each of these systems is linked to forms of social and economic organization which appear to provide a basis for the leadership systems described.[12]

Type I: Egalitarian Leadership

The forms of egalitarian leadership described in Type I are found in many of the societies anthropologists term *simple* or *primitive*. They are all characterized by the widespread availability of leadership roles, the ease of access to such roles, and the use of influence as the main mode by which

FIGURE 3-1   Leadership Systems

SYSTEM TYPE	MODE OF DISTRIBUTION	MODE OF ACCESS	MODE OF MOBILIZATION
Type I EGALITARIAN	OPEN	ACHIEVEMENT	INFLUENCE
Type II A. SEMIEGALITARIAN: CATEGORICAL	OPEN	ASCRIPTION	INFLUENCE
B. SEMIEGALITARIAN: MANAGERIAL	CLOSED	ACHIEVEMENT	INFLUENCE
Type III RANK	CLOSED	ASCRIPTION	INFLUENCE
Type IV A. STRATIFORM: AUTHORITARIAN	CLOSED	ASCRIPTION	POWER
B. STRATIFORM: DEMOCRATIC	CLOSED	ACHIEVEMENT	POWER

leadership is exercised. All these forms are associated with economies where the basic productive resources of society are open to all and in which there is little connection between leadership and the control of major productive resources.

Egalitarian leadership exists where a wide variety of factors serve to prevent or inhibit more permanent forms of leadership. The classic cases of egalitarian leadership are found in those societies where the main economic activities are organized around the hunting and foraging of wild animals, fruits, and vegetables. Societies characterized by such forms of leadership are often regarded as the simplest of societies and examples include the Eskimo, the Australian Aborigines, and the !Kung hunter-gatherers of the Kalahari Desert in Namibia. Of all these peoples, the best described are the hunting-and-foraging groups of the Kalahari, whose lifeways often form the basis of anthropological discussions of simple societies.

For a variety of reasons there seem to be no formally recognized leaders in !Kung society. Of major importance here seems to be the basic instability of the residence groups which make up !Kung society. There always seems to be a core residence group which is associated with one or more permanent water holes. This group is regarded as the "owners" of the water and adjacent territory, although the concept of ownership here comes to involve only nominal supervisory rights over access to these areas.

The instability of these groups seems to be a function of changes in water supply as well as changes in the availability of wild animals and plants in any given area. As a result of ecological shifts, the composition of any residence group changes as individuals alter their place of residence according to individual need and local custom. Here one must imagine many small clusters of people combining, separating, and recombining, with a constant shift of personnel among the clusters. This phenomena, known as "residential flux," seems to inhibit formation of the kinds of enduring social relations which might result in more permanent forms of leadership.[13]

According to Lee, the basic !Kung ideology is that there are no leaders.[14] When asked whether there are any headmen the !Kung have replied: "of course we have headmen . . . each of us is headman over himself." But, in fact, there do exist individuals who seem to take on leadership roles, despite the fact that these remain unacknowledged and such kinds of leadership roles seem to depend entirely upon the most indirect and subtle forms of persuasion. Moreover, such leaders are well integrated into the daily life of the small bands of between ten and twenty persons which make up !Kung residential units.

According to Lee, access to leadership seems to involve the fulfillment of one or more of the following traits:

1) Seniority in a large family. Here the eldest members of a family grouping are often placed within leadership roles within their own grouping. To the degree that a camp is composed primarily of one family, such persons stand a high chance of falling into leadership position.

2) Land "ownership." Individuals who are members of land "owning" groups also seem to have access to leadership positions. This seems to be a major way in which women come into positions of leadership.

3) Marriage into a land "owning" group. This seems to be the major way in which men come into leadership. Here energetic and capable men from other camps marry into such positions or share them with their spouses.

4) Personal qualities. Here entrance into leadership positions seems largely based upon personal characteristics which would attract followers. Most important among these seems to be speaking and mediating skills, but good hunters and ritual specialists also are capable of attracting followers.

According to Lee, there is a surprising lack of commonly held personality traits among such persons except that aggression and arrogance automatically disqualify individuals for leadership positions.

In !Kung society, then, there seems to be a variety of ways in which individuals are placed into leadership positions. Yet, these positions seem to carry little weight; leaders neither give orders nor do they make any demands. Significantly, their material life-style is often below that of other members in their camps. In sum, then, leadership among the !Kung seems to involve the decisions of individuals to take up positions which influence the course of decision making. The routes to such social positions seem so varied that, in fact, one might decide that leadership among the !Kung simply involves the decision to act like a leader. The main issue among the !Kung seems to be who is ineligible for such roles (that is, who is too aggressive or arrogant) rather than who is eligible for the roles.

Type II: Semiegalitarian Leadership Systems.

In this paper, I define *semiegalitarian leadership* as existing in those leadership systems where men rather than women tend to monopolize leadership positions. As in egalitarian leadership systems, the ability of a leader seems largely to depend upon his ability to persuade. Moreover, such systems also rest upon a generally egalitarian economic base, in which the major resources of society are open to all. Yet, there is also clear ascription in the sense that women are generally excluded from leadership positions. At the same time, leadership positions are themselves so tenuously constructed that they often exhibit the transient ephemeral qualities found in egalitarian systems.

Categorical Categorical leadership places whole groups or categories of persons into positions of leadership by means of rather broad-based ascriptive criteria. A good example are the many societies where age and sex categories become the basis for leadership positions. Perhaps the best described of such systems occur among the cattle-keeping peoples of East Africa such as the Masai and the Samburu, where the male population is organized into specific age groups, all of whose members come to assume leadership roles as the group passes into maturity.[15]

All contemporary ethnographers will undoubtedly agree that there is clear male bias in such systems. Here leaders are senior men who come into leadership positions, as a group, when they reach their midforties. Significantly, such systems seem to develop in a context of routine intertribal warfare and in economies demanding a fair amount of mobility in order to accommodate the needs of cattle, sheep, and goats. Both these factors tend to favor the emergence of male bias in leadership.

Societies of this type are sometimes termed *gerontocracies* to point out the dominant character of the older men. The dynamics of the system of leadership are relatively simple. As each age group matures it moves through specific socially defined categories. Among the Samburu and Masai these are 1) Warrior, 2) Junior Elder, 3) Senior Elder, and 4) Nominal Elder. For a certain period of time the age group is in the Warrior category, but eventually it is pushed out and replaced by men of another age group. Age groups achieve leadership when they reach the Senior Elder category. Yet the leadership role available to elders is limited to about fifteen years. As the age group moves out of the Senior Elder category, its members, still regarded as elders, begin to lose influence in a very dramatic way, opening up the role for those people who replace them.

Thus for the men, at least, all positions of leadership are open to all. Women, on the other hand appear to have very little influence and as a result these societies are best thought of as having semiegalitarian leadership systems.

Managerial A second type of semiegalitarian leadership can be termed *managerial leadership.* Managerial leaders are typically associated with village societies where small-scale agriculture predominates but where there is usually a considerable amount of intervillage and intersocietal trade of prestigious goods. In such systems managerial leaders emerge and appear to play a key role in the organization of productive activities for trade.[16] Typically, the number of managerial leaders in a society is relatively small, although there are some cases, such as among the Tsembaga of New Guinea, where the number of such leaders is so great that they suggest a situation closer to the kind of conditional leadership found among hunting-and-gathering peoples.[17]

Individuals gain access to managerial roles largely through their own effort. Normally, managerial leaders are among the hardest workers in a village and among the most politically and economically astute as well. In much of the anthropological literature, managerial leaders have come to be known by the rather archaically sexist title of "Big Men." Managerial leaders seem to have specialized roles with respect to the organization and management in society. At the same time, they exist as leaders only on the basis of their personal skills. This latter element is such a major component of their leadership that they have sometimes been termed *natural leaders.*

Managerial leaders are hard workers; they are usually more productive than other villagers; they tend to initiate activities such as gardening and repair work; and they are usually prominent in local discussions. Their physical stamina and verbal ability cause them to stand out in society. At the same time managerial leaders are limited by their persuasive ability. They can cajole, beg, and embarrass people into productive activities but they cannot order anyone. Most significantly, they function in nonstratified societies. They lead in contexts where all individuals, leaders or not, have free, equal, and unencumbered access to the productive resources of society. Managerial leaders attain leadership by placing themselves in the center of a network of production and exchange and their success as producers and traders makes them individuals of influence in society at large.

The trading network of the New Guinea Highlands provides a good example of the sort of pivotal organizational role which typically brings managerial leaders into public limelight.

In New Guinea there are many societies in which the status of Big Man is linked to exchange systems in which pigs, shells, bird skins, and stone axes are traded. The trade is carried out by partners who are both Big Men and relatives by marriage. The trade is governed by a customary prohibition against individuals consuming pigs that either they or their close relatives have raised. Thus all the people must trade in order to eat. Pigs produced by one group of kin are traded to other groups of kin who are related by marriage. The Big Men in this trading system are those who organize the exchanges in pigs. In order to obtain pigs, a Big Man works very hard in managing the production of his own herd as well as exhorting his own kinsfolk to provide pigs for the trade. But the trade is a tricky business, for he must satisfy his own kin with pigs if they are to continue to produce for him, while at the same time he must satisfy his trading partner. All must feel the trade is equitable.

Because the managerial leader functions within the economic heartland of village society, a very important component of the leadership roles involves a process known as *redistribution*.[18] This is termed redistribution because it involves the collection and centralization of goods on the one hand, and the redistribution of these same goods to the population at large on the other. In this process, managerial leaders stand out as redistributors, that is, as persons who manage the collection, centralization, and redistribution of goods. Sometimes the goods involved are simply pooled for a short period of time and then immediately redistributed. At other times, the goods may be held in storage until an appropriate time for their redistribution emerges. What is critical, however, is the existence of customary channels by which the movement of goods to a central organization takes place and the existence of similar channels by which the goods are moved out again to the population at large.

The entire process of redistribution, the sometimes ceremonial displays in which the fortunes of trade are dispensed to followers, provides a great deal of prestige to the managerial leaders. Managerial leaders have been known to literally impoverish themselves in order to please their dependents.

Where people become managerial leaders it seems reasonable to assume that personal influence and the occasional gratitude of followers must be the major incentive. For managerial leaders, there is no clear economic advantage to leadership. They do not enjoy a higher standard of living than their followers, and occasionally experience a far lower standard of living. To this extent, leadership in such situations must carry its own personal rewards.

Type III: Rank Leadership

Rank leadership systems seem to be associated with societies of somewhat greater complexity than those associated with egalitarian leadership systems. More specifically, rank leaders exist in those societies whose systems of production and trade are more intensive and widespread. Rank leaders and managerial leaders share many characteristics in common. There is reason to believe that rank leaders may often develop out of their more egalitarian counterparts. What distinguishes the rank leader, however, is that access to leadership positions in rank setting is clearly ascribed and limited to categories and groups (usually kin groups such as lineages and clans) of persons who have socially recognized claims to such positions. Rank leaders in many primitive societies have been described as chiefs, kings, sheikhs, and other titles. Moreover, their rights are often validated by belief systems which give divine sanction to their leadership. Despite the fact that rank leaders are elevated from the rest of society by socially prescribed and enduring status distinctions, such distinctions afford them few, if any, economic privileges. Typically, their standard of living is no higher than that of their followers and more significantly, they are also bound by the use of influence and persuasion to achieve their ends.

The link between leadership and redistribution is especially prominent in rank societies, but where the managerial leader created a following by personally creating a small redistributive network, rank leaders essentially control a highly institutionalized redistributive system. In fact, redistribution becomes a far more elaborate and ceremonial act under the control of rank leaders than among managerial leaders. The Potlatch, for example, a fantastic celebration, feasting, and whole-scale giveaway of material goods and food found among the Indians of the northwest coast of the United States and Canada in the nineteenth century was part of the system of rank leadership found there. Elaborate displays of wealth were arranged by chiefs who then redistributed the wealth to followers. As in a managerial leadership, the need to attract followers through the redistribution system is of equal importance and a key to the influence of the rank leader.[19]

In some rank systems the process of redistribution affects not only produced goods but the basic resources of society as well. A good example of this is the special role the "king" of the Lozi (a tribal people in Zambia) played in the redistribution of land.[20] Among the Lozi the rights in land were distributed in hierarchical fashion. These were not rights of ownership as we know them but rights to administer land. Some Lozi say the king owns the land, but this is only in the sense that he grants administrative rights to others. Normally the Lozi king grants administrative rights termed *secondary estates* to village heads. These, in turn, grant tertiary estates to the various heads of the households which make up a village. Administrative rights are held in perpetuity so that the granting of them to village heads is largely symbolic. The village heads have actually inherited the estates from their fathers. Just as important, the kind cannot take away the rights he symbolically grants. What then are the king's administrative rights? These are largely reversionary rights to assign control over land which falls out of use. If households move away, or villages break up, either the village head or the king then controls the land. They, in turn, however, will give it to new settlers or villages when the land is required for productive use.

The Lozi distinguish between the rights of persons to assign or control land, and the rights of persons to use land. While the former is a prerogative of kings and village and household heads, the right to use land productively is a right of citizenship which cannot be denied to anyone. Thus, despite the existence of administrative estates, all people have rights to the basic productive force of society: land. The right to organize the redistribution of land does not give the Lozi king greater control over production. The Lozi say, "The king is also a beggar," indicating that if he wanted land he would have to ask for it as would any other person. But whereas the managerial leader created a following by personally creating a small redistributive network, rank leaders essentially control a highly institutionalized redistributive system.

The prerogative of rank, however, often provides rank leaders with economic control unavailable to managerial leaders. In contrast to managerial leaders, rank leaders often do not participate directly in the production process. Instead, their control over redistribution permits them to siphon off sufficient surplus themselves and select followers without direct input of labor. The gleaning of surplus permits the support of part-time specialists, which further extends the rank leaders, control over the economy.

A good example of this was found among the Trobriand Islands near New Guinea.[21] All Trobrianders fell into one of two major social categories. They were either commoners or members of one of the four mythically defined chiefly subclans. A key to understanding the role of the Trobriander chief was that polygamy was a privilege of rank and that chiefs alone were permitted to take more than one wife. Among the Trobrianders, marriage involved a man in a set of customary exchanges with his wife's brother. The main agricultural crop on the island was yams. Each year, at harvest time, a man was entitled to receive a substantial portion of the yearly yam crop from his wife's brother. He, in turn, was obligated to give a substantial portion of his own crop to his sister's husband.

It is obvious that from the point of view of a chief, payments in yams were much more extensive than for commoners. A chief with many wives was the recipient of many yams. Thus, the customary obligations of marriage placed the chief in a uniquely advantageous position to build his own status and prestige as a great and generous redistributor.

The control over surplus permitted the chief to extend his involvement in external trade. The Trobriand Islands were part of a common system of trade which linked many different islands together. The surplus goods permitted a chief to support part-time canoe building, and thus chiefs could become major sponsors of other island trading expeditions. Such expeditions brought back goods which were highly valued in Trobriand society. They contributed greatly to the influence of the chief.

It is important to note that not all villages were headed by chiefs. Some villages were led by headmen whose status was remarkably similar to that of the managerial leader. But the achievement of leadership positions by Trobriand managerial leaders was limited by the ranking system and its customary prerogatives. Limited to monogamy, managerial leaders could exercise their influence only over their own village, unlike chiefs, whose wives and influence could extend over several villages. But the fact that villages could be legitimately led by commoners meant that people could escape the influence of a chief by forming or joining a new village outside the chief's control.

Nevertheless, there were clear economic advantages for commoners to align themselves with chiefs since the latter could provide them with the means to participate in trading relationships of great importance to the islanders.

But despite the fact that rank leaders have privileges not associated with egalitarian leadership systems, they still depend largely upon the good will of followers who continue to have open access to the economic resources of society. Like their egalitarian counterparts, they spend the bulk of their time creating, not ruling, a following.

Type IV: Stratiform Leadership

Stratiform leadership systems occur where there is a hierarchical distinction between those who control the productive resources of society and those who are the direct producers.

Stratified societies revolve around the relationship between those who control production and those who do the producing. These are not the only interesting and important relationships in such systems, but this relationship provides the central dynamic. Moreover, although there may be a certain degree of individual mobility—both upward and downward—the system of stratification must remain relatively stable. The existence of stratification also involves an unequal distribution of status, prestige, and privileges. Control over production is typically associated with high status, prestige, and often remarkable levels of consumption. In short, stratified societies are marked by major economic, social, and cultural distinctions between the controllers and the producers.

The history of stratified societies is, of course, complex. Stratified societies are not characterized by common organizational or productive activities. Feudalism, capitalism, and state socialism represent very different ways in which society can be organized. What these systems share, however, is that as social systems they depend upon the structured inequality between controllers of the conditions of production and the direct producers. In other words, since the emergence of economic stratification, much of the history of the world has been dominated by societies which, though very different from one another, deny the vast majority of their populations direct control over productive resources.

Similarly, since the emergence of stratified societies, political leaders have often been drawn from groups and categories of persons who have greater control over economic resources. Such leaders represent, directly or indirectly, these dominant groups and categories, although at much the same time they are often perceived as and perceive themselves as representing society as a whole. Since the emergence of stratified societies, leadership systems have invariably been closed. Moreover, leaders in such systems invariably have recourse to the use of power in order to ensure the continuity of society.

Stratiform leadership systems function within an economic environment largely determined by these facts. At the same time there are clear differences among stratiform systems. The typology suggests that two broad forms exist: authoritarian and democratic. In authoritarian systems there is greater cohesion between economic structures and political structures so that political leaders directly orchestrate the economy as well. In more democratic systems, there appears to be a disjunction between economic and political systems, and political leaders are less directly in control of economic matters.

Authoritarian leadership   Authoritarian leadership systems seem to exist in societies where the economy is directly subordinated to the political leadership system. Authoritarian leadership systems were common in the ancient world with Egypt, Mesopotamia, China, and India providing prime examples. Similarly, the ancient civilizations of the Maya and the Aztec also were characterized by authoritarian regimes. In more recent times Nazi Germany, Fascist Italy, the Soviet Union, and China all provide instances of the great variety of political leadership systems which can be understood as authoritarian.

Authoritarian regimes can be characterized by the relatively autonomous and unchecked use of power on the part of political leaders. Obviously in all leadership systems power is channeled and institutionalized and subject to various checks and balances. In authoritarian systems, however, checks over power of political leadership are generally far weaker than exist in more democratic systems. In fact, a hallmark of authoritarian leadership systems is that such leaders normally utilize the state apparatus in which they function to eliminate, insofar as it is possible, autonomous, independent sources of power which do not emanate from the state system itself.

In ancient authoritarian regimes, such sources of power emanated from family or kinship ties or might have been linked to religious instructions and orders which stood relatively autonomously from the state. In all systems where authoritarian leadership existed, such leaders attempted to consolidate state power by breaking up alternative sources of power and authority. Henry Tudor's struggles with the Roman Church are only one example of a process which characterizes the problematic relationship between centralized power and authority and alternative power bases in society.

Alternative sources of power and authority have also emanated from different modes of economic organization. The pastoral societies existing on the fringes of ancient Chinese civilization always represented a challenge to the state and state leadership, since their ways of life could not be brought under state control. Similarly, ancient states often brought about the destruction of economics based upon hidden agriculture which also stood outside of the managed environment of state production. Finally, petty capitalism inside Communist states provides a challenge to state authority which the state has sometimes attempted to destroy and at other times to control.

A main characteristic of the societies in which authoritarian leadership systems flourish is the extreme embeddedness of the economy in the political system. This has been discussed by Wittfogel[22] in his distinction between semimanagerial and managerial regimes. Wittfogel placed many of the civilizations of the Old and New Worlds into the semimanagerial category and located modern-day Soviet Union and China into the managerial category. Wittfogel specifically argued that the ancient authoritarian regimes developed out of the need to coordinate and manage large irrigation systems. Leadership in these regimes emerged out of the enormous and complex bureaucratic structures which essentially carried out managerial, supervisory, and defensive tasks. At the same time, however, the political structures became more powerful than society in the sense that the economy soon came to support the growth of the bureaucratic and leadership systems which it created. The political system, in this sense, conquered the economy and converted the various modes of production and exchange of society into its own direct use. Wittfogel used this model to explain the structure of modern-day Soviet Union and China. The latter, he argued, were actually more despotic versions than their ancient counterparts. In this case, the historically constructed bureaucracy absorbed and overrode changes in the economy brought about by revolution, creating a so-called Asiatic

Restoration, namely the subversion of a modern revolution by an ancient bureaucracy.

Other critics of state socialism have echoed similar themes. Djilas,[23] for example, specifically argues that the historical development of the economy in Communist societies is a reflection of the development of the political systems from a revolutionary dictatorship to a reactionary despotism. The dominance of political structures over the economy is the hallmark of Communist political systems. Moreover, much of Communist ideology is designed to support the need for state and political intervention into the economy. Typically, nonsocialist economies, whether capitalist or peasant, are seen as anarchic and irrational and incapable of supporting human collective needs. Thus state political intervention into the economy becomes mandated in order to rationalize the economy, so as to meet such needs.

Leadership roles in authoritarian systems are invariably closed, although there are certainly a great many variations in the number and form of key leadership positions. The closed centralized character of authoritarian leadership systems is often justified in terms of the great managerial tasks with which the society is faced. In ancient authoritarian systems leadership roles might be limited to one or two persons with divine pretensions. In more modern systems leadership roles are usually shared among key officials with definite spheres of power and authority.

Access to the structures of power are often highly ascribed. In ancient authoritarian systems leadership was largely gained through principles of kinship and inheritance. In many authoritarian societies the military or the bureaucracy may, in fact, constitute a class out of which potential leaders are drawn, making it difficult or impossible for individuals outside such ascribed categories to reach significant positions of leadership. Nevertheless there are major elements of achievement involved in reaching main leadership roles. Individuals, once having met the more formal and ascriptive criteria, must still achieve leadership posts, largely through a difficult climb through the bureaucratic structures of the leadership system. Individuals desiring leadership posts will invariably have to seek out patrons, mobilize clients, appeal to successful interest groups, beat opponents, and create an aura of charisma around themselves so as to "make it" into leadership positions.[24] Significantly, once a person meets the basic ascriptive criteria, the process of becoming a leader in an authoritarian regime requires many of the same skills required to become a leader in almost any political system. One possible exception is that displays of overt power are often a significant variable in determining achievement in such contexts. Thus control over the police or the army, a factor which might eliminate a person from political competition in more democratic systems, might serve to enhance a person's political position in more authoritarian structures.

Finally, the power available to leaders in authoritarian systems is normally greater than that available in more democratic systems. In ancient authoritarian states the power of the leader was often exercised in displays of physical cruelty. Physical punishment was often routinized and bureaucratized, both as a means of mobilizing the labor force as well as for controlling members of government bureaucracies. In many instances the executioner was a permanent fixture of the royal court. In more modern systems, the secret police or the state police have often primarily served as a political force during dissent through the routine use of physical force and torture. Similarly the courts and the law can become harnessed to state systems of political control.

In sum, authoritarian leadership systems have existed where the state has attempted to gain complete control over the rest of society, especially in the management of the economy. The enormous tasks involved in such an enterprise are used, in fact, to justify the centralized and authoritarian control of leaders within such systems. Moreover, it may well be that once a state system sets as its goal complete management of an economy, this is bound to lead to the expansion of power and authority within the leadership system. But, since such control is probably elusive, it may serve as an unrealizable goal toward which authoritarian leadership is ever harnessed and justified.[25]

Democratic leadership   Democratic leadership systems also function within highly stratified economic systems. At the same time, such systems seem to flourish largely where there is a major disjunction between the political and the economic system. Thus while politics and economics may be heavily integrated, the political structures seem to be more dependent upon economic considerations than is the case in more authoritarian systems.

A correlation between capitalism and democracy has been championed by Milton Friedman.[26] Friedman has basically argued that the near anarchic and highly competitive character of the market system effectively removes the economy from control of political authority and thereby reduces the concentration of power. The essential argument is that separation of political and economic power is great enough so that economic power can be used to check the abuse of political authority. Essentially, the decentralization of the economy creates nongovernmental sources of power.

Socialist critics of capitalism have often agreed in part with Friedman. They have basically argued that capitalism is anarchic and irrational and, as mentioned earlier, thus fails to satisfy collective needs.[27] In this sense they see political freedom purchased at high economic cost. Under some utopian socialist visions, increased state intervention would solve the problem of capitalist anarchy and irrationality without limiting political freedom.[28] In reality, however, wherever massive state intervention in the economy has occurred, political freedoms of the kind usually known under capitalism have been curtailed. Put simply, authoritarian and managerial states and leadership systems have usually sought to impose economic rationality at the cost of political freedom. Some critics of capitalism have argued that the day of "anarchic" capitalism has passed and that the future of capitalism is essentially one of monopoly capitalism in which the state will come to intervene in the economy in as equally a pernicious way as that found in other authoritarian systems. While obviously this could come to be true, the equation between capitalism and political freedom still remains quite strong.

It is clear that in the United States and elsewhere where capitalism has flourished, the relative anarchy of the economic system has served to create multiple centers of power which have effectively inhibited the emergence of societywide leadership systems with the coordinative and coercive power embedded in authoritarian leadership systems. Obviously in some areas there have been alliances which have cut across political and economic boundaries. The well-worn concept of the military-industrial complex points specifically to a fusion and integration of power which is fundamentally regarded as unhealthy in this country. But even high-ranking leaders have been fearful of this. As is well known, it was the rather conservative President Dwight D. Eisenhower who was among the first to point out the dangers of this coordination of power and economics in the United States.

The societywide leadership system in capitalist societies such as the United States must invariably come to deal with the system of supports and constraints which the leadership system provides. Like other stratified systems, democratic leadership systems are relatively closed, and power based. In most representative democracies, leaders are usually drawn from the economic elite although, in the United States, several have come from relatively modest economic backgrounds. (Nevertheless, whatever route individuals may take, by the time they are in a position to become societywide leaders, they usually have come to represent various sources of power in American society and have had to harmonize their personal interests with these sources.) In this sense, it is difficult if not impossible for radicals of left or right to have more than local regional impact, since recruitment into societywide leadership positions involves a process of accommodation to the multiple centers of power, and thus has a moderating effect upon political ideology. Thus leadership involves more than a simple climb through the bureaucracy in democratic states since not all power is centered in the political bureaucracy. Leaders must build extensive networks or contacts with sources of power outside the formal national political system. This involves compromises with business, labor unions and even, at times, criminal elements. Thus, while certainly a relatively closed system in terms of role distribution, access to political power depends very much more upon achievement than in more authoritarian systems.

Finally, because capitalism creates the kind of alternative centers of power which in the ancient world were embedded in family and religious institutions, it is much harder for democratic leaders to exercise unilateral power. In a sense, gaining access to leadership position involves gaining access to a position of power as well as surrendering power to those forces through whom a leader must work in order to lead. While capitalism is not the only force which might serve to decentralize political power in the state it has, in the last two hundred years, proved to be a powerful check upon authoritarian rule.

CONCLUSION

In this chapter, I have provided a typology of leadership systems which covers a variety of societies from simple to complex. It has been argued, broadly speaking, that over the course of human history leadership systems have become more centralized, less accessible to the populace at large, and more dependent upon the use of power. It has also been shown that the linkage between the political system and the economic system seems to be of principle importance in understanding the nature of the leadership system. In simple or primitive societies there often seems to be a complete break between politics and the organization of principle economic resources. Where leadership roles are directly and unambiguously linked to economic issues, they are so only with respect to the distribution of prestige goods in society. Thus, leadership appears to be compartmentalized as a separate sphere of activity which does not usually spill over and dominate other activities of society. Leadership seems largely uninvolved in the production of basic resources, which is carried out by autonomous and independent individuals and households. Moreover, where leadership is so disconnected from control over production of basic material goods there seem to be severe breaks upon leaders' attempts to create a following. In more complex, state-level societies, leadership and control over the economy are more firmly wedded to each other. Yet here also the degree of embeddedness seems to have an important effect upon the power invested in leadership systems. Where the economy is tied to political goals leadership seems more closed, ascriptive, and power based than in situations where the economy remains relatively decentralized. While egalitarian leadership systems and democratic stratiform systems are very far apart from one another, the degree of freedom that people have from coercive leadership seems to be a function of the degree of separation of the sphere of politics from the sphere of economics. In egalitarian societies this rests on the almost complete separation of economics from leadership, while in democratic societies it seems to rest upon the centripetal qualities of capitalism which serve to continually decentralize the power base. The latter seems, at this point in history, to counteract centralizing tendencies in the development of state-level leadership. Put another way, the development of society from simple to complex seems to suggest that if one is concerned with limiting the power of leaders, a little bit of anarchy is no dangerous thing.

NOTES

1. Michael Banton, *Roles: An Introduction to the Study of Social Relation* (New York: Basic Books, 1965), pp. 28–29.
2. The ideal type as understood by Weber is a type case which serves as a hypothetical construction of a class of phenomena. Observational data are usually compared in terms of their greater or lesser fidelity to such ideal types. *See* Max Weber, *Economy and Society* (Berkeley: University of California Press, 1978).
3. Stanley Diamond, *In Search of the Primitive* (New Brunswick, N.J.: Transaction Books, 1969).
4. Eleanor Leacock, "Women's Status in Egalitarian Society: Implicators for Social Evolution," *Current Anthropology*, 19 (1978), pp. 247–75.
5. The distinction between achievement and ascription, although widely used without specific attribution in anthropology and sociology, was originally made by Ralph Linton, *The Study of Man* (New York: Appleton-Century-Crofts, 1963).
6. *See* Elsie Begler, "Sex, Status, and Authority in Egalitarian Society," *American Anthropology*, 80 (1979), pp. 571–88 for an excellent review of this issue. *See also* Adams's distinction between independent and dependent power, which essentially revolves around a similar behavioral dichotomy. Richard Adams, "Power in Human Societies: A Synthesis," in Raymond D. Fogelson and Richard N. Adams, eds., *The Anthropology of Power: Ethnographic Studies from Asia, Oceania, and the New World* (New York: Academic Press, 1977).
7. Weber, *Economy and Society*.
8. Morton Fried, *The Evolution of Political Society* (New York: Random House, 1967); Elman Service, *The Origin of the State and Civilization* (New York: W.W. Norton & Co., 1962); Ronald Cohen and Elman Service, *Origin of the State* (Philadelphia: ISHI Publishing Company, 1978).
9. Michele Rosaldo, "Women, Culture and Society: A Theoretical Overview," in Michele Rosaldo and Louise Lamphere, eds., *Women, Culture and Society* (Stanford: Stanford University Press, 1974), pp. 17–42.
10. Leacock, "Women's Status in Egalitarian Society."
11. Karen Sacks, "Engles Revisited: Women, the Organization of Production and Private Property," in Rayna Reiter, ed., *Toward an Anthropology of Women* (New York: Monthly Review Press, 1975).
12. In this typology the combination of variables (closed, open, achieved, ascribed, power, and influence) are used to generate potential "ideal type" classificatory constructs. Only some of them, however, appear either logically or empirically possible.
13. Colin Turnbull, "The Importance of Flux in Two Hunting Societies," in Richard B. Lee and Irvin De Vore, eds., *Man the Hunter* (Chicago: Aldine Publishing Company, 1972), pp. 132–37.
14. The description of the !Kung is drawn from Richard B. Lee, "Politics, Sexual and Non-Sexual in an Egalitarian Society: The !Kung San," in Gerald B. Berr-

man, ed., *Social Inequality: Comparative and Developmental Approaches* (New York: Academic Press, 1981).

15. Paul Spencer, *The Samburu* (Berkeley: University of California Press, 1965).
16. Marshall Sahlins, *Social Stratification in Polynesia* (Seattle: University of Washington Press, 1958); Douglas Oliver, *A Solomon Island Society* (Cambridge: Harvard University Press, 1955).
17. Roy Rappoport, *Pigs for the Ancestor* (New Haven: Yale University Press, 1968).
18. *See* Marshall Sahlins, *Stone Age Economics* (Chicago: Aldine Publishing Company, 1972), for basic review of precapitalist economic systems.
19. Helen Codere, *Fighting With Property* (Seattle: University of Washington Press, 1950).
20. This description of the Lozi is drawn from Max Gluckman, *Politics, Law and Ritual in Tribal Society* (Oxford: Oxford University Press, 1965).
21. Bronislaw Malinowski, *Argonauts of the Western Pacific* (New York: Dutton, 1912).
22. Karl Wittfogel, *Oriental Despotism: A Comparative Study of Total Power* (New Haven: Yale University Press, 1957).
23. Milovan Djilas, *The New Class* (New York: Praeger Publishers, Inc., 1957).
24. Robbins Burling, *The Passage of Power: Studies in Political Succession* (New York: Academic Press, 1975).
25. Hanna Arendt, *On Revolution* (New York: Viking, 1963).
26. Milton Friedman, *Capitalism and Freedom* (Chicago: University of Chicago Press, 1965).
27. Stanley Diamond, "Critical versus Ideological Marxism," in Stanley Diamond, ed., *Towards a Marxist Anthropology* (The Hague: Monton and Company, 1979), pp. 1–10.
28. Charles Anderson, *The Political Economy of Social Class* (Englewood Cliffs, N.J.: Prentice-Hall, 1974), p. 242.

LEADERSHIP AS A POLITICAL ACT

4

Barbara Kellerman

One would imagine that political science has paid political leadership considerable heed. Surely it is central to a discipline that concerns itself with the application of scientific methods to the study of politics and political behavior. And indeed some of our most eminent contemporary political scientists confirm its importance. Dahl and Neubauer write that "perhaps no question is as central to political discourse as that of political leadership. For, if there is an 'irreducible fact' of politics, it is that in any political society some shall be the rulers and some the ruled."[1]

Astonishingly, however, political leadership has been the subject of sharp neglect. Significant evidence in support of this assertion may be found in the titles of articles published in the *American Political Science Review*. "The computerized keyword index . . . of 2,614 articles that appeared . . . from 1906 to 1963 makes it easy for us to discover that the words 'leader' or 'leadership' appeared in such titles only seventeen times."[2] The reasons for this inattention—which is slowly starting to give way— need not concern us here. But the durable neglect of a subject by a group that should by all rights have given it close scrutiny suggests that there is something elusive about it, something about political leadership that does not lend itself to ready study or analysis.

Although political scientists have written at least three excellent books on leadership in recent years—Glenn Paige, *The Scientific Study of Political Leadership;* James MacGregor Burns, *Leadership;* and Robert C. Tucker, *Politics as Leadership*—good work in this area is just beginning. This chapter will nudge the effort forward by presenting key perspectives on political leadership as viewed by one political scientist. The chapter is not an overview; nor is it inclusive. Rather I will pose a very few critical questions and attempt to answer them with reasonable thoroughness while necessarily meeting the demand for economy. In particular I will ask: What is political leadership? Who leads? Why do we follow? What makes good leadership? I do not, of course, suggest that these are the only questions, nor even necessarily that they are the most important ones. Rather they are some of those manifestly pertinent to a political science prepared to develop more fully a literature on political leadership.

But before turning to these general questions, there will be a brief discourse on the specific issue of political leadership in America. Grounding the broader discussion in a familiar setting should facilitate connections between leadership *theory* and the *practice* of leadership. Thus, for example, the answers to "Why do we follow?" may well take on greater clarity if they are applied to the American experience. What will be attempted, in other words, is a far-ranging discussion that is anchored—sometimes explicitly, more often implicitly—in the American political culture.

LEADERSHIP IN AMERICA

From the beginning—even before 1776—Americans have tended to be ambivalent about their political leaders. They long for, and at the same time resist, strong leadership in both theory and practice. On the one hand Americans have continued throughout over two hundred years of history to wail about their "crisis of leadership"—a lament which suggests nothing so much as a collective wish for powerful as well as competent leaders. But on the other hand many Americans are suspicious of those—elected or appointed—who exercise what they see as too much power, and thus they undercut those who seem to get their own way too often. In short, more often than not, sooner or later Americans turn down and out those who would be their leaders—those who persist in defining public goals, and instructing on exactly how to reach them.

The term *political culture* refers to those widespread ideas, habits, norms, symbols, and practices that are politically relevant to a given system, especially as they pertain to the legitimate use of power. Each nation's political culture is peculiar unto itself, shaped, naturally, by its own idiosyncratic history and development. Of America it may be said that, with regard to leadership, its political culture is characterized by *ambivalence* and *reluctance*. Americans have, in Tocqueville's words, "a weak confidence in the superior attainments of certain individuals." Moreover, they are not naturally disposed to take one of themselves for a guide.[3]

In part, this lack of certainty about what properly constitutes leadership grows out of America's revolutionary heritage. The Founding Fathers' aversion to monarchy, to the very notion of great power residing in one man, made the question of just how much authority would be granted the president—who would inevitably have more authority than anyone else—perhaps the most contentious one of the day. *The Federalist Papers,* that great collection of letters to the public penned by Alexander Hamilton, James Madison, and John Jay in defense of the Constitution,* vividly depicts the passions that marked the debate. Interestingly, it was Hamilton—an advocate of strong leadership—who took on the task of distinguishing between the president and the much hated king of Great Britain. Clearly, Hamilton felt obliged to hide his own preferences behind the litany of constraints that would be imposed on America's chief executive.

The President of the United States would be an office elected by the people for *four* years; the king of Great Britain is a perpetual and *hereditary* prince. The one would be amenable to personal punishment and disgrace; the person of the other is sacred and inviolable. The one would have a qualified negative upon the acts of the legislative body; the other has an *absolute* negative. The one would have a right to command the military and naval forces of the nation; the other, in addition to this right, possesses that of *declaring war,* and of raising and *regulating* fleets and armies by his own authority. The one would have alike concurrent authority in appointing to offices; the other is the sole author of all appointments. The one can confer no privileges whatever; the other can make denizens of aliens, noblemen of commoners. . . . The one has no particle of spiritual jurisdiction; the other is the supreme head and governor of the national church! What answer shall we give to those who would persuade us that things so unlike resemble each other? The same that ought to be given to those who tell us that a government, the whole power of which would be in the hands of the elective and periodical servants of the people, is an aristocracy, a monarchy, and a despotism.[4]

It would be hard to overestimate the continuing impact of this endemic suspicion of strong leaders on America's collective consciousness, and on the practices of its political life. It is a distrust that endures, because of the persistence of national ideals such as liberty, equality, individualism, and democracy. Americans are still suffused with tales and symbols that insist that they are all equal, and free to participate equally in the making of collective decisions. Moreover, Americans are temperamentally disinclined to either follow, or think first in terms of groups or communities.

---

*Specifically, their attempt was to obtain ratification of the Constitution as it had been drafted at the Constitutional Convention in Philadelphia in the summer, 1787.

America's heroic archetype is the "lonesome cowboy," or "self-made man." There is admiration, but not reverence, for the organization man, or self-effacing team player. Thus, although America's antiauthority ideals may be only imperfectly realized, the fact is that they permeate its political culture. The result: Americans do not ordinarily grant anyone the right to lead them anywhere for very long.

It may be noted that the ideal of a leaderless society has also been fostered by the academy. The most widely accepted analysis of power in America is the pluralist analysis, which argues that leadership in any particular area depends on who cares and who is involved. Necessarily, then, no single leader or leadership group predominates. In other words, any American can be a leader, at least in some areas, if he or she really *wants* to be a leader—which is another way of saying that no single person is likely to be a leader all the time, in all situations.

Samuel Huntington's recent book *American Politics: The Promise of Disharmony* explores the impact of America's democratic ideals with a new elegance. Indeed, it is perhaps his main point that "the distinctive aspect of the American Creed is its antigovernment character. Opposition to power, and suspicion of government as the most dangerous embodiment of power are the central themes of American political thought."[5] Huntington theorizes that it is precisely the gap between the ideals of American democracy and the performance of American politics that has led to four political upheavals in our history and, more importantly, to a chronic frustration about America's inability to achieve a more competent and satisfactory political system.

If we can agree that America's ambivalence toward, or even opposition to, power and strong leadership is as old as the Republic and fully ingrained, perhaps we might also agree that there have been moments in America's history when this suspicion was exaggerated. At certain points, for a complicated mix of social, political, and economic reasons, public hostility toward those who have political power heightens. (Huntington asserts that this occurs cyclically, with every third generation.) Then, some years later, the anger is spent, the tension ebbs, and a kind of paralysis sets in. Americans appear to forget where they were going and there is no obvious leader to point the way. It is a national malaise, as it were—a feeling that somehow, America has lost its bearings.

An argument can be made for the proposition that the late seventies and early eighties are just such a time—Ronald Reagan's personal popularity notwithstanding. John Gardner, in a prophetic 1965 speech titled "The Antileadership Vaccine," sounded the warning. He cautioned that "we are immunizing a high proportion of our most gifted young people against any tendencies to leadership." Although Gardner acknowledged that America's educational institutions effectively prepare their students for the job market, he argued that this narrow professional conception "leaves little room for leadership in the normal sense. . . . Entry into what most of us would regard as the leadership roles in the society at large is discouraged. [This is unfortunate for] leadership, properly conceived, serves the individual human goals that our society values so highly, and we shall not achieve those goals without it."[6]

Just about the time that the political energy of the sixties and early seventies was spent—Huntington labels these years "America's fourth major creedal passion period since independence"—Watergate broke. Not surprisingly, Watergate reduced still further our trust in government. According to Gallup, some 67 percent of those polled reported that the Watergate situation reduced their confidence in the federal government "somewhat" (37 percent) or a "great deal" (30 percent).[7] And so it was that the antileadership vaccine, the disenchanting close of a creedal passion period, and the exposure of corruption at the top level of American government combined to create a situation in which, according to *Time*, leadership was the "biggest issue." On the occasion of the 1976 *Time*-sponsored "Leadership Conference," the news weekly reported that trust in government had declined from 76 percent in 1964 to 33 percent in 1976, and that 83 percent of American voters said that they did not "trust those in positions of leadership as much as they used to."*[8]

The trend continues. In 1981 Gallup reported that its current findings "give further evidence of the poor public image of politicians in the United States." US congressmen and state and local office holders are—in terms of Gallup's "ethics scale"—"among the lowest rated of the occupations tested."[9]

Tellingly, during the 1976 presidential campaign both Jimmy Carter and Gerald Ford stressed their leadership qualities. Carter's television ads described him as "a leader, for a change." Ford's spots said of the then incumbent president: "He has virtually a lifetime of leadership."

Of course, some of this was media hype. Leadership has recently been something of a "hot topic." But at the same time there has also been a more serious effort to examine what exactly political leadership is, and why Americans seem to have so much trouble now recruiting "the best and the brightest" to fill their leadership roles. In considerable part this new push to examine political institutions and processes in the light of leadership issues is the result of the manifest fragmentation of America's political community. Single issue politics have replaced the more broadly based party politics, and the coalitions of old, which made governing possible in America's fractured system of checks and balances, have been gravely weakened.

---

*Apropos the above mentioned ambivalence toward leadership, it is amusing to note that *Time*'s long article on the need for good leaders concluded with the following absurdity: "In a democracy, to some extent, all must be leaders."

Moreover, there is nothing to replace them. Political scientist Bruce Miroff suggests that what happened was the cracking of concensus politics: "Consensus was to be, in the prevailing 1960s view, the grand contemporary achievement of American politics." Our political leaders would overcome America's persistent tendencies toward fragmentation and stalemate by skilled leadership which would concentrate on the pursuit of broad public objectives. But, argues Miroff:

> The consensus constructed so artfully in the first half of the 1960s cracked extensively in the second half of that decade. The phenomena that cracked it were, of course, the Vietnam War and racial polarization, along with the later addition (around 1970) of economic "stagflation." By the 1970s all the major premises of consensus politics—economic growth with stable prices, the absence of fundamental political conflict, the efficacy of expert problem-solving, Cold War unity—had become problematical.[10]

Miroff concludes that the demise of consensus politics revealed fundamental flaws in the theory of consensus leadership (which cast the leader in something of a heroic role), but that alternative theories have yet to stake strong claims.

The fact that America is indeed in a time of particular uncertainty about the proper role of authority is documented in David Broder's 1981 book *Changing of the Guard.*[11] Broder interviewed hundreds of people who may be said to constitute the new generation of American leaders, "men and women who have spent the last 20 years bringing about the changes with which they are now confronted."[12] Above all he looked at what has happened to leadership in the most venerable of America's political institutions: the presidency and the congress.

Broder writes that the first two post-Vietnam presidents—Gerald Ford and Jimmy Carter—"were notably ineffectual at leading the government or rallying public support."[13] In part, of course, this had to do with the personalities of the two men. Neither had what it takes to inspire. But in Broder's conversation with Stuart Eizenstat, then a top aide to President Carter, six points emerged which spoke to the broader fragmentation of intellectual and political authority. Each of them directly addressed why our current political leaders have trouble getting us to follow.

1. There is a basic conflict between the public's desire for greater services and its resistance to government spending and regulation.
2. The task of reconciling these conflicts is impeded by the lack of tested doctrine to solve the most complicated policy riddles such as "stagflation."
3. The struggle for scarcer resources has heightened tensions among competing groups.
4. Increasingly well-organized economic-interest groups have mobilized their forces to defend, and even expand, their claims on the federal budget.

5. Congress has seen that a fragmentation of its institutional authority as power has been dispersed among small subcommittees, each of which is vulnerable to interest-group pressures from its own clientele.
6. The influence of party loyalty has been so diminished that appeals for unity based on that allegiance are of negligible impact.[14]

A similar message came from the legislative branch. Christopher Dodd, then a congressman and now a senator from Connecticut, was quoted as having said that "it's awfully hard" to mobilize Democrats on any legislative issue. Even younger members "don't want to feel as though they have to be responsible to the leadership. They see *themselves* as being leaders. And that is why I question the ability of the institution to come to terms, in the long run, with the problem, unless we decide that some people have got to be the pawns or the foot soldiers and others are going to have to be the leaders."[15]

At the end of *Changing of the Guard* Broder raises what may be regarded as the fundamental question about those who would be our political leaders. Do they have what it takes? His suggestion is that our reluctance to exert power may equal our reluctance to bow to it.

> So the challenge to the young people will not be to abolish bureaucracy or escape from it, but to tame it and to lead it. [But] there were some moments when I thought I heard them saying that that was a task from which they might shrink. . . . None of these individualists . . . is eager to accept the discipline involved in any hierarchical power structure.
>
> What was puzzling . . . was the sense I occasionally had that some of these young people might be as uncomfortable giving orders as most of them are in taking them. . . . Many of them felt called upon to deny that their love of politics had anything to do with the pursuit of power for power's sake. There is no harm . . . in their striking such an attitude, as long as they know it is a pose. For leadership *is* the exercise of power, and leadership is what the country will demand of this generation.[16]

As I said at the beginning, the rest of this chapter will be much less concerned with the specific issue of political leadership in America. But before turning to the broader questions, one final point: The role of leadership during times of crisis, or in societies or systems that are rent by sociopolitical conflicts, is always easier to understand than the role of leadership in settled situations in which politicians "seem to be limited to routine, unimportant decisions and to bargaining over incremental changes in government policies."[17] Yet given America's circumstance, it is precisely the nature of, and possibilities for, this second kind of leadership that we need to clarify.

WHAT IS POLITICAL LEADERSHIP?

I have spoken about the ambivalence of Americans toward *political leadership*. But so far the term has not really been defined. Let us begin that task by splitting the term in two, starting first with the noun.

It has been said that there are almost as many definitions of *leadership* as there are leadership theories. The social science literature is replete with definitions that associate leadership with, for example, the exercise of power, influence, command, authority, and control. The following list gives some further idea of how, variously, *leadership* may be defined and conceived.

1. *Leadership as the Focus of Group Process.* Leadership results in group change and activity.
2. *Leadership as Personality and Its Effects.* Leadership is a combination of traits that enables a particular individual to motivate others to accomplish given tasks.
3. *Leadership as the Art of Inducing Compliance.* Leadership is the undirectional exertion of power or influence that molds the group to the leader's will.
4. *Leadership as the Exercise of Influence.* Leadership exercises a determining effect on the behaviors of group members; but the relationship between leader and followers is characterized by voluntary responses.
5. *Leadership as Behavior.* "Leadership may be defined as the behavior of an individual while he is involved in directing group activities."[18]
6. *Leadership as a Form of Persuasion.* Leadership is the management of people by persuasion and inspiration rather than by coercion.
7. *Leadership as a Power Relation.* Interpersonal power is conceived as "a resultant of the maximum force which A can induce on B minus the maximum resisting force which B can mobilize in the opposite direction."[19]
8. *Leadership as an Instrument of Goal Achievement.* Leadership is defined in terms of the accomplishment of group goals.
9. *Leadership as a Differentiated Role.* The leadership role is required to integrate the various other roles of the group, and to direct the group effort toward goal achievement.
10. *Leadership as the Initiation of Structure.* Leadership results in the initiation of group interaction.[20]

What single definition of *leadership* might we then extract? We can say that leadership is the process by which one individual consistently exerts more impact than others on the nature and direction of group activity. Or, more simply, the leader is the one "who makes things happen that would not happen otherwise."[21]

We can also make a distinction between leadership as defined by position, or *headship*, and leadership as defined by the relationship between leader and followers, or *leadership*. Headship is associated with the "rights and duties of an office or status in a hierarchical structure, whether a formal organization or an informally stratified collectivity."[22] Headship is identified with superior position, and followership with subordinate ones. It is maintained through an organized system, and it implies a considerable distance between the group members and the head. Leadership, too, is associated with the one who shapes the actions of others. But the focus here is not on role, or position, but on the special nature of the relationship between leader and followers. Leaders, in contrast to heads, are accorded their authority spontaneously by group members who, it turn, follow because they *want* to rather than because they *must*.

But what of the adjective at issue here? Can *political* leadership be distinguished from other forms of leadership? Yes, to a degree. Ordinarily, political leadership refers to control over public policy decisions. Political leaders derive their authority from the fact that they occupy a high office in a legally sanctioned government which, by virtue of its legitimacy, has the power and authority to choose between alternative goals and courses of action. In other words, the *political* of political leadership "establishes the general organizational context. Explicitly or implicitly, political is taken to refer to the state and to governmental processes."[23]

Of course, the adjective "political" need not refer only to matters of state. We need only recall that manipulative corporate executives are tagged "politicians" just as readily as ambitious congressmen. More broadly, then, political leadership implies some kind of partisan (or ideological) leadership, *a personal push for particular changes* in group goals, activities, or structure. I should perhaps point out that implicit in both definitions of *political* leadership—that is, in those that refer specifically to matters of state and in those that suggest no more than partisan infighting—is the suggestion of an ongoing struggle for control among competing individuals who have different notions of what should be done and how, and who should get what and why.

Paige has suggested that one way of coming to understand political leadership is to look at how leaders themselves view what it is they do. A sampling:

Leadership as Persuasion: "A leader is a man who has the ability to get other people to do what they don't want to do, and like it." (Harry Truman)

Leadership as Class Dominance: "The working class leads everything." (Mao Zedung)

Leadership as Influence by Example: "Clean examples have a curious method of multiplying themselves." (Gandhi)

Leadership as Creative Brutality: "Whatever goal man has reached is due to his originality plus his brutality." (Adolf Hitler)

Leadership as Revolutionary Expression: "The art of the politician . . . consists in the correct appraisal of the conditions and the moment when the vanguard of the proletariat can successfully seize power. . . ." (Lenin)

Leadership as Master of Circumstance: "If we do not win, we will blame neither heaven nor earth but only ourselves." (Mao)[24]

Leadership as Interpretation of "the Sense of the Community":

Practical leadership . . . must daily feel under its own feet the road that leads to the goal proposed, knowing that it is a slow, a very slow, evolution to wings, and that for the present, and for a very long future also, Society must *walk.* . . . In the words of the master Burke, "to follow, not to force, the public inclination,—to give direction, a form, a technical dress, and a specific sanction, to the general sense of the community, is the true end of legislation." That general sense of the community may wait to be aroused, and the statesman must arouse it; may be inchoate and vague, and the statesman must formulate and make it explicit. But he cannot and he should not do more. (Woodrow Wilson)[25]

To be sure, the above sampling of leaders on leadership is as confusing as it is illuminating. There is something jarring about finding Hitler and Wilson on the same list, both talking about more or less the same phenomenon, but in such strikingly dissimilar tones. Hitler speaks of leadership as something that emanates from within the all-powerful, even brutal, ruler. Wilson talks of a different wellspring altogether; he sees leadership as a process that must begin not with the leader but with those whom he would "lead." There is, moreover, a moral element in Wilson's vision of leadership, one which is obviously absent from anything Hitler ever said on the subject.

What is emerging from the discussion is the fact that political leadership is a complicated concept. Just the noun, *leadership,* is saddled with many, sometimes mutually exclusive, definitions. And we have seen how differently the term is conceptualized by those who theorize about leadership, as well as by those who practice it. It would be fitting, then, to conclude this section with a glance at the question of historical causation. For it is a plausible hypothesis that one reason we are having so much trouble formulating a widely acceptable definition and/or conceptualization of leadership is because we have no clear idea of what social and individual needs motivate it. We cannot agree on whether man does or does not have an innate need to look up to some higher authority; we cannot agree on whether society can, or cannot, be organized along lines that are anything other than hierarchical; and we cannot agree on what role, if any, is played by the hero in history.

In large part, your position on these questions will depend on your conception of the fundamental nature of man. If I were to take the Hobbesian view that life is nasty and brutish, and that without firm sociopolitical controls man would be out of control, I would inevitably come to certain conclusions about the need for leadership and the requisite nature of leadership. If, to the contrary, I were to adopt Rousseau's view that man in a state of nature is decent, good, and true, and that it is precisely "civilized" society that provokes us to "uncivilized" behavior, I would conclude something altogether different.

Some of these issues are addressed in the well-known "hero in history" debate, which is directly concerned with the question of historical causation. Basically, there are two camps. One claims that history is shaped by the leadership of great men:* Without Moses the Jews would have stayed in Egypt; without Lenin there would have been no Russian Revolution; without Churchill the Nazis would have conquered Great Britain. This position presupposes that all people are *not* created equal, and that, in fact, some few persons are endowed with unique qualities which make them a superior few.

The other camp argues that leaders emerge as the result of task, time, place, and circumstance. Even the occasional "great man" is merely responding to his environment. He profits from both the objective events and the work of others.

Recently these two camps have been joined in an uneasy alliance. The personal-situational theorists claim that leadership can be explained only by the *conjunction* of 1) the nature of the leader; 2) the nature of the group; and 3) the nature of the event, or problem, or task, confronting the group.

But it is, as I said, an uneasy alliance. Who would dare to argue that there has never been a "great man," someone so extraordinary that, no matter what the situation, he would have emerged on top? And, conversely, who would dare to argue that there have never been group needs so specific as to have determined, in effect, who the leader would be? Yet the debate and the resolution are indicative. As I said earlier, we are dealing here with complex materials that have so far eluded simple definitions, a uniform conceptualization, and easy explanations.

WHO LEADS?

After asking "What is political leadership?" the next question seems obvious: "Who are the political leaders?" Let us dispense first with the matter of identification.

In line with the above-mentioned distinction between heads and leaders, political leaders can be identified in two ways: 1) they occupy formal offices or are members of official ruling groups or decision-making bodies; or 2) it can be demonstrated that what happened did so because leaders made it happen. We can prove leadership only "when it can be shown that those said to be followers would otherwise have behaved differently."[26]

But to ask who are the political leaders is to introduce a more complicated question. It is to ask what types of people aspire to and finally gain

---

*With reluctant deference to how it has typically been, I will refer to the leader as "he."

positions of political leadership. As such, it is to raise the issue of the role of personality in politics.

It must be stated at the outset that personality—and we return here to the hero in history issue—does not always matter very much. To quote Fred Greenstein's well-known formulation, the likelihood of personal impact 1) increases to the degree that the environment admits of restructuring; 2) varies with the actor's location in the environment; and 3) varies with the personal strengths and weaknesses of the actor.[27] In other words, individual actors are likely to make a political difference only when the environment is hospitable (that is, malleable), when they are located at or near the top of the heap, and/or when their particular skills meet the requisites of the particular situation. In this view, a leader will emerge as the result of a good fit between the personality of the individual actor and the characteristics of the setting.

Erik Erikson wrote that true leaders (as opposed to heads) *can* only grow out of that special fit. He argued that the answer to "Who leads?" depends on the answers to "What is the setting?" and "Who are the followers?" Indeed, Erikson combined psychological (inner world) and contextual (outer world) analysis to produce a new kind of inquiry. His psychobiographies of Luther and Gandhi have done no less than transform our notion of the biographical enterprise.[28]

Psychobiography is any life history that employs an explicit personality theory. Theories of personality work on the assumption that individual behavior has organized internal dispositions, and that these are relatively stable over time.[29] Thus, psychobiographers pay special attention to psychology, sometimes, unfortunately, to the neglect of economic, social, and political factors. Indeed, psychobiographers quite frequently stand accused of reductionism, the charge that they explain away complex events by facile Freudian references to infantile motives and neurotic conflicts. But Erikson avoided the pitfalls. And he convinced many of us that great leaders are not born. Rather, as he explained it, they grow out of the extraordinary resonance they have with those whom they would lead.

> From the psychohistorical viewpoint, then, the question is not, or not only, whether a man like Gandhi inadvertently proves some of Freud's points (such as the power of the emotions subsumed under the term Oedipus Complex), but why such items which we now recognize as universal were re-enacted in different media of representation. . . by particular types of men in given periods of history—and why, indeed, their time was ready for them and their medium: for only such complementarity makes a confession momentous and its historical analysis meaningful.[30]

Leadership, as Erikson defines it, depends then on the interaction between leader and followers. The powerful interaction that particularly interests Erikson often takes place within sociopolitical movements rather than in political systems operating routinely through established institutions. Thus, it is plausible that psychohistory is more suited to the analysis of those whom Robert C. Tucker calls nonconstituted leaders (of social movements) than to constituted, or official leaders.[31]

It can reasonably be argued, in any case, that the good psychobiography will excel at providing both a thorough analysis of the individual leader, and a rigorous description of the context in which leadership took place. But support for this proposition raises a problem that must confront those who would also answer our original question, "Who leads?" For the assumption that underlies psychobiographies is that their subjects can be understood only as idiosyncratic actors. By definition, psychobiographies address what is unique. Even conventional biographies have a narrow concern: the personal and professional development of their subjects. Life histories of political leaders do not, then, typically address the broader question of how their subjects do, or do not, compare to other leaders in other situations.

But if all leaders are unique, and have singular tales to tell, how can we ever hope to know what motivates them—as a group—to seek out positions of political leadership? And, if the environment is never the same, how can we begin to explain why some succeed and others do not? Is it in fact true that each case is sui generis? Or are there regularities that can be extracted from the ever accumulating abundance of biographical detail?

Some fifty years ago Harold Lasswell, in his pioneering work *Psychopathology and Politics*, responded to these questions by proposing that it was possible to classify leaders as particular types.[32] To speak of type is to say that although each leader is, of course, different in fine detail, important similarities can be extracted. These similarities allow for the claim that two or more leaders are of the same type.

Using what were then the most modern psychoanalytic findings as his theoretical base, Lasswell conducted a series of prolonged interviews with people "who play on the public stage." As a result of these interviews he postulated three types of political leaders: the Agitator (for example, Old Testament prophets), the Administrator (Herbert Hoover), and the Theorist (Marx).

> The essential mark of the agitator is the high value which he places on the emotional response of the public. . . . The agitator has come by his name honestly, for he is enough agitated about public policy to communicate his excitement to those about him.[33]
> [The administrator is tied] to the members of his own environment, whose relations he seeks to co-ordinate. The administrator is a co-ordinator of effort in continuing activity.[34]
> Marx, [a theorist], wanted to impress himself upon mankind, certainly. . . . But more: Marx wanted unreserved admiration for the products of his mind. He toiled through years of isolation and poverty to make his

assertions impregnable. It was more important to gain theoretical complete-ness than to modify his technique of social intercourse.[35]

Lasswell concluded that although individual responses to particular situations accounted for the three different types, the same general formula explained why they became political men: "p $\}$ d $\}$ r = p, where p equals private motives; d equals displacement onto a public object; r equals rationalization in terms of public interest; P equals the political man; and $\}$ equals transformed into."[36] This broad conceptualization of why people chose to "play on the public stage," that is, to become political leaders, has gained wide acceptance.

Another effort to posit a particular type—the revolutionary leader—may be found in E. Victor Wolfenstein's *The Revolutionary Personality* or Bruce Mazlish's *The Revolutionary Ascetic*.[37] Wolfenstein offers what is an essentially Freudian interpretation of Lenin, Trotsky, and Gandhi. He finds that at critical stages the three leaders had fundamental things in common, for example, during adolescence:

> Turning then to adolescence, we found the following situation to be common to all three men. Each had an unusually ambivalent relationship with his father. . . . When the nature of the youth's relation to paternal authority is very much at issue, it is extremely likely that the individual will be responsive to occupations, of which revolutionary activity is one, which allow him to work through his conflicts and hopefully resolve them. . . . The revolutionary is one who escapes from the burdens of Oedipal guilt and ambivalence by carrying his conflict with authority into the political realm.[38]

Mazlish posits a type he labels "the revolutionary ascetic"–a modern variant of the revolutionary personality who "emerged full-blown in Europe at the end of the nineteenth century, and quickly became an international figure in the twentieth century" (for example, Lenin or Mao).

> The revolutionary ascetic is a professional revolutionary who devoted his whole life, and love, to his profession. . . . His key problem is control: of himself, of his followers, and of society at large. We have tried to analyze that problem of control primarily in terms of the Freudian concepts of libido, i.e. love, and aggression. . . . In our analysis we have been concerned with both the creativity involved in the revolutionary ascetic's achievement of self-control, and thus the ability to break with an old world order to create a new one. . . . [39]

But perhaps the best known typology of political leaders is James David Barber's. Put briefly, two dimensions interact to produce four types of American presidents. The dimensions are Level of Activity (active or passive) and Affect Toward the Activity (positive or negative). The four types are:

Active-positive. There is a congruence ... between much activity and the enjoyment of it, indicating relatively high self-esteem and relative success in relating to the environment. ... [for example, Truman]

Active-negative. The contradiction here is between relatively intense effort and relatively low emotional reward for that effort. The activity has a compulsive quality, as if the man were trying to make up for something or to escape from anxiety into hard work. ... [for example, Lyndon Johnson]

Passive-positive. This is the receptive, compliant, other-directed character whose life is a search for affection as a reward for being agreeable and cooperative rather than personally assertive. ... [for example, Harding]

Passive-negative. Why is someone who does little in politics and enjoys it less there at all? The answer lies in the passive-negative's character-rooted orientation toward doing dutiful service; this compensates for low self-esteem based on a sense of uselessness. ... [for example, Eisenhower][40]

This glance at some of the important work of Lasswell, Wolfenstein, Mazlish, and Barber suggests, then, that we can reasonably talk about particular types of political leaders. Inevitably, to typecast a leader is to lose the textural richness that characterizes the best of the conventional biographies, or psychohistories. But the good typology will, with economy, convey important information about *personality* and *political behavior.* By freeing us from the necessity of considering each leader sui generis all the time, typologies serve a useful function.

Yet, typologies that focus on political leaders convey little or nothing about political setting (this includes followers). And, as I asserted earlier, it is the interweave between personality and setting that especially interests us. Let me turn very briefly, then, to the political environment.

In a 1965 essay, Robert C. Tucker asserts that the totalitarian dictator is a paranoid personality type who has a profound inpact on the system in which he operates. Tucker claims that "the evidence disclosed by the Stalin and Hitler cases on the connection between dictatorial psychopathology and the politics of totalitarianism strongly suggests that the personal factor should be included in the theoretical model of a totalitarian system."[41] I bring this up because, as Tucker indicates, the more conventional approach has been to see totalitarianism as a system in which the leader plays only one of many parts. In other words, the assumption has been that even a dictator is shaped by the system rather than the other way around.

To gain insight into what we might label the systemic demands on leadership, consider the two extremes: the totalitarian state and the democratic (pluralist) state.

Totalitarianism is a single-party system in which the government nevertheless strives to achieve mass political support on the basis of a powerful, visionary ideology. Once in power, the political elite and, in particular, the dictator impose a rigid tyrannical rule which blankets both the public and private sectors of activity. A strong, centrally controlled bureaucracy, buttressed by its access to the technology of mass communication, accomplishes the system's routine tasks. In order to maintain total dominance, the state employs widespread and frequently random terror. Indeed, there is no totalitarianism without terror.[42] Finally, the totalitarian state is relatively isolated. To maintain their preeminent position, totalitarian elites must enforce a closed society in which contact and communication with the outside world are heavily restricted. As for the dictator, all scholars agree that he is an essential part of the political process. Some, however, see him as merely fulfilling a function in the totalitarian system, whereas it is Tucker's contention that he is much more. Tucker claims that in a totalitarian state the leader has perhaps the greatest single impact on political decision making.

Democratic or pluralist systems are characterized by a variety of sources of influence and their dispersal among a wide range of individuals and groups. Pluralism implies the lack of a single, central political and/or economic elite. Instead, the political system is run by different elites which are associated with particular issue areas. Thus, on labor issues, labor unions play a dominant role; on national political issues Washington politicians have the major say; on matters pertaining to business those in the corporate sector make the important decisions; and so on. In other words, particular aggregates are highly influential in some areas, but no aggregates are consistently influential in *all* areas.[43] In a democracy, then, it is the leader's task to articulate and cumulate the interests of the various subgroups in the population. He must cajole or persuade them to follow him in particular. The democratic leader must, in other words, convince his followers that they stand to benefit if they do things his way.

It is impossible to establish hard and fast rules about the importance of the individual vis-à-vis the importance of the setting in the analysis of leadership dynamics. You will, however, recall that Greenstein proposed three circumstances in which the likelihood of personal impact will increase. If we take the converse of these we have useful indicators of those circumstances in which systemic demands, and systemic routines, act to *minimize* the importance of individuals. Thus, the likelihood of systemic impact 1) increases to the degree that the environment does *not* admit of restructuring; 2) increases to the degree that individual actors *fail* to sustain preeminent positions of leadership over long periods of time; and 3) increases to the degree that no single actor has *exceptional* leadership skills.

Of necessity, this discussion has been simplified. The following description of political leadership suggests how complex the process is when analyzed in fine detail: "Patterns of political leadership behavior are a function of personality role, organization, task, values, and setting factors in reciprocal interaction. . . ."[44] But I trust the basic point was made. To understand who leads and why, look first through a wide-angle lens that allows you to see the whole.

WHY DO WE FOLLOW?

It takes two to make leadership: the leader, and at least one follower. In fact, they depend on each other utterly, and define, stimulate, and reinforce each other. A case has even been made for the proposition that "the leader does not exist, fully formed, before the encounter with the group he is to lead."[45] Still, the study of leadership has tended to focus on the presumably glamorous leader, the celebrity as it were, at the expense of the more mundane followers. It is this misleading imbalance that will be addressed in this section.

"Why do we follow?" seems to me to be the basic question.* Of course, we do not always follow; but, more often than not, we do. In informal small groups, in the organizational settings that typically characterize our work lives, and as members of large political aggregates (for example, in our roles as United States citizens), we tend more often than not to obey the chain of command that tells us what to do and when and how to do it. Even in contemporary America–in which, as I said at the beginning, many of us appear to have been inoculated with an antileadership vaccine–if we fail to unite solidly behind our leaders, we at least do enough following to prevent anarchy. Why?

There are two basic reasons: Leaders satisfy certain individual needs, and leaders satisfy certain group needs. I will address both and divide the two categories—individual and group needs—into sections based on types of leadership: transactional and transforming.

James MacGregor Burns, in his pathbreaking book *Leadership*, suggests that there were "two basic types of leadership": the *transactional* and the *transforming*.

> The relations of most leaders and followers are transactional–leaders approach followers with an eye to exchanging one thing for another: jobs for votes, or subsidies for campaign contributions. . . . *Transforming* leadership, while more complex, is more potent. The transforming leader recognizes and exploits an existing need or demand of a potential follower. . . . The result of transforming leadership is a relationship of mutual stimulation and elevation that converts followers into leaders and may convert leaders into moral agents.[46]

I would claim that both transactional and transforming leaders serve both individual and group needs. But I am taking license with Burn's definition of *transforming*. Burns defines the transforming leader as necessarily moral; he elevates his followers and is elevated by them. I am borrowing the designation *transforming* but, for the purposes of this chapter,

*This section addresses only noncoercive leadership.

I am putting aside the moral aspect. As the term will be used here, the transforming leader will do no more and no less than transform. (The transformation for which he is responsible can be either elevating, as Burns would have it, or debasing.)

Individual needs. The transactional leader gives his followers something that *they* want in exchange for something that *he* wants. It is a barter of sorts in which both sides gain and neither side loses. Put another way, the transactional leader satisfies his followers' private needs by engaging them in a relationship of mutual dependence in which the contribution of both sides is acknowledged and rewarded. Thus we follow the transactional leader because it is obvious to us that it is in our own interest to do so. We follow because in exchange for our support, the transactional leader gives us something that we specifically want and/or need.

The transforming leader satisfies needs that are, sometimes, less consciously articulated than those that are met by transactional leaders. Burns derives his conception of the transforming leader in part from Abraham Maslow's need hierarchy. According to Maslow, individual needs are arrayed along a hierarchy which ranges from physiological needs, to safety needs, to the need for affection and belonging, to the need for esteem and efficacy, and so on. Burns states that it is the transforming leader's special mission, and skill, to tap into those individual needs that are at at the upper end of the hierarchy. Burns implies that transforming leadership has less to do with providing followers with enough food to eat, and more to do with engaging followers in such a way that "leaders and followers raise one another to higher levels of motivation and morality. . . . Transforming leadership ultimately becomes *moral* in that it raises the level of human conduct and ethical aspiration of both leader and led, and thus it has a transforming effect on both."[47]

It seems plausible that the leader who engages us strongly enough to raise the level of our collective behavior has a capacity for touching something in us that draws us to *him* in particular. It is precisely this point that Freud (and some of his disciples) made on the subject of leadership. The following excerpt is from *Moses and Monotheism:*

> Let us agree, therefore, that the great man influences his contemporaries in two ways: through his personality and through the idea for which he stands. . . . Why the great man should rise to significance at all we have no doubt whatsoever. We know that the great majority of people have a strong need for authority which they can admire, to which they can submit, and which dominates and sometimes even ill-treats them. . . . It is the longing for the father that lives in each of us from his childhood days. . . .[48]

Lawrence Frank, in a 1939 article in *Psychiatry,* made the same point from a slightly different perspective.

Individuals, with the rarest exceptions, do not know what to do with their lives—how to act, what to desire and hope for—and so we need leaders to guide our aspirations, to project goals and to spur us on toward those purposes. . . . Leadership . . . fulfills the personality needs of the followers who crave the security of a firm and coercive program in which they can, by obedience and submission, find their place in life.[49]

Of course, Burns might reject the suggestion made here that those whom he would label transforming leaders tap into our "need for authority," or our craving for the "security of a firm and coercive program." Still, the evidence suggests that it is precisely transforming leaders (for example, Mao) who touch us at the deepest, unconscious, level. Moreover, some leaders get us to follow for reasons that are not altogether obvious, or logical. Sometimes, transforming leaders as I am defining them get us to follow when to do so means violating the most basic need of all: survival. One thinks, for example, of Jim Jones leading his followers to mass suicide in Guyana. There are, in short, leaders whom we voluntarily—even eagerly—follow because they apparently satisfy what Freud has labeled a "strong need" on the part of "the great majority."

Obviously, what is being addressed here is somewhat elusive material, subject to conjecture and disagreement. Let me then end this part of the discussion with what is only a modest claim: Some persons, under some circumstances, experience the need, or wish, to look *up*. This individual or personal need is more likely to be satisfied by transforming leaders, than by transactional ones.

Group needs. When I addressed what it is that the transactional leader does for individuals, I said that he gives them something "that *they* want in exchange for something that *he* wants." I added that it was "a barter of sorts" in which both sides stood to gain. The same can be said about what transactional leaders do for groups. In particular, in exchange for the power and prestige that the followers *cum* group bestow upon their leaders, the latter take upon themselves the tasks of maintaining public order and conducting the public business.

Every group is faced with group—as opposed to individual—tasks. That is, collectives are faced with issues that 1) grow out of their being a collective, and 2) are more efficaciously addressed by the group than they could possibly be by individuals acting separately. To deal with these collective concerns the group can do one of two things: It can cope as a whole group, that is, it can function so that *each* member of the group decides on *every* matter that confronts the group; or it can select representatives from the group who will assume responsibility for managing the public business, for governing.

If the group is small, having everyone participate may work. The New England town meeting is a commonly used example of this type of collective leadership (although, to be sure, by no means does everyone participate all the time). But if the group is large, it is faced with what Michels has called the "mechanical and technical impossibility of direct government by the masses."[50]

> The regular holding of deliberative assemblies of a thousand members encounters the gravest difficulties in respect of room and distance; while from a topographical point of view such an assembly would become altogether impossible if the members numbered ten thousand. Even if we imagined the means of communication to become much better than those which now exist, how would it be possible to assemble such a multitude in a given place, at a stated time, and with the frequency demanded by the exigencies of party life?. . . . Hence the need for delegation, for the system in which delegates represent the mass and carry out its will. . . . [51]

In large collectives the delegates that Michels refers to will tend to be professionals. That is, they will, by dint of their growing expertise at governing, evolve into a cadre of political leaders, professional pols if you will. Thus, it will become gradually more efficient for those with technical and administrative competence to occupy the positions of political leadership.

In terms of group needs, then, the transaction is as follows. The group bestows the positions of leadership, and all the rewards that they entail, to a corps of relatively qualified and trained professionals. These professionals—transactional leaders—generally get what they are after: in this country, the status, authority, and material benefits that go with being a president, senator, congressman, governor, mayor, state legislator, and so forth. In exchange, these professional leaders perform the tasks that need to be done to maintain and perpetuate the system. In other words, the masses have their collective work done for them. They can afford to participate only minimally (for example, to vote), or to not participate at all. Even completely inactive citizens will enjoy collective benefits such as clean air, a fire department, and a strong national defense.

Once again the transforming leader addresses different group needs, and once again these needs may be less consciously articulated than those that are met by transactional leaders. Redl writes about "group emotion and leadership." By group emotion he means the "instinctual and emotional events taking place within persons under the pressure of group formative processes."[52] He theorizes further that all groups have a central person. "By *central person* is meant person 'around whom' group formative processes take place. . . . The term *central person* designates the one through emotional relationship to whom the group formative processes are evoked in the potential group members."[53] Clearly Redl's argument that leaders (central persons) serve as the nucleus of group energies and attentions can, under certain circumstances, have important political ramifications.

Perhaps the "emotional relationship" between the group and the central person is most dramatically evidenced by the genuinely charismatic leader. Tucker's essay on Weber's concept of charismatic authority states that "the charismatic leader is one in whom, by virtue of unusual personal qualities, the promise or hope of salvation—deliverance from distress—appears to be embodied."[54] Tucker observes further that by virtue of his extraordinary qualities, the charismatic leader has a special hold over his followers. He exercises a kind of spell over them which binds them to him, and to each other.

This relationship—in which the leader evokes so strong an emotional response that his misdeeds and mistakes are ignored or trivialized—can lead to "elevation" or disaster. If the charismatic leader is transforming, he will, according to Burns, capitalize on the strength of his followers' devotion and engagement to "raise the level of human conduct and aspiration." But another kind of charismatic leader—a Hitler, a Jim Jones—will lead his still willing followers to destruction. Yet whether we who are outside the group judge the charismatic leader to be benign or malignant, the main point here is that he apparently emerges in response to some deeply felt group need or wish.

But charismatic leaders are not the only ones able to tap the emotional relationship that Redl writes about.* All transforming leaders must draw on and use what Mazlish refers to as the group's "psychic repository" or culture. "We can conceive of this repository as embodying recurrent themes, ideals, values, fantasies, imagery, symbols, myths and legends."[55] Thus, group needs other than those that are manifestly functional are most apt to be satisfied by transforming leaders. By invoking the psychic repository, and possibly adding to it, the transforming leader confers upon the group a sense of its own identity. He defines what the group is and who constitutes it, where it ought to go and how, and he distinguishes and separates the group from all that is outside.

I began this section by stating that we follow for "two basic reasons: leaders satisfy certain individual needs, and leaders satisfy certain group needs." Indeed, the preceding discussion has elaborated on this claim. Yet I cannot let the question "Why do we follow?" rest until I have made at least fleeting reference to the biobehavioral perspective. For what it offers is an astonishingly simple answer: We follow because we are programmed to follow. It is our nature. Put succinctly: "There seem to be good reasons to believe that man's biological nature incorporates strong propensities to

---

*Redl lists ten different types of leadership. All of these draw on the above mentioned emotional relationship, including those Burns labels *transactional leaders.*

establish and sustain dominance-deference hierarchies within his social groupings; that is, the stratification of political authority, power and influence may be *by nature* intrinsic to human social existence."[56] As I said, there is at least one ready answer to what would appear to be a complex question.

WHAT MAKES GOOD LEADERSHIP?

Given the fact that there is no historical, psychological, economic, political, cultural, or biobehavioral evidence to suggest that political leaders are a vanishing species, it is appropriate to close this discussion with a look at what constitutes *good* leadership. There are, of course, some general answers. Plato insisted on the absolute necessity of philosopher-kings:

> Until philosophers are kings, or the kings and princes of this world have the spirit and power of philosophy, and political greatness and wisdom meet in one, and those commoner natures who pursue either to the exclusion of the other are compelled to stand aside, cities will never have rest from their evils,— no, nor the human race, as I believe,—and then only will this our State have a possibility of life and behold the light of day.[57]

Machiavelli had a rather different model.

> So, as a prince is forced to know how to act like a beast, he should learn from the fox and the lion; because the lion is defenseless against traps and a fox is defenseless against wolves. Therefore, one must be a fox in order to recognize traps, and a lion to frighten off wolves. . . . So it follows that a prudent ruler cannot, and should not, honor his word when it places him at a disadvantage. . . . If all men were good, this precept would not be good; but because men are wretched creatures who would not keep their word to you, you need not keep your word to them.[58]

Clearly, Plato and Machiavelli, though addressing themselves to the same general phenomenon, had different constituencies in mind: Plato spoke to the issue of how the *people* (followers) would fare best, while Machiavelli's intention was to prescribe how *leaders* would succeed.

But let me depart here from the broadly theoretical and conclude with the more narrowly practical. Let me return finally to the question of political leadership in late twentieth-century America.

It will be recalled that I made two main points on the subject: first, Americans have always been deeply skeptical about strong political leadership, and second, the 1980s are a time of particular doubt, fragmentation, and even disintegration. The key questions then are: Does the focus on leadership contribute anything to the analysis of our contemporary malaise? Can leaders do much to ameliorate problems that are deeply entrenched?

As will be obvious by now, answers to such questions are complicated. For example, it is clear that the individual political leader—however outstanding or charismatic—can only provide partial relief. Our problems run deep and require the most fundamental reexamination of, above all, our antileadership ideology, our antiauthority political culture, and our political economy which contributes generously to the creation of hierarchies of power and influence. Indeed, it may fairly be said that tensions in our society emanate in no small part from the disharmony between our traditional claim to *political* equality, and the fact of our *economic* inequality. No society that places such a high value on the self-made man, on independence as opposed to dependence, can tolerate 10 percent unemployment without suffering considerable strain.

But if the complete answer to the question about what makes good leadership is beyond the scope of this essay, a partial response may nevertheless be assayed. I will look at three factors very briefly: institutions, persons, and processes.

In terms of public perceptions, large *institutions* in American society—public and private—are in trouble. Americans have lost faith in the ability of big government, big business, and big labor to manage their public and private affairs. Consider just one example: the advice financial experts give these days on what was until just recently a rock-ribbed institution: social security. "Don't trust the government to manage your old age anymore," Americans are told. "Fend for yourself. Make your own arrangements."[59]

It behooves those who manage America's large institutions to take responsibility for restoring public faith in both their efficacy and legitimacy.[60] To accomplish this, institutional leaders will have to take risks, and they will have to hold themselves accountable.[61] They will have to rethink: 1) the internal (bureaucratic) structures of their institutions; 2) the relationships among those who populate their institutional communities; 3) the relationship between the institution and the world outside; and 4) the viability of their institution as it is now constituted in light of rapid social, political, economic, and technological change.

About *persons,* especially political leaders, we can make the following assessments. First, if they are to stay in touch with those whom they would lead, they will certainly have to be drawn from a larger pool. No longer can America afford, for example, to have a Congress so dominated by white males who are overwhelmingly either businessmen or lawyers. Second, Americans who have traditionally thought of themselves as, and indeed have been, followers, will have to rethink their roles. No longer can they let those whom they conveniently label *political professionals* be the *only* consistently active participants in the political process. The pros will, at the least, have to be supplemented by new leaders who hail from heretofore untapped quarters, and who represent those interests and constituencies that are now, for all practical purposes, disenfranchised.[62] And, finally, those who assume leadership roles will have to forego any impulse to "go it alone," in favor of coalition and cooperation. Even leaders such as the Reverend Jerry Falwell, who have been highly successful with certain groups, will have to reach beyond their still relatively narrow constituencies if they are to make more than a limited, short-term difference.

Let me say a last word now about leadership *processes*, the dynamics that ensue when leaders (or heads) try to get others to follow. I said earlier that the coalitions of old have been gravely weakened. To compensate, or to cope with the dissensions, three possibilities seem to me to exist: 1) America's political leaders adopt an authoritarian style in which they reward those who follow, and punish or repress those who do not; 2) Americans wait for an extraordinary leader who will get them to move, to follow, by the sheer force of "charisma"; or 3) Americans proceed to find themselves leaders who listen as well as orate, who respond as well as control, who facilitate as well as dominate, and who inspire rather than conspire.

A repressive society would be in the interest of, at most, the few; to wait for the extraordinary leader is to trust fate to dumb luck; and so America is left with alternative number three. The American people have little choice but to generate political leaders who are skilled at integrating, adept at keeping their eye on the important long-range goals (rather than short-term rewards), and who are able to mobilize us on our own, shared, behalf.[63] Only political leaders who accomplish the above will finally make a positive, substantive, and durable difference on behalf of the *many*.[64]

NOTES

1. Robert Dahl and Deane Neubauer, *Readings in Modern Political Analysis* (Englewood Cliffs, N.J.: Prentice-Hall, 1968), p. 251.
2. Glenn Paige, *The Scientific Study of Political Leadership* (New York: Free Press, 1977), p. 11.
3. For elaboration of the concept of political culture *see* especially Gabriel A. Almond and Disney Verba, *The Civic Culture: Political Attitudes and Democracy in Five Nations* (Princeton, N.J.: Princeton University Press, 1963), and Lucian Pye and Sidney Verba, eds., *Political Culture and Political Development* (Princeton, N.J.: Princeton University Press, 1965). It should be noted that the concept of political culture is similar to Erich Fromm's "social character," which refers to a cluster of traits shared by members of a group such as a class, or nation. The Tocqueville quote is from Alexis de Tocqueville, *Democracy in America* (New York: Knopf, 1953), II, p. 258.
4. Alexander Hamilton in *The Federalist Papers* (New York: Mentor, 1961), p. 422.
5. Samuel P. Huntington, *American Politics: The Promise of Disharmony* (Cambridge: Harvard University Press, 1981), p. 33.
6. John Gardner, "The Antileadership Vaccine," Carnegie Foundation Report, 1965.
7. The Gallup Opinion Index, Report No. 99, Political, Social and Economic Trends (September, 1973), p. 8.

8. "Leadership: The Biggest Issue," *Time*, November 8, 1976.
9. The Gallup Report, Report No. 192, Political, Social and Economic Trends (September, 1981), p. 3.
10. Bruce Miroff, "After Consensus: The Dilemmas of Contemporary American Leadership," in *Presidential Science Quarterly* (Summer 1981), p. 416.
11. David Broder, *Changing of the Guard: Power and Leadership in America* (New York: Penguin, 1981).
12. Aaron Wildavsky, "The New Establishment?" *New York Times Book Review*, August 31, 1980.
13. Broder, *Changing of the Guard*, p. 72.
14. Ibid., p. 122.
15. Ibid., p. 76.
16. Ibid., pp. 473–74.
17. Andrew McFarland, *Power and Leadership in Pluralist Systems* (Stanford: Stanford University Press, 1969), p. 175.
18. Hemphill in Bernard M. Bass, *Stogdill's Handbook of Leadship* (New York: Free Press, 1981), p. 10.
19. French and Raven and French in Ibid., p. 11.
20. Homans in Bass, *Stodgill's Handbook of Leadership*, p. 14. The list of leadership definitions and conceptions is taken from Bass, pp. 7–15.
21. McFarland, *Power and Leadership in Pluralist Systems*, p. 155.
22. Lewis J. Edinger, "The Comparative Analysis of Political Leadership," *Comparative Politics*, 17 (January 1975), p. 255.
23. Ibid., p. 257.
24. Paige, *The Scientific Study of Political Leadership*, p. 66.
25. Excerpt from "Leaders of Men," an address by Woodrow Wilson delivered on June 17, 1890. I am grateful to Juliette George for drawing my attention to this speech.
26. Edinger, "The Comparative Analysis of Political Leadership," p. 259.
27. Fred Greenstein, *Personality and Politics: Problems of Evidence, Inference, and Conceptualization* (Chicago: Markham, 1969), pp. 42–45.
28. Eric H. Erickson, *Young Man Luther* (New York: Norton, 1958), and Gandhi's *Truth* (New York: Norton, 1969).
29. This definition is taken from Jeanne H. Knutson, "Personality in the Study of Politics," and Betty Glad, "Contributions of Psychobiography," both in Jeanne H. Knutson, ed., *Handbook of Political Psychology* (San Francisco: Jossey-Bass, 1973).
30. Eric H. Erickson, "Cn the Nature of Psycho-Historical Evidence: In Search of Gandhi," in Dankart A. Rustow, *Philosophers and Kings: Studies in Leadership* (New York: Braziller, 1970), p. 41.
31. For more on nonconstituted leaders *see* Robert C. Tucker, *Politics as Leadership* (Columbia, Mo.: University of Missouri Press, 1981), pp. 77 and following.
32. Harold Lasswell, *Psychopathology and Politics* (Chicago: University of Chicago Press, 1930). I am not, incidentally, suggesting that Lasswell was the first to classify leaders as particular types, merely that he was the first of the more contemporary social scientists to do so.
33. Ibid., p. 78.
34. Ibid., p. 127.
35. Ibid., p. 53.
36. Ibid., p. 75.

37. E. Victor Wolfenstein, *The Revolutionary Personality* (Princeton, N.J.: Princeton University Press, 1971), and Bruce Mazlish, *The Revolutionary Ascetic* (New York: Basic Books, 1976).
38. Wolfenstein *The Revolutionary Personality*, pp. 305 and following.
39. Mazlish, *The Revolutionary Ascetic*, pp. 213–14.
40. James David Barber, *The Presidential Character* (Englewood Cliffs, N.J.: Prentice-Hall, 1977), pp. 12–13.
41. Robert C. Tucker, "The Dictator and Totalitarianism," in Fred Greenstein and Michael Lerner, eds., *A Source Book for the Study of Personality and Politics* (Chicago: Markham, 1971), p. 465.
42. *See* especially, Hannah Arendt, *The Origins of Totalitarianism* (New York: Harcourt, Brace and World, 1951) and Carl J. Friedrich and Zbigniew Brzezinski, *Totalitarian Dictatorship and Autocracy* (Cambridge: Harvard University Press, 1956).
43. For the classic pluralist view *see* Robert Dahl, *Who Governs?* (New Haven: Yale University Press, 1961). Of course, the elite theorists implicitly take issue with Dahl's pluralist hypothesis. For a classic statement on that position, *see* C. Wright Mills, *The Power Elite* (New York: Oxford University Press, 1956).
44. Paige, *The Scientific Study of Political Leadership*, p. 105.
45. Bruce Mazlish, "Leader and Led, Individual and Group," *The Psychohistory Review*, 9, no. 3 (Spring 1981), p. 218.
46. James MacGregor Burns, *Leadership* (New York: Harper & Row, 1978), p. 4.
47. Ibid., p. 20.
48. Sigmund Freud, *Moses and Monotheism* (New York: Vintage, 1967), p. 141.
49. Lawrence K. Frank, "Dilemma of Leadership," *Psychiatry*, 2 (1939), pp. 343–44.
50. Robert Michels, *Political Parties* (New York: Free Press, 1962, originally published in 1911). *Political Parties* is, deservedly, one of the twentieth century's most influential books. And it is a must for anyone seriously interested in the study of leadership.
51. Ibid., pp. 65–66.
52. Fritz Redl, "Group Emotion and Leadership," *Psychiatry*, 5 (1942), p. 575.
53. Ibid., p. 576.
54. Robert C. Tucker, "The Theory of Charismatic Leadership," in Rustow, *Philosophers and Kings*, p. 80.
55. Mazlish, *The Revolutionary Ascetic*, p. 220.
56. Fred H. Willhoite, Jr., "Primates and Political Authority," *The American Political Science Review* (December 1976), p. 1110.
57. Plato, *Republic*, from Book V.
58. Machiavelli, *The Prince* (Middlesex, England: Penguin, 1961), p. 100.
59. *See*, for example, Jack Egan, "The Offer You Can't Afford to Refuse," *New York*, November 30, 1981.
60. Rosabeth Moss Kanter made this point in "An Agenda for Leadership in America," *Roundtable on New Leadership in the Public Interest* (NOW publication, 1980), p. 21.
61. Dennis F. Thompson claims that "the pursuit of personal responsibility provides the best foundation for understanding the role that human agency plays in good and bad government." In "Moral Responsibility of Public Officials: The Problem of Many Hands," *The American Political Science Review* (December 1980), p. 905.
62. For tales of leaders "from below" *see* Harry C. Boyte, *The Backyard Revolution* (Philadelphia: Temple University Press, 1980).

63. For more on a similar theme *see* Lynn Rosener and Peter Schwartz, "Women, Leadership and the 1980's: What Kind of Leaders Do We Need?" *Roundtable on New Leadership in the Public Interest,* pp. 25–36.
64. For some answers to the question of how leaders make a difference, *see* Valerie Bunce, *Do New Leaders Make A Difference?* (Princeton: Princeton University Press, 1981).

THE SOCIAL, ORGANIZATIONAL, AND CULTURAL CONTEXT OF EFFECTIVE LEADERSHIP

5

Martin M. Chemers

The primary focus of this chapter will be on leadership as an interpersonal process. Although there are managers who do not interact with other people, (for example, a manager of data processing), *leadership* is a social phenomenon. Thus, much of the research and the theoretical perspectives to be discussed here concern themselves with the dyadic or small-group aspects of leadership. Although one can discuss management at the organizational level in terms of corporate planning and actions, leadership is meant to be the processes of interpersonal influence which take place in the small group. Most of the research reported in this chapter was done on small groups.

It is equally true, however, that the leadership process is not divorced from the broader situational context. Aspects of the group's task, the authority system of the larger organization, and the social, economic, and cultural characteristics of the society in which the organization is embedded are critical influences on the nature of leadership. The aim of this chapter is to organize these various factors of leadership into a coherent whole, which allows us to discern the common themes in contemporary theory and the potentially productive avenues of future research.

THE NATURE OF LEADERSHIP

Organizational Functions

A first principle in the study of group effectiveness is that a group is relatively inefficient. A group, as opposed to an individual working alone, must coordinate the knowledge, abilities, and actions of its members.[1] The time, effort, and resources devoted to coordination represent potential decrements in performance. However, there are many tasks which cannot be accomplished by a single individual. Such tasks necessitate the creation of groups. Many tasks further require the coordination of several groups into larger organizations. The dictionary defines the word *organize* as "to make into a whole with unified and coherent relationships." Thus, a primary function of any organization is to create this unified set of groups in coherent relationships. All organizations must attend to two major functions in accomplishing this goal.

One function, which can be called *internal maintenance,* refers to the efforts of the organization to maintain the integrity of its various subsystems. An apt analogy is to the internal maintenance activities of the human body. Any living organism must coordinate its various parts to maintain a steady state or equilibrium which permits life to proceed. A human being must maintain a relatively constant body temperature, blood saline level, neuronal activity level, and so forth. The organism accomplishes this function through the activities of preprogrammed systems which respond to stimulation from sensing devices within the system. Task-directed organizations have a similar function. Day-to-day activities within the organization must be reliable and predictable. Job descriptions, standard operating procedures, and chains of command are examples of preprogrammed organizational systems designed to maintain equilibrium. Payroll forms, monthly reports, and inventory statements are sensing devices which establish and maintain the accountability of subsystems. Thus, the modern organization is built around a pervasive set of rules, regulations, and functions which ease the performance of standard duties and routine activities. The maintenance of these internal regularities is so essential to organizational functioning that it is possible to lose sight of another essential responsibility of organizations, *external adaptability.* An organization which overemphasizes internal maintenance turns inward, losing touch with the demands of its environment.

External adaptability requires that an organization be sensitive to its environment and internally flexible enough to respond to change. An effective organization is one which balances the functions of internal maintenance and external adaptablity. Control and order coexist with responsiveness and change. The requisite amount of emphasis on each function is influenced by the larger environment of which the organization is a part.

An adaptive human being changes his or her wardrobe as the seasons change. Likewise, an effective organization attends and responds to changes in the supply of resources, the demand for a product, the availability of capital, or other critical aspects of its environment.

Small-Group Functions

Organizational functions have their analogues at the level of the small group or unit. Here the function of internal maintenance is translated into the *motivation* and *control* of group members. The leader must direct the activities of subordinates and motivate them to carry out those activities efficiently. The rules, regulations, and systems of the larger organization, or general context, guide the leader in the direction of subordinates. A well-defined and structured task specifies the group's goal and procedures for reaching the goal. However, just as an organization's environment presents new challenges requiring response, so also a work unit or small group will be confronted with tasks for which no standard operating procedures exist. The leader and the group must then engage in the functions of *information processing* and *decision making*. Goals are defined, problems are solved, and procedures for attaining objectives are developed.

An extensive body of leadership research has demonstrated that the styles, behaviors, and activities of leadership which can accomplish these disparate organizational and small-group functions are quite different. Current organizational and leadership theory adopts the notion of "contingency." This notion argues that the organizational structure or leadership style which will be most effective depends or is contingent upon the nature of the task environment. Contemporary research attempts to identify and categorize the most critical features of the leadership situation and relate them to the most important aspects of leadership style and behavior.

CONTEMPORARY
LEADERSHIP THEORY

A Brief History

The scientific study of leadership can be roughly divided into three periods: the trait period, from around 1910 to World War II, the behavior period, from the onset of World War II to the late 1960s, and the contingency period, from the late 1960s to the present.

Traits. The early research on leadership emergence and leadership effectiveness proceeded from the premise that, somehow, those who became leaders were different from those who remained followers. The objective of the research was to identify specifically what unique feature of the individual was associated with leadership. The success of the mental testing movement in the early part of the century encouraged researchers to employ the recently developed "personality tests" in their search for the leadership trait. A large number of studies were done in which leaders and followers were compared on various measures hypothesized to be related to leadership status or effectiveness. Measures of dominance, social sensitivity, moodiness, masculinity, physical appearance, and many others were used. The typical research design involved the administration of one or more individual difference measures to members of an organization that had leaders and followers (for example, a military unit, industrial organization, or university student bodies). The scores of leaders and followers on the measures were compared for significant differences.

In 1948, Ralph Stogdill[2] reviewed over 120 such trait studies in an attempt to discern a reliable and coherent pattern. His conclusion was that no such pattern existed. The mass of inconsistent and contradictory results of the trait studies led Stogdill to conclude that traits alone do not identify leadership. He pointed out that leadership situations vary dramatically in the demands which they place upon the leader. For example, compare the desirable traits and abilities for a combat military officer with those for a senior scientist on a research team. Stogdill predicted that leadership theorizing would be inadequate until personal and situational characteristics were integrated.

Behaviors. The failure of the trait approach and the growing emphasis on behaviorism in psychology moved leadership researchers in the direction of the study of leadership behavior. A classic study of leadership styles was conducted by Kurt Lewin and his associates.[3] These researchers trained graduate research assistants in behaviors indicative of three leadership styles: autocratic, democratic, and laissez-faire. The autocratic style was characterized by the tight control of group activities and decisions made by the leader. The democratic style emphasized group participation and majority rule, while the laissez-faire leadership pattern involved very low levels of any kind of activity by the leader. Groups of preadolescent boys were exposed to each leadership style and the effects measured. Results indicated that the democratic style had somewhat more beneficial results on group process than the other styles. The importance of this study is not so much in its results but in its definition of leadership in terms of behavioral style. Also the emphasis on autocratic, directive styles versus democratic and participative styles had a profound impact on later research and theory.

In the 1950s, the research focus turned even more basic and behavioral. A number of independent researchers using rating scales,[4] interviews,[5] and observations[6] attempted to identify the specific, concrete behaviors in which leaders engaged. Here the emphasis was to move away from the focus on the internal states of leaders (that is, their values or personalities, as well as any preconceived leadership styles) to the more basic question of what it is that leaders actually do.

The most comprehensive study of leader behavior employed a rating scale labeled the Leader Behavior Description Questionnaire (LBDQ).[7] After extensive observation and rating of large numbers of military and industrial leaders, it was found that most of the variation in leader behavior could be described by two major clusters or factors of behavior. One factor which included items relating to interpersonal warmth, concern for the feelings of subordinates, and the use of participative two-way communication was labeled *Consideration* behavior. A second factor whose items stressed directiveness, goal facilitation, and task-related feedback was labeled *Initiation of Structure*. A number of other research projects confirmed the existence of these two general behavioral configurations, although they might be labeled *employee oriented* versus *production oriented*[8] or *task* versus *socioemotional*.[9]

The identification of two reliable dimensions of leader behavior was a major step forward for the field of leadership. Optimism was high that research had finally cracked open the complexity of leadership effects. Unfortunately, attempts to relate the behavioral factors to group and organizational outcomes proved quite difficult. Although the leader's consideration behavior was generally associated with subordinate satisfaction, this was not always the case. Furthermore, the relationship between leader-structuring behavior and group productivity revealed very few consistent patterns.[10]

During both the trait and behavior eras, researchers were seeking to identify the "best" style of leadership. They had not yet recognized that no single style of leadership is universally best across all situations and environments. For this reason, leadership theorists were quite disappointed when the behavior patterns which they had identified were not consistently related to important organizational outcomes such as group productivity and follower satisfaction.

Current Theory

Contingency approaches.   The reliable prediction of the effects of leadership style on organizational outcomes awaited the development of the modern contingency theories. The first of these was developed by Fred Fiedler.[11,12] Fiedler's approach centered on a personality measure called the "esteem for the least-preferred co-worker" or LPC scale which he found to be related to group performance. The person who fills out the scale is asked to rate an individual with whom the rater had difficulty accomplishing an assigned task. The most widely accepted interpretation of the meaning of this measure is that a person who gives a *very negative* rating to a poor co-worker is the kind of person for whom task success is very important. Such a person might be labeled "task motivated." A leader who gives a least-preferred co-worker a relatively positive rating would appear to be more concerned with the interpersonal than the task aspects of the situation, and is called "relationship motivated."[13,14,15]

A considerable body of research[16] indicates that the task-motivated leader is more attentive to task-related aspects of the leadership situation, more concerned with task success, and under most circumstances, more inclined to behave in a structuring, directive, and somewhat autocratic style. The relationship-motivated leader, on the other hand, is more attentive and responsive to interpersonal dynamics, more concerned with avoiding conflict and maintaining high morale, and more likely to behave in a participative and considerate leadership style.

After a very extensive series of studies covering some fifteen years, Fiedler[17] determined that leadership style alone was not sufficient to explain leader effectiveness. He set about to develop a model which integrated situational parameters into the leadership equation. He saw the most important dimension of the situation to be the degree of certainty, predictability, and control which the leader possessed. Fiedler developed a scale of *situational control* based on three features of the situation. These were: 1) leader-member relations, that is, the degree of trust and support which followers give the leader; 2) task structure, that is, the degree to which the goals and procedures for accomplishing the group's task are clearly specified; and 3) position power, that is, the degree to which the leader has formal authority to reward and punish followers. The research results indicate that neither style is effective in all situations. In *high control* situations, where predictability is assured by a clear task and a cooperative group, the task-motivated leader is calm and relaxed but maintains a strong emphasis on successful task accomplishment, which is very effective. However, under conditions of *moderate control,* caused by an ambiguous task or an uncooperative group, the task-motivated leader becomes anxious, overconcerned with a quick solution, and sometimes overly critical and punitive. The more open, considerate, and participative style of the relationship-motivated leader can address the problems of low morale or can create an environment conducive to successful problem solving and decision making, making the relationship-motivated leader more effective under these conditions. The crisis nature of the *low control* situation calls for a firm and directive leadership style which is supplied by the task-motivated leader. Such a situation is too far gone to be quickly solved via a participative or considerate style, although such styles may be effective in the long run.

The Contingency Model, as Fiedler's theory is called, has been the subject of considerable controversy.[18,19,20] Arguments have raged over the meaning of the LPC scale, the appropriateness of situational variables, and the general predictive validity of the theory. However, a recent extensive review[21] indicated that the predictions of the theory are strongly supported by data from both laboratory and organizational studies.

Research on the Contingency Model has been quite extensive and broad. The person/situation perspective has provided insights into leadership phenomena which were obscured by "one best way" approaches. One example is in the area of leadership training. Reviews of research on leadership training[22] had concluded that such training had few consistent effects on group performance or subordinate satisfaction. However, Contingency Model research on the effects of leadership training[23,24] has shown that training has its most powerful effects on the leader's situational control. Training provides the leader with knowledge, procedures, and techniques which increase his or her sense of control over the group's task activities. Since the relationship of leadership style to group performance varies across different levels of situational control, the increased control provided by training can either improve or lower a particular leader's performance. For example, if a situation was of moderate control for untrained leaders, the relationship-motivated leaders would perform most effectively. Leadership training which clarified and structured the task would change the situation into one of high control. Under these conditions, the task-motivated leaders would perform better than the relationship-motivated leaders. With the task-motivated leaders getting better and the relationship-motivated leaders getting worse, the net effect of training would appear to be null. However, when both leadership style and situational control are analyzed, the effects of training become clear. These findings helped to explain why leadership training has not been found to be a consistent positive factor in leadership effectiveness. More importantly, the utility of the situational-control dimension as a mediator of leadership effectiveness gained further support, suggesting that aspects of certainty, predictability, and control could well be the most critical factors in the leadership equation.

A number of other contingency-oriented leadership theories have also addressed the relationship of leadership decision-making style to group performance and morale. The best known of these approaches is the Normative Decision Theory presented by Vroom and Yetton.[25] These authors have identified a range of decision-making styles. These include *autocratic* styles, in which the leader makes a decision alone without consulting subordinates; *consultative* styles, in which the leader makes the decision, but after consulting with subordinates; and a *group* style, in which the leader allows subordinates to share in the decision-making responsibility. The dimension which underlies the range of decision styles is the degree to which the leader allows the followers to participate in the process of decision making. As the word *normative* in the name of the theory implies, the model specifies which of the styles is most likely to yield effective decisions under varying situations. Like Fiedler's Contingency Model, and other contingency theories, it is assumed that there is no one best way to make decisions, and that the most effective style will depend on the characteristics of the situation.

The situational characteristics which are considered most important in this model are 1) the expected support, acceptance, and commitment to the decision by subordinates and 2) the amount of structured, clear, decision-relevant information available to the leader. Three general rules determine which styles or sets of styles will be most effective. The first rule is that, other things being equal, autocratic decisions are less time-consuming and, therefore, more efficient. However, the second rule specifies that if the leader does not have sufficient structure and information to make a high-quality decision, he or she must consult with subordinates to gain the necessary information and enlist their aid and advice. The third general rule specifies that if the leader does not have sufficient support from subordinates to be assured that they will accept the decision, the leader must gain subordinate acceptance and commitment through participation in decision making.

Research support for the Normative Decision Theory is somewhat sparse.[26,27] Managers who are asked to recall and describe the characteristics of good and poor decisions that they have made in the past have been shown to usually describe situations and styles that would be predicted by the theory. Such recollective analyses are clearly open to distortion and bias. However, a comparison of Normative Decision Theory with the Contingency Model, described earlier, helps to strengthen and clarify both theories.

The two most important features of Fiedler's situational-control dimension are leader-member relations and task structure, which are extremely similar to Vroom and Yetton's characteristics of follower acceptance and structured information availability. Thus, the various situations presented in Vroom and Yetton's analysis would fit closely into Fiedler and situational-control dimension. Further, Fiedler's task-motivated and relationship-motivated leaders are typically described as using decision styles which fall toward the two poles of Vroom and Yetton's dimension of style. Task-motivated leaders are more likely to tend toward autocratic or minimally consultative styles while relationship-motivated leaders more often use group-oriented and participative styles.[28,29,30] The two theories make very similar predictions. Autocratic decisions are likely to be efficient and effective when the leader has a clear task and the support of followers. Relatively more participative decisions will fare better when either support or clarity are absent.

Despite the similarity of the two theories, they diverge sharply on the question of the ability of people to modify and change their decision styles. The normative model assumes that leaders can quickly and easily change their behavior to fit the demands of the situation, while Fiedler sees leadership style arising out of stable, enduring, well-learned personality attributes which are quite difficult to change. Some research by Bass and his associates[31] on decision styles is relevant to this question. Bass and others identified five decision styles which are quite close to those already discussed. These are called directive, negotiative, consultative, participative, and delegative. In a large survey conducted in several organizations, Bass asked managers to rate a number of features of the leadership situation which affect or are affected by these decision styles. The results do indicate that the effects of decision style on group performance and subordinate satisfaction depend on the situation, although the pattern of results in these studies is not yet clear and consistent. However, of great interest was Bass's finding that the various leadership styles were not independent of one another. The directive and negotiative styles seem to form one related set, while consultative, participative, and delegative form another. This suggests that some leaders across many situations tend to use more directive, task-oriented, autocratic styles while another type of leader is more likely to employ the participative, open, relationship-oriented styles. The possibility, then, that leadership decision and behavioral style are stable and enduring aspects of the individual leaders seems reasonable.

Another prominent contingency theory of leadership is the Path Goal Theory.[32,33] This is a more restricted theory which deals primarily with the effects of specific leader behavior on subordinate motivation and satisfaction, rather than the more general issues of decision making and performance. The Path-Goal research has studied the effects of the Leader Behavior Description Questionnaire categories of considerate and structuring behavior. The theory predicts that leader-structuring behavior will have the most positive effects on subordinate psychological states when the subordinate's task is unclear and/or difficult, that is, unstructured. The structure provided by the leader helps to clarify the *path* to the *goal* for the subordinates. On the other hand, consideration behavior will have its most positive effects when subordinates have a boring or distasteful job to perform. Subordinates then appreciate the "strokes" provided by their boss, more than they would if their job were intrinsically satisfying.

It is difficult to integrate Path Goal Theory with the more general theories of leadership discussed earlier. It is not concerned with participative decision styles. In fact, it is not concerned with decisions at all, and might more properly be thought of as a theory of supervision under conditions where the supervisor has high clarity and follower support. However, even with this model, the dimension of clarity, predictability, and certainty of the situation is a variable of critical importance. Research support for the Path-Goal Theory is variable. The most clear and consistent results show up on studies of follower satisfaction rather than group performance. However, a most interesting recent finding by Griffin[34] indicates that in addition to job characteristics, the needs, attitudes, and expectations of the follower have an important effect on the follower's reaction to leader behavior. Griffin found that managers who scored high on a measure of the need for personal growth preferred not to receive structuring supervision, even under conditions of ambiguity. These subordinates would rather work the problem out for themselves. Conversely, subordinates low in growth need were not upset by a boring, routine job. The supervisor's considerate behavior had little effect since the subordinates were not really suffering. This result is especially important because the theoretical orientations of the three theories described so far tend to largely ignore the characteristics of subordinates.

Transactional approaches.   The theories discussed above might all be regarded as "leader oriented" approaches. They tend to focus most of their attention on the leader's actions and attitudes. Although followers make their appearance in features related to leader-subordinate relationships, the leader is clearly the central figure and prime actor. However, some transactional or exchange theories of leadership addressing the relationship between leader and followers have had considerable impact.

One of the most important bodies of research in leadership are the studies of leader legitimation by Hollander.[35,36] Hollander developed the notion of "idiosyncrasy credit" to refer to the freedom which valued group members are given to deviate somewhat from group norms, that is, to act idiosyncratically. Idiosyncrasy credits are earned through the demonstration of competence and shared values which serve to make the group member more indispensable to the group. The individual's achieved value, which is the same as status, allows him or her to introduce new ideas and new ways of doing things into the group or society, thus creating adaptability and change. Hollander's work shows us that the legitimation of leadership is a process of social exchange. Members of groups exchange their competence and loyalty for group-mediated rewards which range from physical rewards such as income or protection to the less tangible rewards of honor, status, and influence.

The work of George Graen and his associates[37,38,39] has shown that the nature of exchange processes between leaders and subordinates can have far-reaching effects on group performance and morale. Research with the Vertical Dyad Linkage model has shown that a leader or manager develops a specific and unique exchange with each of his or her subordinates. These exchanges might range from a true partnership in which the subordinate is given considerable freedom and autonomy in defining and developing a work-related role to exchanges in which the subordinate is restrained, controlled, and little more than a "hired hand." As might be expected, the more positive exchanges are associated with higher subordinate satisfaction, reduced turnover, and greater identification with the organization.[40]

On the one hand, these findings are not surprising. Good interpersonal relationships in dyads make people feel better about each other, themselves, and their work. The importance of this research is that it redirects our attention to the relationship between leader, follower, and situation, and encourages a broader and more dynamic approach to the study of the leadership phenomenon. However, the Vertical Dyad Linkage Model does not elucidate the causes of good and poor exchanges.

Over the years, a number of studies have examined follower effects on the leadership process. Although not organized into a comprehensive theory, the research makes some interesting and important points. For example, a number of studies[41,42,43] have shown that leader activity, specifically the leader's willingness to engage in attempts to move the group toward its goals, is dramatically affected by followers' responses to the influence attempts. Leaders lead more with follower acceptance.

Individual differences in follower attitude or personality traits have long been associated with leadership effects. Early studies by Haythorn[44] and Sanford[45] showed that differences in authoritarian versus egalitarian attitudes of followers determined reactions to leader's style. A recent study by Weed and others[46] updates the same effect. They found that followers who are high in dogmatism respond better to leaders who engage in high levels of structuring behavior. Low-dogmatism followers perform better with considerate leader behavior.

A number of other characteristics, including need for achievement,[47] work values,[48,49] and locus of control[50,51] have been shown to impact on leader behavior and follower attitudes. At this point, the literature on follower characteristics is not well integrated. However, the results occur frequently enough to suggest that leadership theorizing will benefit from attention to leader *and* follower characteristics and to the resultant relationship.

Cognitive approaches. Perception and cognition have played a major role in leadership research. Many dependent measures such as leader-behavior ratings, satisfaction, and role ambiguity, are judgmental or memory processes. Social psychology has been strongly influenced by attribution theory[52,53,54] which is concerned with the cognitive processes which underlie interpersonal judgments. Recently, leadership theorists have begun to apply attribution-theory-based propositions to judgments involved in the process of leadership.

One of the key features of interpersonal judgments is the strong tendency for an observer to develop causal explanations for another person's behavior. Explanations of a person's behavior often center on the question of whether the behavior was determined by factors internal to the actor, such as ability or motivation, or factors external to the actor, such as situational forces, role demands, or luck. Reliable findings indicate that observers have a strong bias to attribute an actor's behavior to internal causes.[55] This tendency may result from the observer's desire for a sense of certainty and predictability about the actor's future behavior. Further, if the observer might be considered responsible for the actor's behavior, internal attributions to the actor remove that responsibility. For example, a teacher might be inclined to attribute a student's poor academic performance to a lack of ability, thereby relieving the teacher of responsibility for that performance.

Recent work by Green and Mitchell[56] has adapted some of the propositions of attribution theory to the processes which leaders use to make judgments about subordinate performance. They have shown that these processes are affected by factors which are not directly related to the subordinate's actual behavior. Studies[57,58] indicate that supervisors make more negative and more internal attributions when the negative outcomes of a subordinate's behavior are more severe. This happens even when the behavior in the two situations is identical. For example, nursing supervisors asked to judge a hypothetical subordinate's performance made more negative judgments of a nurse who left a railing down on a patient's bed if the patient fell out of bed than if the patient did not. These judgments have important implications for later actions the supervisor might take with respect to promotion, termination, or salary. The role-making processes which are discussed in the Vertical Dyad Linkage model might benefit from an analysis of the ways in which supervisory judgments affect leader-follower exchanges.

Calder's[59] attribution theory of leadership argues that leadership processes and effects exist primarily as perceptual processes in the minds of followers and observers. In fact, most of the measuring instruments used in leadership research ask the respondent for perceptions of the leadership process. These perceptions, judgments, and attributions are distorted by the biases which the perceiver brings to the situation. Each individual holds an implicit personal theory of leadership which serves as a cognitive filter to determine what the observer will notice, remember, and report about the leadership process.

A number of recent studies[60,61,62] indicate that such implicit theories are especially problematic in ratings of leader behavior. Raters who are led to believe that a group has performed well or poorly will modify their ratings of leader behavior to conform to the performance feedback. In other words, if I think that good leaders are very considerate of their followers, I am more likely to notice and report the consideration behavior of leaders whom I believe have performed well.

Ayman and Chemers[63] have found that the structure of leader-behavior ratings depends more on the culture of the raters than on the behavior of the leader. These researchers factor analyzed leader-behavior ratings made by Iranian subjects. They found that the structure of the behavior ratings was very different from the structure normally found in studies in the United States and Europe. In most leadership studies done in Western Europe and the United States, analyses of leader-behavior ratings yield two distinct and independent behavior clusters. These are the familiar structuring, task-directed behaviors and the considerate, relationship-directed behaviors. However, the Ayman and Chemers analysis of ratings made by Iranian followers resulted in a single category of behavior which included both structuring and considerate items. This global factor depicting a directive but warm supervisor was labeled "benevolent paternalism." Furthermore, the factor was found to be strongly related to group performance as assessed by superiors and to satisfaction with supervision expressed by subordinates. Interestingly, this unique pattern of behavior ratings was found when the leaders being rated were Iranian or American. This led Ayman and Chemers to conclude that leader-behavior ratings are more a function of the implicit theories which guide the "eye of the beholder" than they are of what the leader actually does.

On the one hand, these distortions in the observation of leadership effects are very problematic. This is especially true for research with certain theories (for example, Path-Goal Theory, the Normative Decision Theory, and the Vertical Dyad Linkage Model) because in many tests of these theories subjects are asked to rate several aspects of the leadership situation, for example, their leader's behavior and their own satisfaction. The relationships observed among these measures may reflect the implicit theories held by the subjects rather than accurate reflections of the constructs studied. However, it is also true that perception, judgments, and expectations form the core of interpersonal relationships. The desire and expectations of a subordinate for some type of leader behavior (for example, consideration) may elicit or compel that behavior. This represents an interesting and necessary area for future research.

Cross-cultural approaches. Berry[64] has argued that American psychology is "culture bound" and "culture blind." The generalizability of our findings are bounded by the fact that most of our research is done with European or American samples. Furthermore, because we rarely compare cultures, we are blind to the potential effects of cultural differences. Chemers[65] points out that this problem becomes more salient when we attempt to export our theories and training programs to cultures which are different from those in which the theories were developed. Cross-cultural research can benefit leadership theory in two ways. Comparative studies can show us the generalizability of Euro-American theories, helping us to recognize the inherent limitations in their transfer to other cultures. More importantly, comparative research give us a much broader range of variables which may highlight relationships previously ignored. For example, since most studies done in the developed countries are done on subjects who are relatively well educated and technologically sophisticated, educational level becomes a background variable to which we pay little attention. However, in a broader context, the socialization or educational background of workers may be an important determinant of work-related attitudes and responses.

Leadership researchers have not totally ignored culture, but the results of the research leave much to be desired. Reviews by Roberts,[66] Nath,[67] Barrett and Bass,[68] and Tannenbaum[69] all concluded that the cross-cultural research on leadership has been characterized by weak methodologies and by a paucity of theory, both of which make the interpretation of the scattered findings very difficult. However, a few cross-cultural models do exist. Neghandhi[70] presented a model of cultural effects on organizational structure in which cultural or national differences act indirectly on management practices by affecting the organizational environment. He argues that organizational structure and managerial policy are more important than cultural factors in determining behavior. This view contrasts with earlier views[71] which saw culture as directly determining managerial values, attitudes, and behavior.

The actual role of culture probably lies somewhere between these two views. Neither culture nor organizational structure are static forces. Rather, they interact in dynamic process influencing one another, and both contribute to managerial attitudes and behavior. For example, studies which have compared the attitudes or behaviors of managers have found national differences somewhat moderated by organizational policy.[72] Unfortunately, after we have dealt with the broad question of whether culture is important, we are still left with few theories which make any specific predictions about the role of culture in shaping leadership process.

A potentially useful theoretical framework relating values to managerial and organizational process has been offered by Hofstede.[73,74,75] Comparing responses to a value survey of managers from forty countries, Hofstede found that the pattern of results could be described by four factors. These were 1) power distance, that is, the relative importance of status; 2) tolerance for uncertainty; 3) individualism versus collectivism; and 4) masculinity. Hofstede[76] argues that a culture's standing on these four value dimensions determines the kind of organizational structure and managerial policies that will be most likely to develop. For example, he argues that cultures which have a low tolerance for uncertainty combined with a low emphasis on status are likely to develop highly bureaucratic organizational structures to reduce ambiguity. Cultures which are also low in tolerance for uncertainty but high in power distance will develop autocratic organizational structures, in which the high-status persons resolve ambiguity by fiat.

The validity of much of the cross-cultural research has been questioned by Ayman and Chemers.[77] In a study of the leadership behavior of Iranian managers, these researchers found that traditional measures of leadership behavior and subordinate satisfaction resulted in very different factor structures in their Iranian sample than did those measures when used with European or American samples. Ayman and Chemers[78] and Chemers[79] argue that the imposition of Euro-American theories, measures, and research designs on other cultures may lead to very inaccurate conclusions.

SUMMARY AND CONCLUSIONS

We can now look back on over seventy years of scientific research on leadership in small groups. For much of that time, the literature has been characterized by false starts, dead ends, and bitter controversies. Even today, the student of leadership is consistently confronted with acrimonious debates among theorists, giving the field an appearance of chaotic disarray. In fact, much of the controversy resembles a "tempest in a teapot." Various theories say much the same thing in slightly different ways, and advocates engage in quibbling over relatively minor differences. The current crop of theories has more which unites than separates them. The last twenty years of research has reinforced and clarified certain common threads, and the study of leadership stands poised for a thrust into a new era of growth. Let us examine these commonalities and the directions toward which they point.

At the broadest level, most contemporary theories adopt a contingency perspective. One would be hard put to find an empirical theory of leadership which holds that one style of leadership is appropriate for all situations. At a somewhat deeper level, the similarities continue. The most frequent dimensions on which leader behavior, style, or decision processes are differentiated are 1) the relative focus of the leader on goal-directed task functions versus morale-oriented interpersonal functions, and 2) the relative use of autocratic, directive styles versus democratic, participative styles. These related dichotomies have been part and parcel of the leadership equation since the first behavioral studies of the late 1940s and early 1950s.

Turning to the situational parameters embodied in most current theories, another area of commonality is revealed. Almost all of the contemporary approaches are concerned with the degree of predictability, certainty, and control which the environment affords to the leader. At an even more specific level most approaches integrate interpersonal and task features into the specification of the situation. Indeed, in retrospect, it is hard to imagine how it could be otherwise. Leadership involves a job to do and people to do it with. The likelihood of successful goal accomplishment must, then, depend upon the degree to which the support of the people and the control of the task are facilitative.

Finally, a careful examination of these leadership theories results in a common set of predictions as well. Autocratic decisions and directive styles in which the leader tells followers what to do are most likely to work when the leader knows exactly what to tell the subordinates (that is, a structured task) and when the subordinates are inclined to do what they are told (that is, good follower acceptance and loyalty). When the leader is not so sure what to do or not so sure that followers will go along, considerate and participative styles have the double benefit of encouraging follower acceptance and increasing follower input into the problem-solving process.

The presence of common themes in the research literature does not mean that we have answered all the questions and solved all the problems in leadership. The contingency approaches do provide us with a stable platform from which to step into the next set of issues. However, these issues are quite complex and will require a more integrated, multifaceted, and systemic view of leadership process.

A major gap in most current leadership theories is the lack of attention to the leaders and followers, as people. We focus on behavior or decision style with very little understanding of the values, needs, and motives which give rise to the observed behaviors. It is assumed that any leader can engage in any behavior, and that leaders and followers can easily identify the correct or ideal set of behaviors in a situation. When the possibility arises, as it has recently, that our observation of behavior may be flawed, we are left with nowhere to turn.

The differences in the factor structure of leader behavior across cultures highlights the role of personal values in the social process of leadership. In the research done in the Western industrialized nations, for example, leader behaviors which are directive and task oriented are usually differentiated from those that are more considerate and interpersonally oriented. The two sets of behaviors load on separate and distinct factors. However, Ayman and Chemers's[80] research in developing nations such as Iran and Mexico reveals a different pattern. The leaders who have the highest group performance and the most satisfied subordinates are those who combine directive task styles with interpersonal warmth and consideration. The factor structure of leader-behavior ratings in these cultures indicates that both structuring and considerate behavior correlate within a single global cluster.

In order to understand why leader-behavior factors differ across cultures, it is necessary to have some theory about the manner in which culture affects behavior. The culture, through the processes of socialization, helps to shape the needs, values, and personality of leaders and followers. The personality of the leader will affect the kinds of behaviors most often used. Further, cultural norms create expectations and judgments about the appropriate behavior of leaders and their group members. The cultural expectations of the society's members then influence the patterns of leadership exhibited.

Thus, one interpretation of the differences in leader-behavior patterns across cultures relates to the very strong emphasis on individualism in the Western democracies and on collective, group-oriented values in much of the rest of the world. When individual responsibility and individual autonomy are stressed, considerate supervisory behavior is that which reinforces the autonomy of subordinates; in other words, egalitarian, participative leadership. Thus considerate behavior is generally likely to be somewhat incompatible with high levels of directive and structuring behavior. However, in more collective and authoritarian cultures, in which group members subordinate individuals goals to group needs, a leader can maintain control over subordinates *and* satisfy them, by being directive and structuring in a warm, supportive, "fatherly" manner. Cultural values are reinforced by social norms which prescribe elaborate codes of politeness and make the exercise of a "benevolent paternalism" the most acceptable mode of behavior.

The role of culture in leadership is much broader and more complex than the abbreviated explanation given here. But this analysis does turn our attention to the role of the leader's and the follower's personalities as an influence on behavior and the perception of behavior. The research on follower characteristics makes it very plain that the way in which one individual reacts to the behavior of another is dependent upon individual differences in styles and needs as well as variations in situational characteristics.

The transactional and exchange theories have shown that the relationship between leaders and followers is a dynamic one extending longitudinally in time. Roles are defined, negotiated, and redefined. People move toward or away from one another with effects on motivation, satisfaction, and individual and group performance. Observations and judgments are made which facilitate and enhance positive or negative relationships. Admittedly, such dynamic relationships are difficult to study. It is also true, however, that leadership theory will make major strides forward when we can begin to tie together the ways in which personal characteristics influence judgments which, in turn, influence role perception and performance which, subsequently, determine group behavior and effectiveness.

The simplistic trait approaches were superseded by the behavioral studies which were replaced by the contingency theories. The next major era of leadership research will begin with the recognition that group and organizational performance are dependent upon the interplay of social systems. A social-systems approach will recognize that the leadership process is a complex, multifaceted network of forces. Personal characteristics of leaders and followers interact in the perception of and reaction to task demands and to each other. The small group is further embedded in an organizational and societal context which influences personal characteristics, social roles, and situational contingencies. If general leadership theory can begin to span the gaps between the various levels of analysis (that is, individual, group, organization, society), the resultant theories will provide us with a much stronger base, not only for understanding leadership but also for improving its quality.

NOTES

1. Ivan D. Steiner, *Group Process and Productivity* (New York: Academic Press, 1972).
2. Ralph M. Stogdill, "Personal Factors Associated with Leadership: A Survey of the Literature," *Journal of Psychology*, 25 (1948), pp. 35–71.
3. Kurt Lewin, Ronald Lippitt, and Ralph K. White, "Patterns of Aggressive Behavior in Experimentally Created Social Climates," *Journal of Social Psychology*, 10 (1939), pp. 271–99.
4. Ralph M. Stogdill, Carroll L. Shartle, Willis L. Scott, Alvin E. Coons, and William E. Jaynes, *A Predictive Study of Administrative Work Patterns* (Columbus: Ohio State University, Bureau of Business Research, 1956).
5. Robert L. Kahn and Daniel Katz, "Leadership Practices in Relation to Productivity and Morale," in Dorwin Cartwright and Alvin Zander, eds., *Group Dynamics* (New York: Harper & Row, 1953).
6. Robert F. Bales and Paul E. Slater, "Role Differentiation in Small Decision Making Groups," in Talcott Parsons and Robert F. Bales, eds., *Family, Localization, and Interaction Processes* (New York: Free Press, 1945).
7. Ralph M. Stogdill and Alvin E. Coons, eds., *Leader Behavior: Its Description and Measurement* (Columbus: Ohio State University, Bureau of Business Research, 1957).
8. Kahn and Katz, *Group Dynamics*.
9. Bales and Slater, *Family, Localization, and Interaction Processes*.
10. Abraham Korman, "Consideration, Initiating Structure, and Organizational Criteria—A Review," *Personnel Psychology*, 19 (1966), pp. 349–62.
11. Fred E. Fiedler, "A Contingency Model of Leadership Effectiveness," in Leonard Berkowitz, ed., *Advances in Experimental Social Psychology*, vol. 1 (New York: Academic Press, 1964).
12. ———, *A Theory of Leadership Effectiveness* (New York: McGraw-Hill, 1967).
13. ———, "The Contingency Model and the Dynamics of the Leadership Process," in Leonard Berkowitz, ed., *Advances in Experimental Social Psychology*.
14. Fred E. Fiedler and Martin M. Chemers, *Leadership and Effective Management*, New York: Scott, Foresman, 1974).
15. Robert W. Rice, "Construct Validity of the Least Preferred Co-worker Score," *Psychological Bulletin*, 85 (1978), pp. 1199–1237.
16. Ibid.
17. Fiedler, *A Theory of Leadership Effectiveness*.
18. Ahmed S. Ashour, "Further Discussion of Fiedler's Contingency Model of Leadership Effectiveness: An Evaluation," *Organizational Behavior and Human Performance*, 9 (1973), pp. 339–55.
19. George Graen, Kenneth M. Alveres, James B. Orris, and John A. Martella, "Contingency Model of Leadership Effectiveness: Antecedent and Evidential Results," *Psychological Bulletin*, 74 (1970), pp. 285–96.

20. Terrence R. Mitchell, Anthony Biglan, Gerald R. Oncken, and Fred E. Fiedler, "The Contingency Model: Criticism and Suggestions," *Academy of Management Journal,* 13 (1970), pp. 253–67.
21. Michael J. Strube and Joseph E. Garcia, "A Meta-analytical Investigation of Fiedler's Contingency Model of Leadership Effectiveness," *Psychological Bulletin,* 90 (1981), pp. 307–21.
22. Robert J. House, "T-Group Education and Leadership Effectiveness: A Review of the Empirical Literature and a Critical Evaluation," *Personnel Psychology,* 20 (1967), pp. 1–32.
23. Martin M. Chemers, Robert W. Rice, Eric Sundstrom, and William M. Butler, "Leader LPC, Training and Effectiveness: An Experimental Examination," *Journal of Personality and Social Psychology,* 31 (1975), pp. 401–9.
24. Fred E. Fiedler, "The Effects of Leadership Training and Experience: A Contingency Model Interpretation," *Administrative Science Quarterly,* 17 (1972), pp. 453–70.
25. Victor H. Vroom and Paul. W. Yetton, *Leadership and Decision-Making* (Pittsburgh: University of Pittsburgh Press, 1973).
26. Arthur G. Jago and Victor H. Vroom, "An Evaluation of Two Alternatives to the Vroom/Yetton Normative Model," *Academy of Management Journal,* 23 (1980), pp. 347–55.
27. Victor H. Vroom and Arthur G. Jago, "On the Validity of the Vroom-Yetton Model," *Journal of Applied Psychology,* 63 (1978), pp. 151–62.
28. Martin M. Chemers, Barbara K. Goza, and Sheldon I. Plumer, "Leadership Style and Communication Process: An Experiment Using the Psychological Isotope Technique," *Resources in Education* (September 1979).
29. Martin M. Chemers and George J. Skrzypek, "An Experimental Test of the Contingency Model of Leadership Effectiveness," *Journal of Personality and Social Psychology,* 24 (1972), pp. 172–77.
30. Rice, "Construct Validity of the Least Preferred Co-worker Score."
31. Bernard M. Bass, Enzo R. Valenzi, Dana L. Farrow, and Robert J. Solomon, "Management Styles Associated With Organizational, Task, Personal, and Interpersonal Contingencies," *Journal of Applied Psychology,* 60 (1975), pp. 720–29.
32. Robert J. House, "A Path-Goal Theory of Leadership," *Administrative Science Quarterly,* 16 (1971), pp. 321–38.
33. Robert J. House and Gary Dessler, "The Path-Goal Theory of Leadership: Some Post Hoc and A Priori Tests," in James G. Junt and Lars L. Larsen, eds., *Contingency Approaches to Leadership* (Carbondale, Il: Southern Illinois University Press, 1974).
34. Ricky N. Griffin, "Relationships Among Individual, Task Design, and Leader Behavior Variables," *Academy of Management Journal,* 23, (1980), pp. 665–83.
35. Edwin P. Hollander, "Conformity, Status, and Idiosyncrasy Credit," *Psychological Review,* 65, pp. 117–27.
36. Edwin P. Hollander and James W. Julian, "Studies in Leader Legitimacy, Influence, and Innovation," in Leonard Berkowitz, ed., *Advances in Experimental Social Psychology,* vol. 5 (New York: Academic Press, 1970).
37. Fred Dansereau, Jr., George Graen, and William J. Haga, "Vertical Dyad Linkage Approach to Leadership Within Formal Organizations: A Longitudinal Investigation of the Role Making Process," *Organizational Behavior and Human Performance,* 13 (1975), pp. 46–78.
38. George Graen and James F. Cashman, "A Role-Making Model of Leadership in Formal Organizations: A Developmental Approach," in J. G. Hunt and L.

L. Larsen, eds., *Leadership Frontiers* (Kent, Ohio: Kent State University Press, 1975).

39. George Graen, James F. Cashman, Steven Ginsburgh, and William Schiemann, "Effects of Linking-Pin Quality of Work Life of Lower Participants," *Administrative Science Quarterly*, 22 (1977), pp. 491–504.

40. George Graen and Steven Ginsburgh, "Job Resignation as a Function of Role Orientation and Leader Acceptance: A Longitudinal Investigation of Organizational Assimilation," *Organizational Behavior and Human Performance*, 19 (1977), pp. 1–17.

41. Alex Bavelas, Albert H. Hastorf, Alan E. Gross, and W. Richard Kite, "Experiments on the Alteration of Group Structure," *Journal of Experimental Social Psychology*, 1 (1965), pp. 55–70.

42. Lawrence Beckhouse, Judith Tanur, John Weiler, and Eugene Weinstein, "And Some Men Have Leadership Thrust Upon Them," *Journal of Personality and Social Psychology*, 31 (1975), pp. 557–66.

43. Leopold W. Gruenfeld, David E. Rance, and Peter Weissenbert, "The Behavior of Task Oriented (Low LPC) and Socially Oriented (High LPC) Leaders Under Several Conditions of Social Support," *Journal of Social Psychology*, 79 (1969), pp. 99–107.

44. William Haythorn, Arthur Couch, Don Haefner, Peter Langham, and Launor F. Carter, "The Effects of Varying Combinations of Authoritarian and Egalitarian Leader and Follower," *Journal of Abnormal and Social Psychology*, 53 (1956), pp. 210–19.

45. Frederick Sanford, "Research on Military Leadership," in John Flanagan, ed., *Psychology in the World Emergency* (Pittsburgh: University of Pittsburgh Press, 1952).

46. Stanley E. Weed, Terrence R. Mitchell, and William Moffitt, "Leadership Style, Subordinate Personality, and Task Type as Predictors of Performance and Satisfaction With Supervision," *Journal of Applied Psychology*, 61 (1976), pp. 58–66.

47. Richard M. Steers, "Task-goal Attributes, N Achievement, and Supervisory Performance," *Organizational Behavior and Human Performance*, 13 (1975), pp. 392–403.

48. Milton R. Blood, "Work Values and Job Satisfaction," *Journal of Applied Psychology*, 53 (1969), pp. 456–59.

49. Ramon J. Aldage and Arthur P. Brief, "Some Correlates of Work Values," *Journal of Applied Psychology*, 60 (1975), pp. 757–60.

50. Thomas L. Ruble, "Effects of One's Locus of Control and the Opportunity to Participate in Planning," *Organizational Behavior and Human Performance*, 16 (1976), pp. 63–73.

51. Douglas E. Durand and Walter R. Nord, "Perceived Leader Behavior as a Function of Personality Characteristics of Supervisors and Subordinates," *Academy of Management Journal*, 19 (1976), pp. 427–31.

52. Fritz Heider, *The Psychology of Interpersonal Relations* (New York: John Wiley, 1958).

53. Edward E. Jones and Keith E. Davis, "From Acts to Dispositions," in Leonard Berkowitz, ed., *Advances in Experimental Social Psychology*, vol 2. (New York: Academic Press, 1965).

54. Harold H. Kelley, "The Processes of Causal Attribution," *American Psychologists*, 28 (1973), pp. 107–28.

55. Jones and Davies, "From Acts to Dispositions."

56. Stephen G. Green and Terrence R. Mitchell, "Attributional Processes of Leaders in Leader-Member Interactions," *Organizational Behavior and Human Performance,* 23 (1979), pp. 429–58.
57. Terrence R. Mitchell and Laura S. Kalb, "Effects of Outcome Knowledge and Outcome Valence in Supervisors' Evaluations," *Journal of Applied Psychology,* 66 (1981), pp. 604–12.
58. Terrence R. Mitchell and Robert E. Wood, "Supervisors' Responses to Subordinate Poor Performance: A Test of an Attributional Model," *Organizational Behavior and Human Performance,* 25 (1980), pp. 123–38.
59. Billy J. Calder, "An Attribution Theory of Leadership," in Barry M. Staw and Gerald R. Slancik, eds., *New Directions in Organizational Behavior* (Chicago: St. Clair, 1977).
60. Dov Eden and Uri Leviatan, "Implicit Leadership Theory as a Determinant of the Factor Structure Underlying Supervisory Behavior Scales," *Journal of Applied Psychology,* 60 (1975), pp. 736–41.
61. Robert G. Lord, John F. Binning, Michael C. Rush, and Jay C. Thomas, "The Effect of Performance Cues and Leader Behavior in Questionnaire Rating of Leadership Behavior," *Organizational Behavior and Human Performance,* 21 (1978), pp. 27–39.
62. H. Kirk Downey, Thomas I. Chacko, and James C. McElroy, "Attribution of the "Causes" of Performance: A Constructive, Quasi-Longitudinal Replication of the Staw (1975) Study," *Organizational Behavior and Human Performance,* 24 (1979), pp. 287–89.
63. Roya Ayman and Martin M. Chemers, "The Relationship of Leader Behavior to Managerial Effectiveness and Satisfaction in Iran," *Journal of Applied Psychology,* 68 (1983), pp. 338–341.
64. John W. Berry, "On Cross-Cultural Comparability," *International Journal of Psychology,* 4 (1969), pp. 119–28.
65. Martin M. Chemers, "Leadership and Social Organization in Cross-Cultural Psychology," paper presented to the Meetings of the American Psychological Association, Los Angeles, 1981.
66. Karlene H. Roberts, "On Looking at an Elephant: An Evaluation of Cross-Cultural Research Related to Organizations," *Psychological Bulletin,* 74 (1970), pp. 327–50.
67. Robert A. Nath, "A Methodological Review of Cross-Cultural Management Research," in Jean Boddewyn, ed., *Comparative Management and Marketing* (Glenview, Il.: Scott, Foresman, 1969).
68. Gerald V. Barrett and Bernard M. Bass, "Cross-Cultural Issues in Industrial and Organizational Psychology," in M. D. Dunnette, ed., *Handbook of Industrial and Organizational Psychology* (Chicago: Rand McNally, 1975).
69. Arnold S. Tannenbaum, "Organizational Psychology," in Harry C. Triandis and Richard W. Brislin, eds., *Handbook of Cross-Cultural Psychology, Social Psychology,* vol. 5 (Boston: Allyn & Bacon, 1980).
70. Anant R. Negandhi, "Comparative Management and Organizational Theory: A Marriage Needed," *Academy of Management Journal,* 18 (1975), pp. 334–44.
71. Richard N. Farmer and Barry M. Richman, *Comparative Management and Economic Progress* (Homewood, Il.: Richard D. Irwin, 1965).
72. Tannenbaum, "Organizational Psychology."
73. Geert Hofstede, "Nationality and Espoused Values of Managers," *Journal of Applied Psychology,* 61 (1976), pp. 148–55.
74. ———, "Motivation, Leadership, and Organization: Do American Theories Apply Abroad?" *Organizational Dynamics* (Summer 1980).

75. ———, Culture's Consequences: *International Differences in Work-Related Values* (London: Sage, 1981).
76. Ibid.
77. Ayman and Chemers, "The Relationship of Leader Behavior to Managerial Effectiveness and Satisfaction in Iran."
78. Ibid.
79. Chemers, "Leadership and Social Organization in Cross-Cultural Psychology."
80. Ayman and Chemers, "The Relationship of Leader Behavior to Managerial Effectiveness and Satisfaction in Iran."

6

ORGANIZATIONAL LEADERSHIP
The Contingency Paradigm and Its Challenges[1]

James G. Hunt

As Chemers's chapter indicates, the study of leadership in organizations has evolved considerably over a number of years. It is important to be familiar with this evolution to add perspective in understanding current approaches to organizational leadership.

Thus, this chapter begins by touching on earlier approaches to organizational leadership. These have led up to the currently dominant contingency paradigm. The chapter briefly treats this paradigm and then discusses in detail some ways in which newly emeging work can expand and refine various aspects of the paradigm.

The chapter then moves from refining and extending the paradigm to research which challenges the nature of the paradigm itself. Such work is reflective of what many would term a *paradigm shift* or new way of conceptualizing and researching the organizational leadership field.

The chapter culminates with conclusions about the current state of the organizational leadership research area.

EVOLUTION IN ORGANIZATIONAL LEADERSHIP APPROACHES[2]

As Chemers points out, the earliest leadership approach was concerned with traits. In organizational research this essentially took two forms. In the first, there was a focus on those traits which distinguished leaders from nonleaders or followers. This was essentially an application of the so-called great man perspective, which was the first general approach to studying leadership and had received considerable emphasis by those outside the organizational leadership area. The focus was on those characteristics or traits that separated "great leaders" from the masses.

A variation of the trait approach focused on trying to identify traits that differentiated "successful" (that is, those who had better performing and/or more satisfied individual subordinates or work groups) from less successful leaders in organizations.

Neither variation of the trait approach was successful in revealing a set of universal leadership traits. Thus, those interested in organizational leadership shifted from traits to behaviors. Their focus was on *behaviors* which differentiated successful from less successful leaders in organizations. For example, do leaders who show more considerate behavior have more effective and/or satisfied followers than those lower in consideration?

Early results suggested this behavioral approach was more viable than the earlier concentration on traits. However, later studies showed inconsistent results and led to the development of contingency leadership models by organizational leadership researchers. Fiedler's model was the first of these and was later joined by the work of those such as House and Vroom and Yetton.[3] All of these are treated by Chemers and do not need to be described here. The guiding principal in each of them is that the most appropriate leadership (typically leader behavior, but in Fiedler's model, task or relationship–motivated leadership style) in terms of follower outcomes (for example, performance and/or satisfaction and the like), is a function of "contingencies" facing the leader. Hence, though there are individual differences in each of the models, they are all subsumed within what may be called the "contingency paradigm." That paradigm, along with the trait and behavioral approaches, is summarized in Figure 6-1.

CONCERNS ABOUT THE
CONTINGENCY PARADIGM

The contingency paradigm has been clearly the dominant approach among leadership researchers at least since the late 1960s.[4] Over the last few years, however, there have been more and more questions raised about the paradigm's adequacy. Many of these questions turn on the notion of understanding and prediction. Some have argued that the current paradigm is too narrow and sterile. The job of a leader or manager in an organization is much broader, complex, and dynamic than a contingentcy paradigm suggests, they say.[5] Others take the paradigm to task because it does not predict work group or individual worker outcomes very well. Often, less

Great man and trait approaches

| Personal Characteristics | → | Separation of leaders from nonleaders
or
successful from less successful leaders |

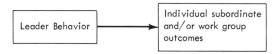

Leader behavior approaches

| Leader Behavior | → | Individual subordinate and/or work group outcomes |

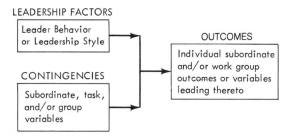

Typical contingency approaches

LEADERSHIP FACTORS

| Leader Behavior or Leadership Style | → | OUTCOMES |

| CONTINGENCIES | → | Individual subordinate and/or work group outcomes or variables leading thereto |
| Subordinate, task, and/or group variables |

Figure 6-1. Evolution in leadership approaches

than 10 percent of the variance in outcomes such as performance is accounted for by the traditional contingency paradigm.[6]

Approaches with implications for dealing with inadequacies in the current paradigm take different directions. This chapter will focus on four of these. The first is concerned with clarifying the relationship between leadership and managerial behavior. The second focuses on refined conceptualizations of leadership. The third emphasizes expanding the nature of the contingencies considered. While all of the previous directions can be treated within a contingency framework, the fourth challenges the framework itself and calls for a paradigm shift.

LEADERSHIP AND MANAGERIAL BEHAVIOR

The terms *leader* and *manager* are often used interchangeably in the organizational literature. Indeed, this chapter has not differentiated the terms up to this point. Yet, as we shall show, it is useful to distinguish between them.

Paradoxically, just as many people fail to discriminate between leader and manager, others differentiate to the point where they fail to consider the relationship between the two. Thus, a whole body of leadership research has developed independently from a body of managerial behavior research. Managerial behavior researchers have traditionally come from different backgrounds and been interested in different questions than have leadership researchers.[7]

It is the contention of this chapter that both of the previously expressed views are counterproductive to the continuing development of organizational leadership research.

A model developed by Mintzberg provides important insight here. Mintzberg systematically observed five chief executive officers over a five-day period. From these observations, he derived the three role categories of: interpersonal, information, and decision making. Within each of these categories were grouped more specific roles as summarized below:[8]

Interpersonal roles. These are concerned with relating to people both inside and outside a manager's organization or unit.

Ceremonial/figurehead	Involves attending ceremonies and representing the organizational system to the rest of the world. These go with being the head of the organization or work unit.
Leader	Entails hiring, training, motivating, evaluating, and rewarding subordinates. Involves integrating subordinates' needs with the needs of the organizational system or work unit.
Liason	Involves giving and receiving information and favors to learn what is going on elsewhere to gain benefits for the organization or work unit.

Informational roles. These are concerned with channeling information into and out of a manager's organization or unit.

Monitor	Involves seeking and receiving relevant information (mail, observations, reports, reading, and the like) for the organization or unit.
Disseminator	Entails transmitting to organization members relevant information for the organization or unit.
Spokesperson	Involves transmitting information outside the organization or unit.

Decision-making roles. These depend on a manager's position and access to information and are concerned with the performance of several roles entailing organization or work unit strategic decision making.

Entrepreneur	Involves seeking opportunities and problems and initiating action in the best interests of the organization or unit.
Disturbance handler	Entails resolving conflicts among individuals or groups in the organization or work unit or between the organization or unit and outside parties.
Resource allocator	Involves making choices among organization or unit resource allocation.
Negotiator	Entails representing the organization or work unit in third-party (for example, government regulators or union officials) formal negotiations.

In terms of the present discussion there are a number of important points to note from Mintzberg's model. First, if one thinks of the total job of Mintzberg's managers, it may be seen that the job is quite broad and encompasses ten specific roles. Second, only one of the roles does Mintzberg consider a leadership one, and it focuses very heavily on selected superior subordinate activities. This is so, even though Mintzberg argues that the leader role is involved in performance of the other roles.

Third, looked at in this way, it is obvious that if one chose to concentrate on the leader role only, a good many additional managerial roles would be neglected.

Finally, the model raises by implication the question of how seriously it should be taken. Is it simply a heuristic device to guide one's thinking or can it be empirically verified; has it helped shape the thinking of scholars and managers? The answer seems to be that there is now a fair amount of empirical support for the model and that it has, indeed, shaped the thinking of scholars and managers. As with any model, there has been criticism as well. One criticism is that the model is useful but that the roles need to be more specific than those originally derived by Mintzberg.[9]

To summarize, Mintzberg's model clearly illustrates the earlier contention that leadership and managerial behavior should be treated as distinct but related concepts. Failure to do this obscures conceptual and empirical distinctions that are important for systematic development of organizational leadership research and practice.

REFINED CONCEPTUALIZATIONS OF LEADERSHIP

In the organization leadership literature, leadership is typically treated as a form of interpersonal influence.[10]

Using a definition of *leadership* as an influence process means that anyone who influences someone else can be a leader in that particular instance. Thus, we can speak of *informal* leaders in work groups as well as the group's formally designated manager, who would be expected to exercise *formal* leadership. Informal leaders are also sometimes referred to as *emergent* leaders—those who emerge to exert influence for certain kinds of activities. While the orientation of this chapter is toward formal leadership as exhibited by managers, it is important to keep in mind that informal and emergent leadership are also considered important in organizations.

Some organizational scholars have argued that simply defining leadership as interpersonal influence is not distinct enough. What is there to justify the term *leadership* as a separate concept, they say.[11]

In response, House and Baetz argue that leadership is a subset of the broader social influence concept and may be uniquely defined

> . . . as the degree to which the behavior of a group member is perceived as an acceptable attempt to influence the perceiver regarding his or her activity as a member of a particular group or the activity of other group members. . . . An action by a group member becomes an act of leadership when that act is perceived by another member of the group as an acceptable attempt to influence that person or one or more members of that group.[12]

Another scholar elaborates on the influence concept of leadership as follows:

> Leadership is both a process and a property. The *process* [emphasis his] of leadership is the use of noncoercive influence to direct and coordinate the activities of the members of an organized group toward the accomplishment of group objectives. As a *property,* [emphasis his] leadership is a set of qualities or characteristics attributed to those who are perceived to successfully employ such characteristics.[13]

Running through both these definitions is an acceptance or noncoercive influence component.

Still other researchers provide definitions which differentiate between leadership and supervision.[14] Leadership involves the influence of group members through interpersonal processes without resort to the authority or power inherent in the employment contract. This is in contrast to supervision, which involves the influence of group members by means of formal rewards and punishments and/or contractual obligations.

The difference between leadership and supervision is utilized, among other places, in conceiving of leadership as a reciprocal exchange process. Here, group members accord greater status and influence to a manager (or informal leader) who demonstrates competence in such activities as seeing that group goals are achieved. The exchange relationship with the manager is constantly evaluated and the manager will not continue to receive the benefits associated with the position unless the group is seen by its members as making satisfactory progress toward its goals.[15] Managers who have built up a good exchange relationship tend to be able to use leadership, as opposed to supervision, for many of their dealings with subordinates.

An important research effort which is built around such an exchange process is the Vertical Dyad Linkage theory (VDL) of George Graen and his associates. Unlike other approaches, this one emphasizes the relationship of the manager with each individual subordinate (the "dyadic linkage").[16]

The VDL approach focuses on the development of different kinds of exchange relationships with different subordinates. Managers are seen as establishing special exchange relationships with given subordinates. These subordinates are granted extra autonomy, influence, and the like in exchange for greater commitment, loyalty, and assistance to the boss in the performance of his or her duties. These individuals are described as "in-group subordinates" and are contrasted to "out-group subordinates" who do not have this special relationship with their boss.

The VDL approach is of special interest because its conception of leadership is a process which must be investigated over time. Hence, the studies have been longitudinal. In this they have utilized techniques designed to get at causality. Unlike earlier studies which naively assumed that leadership *caused* subordinate outcomes, these later studies have shown that different causal relations can exist.[17] Sometimes leadership causes outcomes, sometimes the opposite, and sometimes, as in the reciprocal exchange notion, both occur simultaneously.

A variation of this reciprocal exchange notion of leadership is articulated in so-called operant or reinforcement views of leadership.[18] These perspectives typically are based on three components in the leadership setting: 1) the stimulus or "environment" facing each individual subordinate; 2) the subordinate's response or performance; and 3) the consequences or reinforcements provided by the manager. The stimulus sets the occasion on which a subordinate's response occurs and the reinforcers are administered by the manager contingent upon the subordinate's response, and thus serve as the consequences.

The manager is seen as the one who manages reinforcements such that subordinates engage in the appropriate responses to stimuli in their work setting in order to elicit the desired consequences or avoid unpleasant consequences (from the manager). Reciprocal relations are involved in that subordinates are seen as responding to the manager and the manager in turn adjusts reinforcements depending upon subordinate responses. In terms of leadership, an important question is the kind of leader behavior most appropriate to elicit the desired consequences.[19]

If the managerial behavior literature helps to differentiate leadership or the leadership role from other aspects of a manager's job, then recent refinements such as considering leadership as noncoercive influence, interpersonal influence beyond that inherent in the employment contract, reciprocal exchange, and the like help differentiate leadership from other more general forms of influence. Both the leadership/managerial behavior differentiation and these refinements can help organizational leadership scholars and managers to better understand leadership. In turn, the potential for enhancing the predictability of the contingency paradigm is increased.

EXPANDING THE CONCEPT
OF CONTINGENCIES

Stewart's Work

In addition to its contribution in focusing on managerial roles, the managerial behavior literature also offers considerable insight in understanding important organizational contingencies. A major contribution in this regard is the work of Rosemary Stewart.[20]

Her approach focuses on three general variable categories that serve as contingencies in managerial jobs. These are:

1. *Demands:* what anyone in the job must do, that is, cannot avoid doing without invoking sanctions that would imperil continuing in the job. These provide a minimum description of the core of a manager's job. Some factors influencing demands are bureaucratic procedures, whom a manager must work with, the extent to which output specifications are available, and the like.

2. *Constraints:* the factors internal and external to the organization that limit what the jobholder can do. Some of these are factors that limit the amount and kind of resources; legal, union, and systems constraints; technological constraints, and the like.

3. *Choices:* the opportunities that exist for jobholders in similar jobs to do different work and to do it in different ways from other jobholders. Demands and constraints are seen as limiting choices, at least in the short run. However, over the long run it may be possible to modify demands and constraints to open up choices. Some key choices concern the focus of attention between different job responsibilities; time spent on supervision compared with other work and contracts; amount and nature of delegation and whom the manager seeks to influence. A particularly key choice aspect is concerned with domain, "the area in which the manager gets involved and seeks to have an influence." Domain choices are influenced to a large extent by the kinds of contacts (external, internal, or mixed) which a manager is free to make. As an example of domain choice, it is useful to think of a school superintendent's position. One superintendent may restrict his or her domain to working almost entirely with the principals, either neglecting community relations and a wide range of other duties or delegating them to others. Another superintendent may take an interest in virtually everything happening in his or her school system.

Like Mintzberg, Stewart sees *part* of a manager's job as leadership, which she defines in terms of influence. Demands, constraints, and choices serve as contingencies bearing on the amount and kind of influence available to the manager and appropriate for him or her to use. Domain and kinds of contacts are especially important. These influence the difficulty of relationships and show where leadership is most needed and is likely to require more skill.

As compared with the traditional contingency leadership paradigm, Stewart's model first introduces a set of conceptually rich categories—demands, constraints, choices—which shape the nature of the manager's job and its leadership requirements. Second, like Mintzberg, she embeds leadership within a whole host of managerial job duties. Third, while like leadership researchers she treats leadership as influence, she sees it in a much more dynamic way than is represented by the traditional paradigm. Furthermore, it is not just vertical superior-subordinate influence, but the influence can take horizontal or lateral (influence vis à vis people at or near a manager's same organization level) forms as well. Thus, she has broadened the concept of leadership as well as contingencies. (It is interesting to compare this lateral notion with Mintzberg's liason and spokesperson roles, which he treats separately from the leader role.)

Hierarchical Functions as Contingencies

Stewart's work argues that one of the contingencies influencing the demands, constraints, and choices impinging on a manager's job is hierarchical position or function. This general theme has also received attention from others.[21] Essentially, it is argued that functions or roles of managers will differ, or at least assume a differing emphasis, according to hierarchical position in the organization. This difference in function then is hypothesized to require different skills, competencies, or behaviors on the part of the manager if he or she is to be successful.

One of the earliest hierarchical function approaches was developed at the conceptual level by Katz and Kahn.[22] Its essence is summarized in Figure 6-2. The figure shows upper-level managers to be concerned with functions related to strategy/policy-type decisions. These managers must also interface with and serve as a buffer to external environment conditions. This part of the hierarchy is here termed a top level *zone* to connote the fact that the number of levels included might well vary from one organization to another. The zone would typically include the board chairman and chief executive officer and might also include key immediate subordinates below these levels.

The middle zone, again, can include a varying number of levels between the top and bottom zones of the organization. Middle managers are primarily responsible for departments, divisions, and the like and are concerned with processes involved with interpreting and "piecing out" the general strategy/policy decisions of upper-level managers.

Finally, lower-level managers are primarily responsible for day-to-day operations in one or a few work units. A first-level manager directly supervising employees would fit here, as might managers one or two levels higher in organizations with many levels. In seeing that day-to-day oper-

FIGURE 6-2 Leadership/Management Function and Ability/Skill Emphases as a Function of Organizational Level

LEVEL OR ZONE OF ORGANIZATION	TYPE OF LEADERSHIP/MANAGEMENT FUNCTION OR PATTERN	ABILITY/SKILL EMPHASES	
		COGNITIVE (KNOWLEDGE BASED)	AFFECTIVE (ATTITUDINALLY BASED)
Top	Organization: Creations and alterations in strategic and policy decisions and organizational design	Total organization/ external and system control	Charisma: Gift of grace aura
Middle	Interpolation: Supplementing and "filling out" of top level strategy/policy and organizational design decisions	Subsystem perspective: Orientation upward to superiors and downward to subordinates	Integration of formal role requirements with face-to-face interactions: Human relations skills
Lower	Administration: Use of existing structure	Technical knowledge and understanding of policies and rules	Concern with equity in use of rewards and sanctions

Adapted from Daniel Katz and Robert Kahn, *The Social Psychology of Organizations,* 2nd ed. (New York: John Wiley, 1978), p. 539.

ations are performed, these managers implement the creations and alterations in strategic and policy decisions previously developed higher up. The model argues that a manager's primary function differs by hierarchical position and that the accompanying cognitive and affective abilities and skills differ as well. The figure shows the narrowing of perspective and greater concern with specifics and technical knowledge hypothesized to take place as one moves down the organization.

At the top echelon, for example, there is a heavy system and external cognitive skill emphasis. These are necessary to deal with the strategy or policy process requirements. As the figure shows, Katz and Kahn also believe charisma to be an important attitudinal characteristic at this echelon. They argue that a charismatic orientation will help set the tone for those lower in the organization. (Charisma is dealt with in more detail later in the chapter.)

For middle managers, abilities and skills tend to be oriented toward subsystems, integration, and linking upper and lower levels in the organization. At the bottom, there is an emphasis on technical competency and rewards and sanctions.

It should be noted that Katz and Kahn see the importance of these functions and emphases as differing by hierarchical position. However, the functions are not mutually exclusive. That is, top echelons are seen as needing some technical and subsystem skills, but not to the same degree as those lower down.

Even though the model has not been tested directly, it appears to have influenced the development of "skill mix" models by Robert Katz,[23] Floyd Mann,[24] and most recently, by the United States Army.[25] The Katz and Army models are entirely conceptual while Mann's work has some empirical support.

The Army model visualizes nine leadership/managerial behavior dimensions ranging from communication to planning and ethics (these are far broader than narrow-gauge interpersonal influence concepts). Each dimension is examined in terms of identifiable tasks and behaviors and in relation to hierarchical level. In most cases the dimensions are considered in the context of five levels (first-line supervisory to the highest executive level). However, in some cases it was possible to consider the dimensions in the context of only three levels. The model is applied for not only the officer corps but for the hierarchy of noncommissioned officers as well.

All the models argue on behalf of different skill mix requirements to deal with the hierarchical position differences (contingencies). The Army model is most specific in terms of its identification of skills and levels. In contrast to the Army, the other approaches use three competencies or skills. For example, Mann discusses administrative, human-relations, and technical competence. His model hypothesizes that *administrative competence* is needed for one to coordinate the activities of one organizational unit with another and for one to see the needs of the organization as a system. To integrate organizational objectives with individual employee needs, a manager must have *human-relations competence*. Finally, to perform other tasks, including technical operations, the manager must possess *technical competence*. Mann's data generally suggest that technical and human-relations skills are more important at lower levels while administrative skills become more important higher up. Katz's model is very similar.

To these works can be added a related discussion by Mintzberg of hypothesized managerial role requirement differences by job type and some other contingencies as well.[26]

As a group these studies sensitize us to the importance of the vertical aspects of an organization as contingencies. The idea is intuitively appealing but underresearched in the organizational leadership area.

Second Generation Contingency Models

Stewart's work and consideration of hierarchical functions alerts us to the importance of contingencies beyond those emphasized in the traditional contingency paradigm. A final group of models expands this paradigm further. If one considers the traditional contingency paradigm to be a "first generation" contingency model, then these latter approaches might be termed "second generation" contingency models. All are based on open systems assumptions and, in one way or another, include environmental, technological, and organizational structure aspects.[27] Such models often incorporate other important modifications, such as refined conceptualizations of leadership, as well.

One example is a recently conceptualized approach by Tosi.[28] In it he separates leadership from managerial behavior and considers the relative impact of both on the predictability of work-group behavior patterns. His contingency variables are type of organization (mechanistic—highly structured—versus organic—loosely structured[29]) and hierarchical position (top, middle, bottom).

A second example, an approach developed by Richard Osborn and the author, is called the Multiple Influence Model of Leadership (MIML).[30] It is treated in considerable detail below. The following section then explores the organizational application implications of this second-generation model.

The Multiple Influence Model of Leadership[31]

The MIML assumes that the organization's environment, its context for action (size and technology), and its structure, as well as conditions within the work unit, affect the role of a manager. These conditions do this first by influencing the manager's leader behavior. Second, they serve as contingencies which act in combination with leader behavior to affect work-unit performance and satisfaction-related outcomes such as satisfaction, commitment, involvement, turnover, and absenteeism.

To understand the essence of the MIML it is important to first recognize the way in which a work unit is designed. It is designed to deal with intended or expected conditions which designers anticipate the unit will face. Of course, actual day-to-day events often deviate from those originally anticipated. Thus, one might think of a "gap" between predicted and actual conditions. To illustrate, as an organization's environment, context, and/or structure become more complex, the gap between predicted and actual conditions also increases. Along with this, the opportunities and problems facing a manager become greater.

The MIML explicitly recognizes this gap and argues that it is a manager's job to act as a leader by stepping in to narrow the gap through appropriate behavior. To the degree that the manager is successful in helping to compensate for the discrepancy between planned and actual conditions, it is hypothesized that there will be greater work-unit performance and subordinates who are more satisfied, have less absenteeism and turnover, are more committed and involved, and so forth. At a more prosaic level, we might think of an automobile and its driver. The auto is originally designed to deal with a number of anticipated conditions. Nevertheless, all possible day-to-day driving conditions cannot be anticipated and it is left to the driver to help close the gap between design and reality.

Some details. Figure 6-3 shows details of the MIML. Note the additions compared with traditional first-generation leadership contingency models. Not only does the MIML consider a much broader range of contingency variables but it also conceptualizes leadership as both influencing outcomes and itself being influenced by contingencies. At the same time, the concept of leader behavior is refined by being broken down into required and discretionary components.

Required behavior is considered what is required to accomplish the duties that must be performed by any manager in that position in the organization. These are called forth by the design of the organization. These required aspects involve both vertical and horizontal leadership and in that sense are consistent with Stewart's conceptualization treated above. According to the MIML, a manager successful in required leadership may achieve satisfactory performance and satisfaction-related outcomes. However, to go beyond these, discretionary leadership is needed.

Discretionary leadership involves influence attempts over and above those required by the position. The difference between required and discretionary leadership is similar to the difference between "supervision" and "lead-

Figure 6-3. The Multiple Influence Leadership Model compared with traditional contingency leadership approaches*

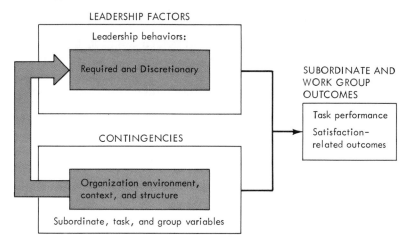

    Indicate additions based on Multiple Influence Leadership Model.

Adapted from John R. Schermerhorn, Jr., J.G. Hunt, and Richard N. Osborn, *Managing Organizational Behavior* (New York: John Wiley, 1982), p. 534.

ership" which was mentioned earlier in the chapter. There is also some similarity to Stewart's earlier mentioned concept of choices.

What kinds of discretionary behaviors can a manager engage in? First, it is important to note that these, like required behaviors, are both vertical and horizontal in nature. Vertically, the manager may act to manage rewards more carefully; reduce uncertainty by providing direction; and strengthen network development by linking individuals to the unit and the unit to the organization. The horizontal counterparts to these three dimensions are: rewarding other units by making a manager's unit responsive to the needs of other units; resolving uncertainty by influencing other unit heads to provide a more predictable flow of resources; and enhancing horizontal network development by establishing linkages to other units to broaden and deepen organizational connections.

Now let us briefly examine complexity in the environment, context, and structure. As previously indicated, the MIML argues that such complexity influences leader behavior and operates in combination with such behavior to influence work-unit performance and satisfaction-related outcomes.

Environmental complexity is considered an overall indicator of conditions outside a given work unit. Complexity is a function of resources outside the unit, the reliance of the work unit on others, and how well the actions of other units can be predicted. A more complex environment is considered one where there are plenty of resources, and a manager's unit is heavily reliant on other units with unpredictable actions.

Contextual complexity is concerned with size and technology. The context for action is considered more complex the larger a work unit, the more sophisticated the technology, and the more varied are the products or services produced by the technology.

Structural complexity is concerned with such things as how specialized the structure is vertically and horizontally and how demanding the control and coordination requirements are. The higher the degree of specialization and the more demanding are coordination and control requirements, the higher the degree of structural complexity is considered.

The model has a number of very specific predictions. However, the core prediction is that, as complexity from any or all of the previous sources increases, a response in discretionary leadership is called for to help narrow the gap between intended and actual conditions. Success in this response, in terms of the three vertical and horizontal behaviors previously mentioned (that is, reward management, uncertainty reduction, network development), will help close the gap and enhance performance and satisfaction-related outcomes.

The model is quite new and so far has been tested only once. Results of the test were interpreted by Hunt and Osborn as providing support for the general logic of the model.[32]

Organizational Application Implications of the Multiple Influence Model

The MIML illustrates the increasing sophistication of the second-generation contingency models as compared with their forebears. A very important question concerns the potential applicability of sophisticated models such as this. That question is addressed here.

As the chapter has shown, a number of individuals have focused on the relationship of leadership in organizations to various work-group or individual employee outcomes. Accompanying this focus, there has often been an emphasis on training to teach managers the appropriate leader behaviors to ensure the desired employee or work-group outcomes. As is now abundantly clear from reviews of the training literature, this approach has not been very successful.[33]

One response to this lack of success has been the work of Fiedler, whose model was discussed earlier by Chemers. Fiedler argues that rather than using training to try to change a manager's leader behavior or style, it is more appropriate to change the contingencies within which the manager operates. He and his colleagues have developed an approach called "Leader Match" which focuses on changes in contingencies to obtain a better match between leadership style and the leader's contingencies. These contingencies are based on those in Fiedler's model, namely: leader-member relations, task structure, and leader position power.[34]

The Multiple Influence Model of Leadership takes Fiedler's work as a point of departure.[35] The model does not, however, ask management to choose between trying to change a manager's leadership or altering contingencies to fit a manager's underlying leadership. Rather, the model allows top management to use training, (but of a more diagnostic nature than that mentioned above) placement, organizational design, or a combination of these in formulating strategy for managerial leadership requirements throughout the organization. Organizational design involves the consideration of complexity in environment, size, technology, and organizational structure. Such complexity, it will be recalled, is an important contingency aspect of the MIML. What follows is a brief illustration of this leadership strategy formulation.

Assume that top management policymakers either currently face or desire to develop one of the following conditions across lower-level work units in their organization:

1. Consistency in performance
2. Variation in performance
   or
3. Some combination of performance consistency and variation.

Consistency in performance.   Here top management policymakers are involved with a set of work units such that the overall performance of the units as a set is a function of the lowest performing ones. "The chain is only as strong as its weakest link." A common situation in which this occurs is where there is high technological dependency across the units. Because of this dependence, substandard performance in one unit affects the performance of the others. Here, the effects of outstanding efforts by some managers will be lost as performance regresses to that of the lowest performing units.

While there are many things that influence the performance of the lowest performing units, top management is concerned about the leadership of the work-unit managers. Given this, the MIML would argue that these managers are relatively poor at responding to small but important variations in the environment, size and technology (context for action), and structure of their work units as compared with the conditions for which the units were originally designed. In other words, these managers are relatively poor at using the discretionary leadership called for by the gap between work-unit design and the actual environmental, contextual, and/or structural conditions encountered.

Consistent with the earlier discussion, top management could deal with this situation by: 1) replacing these managers with those better at discretionary leadership (a placement solution), or 2) training the former to improve their discretionary leadership.

The third alternative—an organizational design one—would be to try to reduce the impact of discretionary leadership via work-unit design changes. Here policymakers would be concerned with lowering complexity in work-unit environment, context, and/or structure to make it less necessary for an individual manager to need to use discretionary leadership.

As an example, let us assume that the production equipment used in the work units is highly sophisticated. According to the MIML, this would indicate a relatively high degree of complexity in the context for action. Since it has been argued that management would like to make discretionary leadership in the set of work groups less important, then complexity needs to be lowered. In this case that might be done by bringing in a staff specialist intimately familiar with the sophisticated equipment. This specialist would then help the work groups to deal with the equipment and, in effect, lower the high degree of complexity created by the equipment.

In turn, according to the MIML, this would lower the need for and the impact of discretionary leadership and help raise the performance of the system as a whole by making the performance in the lower performing units less dependent on the discretionary leadership of the managers in question.

And though it will not be shown in this example, management could also, if necessary, take action to lower complexity in the environment and/ or structure.

Variation in performance. Here top management currently has or desires to have a set of work units where the total output of the work-group set is roughly equal to the average of the component work units. In other words, outstanding performance from one unit can offset less than outstanding performance in another.

Under these circumstances, the MIML would argue that policymakers ought to emphasize conditions in the environment, context, and/or structure which add additional complexities and encourage variations in discretionary leadership across work units. In this case, the high technology production equipment referred to in the example above would be beneficial. It would provide a complex context for action and call for additional discretionary leadership. In turn, where such leadership was aggressively displayed, work-unit performance would be expected to increase and help compensate for lower performance in other units.

If management chose to use placement in lieu of or in addition to the organizational design approach referred to above, then those managers particularly good at discretionary leadership could be identified and placed in the most important units. Finally, training might be used to improve the discretionary leadership capacities of those most in need of such training.

Combination. Here, top management would have a combination or mixture of type units in a set. That is, there would be some units where consistency in performance would be desired and others where an emphasis on variability would be more appropriate. So long as the outputs are not too low, high performing units can partially compensate for lower performing ones. Again, top management would be interested in design, placement, and/or training aspects to influence the importance of discretionary leadership among each of the managers in the set of units. For those where consistency was desired, the strategy would be to downplay discretionary leadership. In those where variability was desired, discretionary leadership would need to be emphasized.

While the MIML has not yet been applied in the manner discussed here in ongoing organizational programs, these implications follow clearly from the logic of the model. They also open up a range of ways in which management can think about leadership/managerial behavior in the organization.

Analysis

All the approaches treated in this portion of the chapter were selected because of their contributions to a greater understanding of the role of contingencies in organizational leadership. Along with this, some approaches also have implications in terms of the managerial behavior/leadership relationship and refined conceptualizations of leadership.

The contingencies introduced vary from many to few. Where there are many specific ones they are usually grouped together into categories, as in Stewart's approach. The MIML goes even further by collapsing these within an overall complexity category. As models attempt to encompass more and more organizational aspects and thus attempt to respond to the "sterility" arguments leveled at the traditional paradigm, the models become more and more complex and unwieldy both theoretically and empirically. Thus, there are strong reasons to use overall categorization schemata to encompass families of variables.

CHALLENGES TO THE CONTINGENCY PARADIGM

The previously discussed approaches have been treated in the context of refining and extending the currently dominant leadership paradigm. However, as mentioned earlier, there are some scholars who argue that we are missing the essence of the leadership phenomenon no matter how elegant or sophisticated are the contingency model refinements and extensions. For them the contingency leadership paradigm must be replaced. They call for a "paradigm shift."

This call for a paradigm shift is not unique to the organizational leadership area. It is also an emerging trend in the organizational behavior area of which leadership is a part. Cummings provides perspective here by pointing out major trends in organizational behavior which he thinks will characterize such work in the 1980s.[36] It is argued in this chapter that trends in organizational leadership research will substantially parallel those in organizational behavior. Hence insight can be gained in terms of where current leadership/managerial behavior research fits and where it might be expected to go in the 1980s.

According to Cummings, organizational behavior research trends in the 1980s can be divided into two broad approaches: conservative and radical. The epistemological base differs dramatically between the two approaches. The conservative approach essentially argues for doing more rigorously what is already being done or extending and refining current models. The radical approach argues that study of the same phenomena, even if done more rigorously, is a dead end. Rather, what is needed is a paradigm shift accompanied by new methods of research. The conservative approach emphasizes four needs:

1. Improved construct validity. For example, as the chapter has shown, there is currently a heavy emphasis within organizational leadership research on clarifying the concepts involved in tapping various aspects of leader behavior.

2. More careful selection and measurement of dependent variables, including a change in those considered important. Old standbys such as performance, satisfaction, absenteeism, and turnover will not only be looked at with increasing sophistication but will be joined by other variables. A manager's impact on various group process variables is a case in point. Basically, this approach argues that whatever variables are added will fit within current paradigms.

3. New applications of longitudinal and experimental research designs. These are designed to get at causality and reflect a more sophisticated continuation of a trend which developed to some extent in the 1970s. As was implied earlier in the chapter, this causality trend is important, regardless of the particular leadership model which is being considered.

4. An increase in, and more appropriate use of, multivariate statistical analysis. Multivariate statistical designs are important: a) in investigating the increasingly sophisticated contingency models previously discussed; b) in dealing with the longitudinal designs mentioned above to get at causality; and c) where one is concerned simultaneously with several dependent variables along with multiple independent and/or contingency variables.

Turning to the radical approach, Cummings sees an emphasis on three needs:

1. Study organizations as social constructions of reality. Those espousing this need argue that the way to understand organizations and their effects is to treat them as social or perceptual constructs rather than as objective realities. An example, as applied to organizational leadership, is developed shortly.

2. Treat the symbolic nature of management as a process. This is illustrated by an emphasis on myths and stories, their transmission in organizations and their significance in terms of socialization and the like. Again, an example related to organizational management/leadership is provided below.

3. Consider processes linking different levels of analysis. An example of this provided by Cummings is to combine organizational sociology and organizational psychology frameworks in studying the impact of environment on an organization. It should be noted though, that within the conservative camp, second-generation leadership contingency models such as the MIML and Tosi's can be partially interpreted as addressing this need.

Let us now turn to some current organizational leadership approaches which provide a major challenge to the contingency paradigm and which are representative of radical thrusts in the organizational leadership area.

Attribution Theory

The first of these streams of work is built around attribution theory.[37] Attributional approaches have been used to focus on either the leader (manager) or work-group subordinates. In the first case, the emphasis is on manager perceptions of subordinates and the attributions managers make to account for the perceptions. In the case of subordinates, the focus is on those particular behaviors enacted by a person (for example, manager) in an organizational context that will cause the perceiver to decide that the manager is, indeed, exhibiting leadership.[38]

Representative of research relating to attributions by managers is that describing the process by which they diagnose causes of poor subordinate performance and then take corrective action. Attribution theory argues that managers are information processors who must integrate cues to decide whether a subordinate's performance behavior is caused by something about the subordinate (internal attribution) or by something in the subordinate's setting (external attribution).[39] For example, one recent study showed that managers were more likely to attribute poor performance to an employee when the employee had a poor work history than when that person had a good one. Furthermore, managers were more likley to direct corrective actions toward the employee rather than toward the work setting.[40]

The major significance of this work in terms of leadership is that it studies the *process* by which a manager diagnoses the work setting as well as providing a basis for behavioral flexibility in response to the diagnosis. Thus, the approach is quite different from the traditional contingency paradigm which focuses upon behaviors exhibited by successful as compared with less successful leaders, given certain contingencies. The attributional focus is on changes in a manager's behavior, dependent upon the manager's interpretation of the causes of a subordinate's poor performance. The interpretation, in turn, is seen as arising from the nature of the situation and an individual's information processing capabilities.[41]

A second key research direction concerns subordinate attributions about leadership. Here subordinates are seen as evaluating the effects of a person's (manager's) actions and then making inferences about the leadership of that person. Leadership, instead of being taken as a given, is seen as being in the eye of the beholder. One of the more important implications of this point is that it can serve as either a positive or negative self-fulfilling prophesy where, "Them that has [or are perceived as having] get." Perception has become reality.[42]

Charismatic and Symbolic Leadership Aspects

Such an attributional approach also reinforces an increasing interest in charismatic leadership (leadership which inspires followers to accomplish outstanding feats)[43] on the part of organizational leadership scholars. Bass articulates the importance of charisma in his recent leadership handbook.

There, following Burns,[44] he talks of "transformational leadership" as opposed to more routine day-to-day "transactional leadership."[45] Dubin briefly describes it in terms of the "gift of grace."[46] Tosi argues that there is a dramatic difference in the imagery of leadership (which is charismatic) and the way it is commonly studied (which consists of research involving mundane, day-to-day acts of lower level managers). "The language of leadership is mystical, the reality mundane."[47] Sayles discusses such charismatic topics as building credibility, anointing, social distance, maintaining leadership momentum, and the like.[48] The military's attachment to the image of the "heroic warrior" is also closely tied to charisma.[49]

Attributional approaches are made to order to examine such charismatic leadership questions or ways in which some people (managers or nonmanagers) pick up the "chosen one" or "gift of grace" aura, and the behaviors of others toward such individuals (providing them with greater acceptance and support).[50]

House has gone the furthest among organizational researchers in terms of systematically considering charismatic leadership.[51] He has developed a model to examine a number of aspects of charisma. He does not specifically use an attributional approach, but attributional concepts could be readily utilized in the model.

For House, charisma describes leaders " . . . who by force of their personal abilities are capable of having a profound and extraordinary effect on followers."[52] He contends, as pointed out earlier, that the term " . . . is usually reserved for leaders who by their influence are able to cause followers to accomplish outstanding feats."[53]

His model first considers a number of characteristics which the literature suggests a charismatic leader should possess. Chief among these are: extremely high levels of self-confidence, dominance, and a strong conviction in the moral righteousness of his or her beliefs. The model then considers some key behaviors of charismatic leaders as suggested by the literature. Role modeling, image building, goal articulation, exhibiting high expectations, and showing confidence and motive arousal are the behaviors upon which House focuses.

House then links these behaviors to some effects on the goals of followers. In an organization, of course, such follower goals are intimately linked with the success of the organization.

Finally, House briefly treats some hypothesized determinants of charismatic leadership.

His model is not without its critics;[54] nevertheless, his work serves as a useful starting point for those serious about investigating charisma in organizations.

Charisma is but one aspect of the symbolic effects of management. These effects have recently become an important new topic of interest for organizational leadership scholars. Symbolic effects are seen as going far beyond the direct leadership effects traditionally investigated by leadership scholars.

Symbolic effects are believed to be intimately tied in with organizational culture. Such culture is concerned with the values, beliefs, and expectations that organizational members come to share. Managers as leaders are seen as both shaping this culture and designing the programs to transmit this culture to the employees. This work on symbolic management/leadership is highly provocative and, though it is beyond the scope of the chapter to pursue the discussion further, it is hoped that the reader's appetite has been whetted enough to pursue the cited references.[55]

CONCLUSIONS

If one were to characterize in one word the organizational leadership area today, that word would be *diversity*. Even though there is a dominant contingency paradigm, the work reported in this chapter shows that the paradigm itself is evolving into a set of second-generation models. Furthermore, some argue that even these are insufficient and that a paradigm shift is needed.

Part of the diversity emerges when, as here, the managerial behavior literature is considered along with more traditional leadership literature. The two areas have developed separately from each other, each with its own literature and with scholars who come from different backgrounds and traditions. It is the contention here that the separation of managerial behavior and leadership is an artificial one that is an accident of the way the areas developed. Scholars from each area have much to say to each other. This chapter suggests that there are the beginnings of a dialogue. To the extent that the dialogue continues, the field will be richer for it.

A second reason for the diversity stems from the diversity in organizational behavior research literature. As has been argued earlier in the chapter, research in the organizational leadership area has developed parallel with that of the organizational behavior area of which it is a part. This has led to two distinct thrusts—what Cummings terms the *conservative* and *radical*.

The traditional contingency leadership paradigm, together with its refinements and extensions, illustrates very well the conservative agenda centering around construct validity, treatment of independent variables, longitudinal and experimental research designs, and multivariate statistical analysis.

The radical agenda is exemplified in the emphasis on attribution approaches, charisma, and symbolic leadership. As a part of the radical thrust these latter approaches are considerd to represent a paradigm shift in the study of leadership. Radical approaches have been slower to develop than conservative ones. A key reason for this is that they do not follow the hard science model embraced by so much of the behavioral sciences and by those studying organizational leadership.

This now appears to be changing. To what extent is as yet unclear. The paradigm shift clamored for by the radicals may indeed supersede new generation contingency models. On the other hand, what may happen instead is that there will be a cross-pollinization of conservative and radical thrusts. At the purist level, the two approaches are antithetical, and their underlying assumptions about how to generate knowledge about organizations are dramatically different. Nevertheless, there is also evidence of the incorporation of radical notions into basically conservative models (for example, processes, attribution, and the like).[56]

On balance, the various developments above suggest that one can probably expect the organizational leadership area to become even more diverse than it is at present. This diversity bothers many people in the area. They argue that much effort has been put forth in the study of leadership with too few results.[57] As has been shown, there have been arguments for scrapping current paradigms, and some have even gone so far as to suggest abandoning leadership as an area of study.[58] Others contend that much of the current leadership research is virtually worthless because it is not immediately relevant to practicing managers.[59]

The position here is that it is unrealistic to look for a magical leadership "pot of gold at the end of the rainbow" (to which everyone, conservatives and radicals alike, will agree and which will alleviate the many perceived difficulties in the area).[60] Rather one should expect diversity into the foreseeable future. This diversity reflects the complexity inherent in an area that appears deceptively simple. As has been argued elsewhere, there will be a plurality of models with "different strokes for different folks."[61] Thus, a model to predict emergent group leadership in a work unit might differ from one to predict managerial impact on organizational performance. Rather than seeing all this as characteristic of a deadend area, it is seen here as an indicator of a fast-changing, healthy research area which is characteristic of the organizational leadership field today.

NOTES

1. Thanks are due to John Blair and Linda Krefting for reviewing an earlier draft of this chapter.
2. The essence of this section is based on Bernard Bass, *Stogdill's Handbook of Leadership* (New York: Free Press, 1981).
3. Fred Fiedler, *A Theory of Leadership Effectiveness* (New York: McGraw-Hill, 1967). Robert House, "A Path-Goal Theory of Leader Effectiveness," *Administrative Science Quarterly*, 16 (1971), pp. 321–38. Victor Vroom and Phillip Yetton, *Leadership and Decision-Making* (Pittsburgh: University of Pittsburgh Press, 1973).
4. John R. Schermerhorn, Jr., J.G. Hunt, and Richard N. Osborn, *Managing Organizational Behavior* (New York: John Wiley, 1982).

5. Morgan W. McCall, Jr. and Michael Lombardo, *Leadership: Where Else Can We Go?* (Durham, N.C.: Duke University Press, 1978).
6. J.G. Hunt, Richard N. Osborn, and Harry Martin, *A Multiple Influence Model of Leadership* (Alexandria, Va.: Army Research Institute for the Behavioral and Social Sciences, in press).
7. Rosemary Stewart, "The Relevance of Some Studies of Managerial Work and Behavior to Leadership Research," in J.G. Hunt, Uma Sekaran, and Chester Schreisheim, eds., *Leadership: Beyond Establishment Views* (Carbondale, Il.: Southern Illinois University Press, 1982), and David Segal, "Leadership and Management: Organization Theory," in J.H. Buck and L.J. Korb, eds., *Military Leadership* (Beverly Hills: Sage Publications, Inc., 1981).
8. Henry Mintzberg, *The Nature of Managerial Work* (New York: Harper & Row, 1973).
9. Neil Snyder and Thomas Wheeler, "Managerial Roles: Mintzberg and the Management Process Theorists," in Kae Chaung, ed., *Academy of Management Proceedings '81* (Wichita: Wichita State University, 1981). J. David Hunger, Neil Snyder, and Thomas Wheeler, "The Management Theory Jungle: A Proposed Integration of Koontz and Mintzberg," in Nan Weiner and Richard Klimoski, eds., *Twenty-Fifth Annual Conference Midwest Academy of Management Proceedings* (Columbus: The Ohio State University, 1982). Steven D. Clement, personal communication, Alexandria, Va., August 31, 1982.
10. Bass, *Stogdill's Handbook of Leadership.*
11. Jeffery Pfeffer, "The Ambiguity of Leadership," *Academy of Management Journal,* 2 (1977), pp. 104–12.
12. Robert House and Mary Baetz, "Leadership: Some Empirical Generalizations and New Research Directions," in Barry Staw, ed., *Research in Organizational Behavior,* vol. 1 (Greenwood, Ct.: JAI Press, 1979).
13. Arthur Jago, "Leadership: Perspectives in Theory and Research," *Management Science,* 28 (1982), p. 315.
14. T. Owen Jacobs, *Leadership and Exchange in Formal Organizations* (Alexandria, Va.: HumRRO, 1971).
15. Based on a summary of leadership exchange by Gary Yuki, *Leadership in Organizations* (Englewood Cliffs, N.J.: Prentice-Hall, 1981).
16. Based on George Graen and James Cashman, "A Role-Making Model of Leadership in Formal Organizations," in J.G. Hunt and Lars Larson, eds., *Leadership Frontiers* (Kent, Ohio: Comparative Administration Research Institute, 1975).
17. For a summary of some of this work *see* Charles Greene, "Limitations of Cross-Lagged Correlational Designs and an Alternative Approach," in Hunt and Larson, eds., *Leadership Frontiers,* and Henry P. Sims, Jr., "The Leader as a Manager of Reinforcement Contingencies: An Empirical Example and a Model," in J.G. Hunt and Lars Larson, eds., *Leadership: The Cutting Edge* (Carbondale, Il.: Southern Illinois University Press, 1977).
18. Based on Sims, "The Leader as a Manager of Reinforcement Contingencies: An Empirical Example and a Model." Fred Luthans, "Leadership: A Proposal for a Social Learning Theory Base and Observational and Functional Analysis Techniques to Measure Leader Behavior," in J.G. Hunt and Lars Larson, eds., *Crosscurrents in Leadership* (Carbondale, Il.: Southern Illinois University Press, 1979), and William E. Scott, Jr., "Leadership: A Functional Analysis," in Hunt and Larson, *Leadership: The Cutting Edge,* also have variations of such an approach.
19. Sims, "The Leader as a Manager of Reinforcement Contingencies: An Empirical Example and a Model."

20. Based on Rosemary Stewart, *Choices for the Manager* (Englewood Cliffs, N.J.: Prentice-Hall, 1982) and Stewart, "The Relevance of Some Studies of Managerial Work and Behavior to Leadership Research."

21. Daniel Katz and Robert Kahn, *The Social Psychology of Organizations*, 1st and 2nd ed. (New York: John Wiley, 1966, 1978). Robert Katz, "Skills of an Effective Administrator," *Harvard Business Review*, 52 (September–October 1974), pp. 90–102. Floyd Mann, "Toward an Understanding of the Leadership Role in Formal Organizations," in Robert Dubin, George Homans, Floyd Mann, and Delmar Miller, *Leadership and Productivity* (San Francisco: Chandler, 1965).

22. Based on Katz and Kahn, *The Social Psychology of Organizations*.

23. Katz, "Skills of an Effective Administrator,"

24. Mann, "Toward an Understanding of the Leadership Role in Formal Organizations."

25. Stephen Clement and Donna Ayers, *A Matrix of Organizational Leadership Dimensions*, Leadership Monograph No. 8 (US Army Administration Center, 1976).

26. Mintzberg, *The Nature of Managerial Work*.

27. Bernard Bass and Enrico Valenzie, "Contingent Aspects of Effective Management Styles," in J.G. Hunt and Lars Larson, eds., *Contingency Approaches to Leadership* (Carbondale, Il.: Southern Illinois Press, 1974), John Miner, "Further Thoughts on the Uncertain Future of the Leadership Concept," *Journal of Applied Behavioral Science* (in press), John Sheridan, Donald Vredenburgh, and Michael Abelson, "Contextual Model of Leadership Influence in Hospital Units," unpublished manuscript, School of Business, Texas Christian University (1981).

28. Henry Tosi, "Toward a Paradigm Shift in the Study of Leadership," in Hunt, Sekaran, and Schreisheim, eds., *Leadership: Beyond Establishment Views*.

29. Schermerhorn, Hunt, and Osborn, *Managing Organizational Behavior*.

30. J.G. Hunt and Richard Osborn, "Toward a Macro-Oriented Model of Leadership," in Hunt, Sekaran, and Shriesheim, eds., *Leadership: Beyond Establishment Views*.

31. Ibid.

32. Ibid.

33. John Campbell, Marvin Dunnette, Edward E. Lawler, III, and Karl Weick, *Managerial Behavior, Performance and Effectiveness* (New York: McGraw-Hill, 1970) and J.G. Hunt, "Another Look at Human Relations Training," *Training and Development Journal*, 22 (1968), pp. 2–10.

34. Fred Fiedler, Martin Chemers, and Linda Mahar, *The Leader Match Concept* (New York: John Wiley, 1978).

35. Based on Hunt, Osborn, and Martin, *A Multiple Influence Model of Leadership*.

36. The discussion in the remainder of this section is based on the author's interpretation, within a leadership/managerial behavior context, of Larry Cummings, "State of the Art: Organizational Behavior in the 1980's," *Decision Sciences*, 12 (1981), pp. 365–73.

37. *See,* for example, Bobby Calder, "An Attribution Theory of Leadership," in Barry Staw and Gerald Salanick, eds., *New Directions in Organizational Behavior* (Chicago: St. Clair Press, 1977).

38. Swee Goh and Andre'de Carufel, "New Directions in Leadership Research: A Review and Some Implications," in Raymond Adamson, ed., *Proceedings of the Annual Conference of the Administrative Sciences Association of Canada Organizational Behavior Division* (Ottawa, Canada: Wilfrid Laurier University, 1982).

39. Ibid.

40. Terrence Mitchell and Robert Wood, "Supervisors' Responses to Subordinate Poor Performance: A Test of an Attributional Model," *Organizational Behavior and Human Performance,* 25 (1980), pp. 123–38.
41. Goh and de Carufel, "New Directions in Leadership Research: A Review and Some Implications."
42. Ibid.
43. *See* Robert House, "A 1976 Theory of Charismatic Leadership," in Hunt and Larson, *Leadership: The Cutting Edge.*
44. James MacGregor Burns, *Leadership* (New York: Harper & Row, 1978).
45. Bass, *Stogdill's Handbook of Leadership.*
46. Robert Dubin, "Metaphors of Leadership: An Overview," in Hunt and Larson, *Leadership: The Cutting Edge.*
47. Tosi, "Toward a Paradigm Shift in the Study of Leadership."
48. Leonard Sayles, *Leadership: What Effective Managers Really Do . . . and How They Do It* (New York: McGraw-Hill, 1979).
49. Segal, "Leadership and Management: Organization Theory."
50. Goh and de Carufel, "New Directions in Leadership Research: A Review and Some Implications."
51. House, "A 1976 Theory of Charismatic Leadership."
52. Ibid.
53. Ibid.
54. For example, Howard Weiss, personal communication, Arlington, Va., June 8, 1982.
55. *See,* for example, Larry Moore and Brenda Beck, "Leadership among Bank Managers: A Structural Comparison of Behavioral Responses and Metaphorical Imagery," in J.G. Hunt, Dian Hosking, Chester Schriesheim, and Rosemary Stewart, eds., *Leaders and Managers: International Perspectives on Managerial Behavior* (Elmsford, N.Y.: Pergamon Press, in press).
56. *See,* for example, the work of Graen and Cashman, "A Role-Making Model of Leadership in Formal Organizations," and Hunt and Osborn, "Toward a Macro-Oriented Model of Leadership."
57. McCall and Lombardo, *Leadership: Where Else Can We Go?*
58. John Miner, "The Uncertain Future of the Leadership Concept: An Overview," in Hunt and Larson, *Leadership Frontiers.*
59. Henry Mintzberg, "If You're Not Serving Bill and Barbara, Then You're Not Serving Leadership," in Hunt, Sekaran, and Schriesheim, *Leadership: Beyond Establishment Views.*
60. Dian-Marie Hosking, J.G. Hunt, and Richard Osborn, "Leadership: Not One Rainbow, Not One Pot of Gold." Working paper, University of Aston Management Centre, Birmingham, U.K., 1980.
61. J.G. Hunt, Uma Sekaran, and Chester Schriescheim, "Beyond Establishment Views of Leadership: An Introduction," and "Conclusion: The Leadership-Management Controversy Revisited," in Hunt, Sekaran, and Schriesheim, *Leadership: Beyond Establishment Views.*

7

FEMINIST
SCHOLARSHIP
ON POLITICAL
LEADERSHIP

Susan J. Carroll

A new scholarship about women emerged during the decade of the 1970s. Although women had been subject to investigation in earlier research, this new scholarship—feminist scholarship[1]—reflected a different consciousness about the study of women. As the editors of *Signs*, a journal devoted to the new scholarship, noted in its first issue, the goals of feminist scholarship are "to compensate for old intellectual evasions and errors, to amass fresh data, and to generate new concepts, tools, and techniques." The new scholarship "tends to question the . . . arrangements that have governed relations between females and males, that have defined femininity and masculinity."[2]

This chapter examines the contributions of feminist scholarship to our understanding of leadership in the political sphere. Although the focus is on *political* leadership, much of the content of this chapter is applicable to the study of leadership more generally.

Two major strains of the new scholarship about women are particularly relevant to the study of political leadership. The first strain is conceptual, reacting against conceptions of leadership as commonly defined by political scientists and practiced by political elites. The second strain of scholarship is largely empirical, produced by researchers concerned with the characteristics, experiences, and attitudes of women who occupy elite

139

positions. While the two bodies of literature reflect the contributions of mutually exclusive sets of individuals, the writings of the more theoretical scholars provide a foundation for important hypotheses that merit attention by scholars engaged in empirical research.

THE FEMINIST CRITIQUE
OF POWER AND LEADERSHIP

In politics and in political science, the concepts of power and leadership have been closely linked.[3] Kenneth F. Janda, for example, has argued that leadership must be viewed as "a particular type of power relationship."[4] Richard E. Neustadt's seminal analysis of power in the Oval Office, *Presidential Power,* is appropriately subtitled "The Politics of Leadership," for Neustadt views presidential leadership and presidential power as inextricably related.[5] Similarly, the two concepts are tied together in the work of James MacGregor Burns, who has written, "To understand the nature of leadership requires understanding of the essence of power, for leadership is a special form of power."[6]

Feminist scholars have noted that power, as discussed in social science literature and practiced in contemporary American politics, has generally been equated with domination and control. Nancy Hartsock has observed:

> Most social scientists have based their discussions of power on definitions of power as the ability to compel obedience, or as control and domination. They link this definition with Bertrand Russell's statement that power is the production of intended effects, and add that power must be power over someone—something possessed, a property of an actor such that he can alter the will or actions of others in a way that produces results in conformity with his own will.[7]

While other definitions can be found in the literature, most political scientists employ definitions of *power* that closely parallel this conception.[8]

Feminists offer different explanations for the common equation of power with domination and control. Socialist feminists such as Nancy Hartsock view this conception of power as derived from the requirements for a capitalist system. Hartsock has argued, "Only in a society based on the market, in which human interdependence is not personal but based on exchange value, can power come to be sought as a value in itself, and domination of others—or the use of power to 'purchase' certain behavior—become the almost exclusive measure of power."[9] Radical feminists, viewing oppression based on sex as the most fundamental form of oppression, place greater emphasis on the exercise of "power over" as a masculine attribute that has helped to perpetuate male dominance over women. Adrienne Rich has suggested:

Power is . . . a primal relationship under patriarchy. . . . [T]he identity, the very personality, of the man depends on power and on power in a certain, specific sense: that of *power over* others, beginning with a woman and her children.[10]

Just as feminist scholars differ in their explanations for the frequent equation of power with dominance, they are not always in agreement about the changes that are desirable. Some feminists, especially those with strong anarchist beliefs, have called for the abolishment of all power relationships.[11] In fact, many feminists, particularly those who had been active in the Civil Rights and New Left movements, attempted to do just that on a small scale during the late 1960s and early 1970s. Movement women, having had their fill of domineering and unresponsive leaders, attempted to structure their own groups and organizations as nonhierarchical and leaderless in order to eliminate the exercise of "power." The clearest examples of this feminist experiment with "structurelessness" were the small consciousness raising groups that sprang up across the country. Nevertheless, even the more structured national organizations, such as the National Organization for Women (NOW) and the National Women's Political Caucus (NWPC), faced internal disputes and splits because many members within their ranks were skeptical of leadership and hierarchy.[12]

During the 1970s, many feminists had second thoughts about this experiment with "structurelessness." Several of the most thoughtful theorists and analysts came to the conclusion that "structurelessness" was a myth and that feminists should no longer reject structure, leadership, and the attendant exercise of power. Feminist groups, in their attempts to abolish structures and leaders, did not so much eliminate power as to mask it. Where there were no formal structures and leaders, informal structures and leaders emerged. When feminists refused to select formal leaders to speak for their movement, the media singled out certain women who, while they occupied no positions of formal authority within the movement, became identified as movement leaders in the public's eyes.[13]

Concluding that the elimination of leadership and power relationships was neither possible nor desirable, many feminist scholars, rejecting the anarchist position, began working toward a reconceptualization of power and political leadership. In writing about power and leadership, these women drew upon the collective experiences of women, as distinct from the experiences of men.

Forming the basis for the writings of one group of feminist theorists was the experience of motherhood. Claiming that the "mother-child relationship is the essential human relationship,"[14] Adrienne Rich drew attention to "the *possibilities* inherent in beneficial female power, as a mode which is absent from the society at large, and which, even in the private sphere, women have exercised under terrible constraints."[15] Although Rich has not specified what the characteristics of this female power might be other than that it would be beneficial, Jane Alpert has been more specific. Alpert has suggested that "the qualities coming to the fore" with a female-based conception of power would be "the same ones a mother projects in the best kind of nurturing relationship to a child: empathy, intuitiveness, adaptability, awareness of growth as process rather than as goal-ended, inventiveness, protective feelings toward others, and a capacity to respond emotionally as well as rationally."[16]

Other feminist scholars have looked not to women's biological experience as mothers but rather to their social experience in families and in the women's movement during its formative years for alternative conceptions of power. Joan Rothschild has argued that the experience of women's work in the precapitalist institution of the family has been based on a set of power relations different from those experienced by men in industrialized society. For this reason, according to Rothschild, women's and men's concept and practice of power differ.

Rothschild has maintained that "women will view power as energy, potential, competence for oneself, rather than 'power over' others. Women will seek to achieve and maintain such power through personalized, supportive, and cooperative means."[17] Nancy Hartsock, noting that we must "look for the theory contained within . . . [the] practice" of feminist organizations, has argued that a definition of *power* as "energy, as the ability to transform oneself and the world . . . as part of a process of change which can be moved forward and directed" is "much closer to what the women's movement has sought" than are conceptions of power based on domination and control.[18]

In spite of differences over whether motherhood or women's social experience should provide the foundation for a female-based conception of power, Rich, Alpert, Rothschild, Hartsock, and other feminist theorists generally emphasize similar qualities as essential to a reconceptualization of power. Supportive and cooperative relationships rather than relationships based on domination are stressed. "Power to" as characterized by energy, ability to get things done, and reciprocity takes the place of "power over."[19]

What does such a reconceptualization of power suggest about the nature of leadership? An effective leader is one who empowers others to act in their own interests, rather than one who induces others to behave in a manner consistent with the goals and desires of the leader. Charlotte Bunch has suggested that leadership should be conceived as "people taking the initiative, carrying things through, having the ideas and the imagination to get something started, and exhibiting particular skills in different areas."[20] Leadership, as reconceptualized by feminists, has both educational and empathic functions. Because leaders often have advantages of breadth of experience and access to information, they have a responsibility to communicate their experience and information to followers in a comprehensible manner. They should always be sensitive to the feelings and desires of their followers, and their actions should reflect such sensitivity. Finally, leaders should nurture the potential of followers and help to build their confidence so that they, too, will attempt leadership.[21]

Although feminist theorists have worked to develop an alternative conceptualization of political leadership, they have not demonstrated that this alternative model of leadership is workable in contexts other than those of small groups and enterprises comprised of feminist women.[22] It will be the task of those scholars who are conducting empirical research on women in positions of political leadership to assess this model's viability in the larger political world.

WOMEN LEADERS IN TRADITIONAL RESEARCH

Much of the traditional literature on leadership and political elites[23] has overlooked women or portrayed them in a distorted manner. When women have appeared in leadership positions, they frequently have been treated as though they were invisible, or barely visible and insignificant. Moreover, statements about women often have been undocumented with empirical evidence and frequently have reflected an underlying assumption that males are naturally suited for leadership while females and female traits are incompatible with the idea of leadership. Three brief examples will suffice to illustrate these patterns.

The work of Robert A. Dahl in *Who Governs?*,[24] a classic study of community leadership by a political scientist, focuses on three issue areas. One of these is education, where women traditionally have played a far more prominent role than in most issue areas. Yet, in New Haven all the leaders in the education field were male, which Dahl seems to accept as natural. He describes two cases of men who, after serving as presidents of the PTA, received appointments to the Board of Education and thereby became educational "leaders." Dahl views these as the "exceptional cases." According to Dahl, "Ordinarily a PTA president is a housewife who lacks the time, experience, interest, and drive to move into the real centers of educational influence."[25] Yet, as Virginia Sapiro has appropriately asked, "If the typical PTA president lacks the time to get into politics, how does she have the time to be president of the PTA? If involvement in a PTA gives one experience and skills . . . why is this not the case for women?"[26] Dahl's own discussion suggests that there may have been a male bias in the selection of Board of Education members from the pool of potential candidates with the necessary experience, many of whom were women. However, Dahl fails to see this bias as noteworthy.

The perceived insignificance of women, even when they appear in substantial numbers, is shown in Dahl's discussion of subleaders. Although he acknowledges that one-third of New Haven's subleaders were women,[27] his discussion of this group proceeds as though all subleaders were men. And except for the statement about PTA presidents cited above, Dahl never considers the question of why the many women who were subleaders infrequently became leaders.[28]

A second and very different work on leadership is *An Anatomy of Leadership: Princes, Heroes, and Supermen* by Eugene E. Jennings,[29] a professor of management. An advocate of the "great man" theory of leadership,[30] Jennings argues that we live in an antiheroic age where we have lost faith in leadership and where leadership is inhibited and suppressed by organizational structures. Not only are the exemplary historical leaders mentioned by Jennings all males but also the various leadership types he describes are given male titles: heroes, princes, and supermen. Only when he discusses the role of leadership in Marxist theory, with which he fervently disagrees, does Jennings apply the title of a female role. In a chapter entitled "The Midwife," Jennings explains that Marxist theory reduces the role of great men to that of midwives: "deliverers of an event which could not be held back if times were ripe."[31] Since physicians as well as midwives deliver babies, one has to suspect that Jennings chose a title clearly designating a female role in order to underscore the gulf between his conception of leadership and the Marxist conception. Since there are no references to women elsewhere in his book, the symbolic message Jennings conveys is that the qualities of women, like the tenets of Marxism, are inconsistent with leadership as he defines it.

While the works of both Dahl and Jennings were written prior to the development of the contemporary feminist movement, James MacGregor Burns's *Leadership* was published in 1978. Burns's treatment of women is an improvement over the earlier works. Nevertheless, the work is characterized by a neglect of the contributions of women leaders and by some of the same biases found in earlier scholarship. Although the book consists of 462 pages of text, the index lists references to women on only five pages.[32] On only one of these five pages does Burns devote any serious attention to the bias against female leadership, noting that one "biological emphasis in the study of leadership is the assumption of male leadership, especially at the higher levels of power."[33] Burns also acknowledges, much as feminist theorists do, that "the male bias is reflected in the false conception of leadership as mere command or control." As the conception of leadership shifts to one of "leaders engaging and mobilizing the human needs and aspirations of followers," women will more often be recognized as leaders.[34]

While most feminist scholars would both agree with Burns and commend him for these insights, they would be troubled by his argument:

> Discrimination by men may be less crucial or less lasting than the consciousness of women themselves of their subordinate or "outgroup" status in politics, though the one has influenced the other. Women in lower political offices, such as convention delegates, saw their roles more as "representative" and less as independent than did male delegates.[35]

Burns cites no studies to substantiate these claims.[36] He seems to offer the fact that women more often than men assume "representative" roles as evidence that women's consciousness of their subordinate status is more severe and persistent than discrimination against women. But if women pay more attention than men to the wishes of those they were selected to represent, why is this not a sign of "leaders engaging and mobilizing the human needs and aspirations of followers"? Why is this necessarily a sign of women's recognition of their inferior status? Is it not possible that men's independent decision making, perhaps in opposition to the wishes of those who selected them, is yet another example of "leadership as mere command or control"? In short, while Burns's work is a clear improvement over earlier scholarship, it is not completely free of questionable interpretations of women's attitudes and behavior.

THE EXAMINATION OF WOMEN LEADERS BY FEMINIST SCHOLARS

Research during the past decade focusing specifically on women leaders was stimulated in large part by a desire to correct the neglect and the biased portrayal of women in traditional research. As more and more women obtained formal positions of political leadership during the 1970s, a number of scholars recognized that the presence of women was likely to be of increasing consequence. However, traditional research offered little guidance as to what the effects of increased representation of women might be. Moreover, as the feminist movement affected the consciousness of a new generation of scholars, a significant number began to question the implicit assumption that the lack of parity between women and men at the elite level was somehow "natural."

Feminist scholarship of an empirical nature, dealing with women in political elites, has focused largely on two questions arising from these concerns. First, why are women so underrepresented in elite positions? What are the factors working against their recruitment and/or election? Second, do female political leaders differ from their male counterparts in background, attitudes, and behavior? If so, how?

The Underrepresentation of Women
in Elite Positions in American Politics

Feminist scholars have pointed to a number of factors that have worked to insure the underrepresentation of women in appointive and elective officeholding positions in the United States.[37] Much of the research, particularly the earlier research, emphasized primarily the importance of family responsibilities and women's own internalized attitudes about proper and improper behavior for women as constraints that limit the pool of potential female officeholders.[38] Several researchers have found that the husbands of female elites are more supportive of their wives' political activities than is the case for the wives of male elites, suggesting that women without supportive spouses almost never seek public office while men without supportive spouses do.[39] Similarly, officeholders with young children are far less common among female than male officeholders, suggesting that the presence of young children more often prevents women from seeking office than is true for men.[40] We also know that women who seek and hold political offices have predominantly liberal views on the role of women in politics and society, indicating that few women with more traditional views about women's roles seek political offices, especially at the higher levels.[41]

While family roles and women's own attitudes about sex-appropriate behavior are important, emphasis on such factors places the burden on women to change their individual lives and attitudes in ways that would minimize conflict with participation in politics. Such changes are perhaps a necessary but not a sufficient condition for increasing the numbers of women in positions of political leadership. As empirical scholarship on female elites developed over the course of the 1970s, increasing numbers of scholars turned their attention to the ways in which other political actors and characteristics of the political system itself work to insure that the numbers of women remain small.

At both state and local levels, it has been demonstrated that the proportion of women serving in elective offices is inversely related to factors such as the desirability of the seats, competition for those seats, and salary.[42] However, this pattern does not seem to be the result of voter prejudice against women candidates. While public opinion polls consistently have shown that a small (and decreasing) core of voters say they would not vote for a woman for various offices,[43] numerous studies have concluded that women candidates are not significantly penalized at the polls on account of their sex.[44] The reason that women seem to fare about as well at the polls as men do, once such factors as incumbency are controlled, probably is due to the existence of a pro-woman vote that counters any anti-woman vote. However, the question of whether there are voters who are predisposed to vote for a female candidate has not been systematically studied.[45]

While voter prejudice may not pose a significant barrier to women moving into elite positions,[46] the attitudes of men who are in leadership positions do. Marcia Manning Lee found that fear of sex discrimination was a major factor inhibiting women activists from running for office and that male activists held attitudes not fully accepting of women as equals.[47] Similarly, a 1977 nationwide study of women officeholders conducted by the Center for the American Woman and Politics found that a large majority of women officeholders at state, county, and local levels agreed that "many men in party organizations try to keep women out of leadership roles."[48] Several studies have found evidence that party leaders seem far more often to be involved in recruiting women as "sacrificial lambs" in races where they have little chance of winning than in situations where prospects for general election victory are good.[49] Recent evidence from studies of women appointed to high-level positions in the Carter administration and in state government suggests a double standard in recruitment, with standards for selection applied more stringently and uniformly to women than to men.[50]

In addition to discriminatory attitudes on the part of male gatekeepers, there is evidence that certain characteristics of the American electoral system help to keep the numbers of women serving in elective office low. Campaign costs for most offices, especially at the state and national levels, are quite high. Although systematic evidence is lacking, many scholars have suggested that raising money is more difficult for women than for men and that this acts as a deterrent to candidacies.[51]

The challenger status of many women also works against them. Incumbents win reelection at a very high rate, and the fact that most women, as newcomers to electoral politics, must run against incumbents keeps the numbers of women in elective office low. Similarly, there is evidence that women fare better in races where several seats are to be filled than in races for a single seat. Yet, races where only a single candidate emerges victorious are far more common.[52]

In response, then, to the question of why women remain underrepresented in elective and appointive positions in government, research has provided a somewhat complex answer. It would appear that family responsibilities, women's own attitudes, discriminatory attitudes of male political leaders, difficulty in raising money, and the fact that most women who run for office must face incumbents and run in races for single seats interact in ways that keep many potential women candidates from seeking and/or obtaining political offices.

Backgrounds, Attitudes, and Behavior
of Women Political Leaders
in American Politics

The other major question addressed by much of the empirical research on female American political leaders focuses on the ways in which women in elite positions are similar to and different from their male counterparts. Women officeholders reflect the class and racial biases found among male officeholders. They tend disproportionately to be Caucasian and to underrepresent the lower socioeconomic strata in the United States.[53]

However, there are important differences between women and men in political elites. Women holding elective office are more concentrated in the middle-aged brackets and have a slightly older mean age than their male counterparts, while women in appointive positions are younger than their male counterparts.[54] Women in elective and appointive offices are less frequently married, and less often have young children.[55] Women elected officials are less likely to have attended graduate school or completed an advanced degree, less likely to have been employed outside the home, and more likely to be concentrated in traditional female occupations (for example, teaching, nursing, social work, and secretarial work).[56] While women elected officials no less frequently than their male counterparts have held a previous public office, they have more experience in parties and organizations.[57] Women may acquire greater experience in parties and organizations which compensates for educational and occupational credentials that are not considered as strong as those of men.

Most of the studies that have examined the attitudes of elective and appointive officeholders have found that the women within each party are more liberal in their views on many issues than their male counterparts within the same party; women also are more supportive of feminist positions on women's issues such as ERA, child care, and abortion.[58] Similarly, there is evidence that female state legislators and members of Congress constitute a more cohesive liberal voting bloc[59] and that they were more likely than males within their party to vote in favor of the ERA.[60]

CONTRIBUTIONS TO THE
STUDY OF POLITICAL
LEADERSHIP

Although it is only during the past decade that women in leadership positions have received serious attention from researchers, feminist scholars engaged in empirical research already have made major contributions to the general study of political leadership. First, feminist scholars have broadened our image of "political leaders" and our knowledge of the experiences that lead to a formal position of leadership in American politics. A campaign advertisement used by Bella Abzug during her 1976 primary race for the US Senate boldly stated, "I'm not what a Senator looks like, but I am what a Senator *should* look like."[61] As this ad emphasized, women leaders *are* different from male leaders. Feminist scholars have only begun to document the nature of those differences, focusing thus far primarily on differences in background and experience, as reviewed above. As more women become political leaders, assumptions based on information gathered during times when all leaders were male, or assumed to be male, will have to change. Increasingly, it is necessary to broaden our image of political officeholders to include not only lawyers and business people but also teachers and social workers; not only those with years of involvement in the Chamber of Commerce and the Rotary but also in the League of Women Voters and the PTA; not only those who are married but also those who are widowed, divorced, or single. As feminist scholars expand the horizons of their research to examine performance and leadership styles of political elites, our working assumptions about political leaders may well undergo further changes.

Feminist scholars engaged in empirical research on political elites also have raised several normative questions regarding equality and representation that should be of concern to those interested in the study of political leadership within a democratic context.[62] Can a system truly be considered democratic when one-half of its citizens are socialized to believe that they are unfit to become political leaders on the basis of an ascribed characteristic such as sex? If the viability of a democratic system depends, in part, on the quality of its leaders, what damage is done if half of the most capable and talented individuals in society are systematically excluded from leadership positions, or discouraged from seeking them, as a result of their sex? Can political leaders (that is, men) whose experience in society is vastly different from that of a group they represent (women) adequately represent the interests of that group?

Finally, through empirical research on women, feminist scholars have expanded the realm of variables considered relevant to the study of political leadership by calling attention to the way in which "private" life impinges upon "public" life. The separation between the private and the public spheres in Western thought extends back to Aristotle.[63] However, feminists have called for a greater integration of the two. Traditional research on elite behavior largely has ignored the role of family as a variable except for its effects on childhood socialization. In contrast, in research by feminist scholars, the role of family has received far more attention, and feminist scholars have found family-related factors to be important not only for women but also for *men*. For example, Diane Kincaid Blair and Ann R. Henry have found that family problems are the major factors leading to retirement from office for male state legislators as well as females;[64] previous research had attributed high rates of legislative turnover primarily to low salaries and had neglected to investigate the importance of family-related variables. Similarly, Virginia Sapiro found that conflicts between family commitments and public commitments, although handled differently by the sexes, were experienced at least as often among male partisan elites as among female partisan elites.[65] Findings such as these suggest that future research on leadership should not overlook the role of "private" factors in affecting "public" pursuits.

QUESTIONS WHICH REMAIN

The most important questions remaining for those involved in empirical research on female political leaders focus on impact and performance. Will women leaders have an impact on public policy different from that of men? Are the issues that most concern them different from the issues of greatest concern to their male colleagues? Do women's and men's leadership styles differ? Do women exercise power differently than men do? What conditions, if any, facilitate the emergence of sex differences in leadership and impact on public policy? Under what conditions, if any, are possible differences suppressed?

Existing research provides only a few hints as to what the answers to these questions might be, and the evidence is somewhat contradictory. Although some research indicates that women candidates may not give higher priority to women's issues than men do,[66] most studies have found women, when compared with men of the same party, more supportive of feminist issue positions and more liberal on a variety of issues.[67] Moreover, some observers who have studied policy related to women have argued that much of the legislation designed to improve women's status never would have been introduced if sympathetic *women* had not held office.[68] The thrust of existing research suggests that women leaders might, in fact, have a somewhat different policy agenda than men, might more often play key roles in initiating policy on women, and might more often vote in a manner supportive of certain types of legislation.

There may be certain intervening conditions that make any differences between women and men more or less evident. For example, the work of Rosabeth Moss Kanter would suggest that the proportion of women serving in a governing body would affect the behavior of women (and men);[69] maybe a critical ratio of women to men is necessary before any distinctive impact of women will be evident. Similarly, the bonding together of women into caucuses or associations, as has happened among legislators within some states and among women holding a variety of offices in other states, might provide the support necessary for women's sex-distinctive priorities and behavior to come to the fore. Clearly, far more evidence based on actual observation of behavior is needed before any firm conclusions can be reached regarding women's distinctive impact, if any, on public policy.

It is even more difficult to speculate about possible differences in leadership styles between women and men in political positions, since this topic has yet to receive serious attention from scholars engaged in actual research. On this question of possible differences in leadership styles, the interests of more conceptual feminist scholars involved in the analysis of power and the interests of more empirical feminist scholars would seem to converge. The writings of feminist theorists such as Bunch, Hartsock, and Rich are fruitful sources for hypotheses about the ways in which women's and men's exercise of power and style of leadership might differ. Similarly, the work of Lynn Rosener and Peter Schwartz, who distinguish between "Alpha" and "Beta" styles of leadership, provides useful hypotheses about possible differences in leadership styles. Alpha leadership, which one would expect to be the dominant style found among men, is characterized by "analytical, rational, quantitative thinking. It relies on hierarchical relationships of authority" and "tends to look for deterministic, engineered solutions to specific problems."[70] In contrast, Beta leadership, which might be more common among women, "is based on synthesizing, intuitive, qualitative thinking. It relies on adaptive relationships for support" and "tends to look for integrated solutions to systemic problems."[71]

Feminist theorists offer suggestions not only about the nature of possible differences in leadership styles between women and men but also about their probable duration. Those who believe, as radical feminists do, that female biology (and childbearing capacity in particular) is a source of differential perspectives between women and men would predict clear and persistent differences in leadership styles of women and men. At the other extreme, those who believe that organizational structures are deterministic, as many socialist feminists do,[72] would expect women moving into formal leadership positions in American society to conform to dominant patterns and to exercise leadership no differently than do men in those positions. More moderate liberal feminists view differences between women and men as stemming from sex role socialization; they would anticipate differences in leadership styles between women and men in the short term that largely would disappear over the years as the socialization of women and men converges.

The theoretical strain of feminist scholarship, then, is quite heuristic in its predictions about the nature and duration of leadership differences between women and men. Feminist scholars engaged in empirical research, having provided answers to questions about sex differences in backgrounds and the underrepresentation of women, have reached a point where they can begin to turn to questions of impact and leadership styles. As feminist scholars focus their attention more directly on testing propositions about sex differences in these areas, we can expect them to make even greater contributions to our understanding of leadership.

NOTES

1. This new research is sometimes called "the new scholarship about women" and sometimes referred to as "feminist scholarship." The use of the word *feminist* is not meant to imply consensus among the scholars to whom it is applied. In fact, these scholars often disagree. However, they do agree that traditional perspectives have often overlooked women or viewed them through a lens shaped by questionable cultural assumptions about women's behavior.
2. "Editorial," *Signs,* 1 (Autumn 1975), p. v.
3. This, of course, has not necessarily been true in disciplines other than political science. See Kenneth F. Janda, "Towards the Explication of the Concept of Leadership in Terms of the Concept of Power," in Glenn Paige, ed., *Political Leadership* (New York: Free Press, 1972), pp. 45–68.
4. Ibid., p. 45.
5. Richard E. Neustadt, *Presidential Power* (New York: John Wiley, 1960), pp. 1–2.
6. James MacGregor Burns, *Leadership* (New York: Harper & Row, 1978), p. 12. p. 12.
7. Nancy Hartsock, "Political Change: Two Perspectives on Power," in Charlotte Bunch, and others, ed., *Building Feminist Theory* (New York: Longman, 1981), pp. 3–4.
8. *See,* for example, Robert A. Dahl, "The Concept of Power," *Behavioral Sciences,* 2 (1957), pp. 201–15; M. Margaret Conway and Frank B. Feigert, *Political Analysis,* 2nd ed. (Boston: Allyn & Bacon, 1976), p. 359; Alan C. Isaak, *Scope and Methods of Political Science,* 3rd ed. (Homewood, Il.: The Dorsey Press, 1981), pp. 77–78.
9. Hartsock, "Political Change: Two Perspectives on Power," p. 4. While Hartsock views this conception of power as a consequence of a capitalist economy, she believes that this conception of power is reinforced by the needs of patriarchy and white supremacy. Power as *power over* works to the benefit of those who are dominant in all three types of relationships.
10. Adrienne Rich, *Of Woman Born* (New York: W.W. Norton & Co., 1976), p. 64.
11. Carol Ehrlich, "An Anarchafeminist Looks at Power Relationships," *Quest,* 5 (1982), p. 77. For a review of such arguments, *see also* Janet A. Flammang, "Feminist Theory: The Question of Power" (unpublished manuscript, Department of Political Science, University of Santa Clara, September 1982), pp. 41–44.
12. *See* Jo Freeman, *The Politics of Women's Liberation* (New York: D. McKay, 1975).
13. *See,* for example, Joe Freeman, "The Tyranny of Structurelessness," in Jane S. Jaquette, ed., *Women in Politics* (New York: John Wiley, 1974), pp. 202–14; Nancy C.M. Hartsock, "Feminism, Power, and Change: A Theoretical Analysis," in Bernice Cummings and Victoria Schuck, eds., *Women Organizing* (Metuchen, N.J.: Scarecrow, 1979), pp. 2–24; Charlotte Bunch and Beverly Fisher, "What Future for Leadership," *Quest,* 2 (Spring 1976), pp. 2–13.
14. Rich, *Of Woman Born,* p. 127.
15. Ibid., p. 73.
16. Jane Alpert, "Mother Right: A New Feminist Theory," *Ms.* (August 1973), p. 92.

17. Joan Rothschild, "Female Power: A Marxist-Feminist Perspective" (paper presented at the 1976 Annual Meeting of the American Political Science Association, Chicago, Illinois, September 2–5), p. 6.
18. Hartsock, "Feminism, Power, and Change: A Theoretical Analysis," pp. 12, 18, 17.
19. The distinction between "power to" and "power over" is particularly emphasized by Flammang.
20. Bunch and Fisher, "What Future for Leadership."
21. Flora Crater, "Leadership Growth and Spirit," *Quest*, 2 (Spring 1976), pp. 60–66.
22. Rothschild describes the pattern of relationships in small, women-run enterprises where such a feminist model of relationships seemed to prevail.
23. In this chapter, the terms *leaders* and *elites* are often used interchangeably although the author realizes that not all members of political elites are necessarily political leaders and vice versa.
24. Robert A. Dahl, *Who Governs?* (New Haven: Yale University Press, 1961).
25. Ibid., p. 158.
26. Virginia Sapiro, "Women's Studies and Political Conflict," in Julia A. Sherman and Evelyn Torton Beck, eds., *The Prism of Sex* (Madison: University of Wisconsin Press, 1979), p. 262. *See* Sapiro's essay for a more extensive discussion of what she calls Dahl's "sexist blinders" (p. 260).
27. Dahl, *Who Governs?*, p. 169.
28. The lack of women among leaders is inferred from Dahl's discussion since he never really shows the sex composition of those he considers leaders.
29. Eugene E. Jennings, *An Anatomy of Leadership: Princes, Heroes, and Supermen* (New York: McGraw-Hill, 1960).
30. Some feminists have expressed skepticism about the "great man" theory. Jackie St. Joan, "Female Leaders: Who Was Rembrandt's Mother?" in Charlotte Bunch, and others, eds., *Building Feminist Theory* (New York: Longman, 1981), p. 232, has observed:

> Women have given birth to, have raised, have comforted, have been brutalized by, and have buried all those Great Men. They have seen him from all sides. Perhaps this is . . . why feminists have been so distrustful of leaders who pretend to be, or are presented by the media as, The Great Woman.

31. Jennings, *An Anatomy of Leadership: Princes, Heroes, and Supermen.*
32. The references to women on two pages concern the role of female citizens in the French Revolution. A third reference notes that women in nineteenth-century Britain had to work outside the system for the right to vote, rather than working within the House of Commons. The fourth reference is one sentence suggesting that there are few means for a female, born into a society that bars women from leadership, to exercise political influence. Burns also makes a few references to individual women. For example, Indira Gandhi is mentioned four times, Eleanor Roosevelt twice, and Golda Meier once.
33. Burns, *Leadership*, p. 50.
34. Ibid.
35. Ibid.
36. Burns's claim that women were more "representative" and less independent probably is based on M. Kent Jennings and Norman Thomas, "Men and Women in Party Elites: Social Roles and Political Resources," *Midwest Journal of Political Science*, 12 (November 1968), p. 487. A recent replication of this study has

found differences between female and male delegates in perceptions of how their decisions should be made to be much smaller than in the earlier study. *See* M. Kent Jennings and Barbara G. Farah, "Social Roles and Political Resources: An Over-Time Study of Men and Women in Party Elites," *American Journal of Political Science,* 25 (August 1981), pp. 476–77.

37. The generalizations drawn here are based on the American case. Despite the recent publication of two excellent anthologies that include several selections on women political leaders in other cultures, comparative research still lags behind research on women in the American context for a number of reasons, including lack of access, the greater difficulty of doing research, and the sheer number of countries and cultures involved. The two recent anthologies are: Joni Lovenduski and Jill Hills, eds., *The Politics of the Second Electorate* (London: Routledge & Kegan Paul, 1981) and Cynthia Fuchs Epstein and Rose Lamb Coser, eds., *Access to Power* (London: George Allen & Unwin, 1981).

38. Edmond Costantini and Kenneth H. Craik, "Women as Politicians: The Social Background, Personality, and Political Careers of Female Party Leaders," *Journal of Social Issues,* 28 (1972), pp. 217–36; Marcia Manning Lee, "Why Few Women Hold Public Office," in Marianne Githens and Jewel L. Prestage, eds., *A Portrait of Marginality* (New York: D. McKay, 1977), pp. 118–38; Emily Stoper, "Wife and Politician: Role Strain Among Women in Public Office," Ibid., pp. 320–37; Marianne Githens and Jewel L. Prestage, "Introduction," Ibid., p. 4; Jeane J. Kirkpatrick, *Political Woman* (New York: Basic Books, 1974), pp. 13–19.

39. Marilyn Johnson and Susan Carroll, "Profile of Women Holding Office II," in *Women and Public Office: A Biographical Directory and Statistical Analysis,* 2nd ed., compiled by the Center for the American Woman and Politics (Metuchen, N.J.: Scarecrow, 1978), pp. 18A–19A; Stoper, "Wife and Politician: Role Strain Among Women in Public Office," pp. 331–32; Sharyne Merritt, "Recruitment of Women to Suburban City Councils: Higgins vs. Chevalier," in Debra W. Steward, ed., *Women in Local Politics* (Metuchen, N.J.: Scarecrow, 1980), p. 92.

40. Johnson and Carroll, Ibid., p. 18A; Merritt, Ibid., p. 91; Irene Diamond, *Sex Roles in the State House* (New Haven: Yale University Press, 1977), p. 38.

41. Johnson and Carroll, Ibid., p. 42A; Susan Gluck Mezey, "Women and Representation: The Case of Hawaii," *Journal of Politics,* 40 (1978), pp. 379–80; Susan Gluck Mezey, "Support for Women's Rights Policy," *American Politics Quarterly,* 6 (October 1978), pp. 485–97.

42. Diamond, *Sex Roles in the State House,* pp. 8–30; Susan Welch and Albert K., Karnig, "Correlates of Female Office Holding in City Politics," *Journal of Politics,* 41 (1979), pp. 478–91.

43. *See,* for example, "Opinion Roundup," *Public Opinion,* 2 (January/February 1979), p. 36; *Gallup Opinion Index* (September 1975).

44. R. Darcy and Sarah Slavin Schramm, "When Women Run Against Men," *Public Opinion Quarterly,* 41 (Spring 1977), pp. 1–12; Albert K. Karnig and B. Oliver Walter, "Election of Women to City Councils," *Social Science Quarterly,* 56 (March 1976), p. 608; Ronald D. Hedlund, Patricia K. Freeman, Keith E. Hamm, and Robert M. Stein, "The Electability of Women Candidates: The Effects of Sex Role Stereotypes," *Journal of Politics,* 41 (1979), pp. 513–24; Laurie E. Elkstrand and William A. Eckert, "The Impact of Candidate's Sex on Voter Choice," *Western Political Quarterly,* 34 (March 1981), pp. 78–87; Susan Welch, Janet Clark, and Robert Darcy, "The Effect of Candidate Gender of Electoral Outcomes: A Six State Analysis" (paper presented at the 1982 Meeting of the American Political Science Association, Denver, September 2–5).

45. The only evidence bearing upon this question of profemale bias comes from those few public opinion polls that have asked voters if they would be predisposed to support a woman candidate. A poll conducted by the Eagleton Institute of Politics in September 1982 found that 26 percent of registered voters in New Jersey claimed they would prefer to vote for a woman if all other things were equal (Press Release, Eagleton Institute of Politics, October 5, 1982).

46. Although women may not fare less well than male candidates in the final judgments of voters, there is evidence that prospective female candidates nevertheless may decide not to run because of anticipated voter prejudice. Women report that their private and family lives are subjected to much more careful scrutiny and questioning by voters than those of male candidates. Women have to walk a finer line in order to establish an acceptable image; voters tolerate less deviation among women. Finally, there may be unwritten "quotas" that are employed by voters (and political leaders); once a certain number of women are serving, there may be a bias against supporting another. *See* Ruth B. Mandel, *In the Running: The New Woman Candidate* (New York: Ticknor & Fields, 1981).

47. Lee, "Why Few Women Hold Public Office," pp. 132–33.

48. Johnson and Carroll, "Profile of Women Holding Office II," p. 39A.

49. Nikki R. Van Hightower, "The Recruitment of Women for Public Office," *American Politics Quarterly,* 5 (July 1977), pp. 301–14; Elizabeth G. King, "Women in Iowa Legislative Politics," in Marianne Githens and Jewel L. Prestage, eds., *A Portrait of Marginality,* pp. 284–303; Irwin N. Gertzog and M. Michele Simard, "Women and 'Hopeless' Congressional Candidacies," *American Politics Quarterly,* 9 (October 1981), pp. 449–66.

50. Susan J. Carroll, "Recruitment During a Period of Elite Circulation: The Case of Women Appointed to the Carter Administration" (paper presented at the 1982 Annual Meeting of the Midwest Political Science Association, Milwaukee, April 28–May 1); Susan J. Carroll, "The Recruitment of Women for Cabinet-Level Posts in State Government: A Social Control Perspective" (paper presented at the 1982 Annual Meeting of the American Political Science Association, September 2–5).

51. For example, Mandel, *In the Running: The New Woman Candidate,* pp. 181–201; Susan Tolchin and Martin Tolchin, *Clout: Womanpower and Politics* (New York: Putnam's, Capricorn Books, 1976), p. 190.

52. Susan J. Carroll, "Women Candidates: Campaigns and Elections in American Politics" (Ph.D. dissertation, Indiana University, 1980), pp. 223, 289; Welch and Karnig, "Correlates of Female Office Holding in City Politics," pp. 478–91.

53. Johnson and Carroll, "Profile of Women Holding Office II," pp. 9A, 12A.

54. Johnson and Carroll, Ibid., p. 16A; Diamond, *Sex Roles in the State House,* p. 38; Carroll, "The Recruitment of Women for Cabinet-Level Posts in State Government: A Social Control Perspective," Table 1; Susan J. Carroll and Barbara Geiger-Parker, "Women Appointed to the Carter Administration: A Comparison with Men" (New Brunswick, N.J.: Center for the American Woman and Politics, forthcoming).

55. Johnson and Carroll, Ibid., p. 18A; Diamond, Ibid., p. 38; Carroll and Geiger-Parker, Ibid.; Susan J. Carroll and Barbara Geiger-Parker, "Women Appointed to State Government: A Comparison With All State Appointees" (New Brunswick, N.J.: Center for the American Woman and Politics, forthcoming).

56. Johnson and Carroll, Ibid., pp. 16A–17A; Diamond, Ibid., pp. 37–39.

57. Johnson and Carroll, Ibid., pp. 17A, 28A.

58. Johnson and Carroll, Ibid., pp. 35A–36A; Carroll and Geiger-Parker, "Women Appointed to the Carter Administration: A Comparison with Men"; Carroll

and Geiger-Parker, "Women Appointed to the State Government: A Comparison With All State Appointees"; Maureen Fiedler, "The Participation of Women in American Politics" (paper presented at the 1975 Annual Meeting of the American Political Science Association, San Francisco, September 2–5).

59. Kathleen A. Frankovic, "Sex and Voting in the U.S. House of Representatives 1961–1975," *American Politics Quarterly*, 5 (July 1977), pp. 315–30; Shelah Gilbert Leader, "The Policy Impact of Elected Women Officials," in Louis Maisel and Joseph Cooper, eds., *The Impact of the Electoral Process* (Beverly Hills: Sage, 1977).

60. Leader, Ibid.

61. Quoted in Mandel, *In the Running: The New Woman Candidate*, p. 33.

62. For excellent reviews of such questions, *see* Kirsten Amundsen, *The Silenced Majority* (Englewood Cliffs, N.J.: Prentice-Hall, 1971); and Virginia Sapiro, "When Are Interests Interesting? The Problem of Political Representation of Women," *American Political Science Review*, 75 (September 1981), pp. 701–16.

63. Jean Bethke Elshtain, "Moral Woman and Immoral Man: A Consideration of the Public-Private Split and Its Political Ramifications," *Politics and Society*, 4 (1974), pp. 452–73.

64. Diane Kincaid Blair and Ann R. Henry, "The Family Factor in State Legislative Turnover," *Legislative Studies Quarterly*, 6 (February 1981), pp. 55–68.

65. Virginia Sapiro, "Private Costs of Public Commitments or Public Costs of Private Commitments? Family Roles versus Political Ambition," *American Journal of Political Science*, 26 (May 1982), pp. 265–79.

66. Mezey, "Women and Representation: The Case of Hawaii," pp. 380–83; Mezey, "Support for Women's Rights Policy," pp. 489–90.

67. *See* note 58.

68. *See*, for example, Freeman, *The Politics of Women's Liberation*, p. 204; Mandel, *In the Running: The New Woman Candidate*, pp. 250–56.

69. Rosabeth Moss Kanter, *Men and Women of the Corporation* (New York: Basic Books, 1977), pp. 206–42.

70. Lynn Rosener and Peter Schwartz, "Women, Leadership and the 1980s: What Kind of Leaders Do We Need? in *New Leadership in the Public Interest* (A Report of the Round Table on New Leadership in the Public Interest, NOW Legal Defense and Education Fund, New York, October 1980), p. 25.

71. Ibid.

72. *See* Rothschild, "Female Power: A Marxist-Feminist Perspective."

8

THE ROLE
OF LEADERSHIP
IN THE
CONSTRUCTION
OF REALITY

Sonja M. Hunt

Sociology deals with those relationships, institutions, and processes which grow out of, and govern, the interaction of individuals with one another; the construction of theories of how society develops, functions, and maintains itself; the achievement of social control; and the antecedents of social change.

As with other social sciences, sociology has been susceptible to the perspectives prevailing in different places and different eras. The attempt to find "laws" of social interaction or social "facts" has inevitably been influenced by contemporary ideologies, morals, and implicit theories of "human nature." Thus, early sociologists such as Herbert Spencer (1820–1903) were much impressed by Darwinian theory and presented views of social structure based upon a misguided attempt to translate the biological concepts of "natural selection" and "survival of the fittest" into the social arena. Later writers such as Charles Cooley (1864–1929) and George Mead (1863–1931) caught some of the enthusiasm of the empirical psychologists and present-day sociologists such as Peter Berger owe something to the popularity of existentialism.

One of the problems, then, for a social science is to transcend the historical perspectives of the age and to move from formulations based on first-order descriptions of the "taken for granted" elements of daily life to second-order analysis of the processes which lead us to take the social world as a given. For this reason sociologists often present a view of "reality" which differs from that which might be given by a person outside the discipline.

Sociology as a distinct discipline dates back only to the mid-nineteenth century, but since that time a significant amount of social change has occurred. Two world wars with their attendant horrors aroused the need to question seriously the origins of human behavior; increased social and geographical mobility changed patterns of family and community life; the enormous developments in mass media both created a common culture and provided the means for the global manipulation of minds and events; and there was a steady growth of technology, giant corporations, bureaucracies, and public institutions.

These events and more have impacted on the kinds of activity engaged in by sociologists and the types of explanatory schemata they have used, from description to investigation, from uninvolved accounts of the social world as it appears to be to a concern with the amelioration of social "problems" and social action, from the accumulation of social data to the social construction of meaning.

Human society and all the activities performed within it, from the family life of the Appalachian miner to the theorizing of the social scientist, is culturally informed by the morals and values of the age. The way in which a society is organized and runs is both a reflection and an expression of such values. Thus accounts of "leaders" and leadership behavior inevitably have the stamp of the era in which they were written. What will be attempted here is to trace the progress of certain ideas pertinent to a discussion of leadership through the works of a few of the more influential European and North American sociologists, and to conclude with the presentation of a modern theory of leadership which comes from a combination and extension of these ideas.

GEORG SIMMEL AND MAX WEBER: LEADERSHIP AS AUTHORITY

Two of the most influential sociologists of the nineteenth century were George Simmel (1858–1918) and Max Weber (1864-1920).

Simmel's method, informed by the views of Kant that knowledge consists of content and form, was to describe all social processes in terms of these two categories. Thus the form of an authority relationship is said to be domination, which may be studied for its content in terms of style, effects, nature, growth, and demise.

Simmel postulated that individuals acquire authority for two reasons: by virtue of outstanding strength and significance in a group such that faith is put in their abilities and trust in their actions, or because certain kinds of institutions such as the church or the army may provide individuals with reputation and the trappings of dignity which they would have been unlikely to acquire without institutional support. In the former case prestige and authority are derived purely from personal qualities which are such as to exert an influence on the followers. In the second case authority is conferred on the person as a consequence of his place within a hierarchy and may occasion the attribution of special idealistic qualities to that person by those who believe in his authority.[1]

In either type of leadership, leader and led have an interactive relationship, since it is impossible to base authority solely on coercion. Thus the led always have the option of following or not following. Simmel commented on the perceived freedom of those under institutionalized and "prestige" leadership, and believed that those who recognize the authority in an appointed office may feel themselves somewhat more "free" than those who become enchanted by a hero or a prophet. On the other hand, people may feel themselves to be following the prestige leader in a spontaneous fashion and perceive themselves as being more constrained by institutionalized authority.

Nevertheless, all leaders are seen by Simmel as subject to the controlling reactions of their followers and he describes the head of a group as, "leading them in their own direction."[2] The leader is conceptualized as the "unitary expression" of the group will, as well as being important for the unification and coherence of the group, and this is said to hold true even in those cases where the group and its leader are in opposition, since the leader as adversary also makes for common cause.

Simmel views the relations between leader and led in terms of a dialectic between obedience and opposition. The leader fulfills the need of the group to have someone take responsibility, but also provides a target for the challenging of power in order that authority should be put in perspective. These antinomian tendencies and their ramifications further strengthen the bonds of the group. In the initial phases of societal development, Simmel believed, leaders must have been exceptionally brave, wise, strong, or possessing in supranormal quantities some other valued characteristic. However, as groups grow larger and membership more diverse it becomes unlikely that any one person will possess such qualities as would appeal to the large numbers of potential observers. Therefore, to the extent that there is significant differentiation within a group, those who would be leaders must shed their individual characters and take on a more generally acceptable and identifiable persona.

Although Simmel is vague on the pathways by which an individual may achieve authority, he makes several points which antedate more modern literature; that the relationship between leader and led is interactive and reactive and that the former cannot maintain authority unless the latter are disposed to believe in his authority; that in order to get and retain power a leader must fulfill the general normative expectations of the group; that although decisions and actions taken by the group may be a consequence of transactions within the group as a whole, it is the leader's function to take responsibility for them.

Max Weber is perhaps best known for his work on the "Protestant Ethic,"[3] but his more general contribution to sociology was the introduction of the concept of *Verstehen,* which may be translated as "meaning" or "understanding." The importance of this can best be seen in contradistinction to the work of Durkheim, who held that there were social "facts" which were of a similar nature to the qualities of natural objects as discovered in physics or geology.[4] Weber was the first sociologist to bring to his craft an appreciation of the role played by psychological processes in social action and of the need for the interpretation rather than mere description of the content and form of social events. He was aware that the sociologist and layperson alike imbue situations with meaning, and this need to make sense of the world in both symbolic and organizational terms is not only an inherent part of human nature but also a driving force in the development of social institutions such as politics, law, and religion. Once constructed, such institutions become a part of the meaning of the social world to the individual. This interpretive sociology defines *action* as "social" only insofar as the actor takes account of the behavior of others by virtue of the subjective meaning he or she attaches to that behavior. The actions of others and the actor are not experienced as "givens" but as a sequence of events which requires interpretation.[5]

In order to understand Weber's accounts of leadership, it is important to grasp that in order to explain social phenomena, he believed it necessary to isolate their critical features into "types" such that all cases of a given phenomenon could be classified by a predetermined definition. However, he emphasized that it was unlikely that any one phenomenon subsumed under that definition would totally correspond in all particulars to the terms of that definition. Weber's "types" of leadership, then, represent one or several aspects of relevant social phenomena and are descriptive rather than analytical. It is improbable that any individual "leader" would fully meet all the criteria associated with the particular type into which he or she fits.[6]

According to Weber's formulation, social actions are controlled and directed by a general belief on the part of the members of a society that a legitimate social order exists. The probability that behavior will be oriented in terms of that order constitutes the basis for its authority. Three ideal types of legitimate authority are postulated, each of which attains its validity in a different way. These are: 1) "rational authority," where patterns of normative rules, originally arising from the interaction of group members, attain legality, and obedience becomes owed to some established *order* within the limits of its scope, for example, educational establishments and the law; 2) "traditional authority," where there is an historically established belief in the legitimate status of those in power and obedience is owed to the *person* of the chief, or leader, and where both parties are thus bound by tradition and exhibit mutual loyalty in a complex pattern of duties and obligations; and 3) "charismatic authority," where some individual is followed and obeyed because of a special trust he induces, his peculiar powers, and his unique qualities.[7]

The concept of charismatic leadership has attracted a great deal of attention and engendered more than a little misunderstanding. Clearly there are some similarities to Simmel's "prestige leadership," but the charismatic leader is part of the expression of schismatic tendencies in society. In contrast to legal or traditional heads he is the antithesis of routinized activities and represents the desire for disruption and change of the prevailing social order. He is a necessary part of the dialectic between the human need for structure and the equally human need for variation and innovation in society.

Charisma is conceptualized as residing in those qualities, often perceived as superhuman, supernatural, or at least totally exceptional, which set one individual apart from all others. It is, of course, necessary for this individual to be acknowledged as exceptional by a significant number of people and such a one cannot be divorced from the "charismatic band"— the group which forms itself around the leader. This is especially the case with religious sects of which an early example would be Christ and His followers and, it has been argued, a more recent example is the group which formed itself around the Reverend Jim Jones.[8]

The sole source of legitimate authority for the charismatic leader lies in the regard of his followers. Such a leader has no institutionalized or traditional claims on power, no career, no prospects of promotion, no ritual trappings of office. All he has is some inner dictate which in some way taps the devotion and aspirations of others. Charismatic leaders and bands are thus completely outside the everyday social routine which is represented by traditional and rational authority.

Weber believed that the rise of charismatic leaders was most apparent at times of great stress in a society and that they emerged not from some bureaucracy or body of experts but rather from the crowd, and particularly from those who live on the margins of the social world. They either possess, or are imputed to possess, special gifts and have their own inner restraints and motives rather than those inculcated by the social order.

Although the term *charisma* is said by Weber to be value free, implying no moral judgment as to the positive or undesirable repercussions of the phenomenon, it is apparent that he believed charismatic individuals to be a necessary antidote to the increasing bureaucratization of society—a process he viewed with distaste.[9] He related the rationalization of the human need for meaning to bureaucracy, which is seen as mechanistic, depersonalizing, routinizing, and representing trends which are inimical to freedom. The rise of bureaucracies is, for Weber, the more negative aspect of the "disenchantment of the world," a process which is discerned by the extent to which magical and fantastic elements of thought are replaced by routines, or the degree to which ideas gain in coherence. At least part of the function of a charismatic leader is to oppose this routinizing process by rejecting rational, economic objectives and redressing the balance toward more "irrational," but more essentially human pursuits. To this end he would not, in ideal form, be concerned for his own private gain or be vulnerable to worldly ties, such as those to family or other legitimated institutions.

The maintenance of leadership under such conditions is precarious, dependent as it is upon the validation which comes from the perception by others that certain peculiar qualities inhere in the leader. There is, thus, a constant need for the charismatic leader to prove himself, so that heroes must perform daring deeds, prophets call forth miracles, and visionaries make appropriate pronouncements. In other words, he must fulfill in a relevant and acceptable manner the expectations of his followers.

Another hazard to the purity of the charismatic band is that in order to survive it must adopt some of the stable characteristics associated with rational institutions. This being the case it may be said that charismatic leadership exists in its true form only while originating. The movement of the charismatic band toward routinization is said, by Weber, to be seen most clearly when the need to find a new leader arises because of the demise, imprisonment, or fall from favor of the original one. During the course of the development of the charismatic band, certain expectations as to the characteristics of the leader will have become more or less fixed. Thus a replacement is usually sought on the premise that someone similar is required. Ways of achieving this will vary according to cultural morae and knowledge of ritual. Thus there may be a thorough search of the community for someone perceived as possessing the required qualities; divine revelation may be awaited or oracles consulted. The former leader may designate his successor or it may be done by fiat of his disciples. Transmission may occur by heredity or by ritual from one leader to another. Each of these cases implies that "charisma" becomes dissociated from the particular qualities of one special individual and evolves into an objectified and transferable set of criteria. Ultimately it may transmute into the "charisma of office"[10] which refers to those distinctive and supereminent attributes attached to, for example, presidents, popes, and kings by virtue of the roles, rituals, pomp and circumstance attached to the status, regardless of the specific personality of the incumbent. Once norms for the recruitment of leaders are established, in particular tests of eligibility or training procedures, the magic of charisma is lost. Nevertheless, one of the signs of charismatic leadership may lie in the ability to leave a significant mark on the subsequent institutionalized structure by giving it some idiosyncratic quality associated with its originator.

Weber has much less to say about leaders in the lego-rational and traditional spheres. Such leaders are, by reason of their "type," unlikely to be important figures in social change since the former are dependent upon the status quo for their livelihood and the latter are the status quo embodied.

Since the time of Weber bureaucratization and rationalization have proceeded apace; multinational conglomerates and huge public organizations make up the major portion of our institutions. Under such circumstances it seems that the emergence of charismatic leadership becomes an unlikely occurrence and the word *charisma* is increasingly applied merely to those attractive public figures who possess a certain charm. Moreover, in the age of public relations the manufacture of leaders via the mass media or "pseudocharisma," as it has been called, may play an important role in maintaining the status quo rather than changing it.[11] It has been suggested that in our day and culture virtually no elected leaders possess charisma in the Weberian sense, perhaps because such people cannot arise out of the institutionalized nature of the modern political process. Charismatic political leaders, if they exist, may be limited to those arenas which are still influenced by magicoreligious elements, for example, Jomo Kenyatta in Kenya, and Mahatma Gandhi in India.[12]

"Charisma" may thus be a social phenomenon which is confined to certain times in history and those places which are not almost wholly dominated by highly organized, technology-dependent institutions. It is also possible that "charisma" is a post hoc type of attribution made with the benefit of hindsight. Attributing "charisma" to Christ, Cromwell, or Columbus is fraught with the problem that we know of them only what their contemporaries and biographers chose to write, and the choices may have been influenced by the events with which they were associated, thus "charisma" could have been inferred after, not before, the occurrences which brought such men to prominence by an understandable confusion between personal qualities and attributions made on the basis of some relevant social action.

In referring to a remark by Nietzche that "success is the greatest liar," Klages commented that success may convince us of the worth of a person even when the success is largely due to chance.[13]

Although Weber was aware of the need for interpretation of individual action in the social world, he took it for granted that the phenomena of social life were a matter of intersubjective agreement. This may be a reasonable assumption on the level of everyday "commonsense" explanations insofar as individuals do experience their acts as meaningful (indeed, if they don't we may regard them as "sick"). They tend to assume also that others do the same. As has been pointed out, however, these commonsense beliefs should not necessarily be used as a basis for the analysis of social processes for fear we will not see past a phenomenon to its origin. The self-evident also requires close scrutiny. Weber seems to accept unexamined the appeal of the charismatic leader and pays small attention to how such people become so designated or what it is exactly that makes them so attractive. He does suggest briefly that those who are disturbed or alienated, in some sense marginal in society, are the most likely to be found charismatic, presumably since they have somehow escaped the full force of previous socialization processes. And he alludes to, but does not clearly state, that the legitimation of charismatic leaders may arise from inferred rather than inherent qualities, while authority relates to the display of appropriate conduct in the face of collective expectations. What Weber does make clear is that the charismatic leader is obeyed because of trust in him and his qualities "as they fall within the scope of the individual's belief in his charisma,"[14] and that traditional and legal authority exist primarily because sufficient numbers of people act out of the belief that they should exist in precisely the way that they do.

CHARLES COOLEY AND
GEORGE MEAD: LEADERSHIP
AS SYMBOLIC INTERACTION

Although there are hints in the writing of Weber that the social world is a human construct which is both a consequence of and a contributor to dominant meaning systems, this view becomes more clearly and carefully elaborated in the works of Cooley and Mead, contemporaries who had an influence both on each other and on the course of American sociology. Their contribution was to emphasize the psychological roots of social action and to show how it is the properties of mind and, in particular cognition, which determine the nature and scope of social phenomena.

Cooley was an exponent of sociological romanticism concerned with the structure and function of social action. Under the influence of neo-Darwinism he construed the study of society as a study of evolutionary processes which possess a natural tendency toward social change, by virtue of some inherent human tendency. Individual variation provides the avenues for change, but can only become effective in the context of group structure, since it is the group which facilitates and encourages the appropriate expression of individual qualities.[15]

Cooley believed that all the phenomena of life and therefore the data of the social sciences were grounded in the imaginative properties of the mind, and that behavior was influenced not so much by internal (psychological) and external (sociological) forces but by what lay between, a reflective and socially derived interpretation of inner and outer events as they are experienced at the time.[16] Thus society is, above all, a relationship between ideas. Social events have their origin in the mind. The "facts" of society are the notions which people have of one another, rather than internalization of an outside reality.

According to Cooley, leadership of any kind exists only insofar as the ideas and images it arouses in the minds of people are communicable and appropriate. A leader must appeal to something in the imaginations of the potential followers. Cooley believed that human beings have an "onward instinct"—that is, a kind of built-in energy which needs direction. It is the ability to appeal to this that constitutes leadership, together with the ability to give a dramatic or visually appealing display of power. Leadership is dependent upon the efficacy of such personal impressions in arousing feeling, thought, or action in others. Since, according to Cooley, all social phenomena are a consequence of a mind's "valuation" of suggestions coming from other minds, in the case of leadership there is something seminal, almost primitive, in the relationship between the impression given by the leader and the mind receiving it. It is the leader's ability to tap unfocused energy, to awaken life, to appeal to instincts, which legitimizes authority.[17]

In spite of this combination of biological and romantic notions of leadership, Cooley acknowledges in his later writings the link between the expectations of the led and the behavior of the leader.

The "natural" leader is he or she who gives the impression of being in charge of the situation. The function of the great and famous is to be a symbol and form, an object of belief, that is, a living definition of what people need to believe, even though actual behavior may fall far short of the ideal, as for example was the case with prereformation popes and medieval monarchs. It is the imagination of the observers under the influence of the idealization of their own need for meaningful symbols that expresses human tendencies. There may thus occur a "halo effect" from specifically admired traits to the whole person. The gap between what the public needs to believe about its leaders and the actual qualities of such leaders may induce deliberate attempts to create a stereotype of the leader which is only remotely connected to the "real" person (compare pseudocharisma). Part of this image building may involve imparting a dramatic air to events which might otherwise be regarded as dull, the timing of announcements for maximum impact, or indulging in dramatic interventions. Thus the leader is obliged, in order to retain power, to behave in accordance with this idealizing tendency of the public mind.[18]

For this reason, Cooley postulated, political problems are often posed in terms of the personalities of the protagonists rather than in terms of, say, abstract socioeconomic analyses. People find it more congenial to accept or reject individuals rather than issues, because such persons are symbolic of the prevalent tendencies of their followers. They are the "embodiment of group desire," rather than anything else.[19] Human proclivities, then, find social expression through the medium of certain human beings who symbolize human needs and motives. The handling of ideas symbolically through the use of designated individuals was believed by Cooley to be important for the flexible functioning of a society. However, it carries the concomitant drawback of closing the collective mind to those who do not fulfill the requisite stereotype and who, therefore, are unlikely to attain positions of leadership. It may also cultivate ignorance concerning the true antecedents of events.

Cooley's views on leadership were not well worked out, but stemmed but his general theoretical stance that individuality can develop only within society. Individuals become "themselves" through the recognition of how they appear to others, and consciousness of self is a consequence of reflections given off by other minds, hence his term *looking glass self*.[20] It follows that "leaders" are a part of this interplay between social action, human need, and imagination.

Cooley made a clear attempt to marry harmoniously psychological and sociological concepts, but a much firmer synthesis was made by Mead, who was able to encompass within his theories the myriad social variables which determine human consciousness and incorporate them within a cognitive model of society. This model postulates that all basic human needs, biological and psychological, are given form and direction by social processes. The interactions of individuals have meaning only insofar as one person plays the "role" expected by the other.[21]

The origins of social action are said to stem from the perception of events by an individual, selective response to these events and the symbolic interpretation of them by reference to the self. The experience of the environment differs from the environment as it was encountered, since some aspects have been reinterpreted, some have been filtered out, and some elements may have been added. The social environment as it is experienced, then, presents the individual with perceptions which form part of the meaning system of the groups to which he or she belongs. The perception and actions of any individual form only a part of the larger communal consciousness, since every group develops a system of symbols, for example, language, gestures, and ritual objects, which are held in common and are significant in the functioning and organization of the group. Insofar as members behave toward one another and take one another into account, they take one another's perspectives toward their own actions and interpret those actions in the light of communal interpretations of reality. Group membership is, therefore, symbolic and the symbols are internalized by the members and influence their individual activities.[22]

Human beings, then, are characterized by their symbolic representation. They construct meanings out of a social world which is also sustained by those meanings, and they act accordingly. The meaning of particular events, persons, offices, statuses, and objects originates in the interpretations made by an observer of the actions of others toward the observer. A society is thus represented inside the individuals of whom it is comprised in the form of a "generalized other" which presents a general system of attitudes and beliefs which are closely linked to the maintenance of social control and the development of self-concept.

Language is, naturally, of prime importance in these processes of symbolization, reflection, perception, and interpretation, since the self develops through, as it were, talking to itself in the terms of the group of which it is a member and "social habits" are internalized.[23]

A universe of discourse develops within groups and societies which is composed of a set of shared meanings relating to the nature of reality and which is a consequence of participation, communication, and symbolization. The world can never be viewed "as it is," but only as filtered and distorted through these processes and meanings. If there is a relationship between the act of one person and the response of another, such that their individual expectations are fulfilled, then meaning is said to exist. The relationship between any event and the later stages of the same social act constitute the field within which meaning exists, and meaning exists only within this universe of discourse. The actions of those in strange groups or foreign societies may appear "meaningless" to us, until we learn to share their processes of communication and interpretation.

Mead portrays a view of the social process in which the personal attributes of any "leader" must be a consequence of the internalization of the "generalized other" to leadership positions. The qualities expected of a leader are, therefore, a function of the prevailing symbols and meaning systems extant within the group: A person will be perceived as a leader to the extent that he or she symbolizes group attitudes and beliefs and can demonstrate in a satisfactory manner those actions and characteristics which exemplify the normative ideals of leadership within a particular universe of discourse.

THE CONSTRUCTION
OF THE SOCIAL WORLD

From Simmel to Mead one can trace the elaboration of certain themes pertinent to the concept of leadership. Simmel recognized that individuals gain power and come to be regarded as "leaders" only insofar as others believe in their authority and their behavior conforms to general expectations. These ideas are extended in Weber's work, where leaders can be seen as fulfilling in part the human need to give meaning to the world whether through legal, traditional, or charismatic means. Cooley and Mead emphasize the cognitive aspects of social action, the internalization of shared meanings, the tendency to seek cause in persons rather than processes, and the maintenance of social control, not by means of external forces such as a police force but by reason of the assumptions, interpretations, and forces originating in social interactions. The social world is thus a product of the human mind, and our ability to construe that world is limited by the extent to which we are members of it and have internalized its symbols.

Human beings do not merely react to the behavior of others: they interpret it and their responses are predicated on the meaning they attach to both their own actions and those of others. Social relations, interactions, and processes are mediated through language and other forms of symbolization. Symbolic interaction implies, too, that an individual acts in ways that he or she believes will be interpreted in a certain way by others. Thus we act and react not solely in terms of the meaning we attach to the behavior of others but also in terms of the meaning we expect others to infer from our behavior. Stable patterns of group existence are made possible only by continuous and shared use of the same schemata of interpretation which, in turn, only persists by being constantly confirmed by the defining acts of others.[24] Out of these shared meanings and mutual acts of interpretation, actions and reactions within a particular universe of discourse, is constructed a view of the world which may be called "social reality."

Social reality refers to those values, beliefs, behaviors, and attitudes which attain validity only through social consensus. For example, physical reality presents us with yardsticks by which to judge manifestations of the physical world; the thickness of wood, whether humans can fly unaided, whether a material is made of tin or brass. But when it is a question of what clothes to wear, which way to vote, or the behavior appropriate to which social situation, we refer to that web of norms, conventions, fads, and moral stipulations which fashion our daily activities and underpin the shifting foundations of the social fabric.

Social reality implies acting in awareness of the behavior and expectations of others and adjusting responses accordingly, although many of the processes involved in this may take place below the level of immediate consciousness. Some responses will have become established so early in life, through the medium of socialization, that they come to seem "natural." Established institutions, organizations, and customary behaviors come to be experienced as something other than the products of human interaction and take on an unassailable quality. At the same time there is a need to explain both the social and the physical world. However, the "causes" of events are sought in the same reticulum of normative interpretations that govern the nature of social reality. This "canopy of legitimations"[25] is part of the socially constructed universe of discourse which enables us to give meaning to our experience and partial knowledge of the world in an integrated way, and offers protection to the institutions erected to bolster the social process.

The ways in which we are constrained to search for explanations are influenced by the same socially shared assumptions about what it is that we should or ought to try to explain. There are thus epistemological issues to be dealt with in the social production of knowledge.

The institutionalization of explanation grows out of socialization and the immersion of the individual in the modes of thought customary to time and place, but it is also a consequence of that search for meaning which appears to be a universal human characteristic. It includes the social roles we take on or are ascribed, the language we use, and the pattern of our perceptions.

Interpreting Perception

Given that the capacity of the brain to process information is limited, any observer of the social and physical world is faced with a myriad of data from which to select. The selection of perceptions is largely influenced by the requirements of the society, institutions, and symbols of the groups to which we belong, given the exigencies and idiosyncracies of individual existence.

The phenomena of the world even after selective perception has taken place are not, however, experienced "tout court" but as we have noted are subject to active interpretation. The observer goes beyond the information available and forms inferences about associations and causal relationships. For example, a series of experiments has shown that observers of two spots of lights of unequal size moving across a screen where one light is larger than the other will interpret the situation as one in which the larger light is chasing the smaller light if the latter is in front, but will experience the smaller light as following the larger if the larger is in front.[26] A great deal of evidence exists to suggest that objects and events are almost never approached as they are but are assimilated into preexisting schemata in the mind of the observer.[27] The search for meaning is so ingrained that it influences the observer to attribute motives, loci of responsibility, emotion, intention, and so on in such a way as to be largely unaware of the contingent nature of such inferences.[28,29,30]

Attribution Theory

The tendency to make inferences about causes of events and behavior, based upon fragmented information and the internalized semantics of social reality, has been formalized in attribution theory, which provides a useful link between empirical studies of psychological processes and the theoretical sociological stance of the symbolic interactionists. This tendency is postulated to stem from a socially and psychologically determined need to understand and predict events in a way which lends stability and coherence to the phenomenal world. This "reality orientation" is seen as linked to the desire to have at least the illusion of control by locating the origin of occurrences.[31]

Attributions may be made situationally or dispositionally, that is, they may be made with reference to social context and social process, or by reference to motives, intentions, and personality traits.

Many studies have shown that observers tend to overestimate the importance of dispositional factors and to underestimate the influence of those forces and pressures which are endemic in the dynamics of social reality. The "fundamental attribution error" is to attribute happenings to the characteristics of the actors in the situation rather than to contextual variables.[32] There is a growing body of literature which stresses the importance of social context rather than personal characteristics as the main influence on the outcome of social interactions.[33] For example, in the Milgram experiments where subjects believed themselves to be administering electric shocks to another individual, it was the combination of contextual variables which was most influential in decisions to deliver what would have been fatal voltages, not some quirk of personality.[34] Similarly, in a prison simulation experiment requiring people to act out the roles of prisoner and guard, the situation itself determined behavior much more than the characteristics of the protagonists.[35] It has been shown that the consistency of personality traits is rather low and that such traits may inhere more in the tendency of the observer to categorize than in the person of the actor. This tendency to infer a consistent "personality" is probably reinforced by the fact that one observes most individuals in only a small sample of situations and that the presence of the same observer may elicit similar behavior from the actor.[36]

The need to explain and predict complex events finds fulfillment to a large extent through the customary socially determined channels. Regardless of the actual content of the attributions there is a tendency to believe that most or all outcomes can be explained by reference to fundamental events, objects, or people. The dispositional view, which explains success, failure, crisis, and change in terms of personal qualities, appears to be common in most cultures. The tendency to seek for an agent of events predominates in cultures and history. This may well be related to animism and the preference for a single source rather than a plexus of interwoven social threads. Moreover, persons as origins imply reversibility of that which, considered as a product of ineluctable social forces, might be more pessimistically viewed as irreversible.

LEADERSHIP AS INFERENCE

The legitimation of social reality refers to the process of rationalizing and explaining the way things are. Part of legitimation is the construction of a vocabulary to objectify and account for human experience. Some of this vocabulary will be apparent in myths, legends, folktales, and so on; for example, explaining events by reference to the powers of gods, demons, magi, witches, or the legendary figures of Icelandic saga. As societies become more institutionalized, reference will be made to theories and bodies of knowledge constructed by persons specialized to do so; for example, scientists, historians and philosophers, and explanations of events may be sought in terms of political lobbying, religious conflict, brain lesions, or the sagacity of great men.

Attributions will, therefore, be made on the basis of the vocabularies and explanatory systems available from the "canopy of legitimations."

The vocabulary of leadership is deeply engrained in the social reality we inhabit at both lower and higher levels of legitimation. The notion of leadership provides a clear-cut and satisfying referent to which political change, social outcome, economic success, personal fate, or organizational failure can be linked. Indeed, it has been suggested that leadership is a residual category to which personal responsibility is assigned for events which would otherwise be unexplainable[37] because they are, in fact, merely the point of focus in a dynamic stream of interacting and complex social forces. Once such a category exists in the vocabulary of legitimation it becomes easy to attribute more and more events to leadership or lack of it. The creation of "leaders" arises out of the need for meaning and the tendency to make inferences within the confines of the prevailing explanatory systems. The meaning of leadership for the group and for the society influences the perceived attributes of leadership and the meaning, at the same time, depends upon a deeply embedded set of beliefs which link behaviors, personal qualities, and sets of happenings. To adopt Weber's phraseology, it may be that with the increasing routinization and disenchantment of the modern world, the need to believe in heroes and great figures becomes greater as the probability of their appearance becomes less likely.

The emphasis on leadership may derive from a desire to believe in the effectiveness and importance of individual action, which is potentially more controllable and understandable than complex contextual variables, a circumstance which is referred to as "the personification of social causality."[38]

The identification of certain roles as having leadership status tends to guide the construction of meaning in the direction of attributing outcomes to the actions of the person occupying the leader role, even though

172 THE ROLE OF LEADERSHIP IN THE CONSTRUCTION OF REALITY

it has been shown that the functions and characteristics said to characterize the leader role are, in fact, spread throughout the members of the group.[39] It has been noted that autobiographies of political leaders may reveal that their actions, although publicly presented and construed as stemming from personal characteristics, whether of foresight or poor judgment, are often seen from the actor's point of view as being inevitable in the face of the particular configuration of situational pressures.[40] Identification of one or two statuses as of prime importance provides a simpler and more readily controllable model of reality. It is easier to conceive of an ameliorization of circumstances where cause is laid at the door of an identifiable individual rather than its being a consequence of social, cultural, economic, and political transactions. The oversimplification is both comforting and optimistic.

There appear to be two ways in which individuals come to be seen as "leaders." They may be assigned to a leader role by reason of birth, that is, they fill a position of traditional hereditary leadership or they may achieve tenancy of a leader role within the rational sphere by virtue of their perceived personal characteristics, such as competence, power, ability to threaten others, techniques of persuasion, or use of "impression management."[41] Individuals then come to be called leaders either because they fill a slot traditionally associated with leadership or because they behave in accordance with notions of how "leaders" behave. Attributions may then be made on the basis of events perceived by observers, even though the actions of the leader subsequently associated with the events have not themselves actually been observed. Consider, for example, the effects of an apparent improvement in the economy soon after the election of a new president. Since inferences are based, as we have seen, on the assumption of more information than is actually possessed, further qualities and powers may be attributed to the leader, especially if his or her behavior is distinctive in some way, and matches socially constructed ideas of how a leader *should* behave. As Calder has pointed out, the behavior and outcomes believed to be a consequence of leadership characteristics provide further evidence for the existence of those characteristics.[42] It has been shown that when asked to choose "leaders" people tend to choose those to whom they attribute the qualities they associate with leadership.[43] Since these characteristics are part of the legitimation vocabulary, there is an inevitability about the choices they make, and the choices they make further strengthen the presumed association between leadership and special qualities. Required to account for some outcome, individuals are likely to search for the most likely "cause." A "leader" is an easily observable antecedent who satisfies the preference for unitary explanations.[44] Moreover, once a stable attribution has been made, individuals are relatively impervious to further and contradictory information.[45]

Although it is suggested here that the attribution of causation to designated persons is a common aspect of human activity which serves to simplify and further legitimate explanatory systems, this should not be taken to mean that the individual as an initiating source of acts is a total fiction. There certainly appear to be circumstances in which one person may trigger, coerce, or facilitate acts in other persons in a rather direct way by the wielding of power, charm, or novel ideas. It may be, however, that such situations are highly circumscribed and much rarer than commonly supposed.

ENACTING THE LEADER ROLE

The exegesis of leadership in terms of inference and a preference for personifying social events poses further questions concerning those individuals who are assigned or who take on leadership roles.

Naturally those who come to be seen as "leaders" share in the same processes of socialization, the same dialectic between society and its explanatory systems, as everyone else. They, too, are socialized into the dominant meaning system and internalize its legitimations. The creation of social identity can be postulated to depend upon the attempts of the individual to locate him or herself existentially in the social world. To some extent this identity will be formulated out of the labels available to the social and cultural context. It is, therefore, embedded in that web of transactions and social interactions which constitute the daily experience of social reality. Thus, self-identification as a leader, or as having aspirations to such a status, is developed and maintained by the customary legitimations within a milieu which accepts the socially constructed concept of leadership.

According to Linton social identity can be judged along the three dimensions of status, involvement, and value.[46] Status refers to a set of beliefs defined by the perceived expectations of the members of a particular social group and is linked to role—a set of observable behaviors displayed by the holder of the role which legitimizes occupancy of that status. (Roles, of course, require intersubjectivity and rather than being static, as implied by Linton, are better construed as processes built out of mutual interpretations.)

The involvement dimension refers to the degree of freedom available to the occupant of a role in relation to the time and energy spent upon it; the more time and energy expended in performing the expected behaviors, the greater will be the involvement. Involvement tends to increase to the extent that an individual internalizes the objectives and values of the group or organization within which the role is located. In particular, representing the group or speaking for the organization in public will tend to increase involvement. Thus the greater the time and energy spent in a role enactment, the more the self comes to be defined by the role. The actor is, as it were, taken in by his own performance. If this occurs, the ability to take other perspectives and view oneself and one's behavior with a certain skepticism may diminish.

The value dimension is related to the credit which is given by observers for the adequate performance of the role and manifests itself in prestige, prizes, promotions, and applause given to those whose performances are most appropriate and convincing. Status, involvement, and value are thus involved in the negotiation of social identity as the individual reconciles his or her roles with the expectations and demands of other people, producing a kind of "working agreement"[47] which represents a continuously maintained correspondence of perception, cognition, and performance.

Borrowing Goffman's dramaturgical approach, one can view these processes of transaction, interaction, and negotiation as moves in a perpetual drama which defines, confirms, and maintains for both audience and participants the conventions of the social world.[48]

Public performances, that is, those acts which are observable by interested others, provide the opportunity for speculations about social identity and self-concept through audience reactions and the amount of "applause" received. The more closely the actor fulfills the expectations pertinent to the held, or aspired to, status, by demonstrating a high degree of involvement in the role, the more acclaim and value will be assigned to the actor.

"Leaders" can now be seen as those who, whether by accident of birth or by increasingly valued performances, act so as to confirm attribution processes emanating from the audience. Leaders may be somewhat aware of the largely fictive nature of their position or may, by reason of the intersubjectivity so necessary for the maintenance of social reality, be taken in by their own performances.

Individuals who typify leader roles are obviously more likely to succeed, and the canny "leader" is one who can identify trends in advance and make it his business to become associated with, for example, an economic boom, a period of prolific productivity, or a breakthrough by a subordinate; and will engage proleptically in all kinds of visible "busywork" for the benefit of the audience.

Conversely, foreseeing trouble, the good performer attempts to dissociate himself or herself in advance from undesirable events by keeping a low profile, leaving others to make the public appearances, or by blaming it all on the previous incumbent. Thus "successful" and, therefore, "good" "leaders" associate themselves with "successful" events and dissociate themselves from nonsuccessful events and confirm the processes of inference involved in attributions, for example, by censoring disconfirmatory evidence and burnishing performances before giving them in public.

CONCLUSION

It has been argued here that in many cases, especially those involving bureaucracy and rationalization, the power and authority in relation to social control customarily attributed to "leaders" is largely illusory except insofar as those in leadership positions perform so as to give substance to the attributions. A "leader " may be better construed as an inference which grows out of the preference for simple as opposed to complex explanations and the tendency to attribute cause dispositionally rather than situationally, based upon a social psychological tendency to have an observable someone, potentially replaceable, be responsible for events rather than intangible and ineffable social forces. The focus on leadership as the center from which major effects emanate can be seen as part of a general tendency to perceive social phenomena at the level of psychological traits of individuals. Values which emerge from the transactions and symbolic interactions of a whole social world are converted into psychic structures. Explaining social phenomena by reference to the personal qualities of actors appeals to the need to understand why things happen and provides readily assimilable information. However, the dangers inherent in this process have been well analyzed by Arendt for their capacity to direct our attention from the true sources of events. In her analysis of the behavior of Eichmann, Arendt implies that the personification of causality leads to the illusion that some individual can be held responsible for social evils. She points out that such a view denies the complex role played by language in providing legitimation for institutionalized action and the force exerted by bureaucratic systems.[49] Under such circumstances the process called by Goffman "bureaucratization of the spirit" occurs.[50] Once procedures have become institutionalized and gained legitimacy, they form a part of the framework of social reality. Thus the origin of orders becomes problematic and their implementation routine.

The notion of leadership and the attributions made to it both grow out of and maintain the human search for meaning and the cognitive constructions of models of reality. The notion that there are "leaders" protects us from metaphysical doubts and terrors. Indeed, it has been hypothesized by Pfeffer that the greater the uncertainty and ambiguity surrounding events and the more they are the consequence of incorrigible social forces, the greater will be the tendency to associate them with personal powers by the institutionalized display of leadership rituals.[51] A further advantage of having a "leader" as the focal point of explanations is the convenience of having a scapegoat who absolves us of responsibility and exonerates us from the blame of participation in undesirable outcomes.

While the analysis of leadership as inference is largely speculative and susceptible to refinement, particularly in respect of the limitations of its applicability, it has been adopted by reason of the view that scientific endeavor should proceed by means of interpretations which attempt to go beyond the accepted framework of social reality.

The traditional language of leadership is part of the language of social reality, which it both encompasses and sustains. As Wittengenstein pointed out, words have many antecedents and their "meanings" are learned by employing them in the customary contexts—a circumstance which may mislead us into assuming that meaning and comprehending are synonymous.[52] Concepts, however, can rarely be divorced from the fabric of historical, cultural, and psychological processes which present us with the contextual framework of the social world. If we wish to understand the phenomena associated with "leadership," it is necessary to try to transcend the assumptions behind the customary use of words and examine the inferences upon which normative "explanations" are based.

NOTES

1. George Simmel, *The Sociology of Georg Simmel,* ed. and trans. Kurt H. Wolff (Glencoe, Il.: Free Press, 1950).
2. Ibid.
3. Max Weber, *The Theory of Social and Economic Organization* (Glencoe, Il.: Free Press, 1947).
4. Emil Durkheim, *The Rules of Sociological Method,* 1895.
5. Max Weber, *Basic Concepts in Sociology,* trans. H. P. Secher (New York: Citadell Press, 1969).
6. Ibid.
7. Max Weber, *On Charisma and Institution Building: Selected Papers,* S. N. Eisenstadt, ed. (Chicago and London: University of Chicago Press, 1952).
8. Doyle Johnson, "Dilemmas of Charismatic Leadership: The Case of the People's Temple," *Sociological Analysis,* 40 (1979), pp. 315–23.
9. Weber, *The Theory of Social and Economic Organization.*
10. Weber, *On Charisma and Institution Building: Selected Papers.*
11. Joseph Bensman and Michael Givant, "Charisma and Modernity," *Social Research,* 42 (1975), pp. 570–614.
12. Karl Lowenstein, *Max Weber's Political Ideas in the Perspective of Our Time* (Boston: University of Massachusetts Press, 1966).
13. Ludwig Klages, *Die Psychologischen Errungenschaften Nietzches* (Liepzig, Barth, 1926).
14. Weber, *On Charisma and Institution Building: Selected Papers.*
15. Charles Cooley, *Social Organization* (New York: Scribners, 1909).
16. Charles Cooley, *Human Nature and the Social Order* (New York: Scribners, 1902).
17. Charles Cooley, and others, *Introductory Sociology* (New York: Scribners, 1933).
18. Ibid.
19. Cooley, *Social Organization.*
20. Ibid.
21. George Herbert Mead, *Mind, Self and Society,* C. W. Morris, ed. (Chicago: University of Chicago Press, 1934).
22. George Herbert Mead, *Selected Writings* (Indianapolis and New York: Bobbs-Merrill, 1964).

23. Mead, *Mind, Self and Society.*
24. Herbert Blumer, "Sociological Implications of the Thought of George Herbert Mead," *American Journal of Sociology,* 71 (1966), pp. 535–44.
25. Peter Berger and Thomas Luckmann, *The Social Construction of Reality* (Garden City, N.Y.: Doubleday, 1967).
26. Fritz Heider and Marianne Simmel, "An Experimental Study of Apparent Behavior," *American Journal of Psychology* (1944), pp. 57, 243–59.
27. Roger Schanck, *Conceptual Information Processing* (Amsterdam, N. Holland, 1975).
28. David Rumelhart, "Understanding and Summarizing Brief Stories," in David LaBerge and S. J. Samuels, eds., *Basic Processes in Reading: Perception and Comprehension* (Hillsdale, N.J.: Lawrence Erlbaum, 1976).
29. Robert Abelson, *Scripts,* invited address to the Midwestern Psychological Association, May 1978.
30. Fritz Heider, *The Psychology of Interpersonal Relations* (New York: John Wiley, 1958).
31. Harold Kelley, "Attribution in Social Psychology," in Edward E. Jones, ed., *Attribution: Perceiving the Causes of Behavior* (Morristown, N.J.: General Learning

32. Lee Ross and Charles Anderson, "Shortcomings in the Attribution Process: On the Origins and Maintenance of Erroneous Social Assessments," in Amos Tversky, Daniel Kahnemann, and Paul Slovic, eds., *Judgement Under Uncertainty: Heuristics and Biases* (New York: Cambridge University Press, 1980).
33. Lee Ross, Gunther Bierbrauer, and Susan Polly, "Attribution of Educational Outcomes by Professional and Non-professional Instructors," *Journal of Personality and Social Psychology,* 29 (1974), pp. 609–18; Stanley Milgram, *Obedience to Authority* (New York: Harper & Row, Pub., 1974); Philip Zimbardo, "The Mind Is a Formidable Jailer: A Pirandellian Prison," *New York Times,* April 8, 1973, pp. 38–60.
34. Milgram, ibid.
35. Zimbardo, "The Mind is a Formidable Jailer: A Pirandellian Prison."
36. Michael Argyle and Roger Little, "Do Personality Traits Apply to Social Behavior?' *Journal of the Theory of Social Behavior,* 2 (1972), pp. 1–35.
37. Lionel Pondy, "Leadership Is a Language Game," in George J. McCall and J. L. Simmons, *Identities and Interactions* (New York: Collier-MacMillan, 1966).
38. Jeffrey Pfeffer, "The Ambiguity of Leadership," in Michael W. McCall, Jr., and Morgan M. Lombardo, eds., *Leadership: Where Else Can We Go?* (Durham, N.C.: Duke University Press, 1978).
39. Alex Bavelas, "Leadership: Man and Function," *Administrative Science Quarterly,* 4 (1960), pp. 491–98.
40. Edward Jones and Richard Nisbet, "The Actor and the Observer: Divergent Perceptions of the Causes of Behavior, in Edward E. Jones, ed., *Attribution: Perceiving the Causes of Behavior.*
41. Erving Goffman, *The Presentation of the Self in Everyday Life* (Garden City, N.Y.: Doubleday, 1959).
42. Bobby Calder, "An Attribution Theory of Leadership," in Barry M. Staw and Gerald R. Salancik, eds., *New Directions in Organizational Behavior* (Chicago: St. Clair Press, 1977), pp. 179–204.
43. Clare Clifford and Thomas Cohn, "The Relationship Between Leadership and Personality Attributes Perceived by Followers," *Journal of Social Psychology,* 64 (1964), pp. 57–64.
44. David Kanouse, "Language, Labelling and Attribution," in Jones, *Attribution: Perceiving the Causes of Behavior.*

45. Mark Lepper, Mark Zanna, and Robert Abelson, "Cognitive Irrelevancy in a Dissonance Reduction Situation," *Journal of Personality and Social Psychology,* 16 (1970), pp. 191–98.
46. Robert Linton, *The Cultural Background of Personality* (New York: Appleton-Century-Crofts, 1945).
47. McCall and Simmons, *Identities and Interactions.*
48. Erving Goffman, *Strategic Interaction* (Oxford: Basil Blackwell, 1969).
49. Hannah Arendt, *Eichmann in Jerusalem, a Report on the Banality of Evil* (New York: Penguin Books, 1977).
50. Goffman, *Strategic Interaction.*
51. Pfeffer, "The Ambiguity of Leadership."
52. Ludwig Wittengenstein, *Philosophical Investigations* (Oxford: Basil Blackwell, 1953).

9

CULTURAL LEADERSHIP AND THE AVANT-GARDE

Monica Strauss

> "Why not" is the most potent question an artist can ask himself; in the fabric of aesthetic imperatives holes develop and wait undiscovered until a spirit sufficiently reckless or driven passes through them.
> *John Updike*[1]

In 1910, two events sponsored by two very different men signaled the gradual conquest of Wilhelmine Germany by the avant-garde. In Berlin, Herwarth Walden, the editor of the newly launched weekly *Der Sturm*, decked the front page of the July 10 issue with a drawing by the Austrian artist Oscar Kokoschka.[2] An illustration for the painter's play *Mörder, Hoffnung der Frauen (Murder, Hope of Women)*—which appeared in the inside pages—it depicted a man standing victorious above a nude woman, preparing to stab her. She, in turn, with a last gesture of defiance, grabs for his genitalia with a clawlike hand. The jagged spikes of line that define the figures heighten the sadoerotic tension of the moment and only the woman's breasts hang soft and vulnerable amid the chaotic hatching. Like the drawing, the one-act drama, with two main characters titled merely Man and Woman, was a stark and immediate rendering of the irrational desperation of passion and its destructive bent.

In September of the same year, The New Artists Association, a group of Munich artists led by Wassily Kandinsky, held their second exhibition.[3] The show, which included works by the members as well as guest artists, had a larger international scope than any previous exhibit of Modernist art in Europe. Among the works on view were Cubist paintings by Picasso,

179

Braque, and Le Fauconnier, Cubist-influenced canvases from Russia, and Kandinsky's nearly abstract *Compositions* and *Improvisations*. The accompanying catalog, edited by Kandinsky, included essays by the French artists Odilon Redon and Le Fauconnier, the Russian contributors David and Vladimir Burliuk, and Kandinsky himself.

Disdain and derision were the result on both occasions. *Der Sturm*, which had only been in existence for a few months, lost subscribers and, as a sign of official disapproval, was banned from sale at railway stations.[4] The New Artists Association Show, besides being declared the work of artists who were "incurably insane," was vilified for its cosmopolitanism.[5] As Kandinsky himself recalled, "The press demanded an immediate closing of this anarchist exhibition composed of foreigners dangerous to ancient Bavarian culture. They emphasized that the Russian artists were especially dangerous. Dostoevsky with his 'all is permitted.' "[6]

Both manifestations challenged traditional German ideas about the function of art. *Mörder, Hoffnung der Frauen*, as drawing and play, was deliberately subversive in content and style.[7] In depicting primitive sexual fantasies, it forced the viewer to confront hostilities that lay unacknowledged below the surface of bourgeois life. Kokoschka was not the first German-speaking painter or writer to point out the restrictive and damaging nature of Victorian sexual attitudes, but he went beyond his predecessors in turning his back on both the Western literary and visual tradition simultaneously.[8] The drawing, with its awkward lines and exaggerated anatomical distortions, revealed the expressive limitations inherent in classical depictions of the nude; the play, with its inarticulate archetypal figures locked in graphic but unexplained conflict, exposed the distancing effect of traditional character development, motivation, and allusive prose.

The same revolution in style—sometimes linked to content, sometimes separate from it—characterized the work exhibited at the New Artists Association Show. There, art's traditional mimetic function—as an imitation of nature—was under siege. In the case of the Cubists, it involved a translation of the real world into a newly devised formal language. To those experimenting with abstraction, like Kandinsky, the real world was becoming less and less important as the original source of inspiration. As Kandinsky put it, ". . . nature and art are essentially, organically, and, by universal law, different from each other . . ."[9] In either case, the spectator, reared on the naturalistic images characteristic of Western art since the Renaissance, came away confused and disturbed.

The creative breakthrough that occurs when an artist questions the limitations of his medium is, in itself, a private act. When performed in the avant-garde context, however, when the artist is conquering territory as yet unacknowledged by the culture, it implies a public process—the proselytizing and publicizing that will finally lead a reluctant audience to recognize the artist's contributions. This is the arena of cultural leadership.

Sometimes the artist himself, but more often writers, impresarios, buyers, and museum directors take on the the job of "raising the consciousness" of the public by offering the avant-garde critical support, opportunities for exposure, and patronage in the face of social hostility.[10]

THE ARTIST AND THE PUBLIC:
THE REVOLUTION OF THE
NINETEENTH CENTURY

Conflict between the artist and his public, an essential condition for the emergence of cultural leadership, played no major role in the visual arts before the nineteenth century. Until then, most artists were entirely integrated in society, worked on commission, and interpreted the religious, political, and social visions of the ruling elite of church and state.[11] Although by the eighteenth century the artist's status had been elevated from that of the medieval craftsman taught in a workshop to handle the tools of his trade, to a "fine artist"[12] who received both a theoretical and practical education in a state-supported academy, he remained a professional trained to render specific services to his society.

The patrons decided what was to be done and who was to do it. When these choices were inspired, as they were in some of the greatest monuments in the history of Western art—the Parthenon, the Abbey of Saint-Denis, the Sistine Chapel—the fusion of a patron's vision with an artist's gifts led to crucial creative breakthroughs.

All this changed after the political and social upheavals of the French Revolution. The new ruling classes, predominantly bourgeois, did not inherit the tradition of patronage, were not confident in their choices, and preferred the reworking of formulas from the past to new responses to the vast social changes of the present.[13] No longer called upon to interpret the ideas of the religious and political sectors, the artist lost his traditional place in society. Once an essential professional with a predictable future, he now became an outsider whose commitment to his métier demanded a high level of dedication and a large element of risk. Forced to make an asset of his precarious position, he embraced the Romantic concept of the artist as "genius," presenting himself as free of all social and theoretical restraints by virtue of his superior gifts.[14] At the same time, artists began to cultivate an adversary stance with regard to society, deliberately baiting the bourgeois with a bohemian life style and a commitment to revolutionary politics.[15]

In truth, art had become a private act, but it was not until the 1860s, with the first experiments of Manet and the Impressionists, that the full implications of this new situation were realized. Their paintings, focusing almost entirely on their immediate experiences, made no overt claim to any larger significance. Depictions of urban crowds, the demimonde, domestic life—all done in a style that emphasized the transient nature of the subjects—were jeered at by a populace used to outworn historical formulas.[16] This gap of comprehension between innovative artists and the public at large was to mark the progress of modern art for the next hundred years. By the twentieth century, it had given rise to the concept of the avant-garde artist moving aggressively forward into areas as yet unthought of or imagined by "official culture."[17]

If avant-garde attitudes had their sources in the battle for recognition led by the Impressionists, modernism—that is, the final break with the mimetic tradition of Western painting—had its roots in the experiments of the next generation. In Post-Impressionist painting, which flourished between 1870 and 1900, explorations of the formal and expressive possibilities of space, color, and line began to change the relationship between art and reality. The motif in a Cézanne still life, for instance, represented both the object observed and the intellectual struggle involved in transferring it to a two-dimensional canvas. The unruly details of nature in a Seurat landscape became part of a system of uniform brushstrokes designed to conform to current optical theories. The brilliant hues, flattened perspectives, and harsh contours used by Van Gogh and Gauguin conveyed subjective rather than objective responses to their subjects. As Van Gogh wrote in one of his eloquent letters to his brother Theo, ". . . instead of trying to reproduce exactly what I see before my eyes, I use color more arbitrarily in order to express myself forcibly."[18]

MODERNISM AND CULTURAL LEADERSHIP IN GERMANY

The earliest Modernist styles—Cubism and Fauvism in France, Expressionism in Germany—emerged in the first decade of the twentieth century. In France, the formal concerns of picture making took precedence over subject matter. Cézanne's attempt to reconcile the three-dimensional object with the two-dimensional surface led to the fragmentation of the object itself in Cubism. Seurat and Gauguin's arbitrary use of color inspired the artificial hues that dominated the Fauve's portraits, landscapes, and interiors. In Germany, Van Gogh and Gauguin's expressive color and distortion of form were the key sources for styles that conveyed a new disaffection of the artist from society. Kokoschka's brazen display of his erotic fears and fantasies or Kandinsky's iconoclastic flights from an increasingly unstable world into abstraction were precisely such expressions.

Resistance to Modernism was harsher, more widespread, more socially and politically oriented in Germany than in France.[19] There were several reasons for this. The separation between the artist and the public, which began in earnest in France in the 1860s with the revolution in style and content launched by the Impressionists, had only begun to have an impact in Germany in the 1890s. Thus the entire development from Impressionism to Modernism was telescoped into a far shorter period and gave the public far less time to adjust.

In addition, since German Modernism had its roots in the French nineteenth-century experiments, it presented a serious threat to German cultural chauvinism. A great many artists and critics still viewed art as an expression of national character. As a result, reviewers of avant-garde exhibits often spent more time casting aspersions on the nationalities of the painters, or the foreign influences upon them, than on the paintings themselves. This nationalist bias transformed essentially aesthetic issues into political ones.

The situation was further exacerbated by a form of Modernism that carried with it an agenda of social transformation. The first German Modernists, for instance, the members of the Dresden *Brücke* (Bridge), although conducting the same kinds of formal experiments as the Fauves in France, did not maintain the same neutrality with regard to their motifs.[20] They depicted their bohemian pursuits (*la vie bohemienne* was a new phenomenon in the German art world) with a youthful exuberance designed to shake up the bourgeoisie. Their revolutionary intent was confirmed in a manifesto published in 1906: "As youth we carry the future and want to create for ourselves freedom of life and of movement against long-established older forces."[21]

The Munich avant-garde also conceived of art as a regenerating force. Franz Marc, one of the leaders of the *Blaue Reiter* (Blue Rider) group, asserted that all the formal experiments of Modernism—Cubism, Fauvism, and so forth—were only surface phenomena veiling a new spiritual content. The function of the modern artist, he insisted, was to create "symbols that belong on the altar of the spiritual religion of the future."[22]

This aestheticization of political and social unrest inspired a different form of cultural leadership in Germany than in France. In the latter country, partisans of Modernism were only called upon to argue for the validity of its formal experiments. In the former, supporters of the new movement shared a vision of art as a socially transforming act.

This was certainly true of the editor Herwarth Walden and the painter Wassily Kandinsky, the two most active supporters of Modernism when it first appeared in Germany. The motivating force behind Walden's passionate defense of modern culture was a desire to shock, to provoke, to goad the hidebound middle classes of Wilhelmine Germany. The impetus for Kandinsky's multifarious activities as a promoter of the international avant-garde was his faith in art as a vehicle of spiritual rebirth. Initially working in separate spheres—Kandinsky in Munich, Walden in Berlin—it was their collaboration after 1912 that proved to be the turning point for the acceptance of the avant-garde in Germany.

The comparative study that follows of the motivations, methods, and achievements of these two men is intended to explore several questions regarding leadership and the avant-garde. What kind of individuals, for instance, take it upon themselves to defend and support artists who function beyond the pale of cultural expectations? What are the qualities required for this kind of risk taking? Is the insider—in this case, Kandinsky—more effective than the outsider? Is there a relationship between the intensity of the individual's commitment to cultural leadership and his concern for social transformation? How does the political environment affect the style of cultural leadership? In the post-Modernist age, when the avant-garde and, indeed, almost any cultural extreme, is beginning to partake of the norm, what can cultural leadership achieve?

HERWARTH WALDEN
AND *DER STURM*

Herwarth Walden, whose original name was Georg Lewin, was born into a middle-class Jewish family in Berlin in 1878. A talented pianist, he resisted his father's attempts to direct him to a more stable profession and finally won permission to attend the Berlin Conservatory.[23] In 1901 he married the poet Else Lasker-Schüler, a woman ten years his senior. Although she was born into an eminent Jewish family in the Rhineland, Lasker-Schüler was a hippie *avant la lettre*. Styling herself the Prince of Thebes or Tino of Baghdad, she went about in oriental garb and wrote lyrical visonary poetry in a gloriously supple German. As a member of a group of young poets advocating radical social and cultural reforms, she put Walden in touch with Berlin's literary avant-garde.[24] Inspired by their fervor, Walden turned his back on his career as a musician and began to function as an impresario and publicist for young authors and composers. Within a few years he had founded the *Verein für Kunst*, a club which sponsored readings and discussions of works-in-progress by both established and experimental writers, published over fifty opera guides, and served as coeditor of a book on Richard Strauss's tone poems.[25]

Like many cultural propagandists, Walden finally found his niche in journalism. By 1908, he was a major contributor to several cultural periodicals and serving as editor of *Der Neue Weg*, a theatrical publication. When, a year later, he was dismissed from this position for publishing the works of August Strindberg and René Schickele, he had such a considerable reputation as a literary connoisseur and impresario that leading German intellectuals, including Max Brod, Elizabeth Forster-Nietzche, and Strindberg himself, sprang to his defense.[26]

Among Walden's supporters on this occasion was the Viennese editor Karl Kraus, a brilliant polemicist and satirist, whose biweekly *Die Fackel* (*The Torch*), was dedicated to exposing the hypocrisy of Viennese language and culture. *Die Fackel* had a wide-ranging influence on German intellectuals from Prague to Vienna, and Walden was no exception.[27] Eager to function as Berlin's cultural gadfly in the same capacity as Kraus, Walden suggested to the Viennese editor that the time had come for a Berlin version of *Die Fackel*. Kraus agreed to subsidize such a venture and the new paper was promptly baptized *Der Sturm* by Lasker-Schüler.[28] Like its Viennese prototype, *Der Sturm* was to publish original poetry and prose by contemporary writers, literary, music, and drama criticism, and biting commentaries by the editor on the press.

As far as the visual arts were concerned, Walden followed Kraus's example and published the writings of the Viennese architect Adolf Loos. Loos, a reformer more than a critic, lashed out at the breaking down of boundaries between fine and applied art, artist and artisan. In his book *Ornament and Crime,* he objected strenuously to the ornate decoration of objects intended for everyday use.[29] Walden's first polemical thrusts in the area of art followed Loos's lead. A series of reproductions of vulgarly decorated theater programs appeared in *Der Sturm,* accompanied by the following sarcastic explanation:

> I fear that one never gets a good enough look at the wonderful cover illustrations with which theater directors decorate their programs, illustrations which have an even greater value now that the prices have increased. I want to bring these modest creations of the artist's hand out of the darkness of the theater into the light of day at last, so that we can be made aware of how close the connections are between our theater and our art.[30]

Kraus was also instrumental in sending Oscar Kokoschka to join the staff of *Der Sturm* after the Vienna performance of *Mörder, Hoffnung der Frauen* had made the artist persona non grata in his native city.[31] Kokoschka worked in partnership with Walden for almost a year and was responsible for bringing about the most fruitful of *Der Sturm's* journalistic innovations: the publication of original graphics. It was the uproar that greeted the macabre, erotic drawings for Kokoschka's play that convinced Walden that avant-garde art might be the most powerful weapon at hand for rousing the ire and gaining the attention of the culturally conservative middle class. From then on Kokoschka's drawings—usually of erotically charged subjects—became a regular feature.

Kraus's influence was on the wane by the second half of 1910 and Walden began to take a closer look at developments in his immediate surroundings. By that time, avant-garde art had become a hot issue in Berlin. The initial exhibit of the New Secession, an artist's organization formed in protest against the growing conservatism of the once liberal Berlin Secession, provided Berliners with their first view of the brash, erotic, primitivizing graphics and paintings of the Dresden *Brücke*.[32] The reaction of the press was hostile in the extreme. One called their work "scribbles,"[33] another suggested that the rejection by the Berlin Secession had not been unjustified.[34] Walden, dismayed by the press's crude condemnation, rallied to the artists' side. He noted the connection of these painters to contemporary movements in France,[35] and backed his critical approval by commissioning illustrations for *Der Sturm* from the participants.[36]

Supportive and analytical reviews continued to appear in *Der Sturm* throughout 1911 as the conflict over the modern movement spread across Germany. Important shows in Düsseldorf and Berlin,[37] featuring the French and German avant-garde, sparked local responses that were both hostile and nationalistic. The "sinful atmosphere" of paintings depicting "naked ladies in gaudy, cannibal-like colors," was attributed to the international connections of the artists.

> The word *Brücke* probably indicates a connection between French and German painters. Most of the exhibited works belong to the new French trends brought in last year . . . by Russians settled in Munich.[38]

How unsettling this "French invasion" really was, was brought home by the last concerted effort of conservative painters to halt the process. They joined forces to publish the *Protest Deutsche Künstler (German Artist's Protest)*, arguing that the integrity of German art was imperiled by French and French-influenced artists.[39] *Der Sturm* stood firmly with those who opposed these chauvinist tactics by printing an excerpt from the counter-statement prepared by the more enlightened sector of the art establishment.[40]

By 1912, Walden had made a certain mark in the German art world. He had commissioned important works of graphic art from young painters in Vienna and Berlin, he had exercised an increasingly vituperative pen against those who questioned the premises of Modernism, and he had pointed out the international scope of the avant-garde to his readers. To celebrate the appearance of the one hundredth issue of *Der Sturm*, Walden decided to plunge in even further and become an exhibitor himself.[41] Renting rooms in a building slated for demolition, he brought two shows to Berlin that he felt the more conservative galleries and exhibition societies would refuse—the debut of the Italian Futurists and the first *Blaue Reiter* exhibition.

The Futurist show, which had appeared earlier in Paris and London, created an international scandal and was labeled an "anarchistic disturbance."[42] It was the ideal event for Walden since it came complete with its own propaganda for the avant-garde and the modern. *The Manifesto of the Futurist Painters*, which Walden published in *Der Sturm* (as well as distributing it on street corners) promoted a new aesthetic approach to modern life.[43] Rejecting the entire artistic tradition of the past, it asserted that the Futurists would only concern themselves with the immediate reality of the urban, industrial present—a reality that was not static but in constant flux and dynamic movement. This dynamism was the subject of the Futurists' paintings—the way images perceived under the influence of light, space, motion, and time are multiplied, deformed, and seen through a network of lines, planes, and irrational perspectives.

The *Blaue Reiter* exhibit, organized by Kandinsky and Franz Marc, and named after an almanac the two artists had edited together, was equally controversial, if less provocative. Like the New Artists Association Show, it was intended to demonstrate the community of interests shared by the international avant-garde. "We do not seek to propagandize a *single*, precise, and special form in this small exhibition, but we aim to show in the *variety* of represented forms how the artist's inner desire results in manifold forms," was the statement that appeared on the front page of the catalog.[44] Included in the show were some of the first abstract and near-abstract paintings yet seen in Berlin.

WASSILY KANDINSKY
IN MUNICH, 1901-1912

Kandinsky was a man of a very different stamp from Walden. Born in Moscow in 1886, he spent the first ten years of his adult life working as a successful lawyer and economist in Russia. Although painting always attracted him, he did not embark on a career as an artist until, at the age of thirty, he declined the offer of a professorship at the University of Dorpat in Estonia and moved to Munich to study art. The sense of vocation that germinated slowly during his early years in Russia, and gave him the strength to turn his back on a promising opportunity in his native country, informed his life.[45] His commitment to art depended upon more than a passionate inclination. It involved a growing conviction that art had something essential to contribute—that it was a spiritual expression conveying more about the world than anything offered by pure intellectual activity. In fact, as Kandinsky described in his autobiography, the splitting of the atom removed the last shred of faith he had in the efficacy of science and freed him to study art.

> The crumbling of the atom was to my soul like the crumbling of the whole world. Suddenly the heaviest walls toppled. Everything became uncertain, tottering, and weak. . . . Science seemed to me destroyed. . . . [46]

This distrust of the material world was a key factor in Kandinsky's intense intellectual commitment to abstraction. An extraordinary synesthetic capacity to experience music as color had convinced him at a very early stage that art, like music, could function as pure form.

> Today the artist cannot progress exclusively with purely abstract forms, as these forms are not sufficiently precise. Limiting oneself to the unprecise deprives one of possibilities, excludes the purely human and, therefore, weakens the power of expression.[47]

By 1911, however, he felt he had achieved that precision and began to paint purely abstract works.[48] His demonstration of the expressive possibilities of pure line and color made him one of the greatest innovators of twentieth-century art. But long before his creative breakthrough, he had begun to function as a leader—as active in the public sphere of the avant-garde as in the private.

As early as 1901, at the very start of his career in Munich, Kandinsky began to organize societies for his fellow artists.[49] They provided opportunities for the young and unknown to exhibit, and displayed the works of artists that could not be seen elsewhere in Munich. *The Phalanx*, which was the first of Kandinsky's organizations, functioned from 1901 to 1904 and presented exhibits of works by Monet, Signac, Toulouse-Lautrec, and Valloton.

To make himself familiar with avant-garde art all over Europe, Kandinsky spent the years from 1904-1908 traveling in Russia, Italy, Holland, Germany, and France. He resumed his activities as an impresario when he returned to Munich in 1909. Totally free of the nationalist bias that still dominated the art establishment in Germany, he was now determined to demonstrate the international character of the avant-garde. The organization he headed this time—The New Artists Association—included Russian, French, and German painters. Their second exhibition, which included contributions from artists all over Europe, was a pacesetter. It provided the precedent for the great international exhibitions of 1912 and 1913—the New York Armory show, the Düsseldorf Sonderbund Exhibition, and the Berlin First German Autumn Salon (sponsored by *Der Sturm*)—that represented the culmination of avant-garde activity before World War I.[50]

When in 1911, the less liberal members of The New Artists Association protested against the growing abstraction of Kandinsky's paintings, he withdrew and began a third association together with Franz Marc.[51] Under the name *Der Blaue Reiter*, it sponsored the exhibition that Walden eventually brought to Berlin.

During these hectic years Kandinsky also proselytized for the avant-garde by sending critical articles and reviews to Russian newspapers and periodicals, editing catalogs, and writing books. His most important work, *On the Spiritual in Art,* provided the theoretical background for his commitment to abstraction. Completed by 1910, it did not find a publisher for two years. Franz Marc finally convinced Reinhold Piper to take the book on, but even Marc's assurance that Kandinsky was "a true prophet, the nucleus of the modern movement in Munich" did not arouse total enthusiasm in the Munich publisher. "I was not exactly delighted by this abstract art," Piper later wrote in his autobiography.[52] He hedged his bet by insisting that the author pay half the expenses of the first edition of one thousand copies. The book sold well, however, and Piper willingly funded the next three printings of one thousand copies each.[53]

Kandinsky's second major literary effort was the *Blaue Reiter Almanac,* which he edited together with Marc. The book was designed to break down the barriers between artists, between creative disciplines, and, above all, between academic art and other forms of visual expression.[54] To support this ecumenical vision, there were fourteen essays by artists, musicians, and critics from France, Russia, and Germany; poetry and quotations; a version of Kandinsky's experimental play *The Yellow Sound;* and three musical scores by Schönberg, Webern, and Berg. Unifying this brilliantly eclectic selection were carefully ordered sequences of illustrations that juxtaposed primitive art with modern masters, Russian folk prints against childrens' drawings, and so forth. As Kandinsky indicated, they served as the linking leitmotiv:

> If the reader of this book is able to lay aside his wishes, his thoughts, his feelings for a while and then leaf through this book and go from a votive image to a Delaunay print, and further from a Cézanne to a Russian folk print, from a mask to a Picasso, from a picture on glass to a Kubin and so on, his soul will tremble and enter then into the world of art.[55]

The first edition of 1260 copies had a cover designed in three colors by Kandinsky, 142 illustrations (four hand-colored), and initials and vignettes contributed by Marc and Hans Arp. By 1914, it had sold out and a second edition of 1000 copies was issued with two new prefaces, an additional plate for a Rousseau self-portrait, and a different woodcut by Marc.[56]

COLLABORATION: 1912-1914

Thus in 1912, when Walden and Kandinsky came into contact as a result of the *Blaue Reiter* exhibition in Berlin, they had much in common. They had functioned as writers, editors, and impresarios; they shared a vision of culture that transcended the boundaries between creative disciplines;

they subscribed to the idea of an international community of artists. Walden, already an admirer of Kandinsky, realized that the artist's contacts with the avant-garde would be of inestimable value to his newly assumed role as an exhibitor and promoter. Kandinsky, on his part, needed someone of Walden's stamp to do battle for him. Clearly Walden would be no ordinary art dealer. His superb managerial and polemic talents, and his personal dedication to the arts, would serve Kandinsky's cause.

Despite his amazing enterprise and initiative, Kandinsky had not achieved public acceptance on a large scale. His artistic experiments were still perceived as extremely radical and he was confronted by the harshest criticism in the press. In addition, he had not yet found a gallery or a publisher willing to give him an active commitment. The meeting with Walden could not have been more opportune. The artist put his publishing and exhibiting activities behind him and began to work with the Berlin editor. Permanent quarters were hired for a *Sturm* gallery and the first show there—a display of French graphics—represented a selection from the second and final *Blaue Reiter* show.[57]

For Kandinsky, personally, the most important achievement of their collaboration was the organization of his first retrospective in 1912 and its subsequent extensive distribution. Walden went to great lengths to promote the exhibition and it traveled throughout Germany, and into Belgium, Holland, and Central Europe during the next few years.[58] When a particularly harsh review of the show appeared in the *Hamburger Fremdenblatt* in February 1913, Walden dedicated a special issue of *Der Sturm* to an organized protest against such irresponsible criticism.[59] Signed by many of the luminaries of the international avant-garde, it brought to light the extent of public support for the artist.[60]

Perhaps the most interesting of Walden's projects for Kandinsky was the publication of the monograph *Kandinsky 1901-1913*.[61] It included a poem dedicated to Kandinsky by the Dutch poet Albert Verwey, over sixty reproductions of the artist's work, Kandinsky's brilliant autobiographical essay *Rückblicke (Reminiscences)*, and a series of "notes," in which Kandinsky described the creative process behind three of his paintings.[62]

Through his connections with Kandinsky and the Futurists, Walden had access to artists all over Europe. The visual and written material they contributed to his paper transformed *Der Sturm* from a local phenomenon—at least in the realm of the visual arts—to a journal of international consequence. Between 1912 and 1914, Walden published the *Futurist Manifesto, The Manifesto of the Futurist Painters*, selections from Kandinsky's *On the Spiritual in Art*, Apollinaire's discussions of Cubism, Robert Delaunay's presentation of his concept of simultaneity, and Léger's definition of Cubist abstraction.[63] The original woodcuts, linoleum blocks, and drawings featured on the front page included works by Picasso, Marc, Macke, Campendonk, Klee, Severini, and Arp, among others.

In the *Sturm* gallery during these years members of the original *Blaue Reiter* group—Macke, Marc, Klee, Münter, and Capendonk—were given one-man shows, while foreign artists such as Ensor, Archipenko, Chagall, the Czech Cubists, Gleizes, Metzinger, and Duchamp-Villon made their German debuts. Walden also sponsored traveling shows, sending exhibitions as far as New York and Tokyo.[64]

In the first issue of *Der Sturm's* fourth year of publication, Walden announced his intention of holding a great international exhibition.[65] Called the First German Autumn Salon after the annual *Salon d'Automne* held in Paris, this show was also the result of Walden's collaboration with Kandinsky and the original members of the *Blaue Reiter* group. The idea for such an event had originated with the Cassirer gallery, a conservative organization eager to catch up on current trends. The *Blaue Reiter* artists, however, rejected Cassirer's peace offering and decided that such a show could only be mounted under the auspices of *Der Sturm*.[66] The First German Autumn Salon opened in September 1913, with contributions from Russia, Czechoslavakia, France, Italy, Germany, Switzerland, and the United States.[67] It was the last great international exhibition in Germany prior to the Great War and demonstrated the extent of Kandinsky and Walden's international network. Many of the young artists shown were to be the leaders of the postwar generation.[68]

In his introduction to the Autumn Salon catalog, Walden trumpeted the triumph of Modernist aesthetics and his own leadership role.

> The *First German Autumn Salon* provides an overview of the new movement, an overview that is intended to expand the awareness of our contemporaries. Our contemporaries have still not learned to see properly. . . . They ask art to reflect their own impressions, yet these impressions are not even genuinely theirs. Being an artist means having one's own perceptions and being able to depict them.
> I am sure that both the uninitiated in art, and the part of the public that, with no right to do so, considers itself artistic, will laugh at this exhibition and at me. I would particularly like to warn these ladies and gentlemen . . . that when Oscar Kokoschka's graphics were published during the first year of *Der Sturm*, connoisseurs and even respected critics laughed at them. Today, three years later, people compete for these derided graphics.[69]

With the outbreak of World War I, the first phase of the avant-garde in Germany came to an end. The German artists left for the front, relations between France and Germany were broken, and Kandinsky went home to Russia. Forced to relinquish his foreign connections, Walden had to create a milieu of his own. He did so with a vengeance. *Der Sturm* became a conglomerate—a *Sturm* theater was founded, and a *Sturm* school. *Sturm* evenings were set up to provide weekly cultural diversions and a *Sturm* publishing house was established to publish artist's monographs and the work of Walden and his friends. Soon enough all the creative people associated with Walden began to be called *Sturm* artists and *Sturm* poets.[70] The gallery continued to show works from Walden's own international collection as well as offering exhibitions to young artists whom Walden now had to discover on his own. Unfortunately, these additions to the roster—primarily minor artists—made clear how dependent Walden had been on his connections with *Der Blaue Reiter* and the international avant-garde for his choice of exhibitors. Now friendship and degree of intimacy appeared to color his judgments, so that by the end of the war the international enterprise of the prewar years had dwindled into a clique with its own limited vocabulary, frame of reference, and conviction of self-importance. In 1920 Walden was assessed by a contemporary:

> Critic, artist, prophet and businessman—that is too much for one individual. But isn't there incredible energy behind the enterprise? I think so! Only one must reproach him for one thing. That in searching for substitutes for Archipenko and Kandinsky, he discovers types like Bauer and Wauer.[71]

With the end of the war, other galleries picked up where Walden had left off, and although the *Sturm* gallery did present some interesting new postwar artists—Kurt Schwitters, for instance—it could no longer consider itself alone in the forefront of the avant-garde.[72] Indeed, through Walden's efforts before the war, artists now had their choice of several galleries to exhibit with, and if many of those who had been encouraged by Walden turned to other affiliations, it may have been the result of the somewhat stifling atmosphere of the *Sturm* clique.

These developments gradually led Walden to lose interest in his role in the art world. Like so many German intellectuals of his generation, his passion for culture was radicalized by World War I and the social revolution that followed. He became an ardent Communist in the twenties, moved to Russia in 1932, and perished in a Russian labor camp in 1941.[73] Kandinsky, on the other hand, continued to function as a leader in the art. In Russia, between 1915 and 1921, he was an active participant in the artistic experiments sponsored by the revolutionary gvernment; in Germany, between 1922 and 1933, he was a leading figure in that utopian institution the *Bauhaus;* and in Paris, during the last decade of his life—1933-42—he had considerable influence on a new generation of abstractionists.[74] His faith in art as an activity of social consequence never ceased.

CULTURAL LEADERSHIP AND THE AVANT-GARDE

As individuals, Walden and Kandinsky shared certain characteristics. They had both rebelled against the expectations of their middle-class upbringing. Walden, the son of a doctor, had to fight to become a pianist instead of the book dealer his father intended him to be. Kandinsky, after a long period of indecision, turned his back on a flourishing career as a lawyer and economist to become a painter. This freed them from the conservative expectations of their class and family backgrounds. Both men were outsiders in the culture they inhabited—Walden as a Jew, Kandinsky as a Russian. As a result they had less to lose in taking an adversary stance. Both Walden and Kandinsky began their careers with an almost messianic faith in their own visions of cultural progress. Almost immediately they took on the role of entrepreneur—Kandinsky as organizer of *The Phalanx*, Walden as the founder of the *Verein für Kunst*. Both were able to bring to bear the verbal facility, organizational talent, and energetic commitment required for the success of initially unpopular enterprises.

And yet there were distinct differences in their styles of leadership. Walden was the classic rebel—more interested in the act of provocation than in the ultimate goal. Indeed, once the goal was in sight—the acceptance of Modernism in the 1920s—he switched to another radical cause and was no longer of any consequence in the art world. A close examination of the content of *Der Sturm* during the crucial years 1910-14 already points to this weakness. Although Walden eagerly published the statements and manifestos of the various Modernist groups, he often failed to distinguish between them, revealing a certain ignorance of the issues involved. In the end, he lumped all of Modernism under the term *Expressionism* and contributed to the semantic confusion that dogs the term to this day.[75]

The artists themselves did not trust him fully. Paul Klee's description of Walden suggests their ambivalence:

> He lives off cigarettes and runs around giving orders like a general. He is someone special but something is missing. He doesn't really love the pictures. He just smells something in them. . . .[76]

Franz Marc, who worked more closely with Walden, was more perceptive regarding his motivation. In a letter he compares Walden with the art dealer Paul Cassirer: "With Cassirer, it's only business, for Walden there can be no doubt that delight plays a role."[77]

Walden was the product of a particular time, a particular environment. He was challenged by more than the Germans' deep cultural conservatism, their resistance to the international character of Modernism, and the nonmimetic implications of Modernist styles. He believed that if the public could be brought to accept the revolution in art, it would be open to social reformation as well. He was not alone in this delusion. Until the Russian Revolution in 1917, many German intellectuals put their faith in culture rather than politics as an instrument of social change. It took the madness of the Great War and the success of the Bolshevik experiment to convince them that their ideas for reform really belonged in the political arena.

Kandinsky, on the other hand, as an artist himself, had a deeper and more knowledgeable commitment to the cause and never wavered from it. He was in the forefront of the Modernist movement until the end of his life and exercised an extraordinary influence on several generations of artists as painter, teacher, writer, and individual of great personal integrity. In 1917, the DaDa impresario Hugo Ball recalled his impressions of Kandinsky before the war:

> At that time Munich was host to an artist who, by his mere presence, placed this city far above all other German cities in its modernity—Wassily Kandinsky. . . . He was concerned with the regeneration of society through the union of all artistic mediums and forces. . . . His aim was to be exemplary in every single statement, to break through convention and to prove that the world was as young as on the day of creation.[78]

Does this mean that Kandinsky, "the insider," was a more effective cultural leader? In the long run, yes. His influence was felt by several generations of artists, while Walden's soon waned. Nevertheless, in the years between 1900 and 1914, when the battle for Modernism was first joined, both were equally influential. Walden's brilliant polemical fervor, precisely because it was that of an "outsider," added to the credibility of the cause. Together, they mounted the daring exhibitions, launched the polemical attacks, and produced the series of unique publications—the *Blaue Reiter Almanac, On the Spiritual in Art,* the Kandinsky monograph, and *Der Sturm* itself—that aroused and informed a hostile public.

Can the successful cultural leadership of these two men be applied to our situation in the post-Modernist age? Experimental artists and the moneyed classes are clearly no longer adversaries. Indeed, since the 1960s, they have even become bedfellows, if somewhat uneasy ones. This does not mean that no barriers remain between practitioners of modern art and the ordinary layman. But there is no longer the illusion that the breaking down of these barriers will serve a useful social function. Artists, critics, impresarios, foundations, and museums now address themselves primarily to an assured constituency. It would appear that only when art is perceived as socially or politically transforming—that is, as pertaining to society as a whole—does it inspire the intense and all-encompassing concern to raise the public consciousness that marked the cultural leadership of Herwarth Walden and Wassily Kandinsky in the early part of this century.

NOTES

1. John Updike, "Gaiety in the Galleries," review of Peter Gay, *Art and Act, The New Yorker,* February 12, 1977, p. 124.
2. *Der Sturm,* I (July 1910).

3. Peter Selz, *German Expressionist Painting* (Berkeley and Los Angeles: University of California Press, 1957), p. 193.

4. Nell Walden, *Herwarth Walden* (Mainz: Florian Kupferberg, 1963), p. 10.

5. *Münchener Neueste Nachrichten*, September 10, 1910. Quoted in Alois Schardt, *Franz Marc* (Berlin: Rembrandt, 1936), p. 70.

6. Wassily Kandinsky, "Franz Marc," *Cahiers d'Art*, XI (1936), p. 273.

7. For an interesting discussion of the play *see* Carl E. Schorske, *Fin-de-Siècle Vienna* (New York: Alfred A. Knopf, 1980), pp. 335–38.

8. Frank Wedekind was an important forerunner.

9. Wassily Kandinsky, "Reminiscences," in Robert L. Herbert, ed., *Modern Artists on Art* (Englewood Cliffs, N.J.: Prentice-Hall, 1980), p. 23.

10. By making this distinction between the private and public aspects of the creative act, it is possible to distinguish artists who are great innovators—Picasso, for instance—from those who are also leaders like Kandinsky.

11. *See* Rudolf and Margot Wittkower, *Born Under Saturn* (New York: W.W. Norton & Co., 1963), passim.

12. Albert E. Elsen, *Purposes of Art* (New York: Holt, Rinehart & Winston, 1971), p. 15.

13. E. J. Hobsbawm, *The Age of Revolution* (New York and Scarborough, Ontario: New American Library, 1962), p. 308; George Heard Hamilton, *Manet and His Critics* (New York: W.W. Norton & Co., 1969), p. 1.

14. Hobsbawm, Ibid.

15. Hugh Honour, *Romanticism* (New York, Hagerstown, San Francisco, London: Harper & Row, 1979), pp. 245–75.

16. John Rewald, *The History of Impressionism* (New York: Museum of Modern Art, 1946), passim.

17. Renato Poggioli, *The Theory of the Avant-Garde* (New York: Harvard University Press, 1971), passim; Roger Shattuck, *The Banquet Years* (New York: Random House, 1955), pp. 24–25.

18. Letter to Theo, August 1888, quoted in Herschel B. Chipp, *Theories of Modern Art* (Berkeley, Los Angeles, and London: University of California Press, 1971), p. 34.

19. Peter Paret, *The Berlin Secession, Modernism and Its Enemies in Imperial Germany* (Cambridge and London: Harvard University Press, 1980), passim.

20. Gerd Schiff, "Arcadia and Human Wasteland," *College Art Journal*, 41 (Spring 1981), pp. 64–69.

21. Selz, *German Expressionist Painting*, p. 95.

22. Wassily Kandinsky and Franz Marc, *Der Blaue Reiter*, new documented edition, ed. Klaus Lankheit (Munich: R. Piper, 1967), p. 31.

23. Walden, *Herwarth Walden*, p. 67.

24. Frederic V. Grunfeld, *Prophets Without Honor* (New York: McGraw-Hill, 1979, 1980), pp. 96–145.

25. Walden, *Herwarth Walden*, pp. 68–69.

26. Genossenschaft Deutscher Bühnenangehöriger, *Ein Protest in Sachen Herwarth Walden* (Berlin: Verlag der Druckerei für Bibliophilen, 1909).

27. For a discussion of Kraus's influence *see* Allan Janik and Stephen Toulmin, *Wittgenstein's Vienna* (New York: Simon & Schuster, 1973), pp. 67–91.

28. Oscar Kokoschka, *Mein Leben* (Munich: F. Bruckmann, 1971), p. 107. Lothar Schreyer, *Erinnerungen an Sturm und Bauhaus* (Munich: List Verlag, 1966), p. 8.

29. Janik and Toulmin, *Wittgenstein's Vienna*, pp. 93–102.

30. *Der Sturm*, I (April 1910).

31. Kokoschka, *Mein Leben*, p. 107.

32. Paret, *The Berlin Secession, Modernism and Its Enemies in Imperial Germany*, p. 210.
33. *Cicerone*, II, no. 19 (October 1910), p. 653.
34. *Kunst und Künstler*, 8 (1909-10), p. 524.
35. *Der Sturm*, I (June 1910).
36. Throughout 1911 most of the drawings and woodcuts that appeared on the front page of *Der Sturm* were designed by *Brücke* artists. These included works by Pechstein, Nolde, Heckel, Schmidt-Rotluff, and Kirchner.
37. The Sonderbund show, Düsseldorf, 1911, *see* Selz, *German Expressionist Painting*, p. 241; Berlin Secession, Spring 1911, Ibid., p. 256; New Secession, Spring 1911, Ibid., p. 194.
38. A review in *Die Kölnische Zeitung* quoted by Walden, *Der Sturm*, II (April 1911).
39. Carl Vinnen, *Ein Protest deutscher Künstler* (Jena: Diederichs, 1911).
40. *Der Sturm*, II (August 1911).
41. Nell Walden and Lothar Schreyer, *Der Sturm* (Baden-Baden: Woldmar Klein, 1954), p. 11.
42. *Kunst und Künstler*, 10 (1911-12), p. 308.
43. *Der Sturm*, II (March 1912).
44. Selz, *German Expressionist Painting*, p. 206.
45. Will Grohmann, *Wassily Kandinsky: Life and Work* (New York: Abrams, 1958), passim.
46. Kandinsky, "Reminiscences," p. 27.
47. Wassily Kandinsky, *On the Spiritual in Art*, trans. and introduction by Michael T.H. Sadler (New York: Dover Publications, 1977), p. 30.
48. Selz, *German Expressionist Painting*, pp. 203–05.
49. For a comprehensive chronology of Kandinsky's activities between 1901 and 1912, *see* Peg Weiss, *Kandinsky in Munich, 1896-1914*, exh. cat., Solomon R. Guggenheim Museum, New York, 1982, pp. 303–06.
50. Selz, *German Expressionist Painting*, p. 193.
51. Ibid.
52. Reinhard Piper, *Briefwechsel mit Autoren und Künstlern, 1903-1954* (Munich: R. Piper, 1979).
53. Reinhard Piper, *Mein Leben als Verleger* (Munich: R. Piper, 1964), p. 299.
54. Kandinsky and Marc, *Der Blaue Reiter*.
55. Ibid., p. 180.
56. Orrel P. Reed, Jr., *German Expressionist Art, The Robert Gore Rifkind Collection*, exh. cat., Frederick S. Wight Art Gallery, University of California, Los Angeles, 1977, p. 107.
57. Donald E. Gordon, *Modern Art Exhibitions, 1900-1916* (Munich: Prestel, 1974), p. 550.
58. Walden and Schreyer, *Der Sturm*, pp. 257–63.
59. *Der Sturm*, III (March, April 1913).
60. Apollinaire, Hans Arp, Marinetti, and Sonia Delaunay-Terk were some of Kandinsky's supporters from abroad.
61. From the correspondence it is not clear who originated the idea, but since Walden took responsibility for the binal organization, choice of texts, and layout, it would appear to have been his initiative. Hans Roethel and Jelena Hahl-Koch, *Kandinsky: Die Gesammelten Schriften*, vol. I (Bern: Benteli Verlag, 1980), pp. 144–45.
62. *Kandinsky 1901-1913* (Berlin: Sturm Verlag, 1913).
63. *Der Sturm*, III (March 1912; April 1912; December 1912; February 1913); IV (August 1913).

64. Walden and Schreyer, *Der Sturm,* pp. 257–59.
65. *Der Sturm,* IV (April 1913).
66. Gustav Vriesen, *August Macke* (Stuttgart: W. Kohlhammer, 1953), p. 124.
67. Some of the artists represented were Giacomo Balla, Carlo Carra, Gino Severini, Umberto Boccioni, David Burliuk, Natalie Gontcharova, Michael Larionoff, Oscar Kokoschka, Piet Mondrian, Lyonel Feininger, Archipenko, Marsden Hartley, Franz Marc, and Gabriele Münter.
68. Max Ernst and Willi Baumeister, for instance.
69. *Der Sturm,* IV (October 1913).
70. Schreyer, *Erinnerungen an Sturm and Bauhaus,* pp. 7–87.
71. Eckart von Endow, *Die Deutsche Expressionistische Kultur and Malerei* (Berlin: 1920), p. 131.
72. *Der Sturm* had only the slightest connections with the new DaDa movement and played no role in the establishment of the Bauhaus.
73. "Herwarth Walden," *Europäische Ideen,* 14, 15 (1976), pp. 10–27.
74. Grohmann, *Wassily Kandinsky: Life and Work.*
75. Donald Gordon, "On the Origin of the Word 'Expressionism,'" *Journal of the Warburg and Courtauld Institute,* 29 (1966), p. 381.
76. Paul Klee, *Tagebücher* (Köln: Dumont-Schauberg, 1967), p. 284.
77. August Macke and Franz Marc, *Briefwechsel,* (Köln: Dumont-Schauberg, 1964), p. 211.
78. Hugo Ball, *Flight Out of Time,* ed. and introduction, notes, and bibliography by John Elderfield, trans. Anne Raimes (New York: Viking Press, 1974), p. 8.

ADULT LEADERSHIP AND ADULT DEVELOPMENT

A Constructivist View

Robert Kegan and Lisa Laskow Lahey

10

Three umpires, so the story goes, were discussing their view of their work. "Some're balls and some're strikes," the first umpire said, "and I calls 'em as I sees 'em." "Some're balls and some're strikes," the second one said, "and *I* calls 'em as they *are*." "Well, some're balls, all right," the third umpire said, "and, sure, some're strikes. But until I calls 'em, they ain't *nothin'*."

The gentlemen were engaged in a philosophical discussion about the nature of reality and the exercise of their authority. In this chapter we define *leadership* as the exercise of authority and we consider it in relationship to a person's implicit "philosophy" or construction of reality. The story doesn't tell us if the umpires' differing views actually caused them to "lead" differently, but we suspect that it might. We also suspect that the *batter's* experience of the umpire's leadership would depend, in part, on the batter's own philosophy about reality. Our suspicions do not derive from what we have learned in baseball parks or philosophy, but the psychological study of adulthood.

While philosophers and poets have long expounded on the different eras of the individual's life course (remember Jacques's discourses on "the seven ages of man" in Shakespeare's *As You Like It*), it is only in the last twenty years or so that developmental psychology has considered life after adolescence. The seminal contributions of Sigmund Freud and Jean Piaget led to understandings of several qualitatively different eras from infancy through adolescence. Each era involved a different organization of inner and outer experience, a different set of motivations and preoccupying concerns, and a different way of making meaning and guiding behavior. Indeed, each era constituted a different "philosophy" (however unrecognizedly) of reality. Although Freud and Piaget thought very differently about these qualitative transformations, a common consequence of their work was the impression that such changes in a person's way of making meaning ended in adolescence. The changes that took place in the latter two-thirds to three-quarters of a person's life were thought to be of a different order, nonregular, and essentially derivative of the fundamental psychological work of earlier years. It is probably safe to say that this is no longer the predominant view of psychological adulthood. While there will always be controversy regarding the role of early experience in the present, and no one suggests there is not enormous variation in possible life courses, there is an emerging picture of adulthood *continuing* a lifelong history of qualitative psychological organizations which, underneath surface variety, have remarkable regularities.

This newer view of adulthood is found in the work of psychologists, many of whom studied childhood and adolescence, and then went on to take the same premises to the study of adulthood as well. Their works, building largely either on Freud[1] or Piaget,[2] or some combination of each,[3] form the beginning of a psychology of the life span. They do not speak in a single voice, are not free of contradiction, and do not always seem to be addressing the same subject. But they do, nonetheless, begin to sketch a rough picture of a sequence of *adulthoods* that people seem to grow through.

Some of the theory, such as Levinson's, views adult life changes as age-related. Using the metaphor of "seasons," Levinson understands the life cycle to contain a series of definable periods or forms, each qualitatively different, through which every adult passes. Development is then conceived of as the response to the specific social and psychological tasks which emerge during predictable age periods. For example, between ages forty-five and fifty, roughly, many people seem to go through a period of reevaluation of, and to greater and lesser extents, reconstruction of, their life purposes and commitments. This can take a variety of forms: it can be a painful and bewildering "midlife crisis" or a smoother, possibly exhilarating "new lease on life"; it can be worked out largely in the private arenas of family, marriage, or new relationships to one's own inner feelings and conflicts, or in more public arenas of career, life-style, friendship networks, or both. A common reconstruction for a man, Levinson would suggest, is a lessening of an identification of himself with his job or career. He may find himself wanting to place work in some bigger context that would allow him more access to a side of himself that has been neglected in the efforts of the preceding decade to establish himself.

The implications of these kinds of self-organizations for the study of leadership are rich and heuristic. One of us, for example, consulted with leaders of a nationally acclaimed public school system. A high-powered organization in which the superintendents and principals demanded much of themselves and each other, these leaders were proud of their dedication and their reputation. When they were asked what would be on a "wish list" to make their work lives better, however impractical, they generated a group of items with a common theme:

1. Sabbatical
2. Daily "time out" (some kind of regular relief from the ceaseless flow of activities)
3. Brief job exchanges (changing jobs with someone in a different role, system, or country for a few days, weeks, or months)
4. More flexible hours ("so we could be with our families more")
5. People to talk with who are not part of the job setting

"The list suggests that we somehow want to keep working here and leave at the same time," one of them said bemusedly. The problem was that many of them had also been harboring this feeling somewhat shamefully or guardedly because each felt it would be taken as a waning of commitment to the organization, and a kind of halfheartedness which was contrary to the leadership ethic of the organization. Some worried that their feelings meant they were slipping as leaders and ought to think about leaving, even though they didn't want to. Actually few, if any, of the leaders felt less committed to their work or the organization. Their current feelings seemed not so much about changes in the *intensity* of their commitment but reevaluations of the *shape* of that commitment. Their own conceptions of leadership had reached some kind of a limit, itself in need of reconstruction, presenting a challenge or opportunity for them, and certainly for the superintendent—the leader of the leaders—as well.

From the Levinsonian point of view, it would not be an accident that these people tended to be about fifty years old. Wortley and Amatea[4] summarized in tabular form what this line of study is uncovering about an adult's twenties, thirties, forties, and so on (included as an appendix to this chapter). The implications of this line of thinking for the study of leadership are manifold: How might the differing life issues particular to a given age express themselves in an individual's leadership or followership? How can the same leader's central preoccupations, focal tasks, expectations, hopes, and dreams be expected to change over time? How might leaders in their sixties and seventies be expected to differ from leaders in their forties and fifties? How does leadership of people in their twenties need to differ from leadership of people in their fifties? And so on.

The line of thinking about adult development and adult leadership to be pursued in the present chapter is a bit different from this Eriksonian-Levinsonian approach, which is tied more to age-related psychosocial tasks. A "constructivist" approach attends to developments in an individual's very *construction* of reality, how he or she makes meaning—in this case, makes meaning of leadership or the exercise of authority. Thus, instead of age-linked responses to the changing conditions of life, constructive theory holds that people respond according to their meaning system. While these developments are strongly related to age in the sense that, very generally speaking, older people's meaning-schemes (or "world views" or implicit "philosophies") tend to be more complicated, differentiated, and encompassing than those of much younger people, they are not a *function* of age. It is quite possible for three adults of identical age to compose three qualitatively different meaning systems or for three adults, each ten to fifteen years older than the last, to compose identical meaning systems. As such, development is not simply a consequence of aging. Instead, development is seen as the qualitative change in a person's meaning system.

The constructivist approach, which grows more out of the Piagetian than Freudian strands of developmental theory, suggests that:

1. Human being is *meaning making*. For the human, what *evolving* amounts to is the *evolving of systems of meaning;* the business of organisms is to organize, as Perry[5] says. We organize mostly without realizing we are doing it, and mostly with little awareness as to the exact shape of our own reality-constituting. Our meanings are not so much something we have, as something we are. Therefore, researchers and practitioners do not learn about a person's meaning-making system by asking the person to explain it but by observing the way the system actually works.

2. *These meaning systems shape our experience.* Experience, as Aldous Huxley said, is not so much what happens to us as what we *make* of what happens to us. Thus we do not understand another's experience simply by knowing the events and particulars of the other but only by knowing how these events and particulars are privately composed.

3. *These meaning systems to a great extent give rise to our behavior.* We do not act as randomly, irrationally, unsystematically, or molecularly as might be thought. Even the most apparently disturbed, irrational, or inconsistent behavior is, as Carl Rogers often suggests, coherent and meaningful when viewed through the perspective of the actor's constitution of reality.

4. Except during periods of transition and evolution from one system to another, to a considerable extent *a given system of meaning organizes our thinking, feeling, and acting over a wide range of human functioning.*

5. Although everyone makes meaning in richly idiosyncratic and unique ways, *there are striking regularities to the underlying structure of meaning-making systems* and to the sequence of meaning systems that people grow through.

What are these different meaning systems in adulthood and how might they give shape to a person's relationship to exercises of authority? We have chosen to answer this question by first introducing in a general way three different meaning systems in adult development. Next we consider how these meaning systems express themselves in each of three very different leadership contexts, ranging from the most intimate and private to the most diffuse and public: leadership in the family (parenting), leadership on the job (running an organization, being an employer), and leadership in the state (political leadership).

THREE SYSTEMS OF MEANING
IN ADULTHOOD

Development is always a process of outgrowing one system of meaning by integrating it (as a subsystem) into a new system of meaning. What was "the whole" becomes "part" of a *new* whole. The first (adult) system is the product of outgrowing a childhood system founded on the hard-won ability to regulate one's impulses to make plans, fulfill goals, and meet needs. As the whole of the childhood self is embedded in its own needs, interests, and goals, the child is able to pursue its own purposes but cannot integrate its own purpose with another's. Instead, the self tends to make other people captive of its own goals, and its single point of view. It is in adolescence that this usually changes, and the hyperindependent school-age child gives way to a more "*inter*personal" meaning system that begins to regulate the (now) *sub*system of individual needs, goals, and a single point of view. Now the person can move back and forth between his or her needs and another's (thus constructing mutually reciprocal relations built around trust rather than fair exchange, and an intrinsic rather than extrinsic value upon relationships themselves), and back and forth internally between one point of view and another within oneself (thus creating a sense of inner dialogue and an orientation to subjective states and "feelings"). What was formerly "the whole" becomes part of a *new* whole.

The strength of this new system (we will call it the Interpersonal System) is that it can see beyond a single point of view and relate to others as something more than facilitators or thwarters of one's own goals and purposes. A limit of this new system is its *own* form of embeddedness which has to do with the absence of a self that can regulate (or take a perspective on) the *interpersonal* definition of reality. Living in the Interpersonal "logic" one *is* the Interpersonal, rather than "having" the Interpersonal. One's self-definitions, purposes, and preoccupying concerns are essentially *co*-defined, *co*-determined, and *co*-experienced. As the limits of a ten-year-old's "logic" are provided for by the constraints and allowances that attend to children, the limits of the interpersonal logic are provided for in the less-than-fully adult privileges and expectations extended to and demanded of adolescents. Still, some persons become chronologically and physiologically adolescent without growing beyond the childhood logic, and we can expect problems as a result. In the same way, some people become chronologically adult without growing beyond the logic more appropriate to adolescence, and we can expect as a result another less well-recognized set of problems—especially if these persons have responsibilities to exercise power, authority, influence, control.

When a person moves on to a new logic, the Interpersonal System becomes a part of a bigger system which now regulates or takes control of it. The system no longer *is* "interpersonal"; it "has" the interpersonal. The person becomes more self-authoring, self-owning, self-dependent, more autonomous—not in the sense of more isolated or separated but in the literal sense of "autonomy," *self-naming*. Rather than having the pieces of oneself co-owned and co-determined in various shared psychological contexts, the person brings the power of determination into the self and establishes the self as a kind of psychic "institution," an organization which the self is now responsible for running and regulating. In common language, the person evolves an *identity*. We call this the Institutional System.

The limit of this system is that it tends to suffer from the malady to which all institutions can fall prey—making the continued maintenance of the organization the very goal *of* the organization, self-perpetuation having become an end in itself. This system of meaning lacks a capacity for self-correction, for reflecting on the fundamental purposes of the organization it is running internally (in the self) or socially (in the world). Having achieved a self-government, it has rescued itself from captivity by the shared realities; but in having no self before which it can bring the demands of that government, it risks the excesses of control that may obtain to any government not subject to a wider context in which to root and justify its laws.

A post-Institutional System involves yet another transforming of the whole into a part of a new whole. The self no longer *is* its particular organization but rather "has" organizations as figures upon a ground, a moving ground more committed to culturing a process than preserving a product. The way in which oneself or one's authority is being organized can be reflected upon and modified because the self is more than its temporary organization. In the Institutional System the person's capacity to maintain a coherent identity is founded on an internally consistent but self-sealing logic which insures that no matter how much information is taken in or how a conflict is resolved, the system's operating principle is always preserved. In the post-Institutional System of meaning the prevailing principle of organization is not ultimate, and a predetermined orientation to conflict and information is transcended.

Describing these systems generally is a difficult and complicated affair because it amounts to an effort to name the most abstract operating principle or underlying logic which holds a system of meaning together. What is exciting about our learnings in this field is that when the underlying logics *are* understood, a great deal of otherwise unrelated phenomena take on a new coherence.[6] But a reader unfamiliar with the field may need the patience to trust more to the cumulative effect of seeing these logics in action over three quite different domains (family, job, state), than to expect to grasp them upon first description. We now turn to the way these different systems influence the exercise of authority in the family.

PARENT AS LEADER

Although it is unusual to consider parenting in the study of leadership (and the reader may be forgiven for thinking, "Leave it to the psychologists to bring Mother into *everything*"), we do not propose parenting as a "special case" tailor-made to psychological analysis. Despite the fact that one is told in first-grade civics class that the most powerful job on earth is the presidency of the United States, we all know that our parents, who have us at considerably closer range over a longer period of time, nearly always have more influence on who we are and who we become than the occupant of the Oval Office. The responsibilities, and the license, of parenting make it truly one of the most powerful jobs on earth, and since most adults do become parents, it may be for many adults, whether they know it or not, their most significant leadership experience.

When we ask parents what they think are the most important things a ten-year-old needs from his or her parents (besides the basics of food, shelter, and clothing), the lists that are generated are usually of this sort:

1. Love
2. Understanding
3. Flexibility
4. Openness
5. Warmth
6. Humor
7. Open-mindedness
8. Ability to listen
9. Respect for the child's individuality
10. Taking an interest in what interests the child

This is a list to warm anyone's heart. These certainly sound like good qualities to us. But is this the whole story of effective parenting, of effective leadership as a parent? We sometimes ask parents to tell us what their lists would really mean in action. "What should you do," we might say, "if you discover your ten-year-old is stealing from the corner drugstore?" The answers: "Find out why." "Talk with him [her]." "Love the child harder." "A child who steals is a child who needs something; find out what she [he] needs and give it to her [him]." Eventually some brave soul in the back of the room says, usually a little defiantly, "I'd scream and yell at my kid so he knew I was angry." "Really?" we say in horror, as the others in the group shrink away from the Neanderthal in their midst. "You'd actually get *angry?* What about 'open-mindedness,' 'understanding,' and 'respecting the child's individuality'?"

What the list is missing is a child's need for parents who can exercise power on behalf of convictions, exert control, be righteously indignant, even express moral outrage (a virtue lauded by the Greeks and in woefully short supply at every level of modern American life). *Power, authority, control* are words that make people uncomfortable, especially in a context such as parenting, which is first of all about *love.* But as far as we can tell as developmental researchers and clinicians, effective parental loving (hence, effective parental leadership) of a ten-year-old must include competent executive functioning, a child's sure sense that someone is in charge who believes in something and will stand for those beliefs. Why is this? Developmentally, children between six or seven and until adolescence are in the process of learning to take charge of their own impulses, to exercise control over themselves so that they can pursue their own goals with a new measure of independence and self-sufficiency, so that they can take pleasure in the competent exercise of social roles (child, peer, pupil) and participation in social institutions. A child at this age is most in need of inclusion and recognition in social institutions which he or she experiences as fair, committed to some shared purposes, and, above all, led by persons who are models of the executive command which is first on the child's own psychological agenda.[7]

The most intimate institution in which the child participates is the family, and the most visceral and instructive lessons the child receives in effective self-leadership comes from the ways she or he experiences *being* led. In a family with an eight-year-old *someone* must be clearly in charge and it had better not be the eight-year-old. *Power, authority,* and *control* make many people uncomfortable, in part because they have seen so many arbitrary and abusive exercises of power (especially at the governmental and corporate levels) that they come to feel that *all* exercises of power must be intrinsically arbitrary or deleterious. On the contrary, the exercise of power as a parent is itself *intrinsic* to effective loving and effective leadership.

But a parent's difficulty with this feature of effective leadership may have to do with the *parent's* developmental position. Certainly an important feature of competent leadership in any context is effective *boundary management,* the ability to recognize and preserve distinctions in membership to different functions and levels of authority. Boundary management—as cold a term as it first appears—might be *the* central feature of effective parenting, the least cold form of leadership imaginable. Imagine how different a parent's resources for boundary management might be if the parent's basic construction of reality is guided by one or the other of the "logics" just described. "A ten-year-old who steals is a ten-year-old who needs something," as one of the parents said. But what he most needs may be *limit-setting* (an issue of boundary management), and it can be very difficult to set boundaries when the parent is always extending the child an option to purchase half of the parent's personal authority. Much of the child will react negatively to the imposing of limits, so where does this loving parent find the resources to inflict grief upon her dear one, especially when the part of the child that does not want to be confined will purchase the option and exercise it at cross-purposes? It is an option purchased by the child at enormous cost to him or her. An effective leader will not extend such an option. Might the adult's developmental position (the prevailing meaning system) have something to do with whether or not he or she does?

While the child may be working on greater psychological self-sufficiency, the parent may be living out of the first of three qualitatively different meaning systems common to adulthood, the Interpersonal System. To expect a parent in this meaning system to exercise power, authority, and control may be expecting a person to do something that he or she is unprepared for, developmentally. Exercising power requires a boundary between the leader and the follower; being a leader demands that one be clear about what the self, *independent of others*, wants and expects of the other. Because the Interpersonal's self-definitions, purposes, and preoccupying concerns are essentially *co*-defined, *co*-determined, and *co*-experienced, there is no self independent of the context of other people. Not only is being the authority a difficult role to fulfill but it is unwelcomed as well. With mutuality as the standard for relationships, this parent is unlikely to voluntarily do anything which threatens the Interpersonal fabric of his or her existence. Instead, this parent is likely to do whatever it takes to keep the child *in* the relationship. Usually, this translates into giving the child what he or she wants. However beneficial this may seem to the child, the net result is not; the child is left with the full responsibility of taking charge of him or herself. By giving in on limits, this parent has failed to provide the child with an outside authority, a leader.

A parent lodged in the Interpersonal meaning system can run into boundary management problems with his or her *adolescent* children, as well. Adolescents are themselves becoming "Interpersonal" and their new capacities for psychological closeness and co-experiencing can end up being unwittingly exploited by the Interpersonal parent's own needs for psychological companionship and support. It is not uncommon for some parents to inappropriately include their children in the intimate details of their marital or private lives, for example, making the child into a confidant. This is the same failure to manage boundaries now in a different form. It can have the same "poisonous fruit" quality to an adolescent that a parent's willingness to give in on limits has to a child; to the child it seems very attractive, but it is purchased at a high price. At bottom it is a default of leadership responsibilities, a failure to exercise those authorities which are required, and a failure that may be traced to the constraints of the leader's underlying system of meaning.

If the Institutional parent is better equipped to exercise the responsibilities of boundary management, this meaning system, too, has its own limitations. Echoing a child's independence at a whole new psychological level, the Institutional parent may be *too* independent. If the Interpersonal System is too vulnerable to the views of others, the Institutional System may be too resistant to consultation and correction.

If the Institutional parent can take charge of a family, espouse values, and stand for them, he or she also tends to become identified with the particular ideology for which he or she stands, and lacks the capacity to hear extra-ideological information as anything other than threatening heterodoxy. A post-Institutional leader as parent, for example, might define his or her leadership goals less in terms of "what the children should become" and more in terms of providing a context which empowers the children to make their own choices as to who they shall be. Such a form of leadership raises boundary management—in this case, distinguishing one's children from oneself—to a qualitatively new level.

Modern American middle-class family life is among the most isolating arrangements in human history. High mobility, the nonparticipation of the parents' parents, the norms against airing the family's linen in public, all point to a small two-generational unit turned in on itself. Societal laws and agencies can address family systems that have become unwholesome only after there are serious casualties, and then only to a certain extent. The only *internal* protection for the "followers" (the children) from family as captivity is internal family leadership that is itself self-corrective. If this is uncommon it may be because the developmental position upon which such leadership depends is uncommon.

Before we look further at the implications of these three developmental positions in a quite different leadership context (employer-employee relations), let us summarize our several hypotheses:

1. Parental loving is as much a matter of *form* as intensity. *How much* a parent loves is not the only crucial determiner of parental success; as important as the love's intensity is *the way it knows*. "How differentiated are the lover and the beloved?"

2. Parental loving cannot be separated from parental leadership. The two are not antagonistic functions but inextricable expressions of a single way of knowing. "How differentiated are the lover and the beloved?" is at once a question about loving, epistemology, and the exercise of authority.

3. Parents who have not developed an Institutional meaning system are at greater

risk of being unable to set effective limits upon their children and themselves *in relation to their children.*

4. Parents who have not transcended an Institutional meaning system are at greater risk of overtly or covertly indoctrinating their children in their own ideology or making loyalty to the family's ideology the tacit price of continued psychological membership in the family.

5. The epistemological form of a parent's leadership (its underlying logic, the way it defines reality) should not be confused with the contents of its ideology. So-called liberal or conservative parents might differ in the values they approve or espouse, but if they are at the same developmental position they are likely to be more alike in their exercise of authority than two liberals or two conservatives in different developmental meaning systems. A "liberal" parent in the Institutional balance can be as authoritarian on behalf of liberal ideology as a conservative parent on behalf of conservative ideology. As a liberal mother said to us, 'I'm going to see to it that no daughter of mine goes off and marries some powerful man before she's had a chance to develop some power of her own."

EMPLOYER AS LEADER

We believe the way a follower experiences another's exercise of authority is also a function of the way the *follower* makes meaning. What a leader does might be differently understood and responded to by followers who are at different developmental positions. We explore this idea in this section, as well as pursuing further the implications of the three meaning systems in a new leadership context. Listen to three teachers all working in the same nontraditional, alternative public school, talking about their employer and leader, the principal:[8]

"I wanted to work in an elementary school because I thought it was a place where I would be accepted. I came here looking for nurturance—you know, if I did something good, people would say 'wonderful' and be real supportive. Or if I had a good idea, people would say, 'Fine, go with it.' But there's no place or time for that sort of thing. I feel I run into a lot of limits and 'buts,' especially from our principal. She has such definite ideas of who we should be."[8] And I suppose that's okay on some level. But she doesn't care about us as people. All she seems to care about is whether each of us is good enough to attend to the individual needs of the kids. I end up spending so much of my classroom time just trying to meet her demands. I never relax, knowing that she's constantly surveying my performance as a teacher. Like she checks to make sure that I individualize every kid's lesson plan. It's not that I'm worried about looking like a bad teacher, because my kids always do well. It's more that I feel she sees me as an automaton, simply carrying out some plan for teaching kids. Anyone could do that. Or when she comes in to observe my classroom, she just sits there taking notes. Meanwhile I'm as nervous as can be, standing up there, alone, while she looks on in her critical, judgmental way. It's not that she ever gives me bad reports, though. I guess you could say she gives me positive ones. Yeah, she even details why she thinks my open classroom is so successful. But I always feel dissatisfied—there's just something missing in those reports. I don't know exactly what."

"It would just be nice . . . just some kind of thanks or some acknowledgment for the effort that I put forward, my investment."[8]
"Teaching is a funny profession. You don't get a lot of feedback all the time. It's just your own feeling about how things are going."[8] And if the kids show some appreciation and respect for what's going on, that, I guess, is the kind of feedback that keeps you going. So I'm enormously grateful for my kids who tell me, in their own way, that I matter a lot to them. That I make a difference."

"As a principal, I think she's terrific. Running an alternative school is no easy task—there really are a lot of people out there who see 'open classrooms' as a playground for exploring the esoteric. Not only do I respect her ability to stand up to those people but I am also in full agreement with her argument for the need for this school. There are plenty of traditional school settings, imposing a monolithic unitary system of education on the kids. What is needed are alternatives, like this place, that don't stultify the individual differences among the kids. Enough of pressing every student into the same mold, of hewing out a single identity from such rich, unique sources. We desperately need to provide different means and allow for different aims for each student. And we *do* it here. Working for what I believe in makes my work worthwhile."
"When I first came here I was a little uneasy about how well I would get along with this principal; she was overtly critical, applying high standards to everyone. I suppose she has to, given all the pressures and complaints from people who don't like what she's doing. Still, I have a hard time with that part of her. I used to worry about what I would do or say if she criticized me. But it didn't take long for me to trust that my standards for myself were adequate for me. I've reached a point where I can say to her, 'I'm sorry, but I have different standards on this.' I have a lot of confidence in myself: I know I'm a hard worker and what I produce is high quality. I get to do my work, and I feel good about how well I work with the kids. I do enjoy working with them. And I have cordial, if not friendly, relations with my fellow workers and the principal."

"It's apparent that she is tremendously loyal to the school. Such commitment certainly has commendable features. Despite continuing threats to the school's survival, I basically believe that we will continue. And that's because our principal is so dedicated to the school's existence. She has a seemingly undying reserve of energy to really hang in during these crises. But there's another side to her responsibility to maintaining this place, and that's her unwillingness to consider other possible ways of running this system. Her focus on preserving the status quo, in defending the school from external and internal attacks, seems to limit the school's potential. Tied to her responsibility to preserve the school, she views most negative reports about the ineffectiveness or impracticality or irrelevance of open classrooms as 'enemies' which need to be co-opted or neutralized. So, occasionally she makes decisions that serve the school's current need but aren't in the best interest of the school in the long run. This place could become multidimensional, full of texture, if she listened to the supposed 'enemy' with a spirit willing to view criticism as seeds for possibilities, or as mirrors in which we could look at our school, its practices, its criteria, rather than only looking from our overly subjective perspective. Of course, it's scary to look at criticism as useful."

"I want to add that I am grateful to work in a school that I think will survive, despite all the fiscal cuts. I suppose my confidence in that has much to do with my confidence in the principal. She's a true fighter. And even if the school remains 'as is,' I know I can always continue encouraging the process I believe in within my classroom. Still, I admit that it saddens me that this place may never realize its full potential."

That three distinct viewpoints of a leader, the principal, should emerge as if three *different* people were being described probably surprises no one. We have always known that people see things differently. But there is a way the constructivist view departs from our more homespun psychological way of thinking about such differences. Typically we assume that different people are seeing the *same* thing in different ways. And we try to explain how those differences arise by appealing to differences in characteristics between the people. For instance, we might want to know if there were age differences, or differences in the number of years of teaching experience, or differences in former work experience—did any of the teachers work in alternative schools before?—or differences in how well they got along with former principals. In other words, we probably would look to their personal history for clues to understand the present differences brought out in these depictions of the same leader.

The constructivist view questions whether it is the *same* thing that is being seen differently or whether a *different* thing is being seen in different ways. Of course, each is talking about the same physical entity, but if each is constructing reality out of a whole different logic, then in the psychological sense three different "objects" do exist (". . . until I calls 'em, they ain't *nothin'*"). Some unseen part of the principal, for example, could not simply be pointed out to a teacher who would then immediately see it. It might require a whole developmental transformation in the teacher for her to see the principal in that new way.

The first teacher, here at "Alternative High," speaks about her want to be accepted, supported, and praised. Two qualities can be noted about these needs. One is that for this person the need to be stroked, praised, and nurtured seem paramount. Longing for these interpersonal needs to be met, there is a way that she is unreceptive to the messages from the principal about the quality of her teaching ability. This teacher's orientation to the relational aspect of her involvement with the principal apparently takes priority over her own performance as a teacher. Not wanting to be seen as an automaton who carries out tasks, who performs, this teacher is making a plea to be seen as a person to be related to and not simply as a worker. Evaluations by the principal may be intimidating or threatening because in these, this teacher feels that the principal is objectifying and dehumanizing her. The principal separates the worker from the person and so this teacher is left feeling unattended to, as if she didn't exist, as if the leader does not *really* care. When her needs to be joined in a more intimate way are fulfilled, she feels worthwhile and valued. Being appreciated by her kids helps her to feel good about herself and what she is doing; they seem to be the fuel that keeps her working.

The other quality is that there is a way in which this individual cannot fulfill these needs by herself. She alone does not seem to be the controller of her well-being; the cooperation of others (for example, giving their support and acceptance to her) is an absolute must. This is not to suggest that those not embedded in the interpersonal do *not* need others for their well-being. The crucial difference is *how* the individual needs the other. The first teacher is a *psychological* employee as well as an economic employee; psychologically speaking, she is not in business for herself. Certainly this must be a crucial feature of her leadership in relation to her students and of her followership in relation to the school's principal.

A different picture of the principal is conveyed in the second teacher's account. No longer *being* her relationships, but *having* them, means that this teacher does not need the principal to vitalize and renew her feelings. Instead, this teacher appropriates the principal to a new context. The principal has a place in the maintenance of this teacher's personal self-system, a self-system about time-bound constructions of role, norm, and self-regulation. The principal—who allows this teacher to exercise her self-definition, her own authority, her own personal achievement; who allows this teacher to live her role—is viewed as a cohort, or a like-minded thinker. Rather than orienting to the principal as a source of approval, this teacher focuses on how they share a particular ideology, specifically about alternative schooling.

Affiliation and acceptance are not ultimate. "Cordial, if not friendly relations" are sufficient. This person's well-being seems linked to her investment in her work; her commitment to teach according to her own principles and her belief in what she does (for example, "Working for what I believe in makes my work worthwhile"); her ability and willingness to set her personal standards ("I can say to her, 'I'm sorry, but I have different standards on this' "); and her making herself the primary *source* of her evaluation ("What I produce is high quality. . . . I feel good about how well I work with the kids"). Stated more generally, this teacher's well-being is linked to the smooth running of her own system, her own institution.[9]

The third teacher presents yet another perspective. Neither seeking acceptance and thus depending on the principal's mutuality, nor looking to keep her self-government stable and thereby seeing the principal as either loyalist or foe, this teacher views the principal as an individual. No longer *being* her institution—the duties, performance, work roles, and careers which institutionality gives rise to—this teacher *has* her career. Because the functioning of her own organization is no longer an end in itself, she cannot join the principal as a fellow organizer, loyal to the status quo at all costs. More specifically, she sees that there is a way that in making the maintenances and protection of the current shape of the school ultimate, so that "right" or "good" is defined by what supports and encourages the continued life of the school as currently defined, the school suffers. Instead of the school being preserved by sidestepping conflicts, it could risk enhancing itself with each open-ended encounter with conflict. That is, the school could be responsive to cumulative development brought about by the acknowledgment and appreciation for contradiction and friction.

It is worth noting that *both* the first and third teachers have problems "following" their leader, but for quite different reasons. This is both a function of *their* developmental position and that of the *leader*. Focusing on the follower's ways of knowing may create the equally false impression that what one "knows" is *independent* of the leader. To illustrate the leader's contributions, we introduce a new school ("Traditional High"), three new teachers, and a new principal. The guiding question is: How might teachers in the same three meaning systems respond to a leader who is in a different meaning system from the first principal? The first teacher in our new set speaks:

"Often I think the attitude of the teachers is a reflection of how they're treated, and of how their principal looks at them. This principal is always very supportive of the teachers and that makes a gigantic difference in my own caring about what kind of job I do. I find her to be very supportive and intelligent and understanding of human beings, and I just think it's rare to find a principal like that. When she comes in to observe in your classroom, for instance, she participates in the activity, whatever it is. And the things she writes up are always on a positive note. But it's not that we're all superduper teachers. She just writes up her comments in a way that makes you feel good and positive reinforcement works with adults just as it works with children— you make them feel as if they're doing a good job and they try even harder."[8]

"Another plus is that she really brings about a sense of community within the school, both among the teachers and between students and teacher. I think everyone shares the good feelings that come from this place functioning as a whole. You know, it's as if she never imposes her own will on us. Well, if she does, then I'd have to say her greatest concern is with the school working as a whole. Because she works so hard to maintain open communications all around. As a consequence, I think we all feel a lot of understanding, compassion, and kindness. I think we all feel the warmth of the school. "I guess it's nice to have other teachers, too. Like it's nice that most of us get along quite well and are a strong source of support for one another. But I think of the principal's support as crucial."[8]

Like the first teacher at Alternative High, this teacher is highly attuned to matters of support and praise. Talk about receiving the principal's support and the importance of positive reinforcement runs throughout her statement, suggesting how very important support is to this teacher. A second quality shared between this teacher and the first at Alternative High is their inability to fulfill their need for approval and acceptance by themselves. For both teachers, the foremost need is to be supported by another; external approval is the first and most vital source of approval. When supported, each can care about his or her work.

Despite parallels in each teacher's logic, there are clear differences in how satisfied each is with the leader, and more generally, with working in the school. This teacher is thriving. Rather than critically observing, this principal participates in classroom activities while "observing" class functioning. Rather than sending reports that have "something missing," this principal sends comments written "in a way that makes you feel good." Positive reinforcement received from the principal makes this teacher feel as if she's doing a good job, so she tries even harder. It is such approval, externally initiated, that motivates her to work harder. Receiving such approval, and working in a community of understanding, compassion, and kindness are supports of the most essential kind for this person. Developmentally speaking, these are life supports. For some reason, to be explored in a moment, the environment created by this principal confirms the teacher's fundamental way of making meaning. Now consider a second teacher:

> "She's a real gem. Within the school she's highly respected, but she's liked, and I really don't know which comes first. The principal's role is important, but it's also the person. I think she is a very special person. She supports the staff in an open-ended way. I feel she will let me do whatever I want; she trusts my ability as a professional. I don't feel I need to go to her when I want to change an aspect of curriculum in my classroom; I know that whatever my decision is, she will back me up. She got me appointed to a planning committee in the central office and has been a real big help to me, introducing me to people it's a good idea for me to meet.
>
> "Yet sometimes I also feel as if things are getting very out of hand here. Not in my classroom because I need to be well organized in there and I always am. But, well, just around. I feel there's no predictable rhythm. It's almost as if the only thing that can be counted on is the unpredictable nature of how things work. She's always presenting yet another side of the coin. And we're supposed to be the ones to generate our own rules. Most of the time that suits me fine, though it *is* draining, but sometimes I wish that she would lay down some of the rules. Or tell us what *she* thinks, or what *she* wants us to do. Especially when it comes to decisions about curriculum—I feel as if she introduces all these different ideas, the pros and cons, how a pro can simultaneously be a con, and all this stuff that never helps me to decide on anything. Something is lacking—maybe it's that she needs to be concrete, more specific when she talks. I guess I get back to wanting her to tell us her opinion, rather than giving us convoluted and largely irrelevant discourses on the given topic.
>
> "Another problem is that there's too much of a premium placed on expressing our concerns and problems. I suppose there's an equal respect on sharing our joys, our triumphs, and the good stuff like that. But that kind of talk doesn't upset me like the more serious talk about problems. With so many opportunities to reflect together on things such as the way we work

together, or whether we are actually aware of the effects of our behavior on one another, stuff like that, there's plenty of opportunities for differences and conflicts to be exposed. You know, people hurting each other, saying things about the other that are very hard to listen to. When that happens, I worry whether we can keep working together. So why do we take these risks? They're basically unnecessary, having nothing to do with teaching. Not according to the principal, though."

Subjected to the maintenance of a personal self-system, this teacher is developmentally like the second teacher at Alternative High. Neither views the principal as an authority who doles out rewards, evaluations, or approval since both, with their self-defining, self-depending, self-authoring capacities can evaluate themselves. Feeling as if "I don't need to go to her when I want to change an aspect of curriculum," this teacher sees support not as personal approval but as having to do with the principal's support of her exercising influence, assuming responsibility and taking initiative. Support is recognizing that the teacher is the originator of her meaning and purposes. Support is looking out for opportunities for the teacher to advance her career. In this respect, both teachers are being adequately (though differently) supported by their leader.

However, this teacher does not seem at ease with the way the school is managed. Unlike the principal of the alternative school, with her loyalty and investment in the continuing life of the school as currently defined, this principal runs things "unpredictably." Unlike the principal who has definite ideas about what teachers should be doing, and who applies her standards to everyone, this principal leaves the reins in the hands of the teachers, a very draining process. An additional problem is that expression of difficult feelings is encouraged. Such irregular means of running the school causes discomfort for this teacher. Being subject to keeping her own self-system functioning, she views the unreliable outcomes of the principal's leadership style as interfering with her most basic need to run herself. Finally, let us hear from a third teacher at Traditional High:

"A wonderfully warm, spirited, and lively woman, our principal is a model principal. She has the gift of seeing the complexity, the multifaceted character of every individual in this school, parents included, so one always feels fully received and deeply respected. Her genuine tolerance and respect for individual differences really helps to create an environment where the prevailing norm is one of individuality. And trust. Both these norms mean that people can feel free to communicate their feelings, to take risks, to experiment with ideas and feelings without having to defend them. Her loyalty is to keeping communication open, which keeps the entire process of this school open to questions, to possibilities, to conflict, to reconstruction. So there's a resulting air of tentativeness around here. I know some teachers actively dislike that kind of hectic, ambiguous existence, but I honestly don't know that we could continue to learn from our experience if we sought to reduce the ambiguity.

"Her style is an unusual mix of directiveness and nondirectiveness. The directiveness is geared toward processing, so an inevitable nondirective quality emerges. I think most teachers here welcome the space she offers them to take their initiatives and to make their own choices. Also the collaborative decision making is generally well received. Most of us feel free to contribute our perspective to the decision process. Again, because of the open communication, conflicting opinions are welcomed. And typical of the spirit of this place, all our decisions remain open to change."

Having separated herself from her self-system, no longer being "subject" to maintaining her institution, this teacher, like the third teacher at Alternative High, is able to objectify the value, purposes, and regulations of a psychic administrator. The form-bound autonomous self has been surrendered to the individual who runs, but is no longer equated with the running of, the system. Letting go of the need to run a self-system as an end in itself also means that the self no longer need be the exclusive originator of meaning for the self. Others are welcomed into that process.

Although both this teacher and the third teacher at Alternative High share this logic, they are experiencing their leaders differently. While this principal and teacher are able to welcome each other into their continuing processing of all kinds of information about their school, the other principal-teacher team cannot. When self-maintenance is no longer the ultimate goal for both, each is able to "give herself up" in a way that permits interdependency. This is not the case in the relationship between the other teacher and the principal from Alternative High. Despite that teacher's ability to share herself and to simultaneously grant the principal her own distinctness, the principal is unable to reciprocate. Being auto-regulative, the principal must guard the boundary between self and other, lest it be penetrated. For that principal, interindividuality is not a possibility; it is a threat to the balance of the system.

William Torbert's understanding of bureaucratic and postbureaucratic structures for organizations speaks quite directly to the differences between those work settings which might facilitate development beyond the institutional and those which, in effect, serve to overconfirm or hold too tightly this particular system of meaning.

In contrast to the usual features of organizations

(a)   which focus on doing the predefined task;

(b)   in which viability of the product becomes the overriding criterion of success;

(c)   in which standards and structures are taken for granted;

(d)   which focus on quantitative results based on defined standards;

(e)   in which reality is conceived of as dichotomous and competitive (success-failure, in-group-out-group, leader-follower, legitimate-illegitimate, work-play, reasonable-emotional, and so on),

Torbert suggests features of what he considers a qualitative evolution in the development of an organization:

(a) shared reflection about larger (wider, deeper, more long-term, more abstract) purposes of the organization;
(b) development of an open interpersonal process, with disclosure, support, and confrontation on value-stylistic-emotional issues;
(c) evaluation of the effects of one's own behavior on others in the organization, and formative research on the effects of the organization on the environment ("social accounting");
(d) direct facing and resolution of paradoxes; freedom-control, expert versus participatory decision making, and so forth;
(e) appreciation of the particular historical moment of this particular organization as an important variable in decision making;
(f) creative, transconventional solutions to conflicts;
(g) deliberately chosen structure with commitment to it, over time; the structure unique in the experience of the participants or among "similar" organizations;
(h) primary emphasis on horizontal rather than vertical work-role differentiation;
(i) development of symmetrical rather than subordinate relation with "parent" organizations.[10]

From a developmental perspective, the question which differentiates these two settings is, "Where does the organization's ultimate loyalty lie?" In Torbert's first organization, the typical bureaucratic setting, allegiances are to the tried and true means of production. Predetermined structures exist to aid the production of a predefined product, which is judged by preset standards of quality. This organization's loyalty is to the institution-as-it-is. In contrast, in Torbert's second organizational model, loyalty lies with evolution or development of the organization. There is a commitment to self-exploration, open-systems information seeking, and possible reconstruction of its goals, practices, and criteria—all of which amount to an "institutional capacity for intimacy." In its attention to the larger purposes of the organization, to the receiving of information about one's way of operating, to opportunities to be confronted, to the facing of paradox, there is a continual message that maintaining the system-as-it-is will not be enough.

Refocusing on the principals, we now ask where each principal's ultimate loyalty lies. Drawing on common items from the reports of the three teachers in the first school, a picture of a principal who is highly committed to maintaining an alternative school is created. Despite her philosophical/ideological allegiance to the processlike methods and goals of an open-classroom education, the *way* she carries out her commitments is inconsistent with her professed ideology. She exercises her commitment in a way that amounts to a defense of the school-as-is. For example, rather than welcoming possibilities which could alter the form of the school, she keeps

218 A CONSTRUCTIVIST VIEW

out of the system all information that could contradict the present structure. This stance toward information characterizes the person Argyris and Schon[11] call a "single-loop learner," the learner who is invested in seeking to maintain and confirm the system. Constructive developmental theory suggests that such investment is not simply a defending of coldhearted ideas; the defense is of a self. What characterizes this principal, then, is her identification with the form of her system, an identification which is rigidly defended, even if the content of the system (its ideology) is about "process" and "openness."

The second principal, with her ability to allow the process of the school's development to be genuinely open-ended, is primarily loyal to that process. Her ability to stand apart from the goal of keeping the system-as-it-is allows her to stand apart from her personal system and seek out information by which it might be modified. Such information seeking typifies what Argyris and Schon call the "double-loop learner." The learning system of this person entails calling into question the system's norms, objectives, and basic policies. An institutional capacity for intimacy is also illustrated by the principal's openness toward collaborative learning about the system. A basic trust of people, of their ability to make and offer decisions, allows her to behave in nonmanipulative and self-fulfilling ways.

We have tried to suggest a number of things in this section on developmental aspects of leadership in the work setting. So it might be well to briefly summarize what amounts to a series of speculations:

1. The same underlying structures which shape an adult's meanings in his or her leadership role as a parent will operate in his or her conceptions and behaviors of leading and following at work.

2. How a person's leadership is perceived by those who follow is a function of both the meaning systems of the followers and the meaning system of the leader.

3. Followers (in this case, employees) are generally dissatisfied with leaders who are operating out of a meaning system less developed than their own.

4. Leaders who are developmentally beyond their followers are vulnerable to having their purposes translated into meanings they do not necessarily intend. (But the basic forms of such translations are not completely random and can be anticipated.)

5. What a follower experiences as *support* from a leader will differ depending on the follower's developmental position. Leaders who can provide support in forms the followers *themselves experience as support* will be more effective.

6. Finally, as we said earlier about parenting, the epistemological *form* of a person's leadership (its underlying logic; the way it defines reality) is not to be confused with the *content* of a person's leadership (its professed values or ideology). A leader who espouses, for example, quite traditional values might actually define and live out a "leadership reality" that has more in common with a developmentally similar "radical" than a leader who espouses the identical traditional values but who lives them out at a different developmental level.

The psychologist Stanley Milgram, wondering what it might be about German society or German people that would permit the atrocities of the
Holocaust, devised an experiment to test people's capacities to disobey
inhumane orders.[12] Subjects were led to believe they were participating in
a university-approved, scientific study on the effects of punishment as in-
ducements to learning. The punishment involved administering increasingly severe electric shocks (as "teacher") to a second subject (the "learner")
who, unbeknown to the first subject, was actually an experimenter-confed-
erate, complaining of a heart condition, yelling in simulated agony from
the next room as each crack of electricity was (only apparently) being
received, and eventually pleading to be let out of the experiment. Meanwhile, the experimenter, calm and earnest in his white lab coat, asks the
subject to continue administering the shocks. Fieldtesting his experiment
locally to get out any procedural bugs, Milgram was horrified to discover
he didn't need to go to Germany to find candidates for Buchenwald staff
positions. The majority of American subjects, from all walks of life, continued to administer possibly fatal levels of electric shock, despite the pro-
tests and audible agony of the recipient. Most of those who did so were
clearly distressed and pained in the performance of their "duties."

Periodically, polls are conducted in this country in which citizens are
asked if they think it would be a good idea, for example, if everyone had
the right to protest any aspect of government policy so long as they did
not advocate violence; or if they think police officers should always be
barred from searching a person's home without his knowledge, even if he
is highly suspected of wrongdoing; and so on. In other words, they are
asked if they approve of each of the rights already guaranteed by the Bill
of Rights. Invariably, the results of these polls are that a majority of citizens
would deny all of us, presumably themselves included, the majority of the
Bill of Rights actually guaranteed us.[13]

Not long ago, more than thirty members of a United States president's
administration, including the president himself, were named as criminal
conspirators or convicted of criminal acts associated with a set of behaviors
notably absent of personal greed, and largely motivated by the conviction
that what was being done was right, if not strictly legal.

In all these cases, what is most impressive is not that there is so much
wrong going on but that it is being done by apparently ordinary, perfectly
decent, upright citizens like you and me, who in general believe their actions
are *right*. Lawrence Kohlberg's twenty-five years of research and writing
on the individual's construction of *moral* reality has lain a theoretical and
methodological foundation for the constructivist approach to the study of
adult development.[14] The results of his work question the common social

psychological explanations for the phenomena such as those found in Milgram's obedience experiments (the view espoused by Milgram himself), or the Watergate affair (*see*, for example, Raven)—the view that social *pressures* (the spell of the scientific laboratory, the demands of the "Nixon team") cause people to act in ways inconsistent with their own values. The actions may actually be quite consistent with their values. Kohlberg's work puts the focus not on the supposedly extreme social pressures but the individual's moral reality (his or her underlying logic) which makes meaning *of* those social pressures.

Kohlberg and his associates actually interviewed a group of Milgram subjects with measures designed to assess the predominant logic in which a person is living. They found that the relation between developmental level and who quit the experiment was not at all random. While most people tended to continue the experiment as we said, most of these independently judged to be at a "postinstitutional" stage of development actually quit the experiment![15]

Social persuasion studies such as those of Solomon Asch,[16] in which subjects actually change their perceptual assessments in the face of unanimously conflicting assessments by fellow assessors who are actually experimenter-confederates, also tend to suggest that all people are vulnerable to the most tyrannized forms of followership. But, again, more recent studies in the Asch tradition, such as those by Liberman,[17] in which the perceptual dilemmas are rooted in the differences of underlying logic (such as those Piaget identified), would lead to quite a different view, one which confirms the finding of Kohlberg's study of the Milgram subjects—namely, that all people are *not* so malleable, that *knowing* (not what a person knows, but *how* a person knows) is not always a weakling. Some of Liberman's subjects do not change their minds, no matter how many people claim to see things differently. When a person's own epistemology reaches a certain level of development, knowledge can be more powerful than princes.

No set of events in recent memory has so stirred public attention and offered such a lesson in the study of political leadership and followership as that of the Watergate scandal. We give it extensive attention here because it provides us the opportunity to bring the specific ideas of this chapter (with which most readers are probably unfamiliar) to the study of important events and circumstances with which most readers are probably quite familiar.

Daniel Candee studied the moral meaning systems of Watergate participants (as gleaned from their Senate testimony and other public statements) and then did meaning-system assessments of 370 ordinary citizens who were asked for their views of the decisions and behaviors of various Watergate participants.[18] He found that nearly all the members of the Nixon team were in the Interpersonal or Institutional meaning systems, and that those citizens who were in these meaning systems themselves agreed with the decisions of the participants more often than did those citizens who were post-Institutional. He also found that the citizens' meaning system was by far the more powerful predictor of their view of the participants' decisions than was their preference for Nixon or McGovern. Post-Institutional citizens, be they Nixon voters or McGovern voters, look much more like one another than their party comrades on questions of what is and is not ethical conduct or appropriate exercises of authority.

Candee's speculations about the differing quandaries of the Nixon "followers" recalls our earlier distinctions between the three adult developmental meaning systems seen in the contexts of family and work.[19] The problem in the Interpersonal system, Candee says, is that "people one would like to make happy often require one to commit conflicting actions. This was the plight of Herbert Porter, an assistant to Jeb Magruder at the Committee to Re-elect the President, as he explained why he told the Grand Jury that money which had gone to Gordon Liddy to finance the Watergate break-in had actually been given for a 'more legitimate' purpose (infiltrating student radical organizations):

PORTER: Well, Senator Baker, my loyalty to one man, Richard Nixon, goes back longer than any person that you will see sitting at this table throughout any of these hearings. I first met Mr. Nixon when I was eight years old in 1946, when he ran for Congress in my home district. . . . I felt I had known this man all my life—not personally, perhaps, but in spirit. I felt a deep sense of loyalty. I was appealed to on this basis.
          [And in a preceding exchange]:
BAKER: At any time, did you ever think of saying, "I do not think this is quite right?"
PORTER: Yes, I did.
BAKER: What did you do about it?
PORTER: I did not do anything about it.
BAKER: Why didn't you?
PORTER: In all honesty, probably because of the fear of group pressure that would ensue of not being a team player."[20]

In the Interpersonal stage, Candee says, "Right is determined by group norms. It is not surprising therefore that Porter is appealed to positively on the basis of favors established by his reference group (the Nixon campaign) and negatively by the fear of sanction by that group. Unfortunately for Mr. Porter, besides being less than fully moral, decisions based on loyalty are not always even practical. When Porter's name was mentioned to the former president on one of his infamous tapes, Mr. Nixon responded, 'Who?'"

The progression to what we call the Institutional stage is marked, Candee says, by "the awareness that individual relationships are part of a larger society. Roles become structures with definite duties and privileges.

The overriding concern in [the Institutional stage] is to maintain a system which allows the society to function smoothly and avoid chaos. "Such a system need not be conventional society; it may be an 'ideal' system, humanistic, religious, or communal. But if the system itself is seen as more basic than the rights of its individual members, it is being viewed from [an Institutional] perspective. A classic instance of such reasoning seems to have motivated former chief plumber, Egil Krogh, to have authorized the break-in at the office of Dr. Field, Daniel Ellsberg's psychiatrist. Recalling his reasoning at the time, Krogh reflects:

> 'I see now that the key is the effect that the term national security had on my judgment. The very words served to block my critical analysis. . . . To suggest that national security was being improperly invoked was to invite a confrontation with patriotism and loyalty and so appeared to be beyond the scope and in contravention of the faithful performance of the duties of my office. . . . The very definition of national security was for the President to pursue his planned course.'"[21]

According to Candee, "As Krogh saw it, his primary duty was to fulfill the requirements of his role, not to insure human rights. The requirement which he viewed as maintaining the nation really meant maintaining the president. Compared to earlier stages, [Institutional] reasoning has a sophisticated view of the law. But it is not wholly adequate; inherent contradictions remain. Since [Institutional] reasoning does not inquire into the basis of law, it has difficulty handling situations where two reasonable conceptions of the law conflict.

"This shortcoming," Candee says, "seems to have led Jeb Magruder to mistake the re-election of the President for a moral emergency. In explaining his role in the Watergate cover-up Magruder stated:

> 'During the whole time we were in the White House and . . . we were directly employed with trying to succeed with the President's policies we saw continuing violations of the law done by men like William Sloane Coffin. He tells me my ethics are bad. Yet he was indicted for criminal charges. He recommended on the Washington Monument grounds that students burn their draft cards and that we have mass demonstrations, shut down the city of Washington. . . . So consequently, when these subjects came up, although I was aware they were illegal, we have become somewhat inured to using some activities that would help us in accomplishing what we thought was a cause, a legitimate goal.'[22]

"Magruder's fatal flaw was that he did not realize that violations of the law are of different kinds. Rev. Coffin's infraction was committed openly, in the belief that it was a crucial and direct link in the saving of lives in Vietnam. Magruder's action was covert and was not necessitated by a concern for human rights. As in the case of President Ford, who justified the pardon of Richard Nixon because it was rendered out of conscience, Magruder justified his perjury (at least at the time) because it was done for a cause he believed in. The problem, which is left largely unresolved at [the Institutional stage], is how to determine when one's conscience is right or when the cause one believes in is just. The solution to this problem requires that one see morality not as a tool for maintaining society but as a reflection of the very reasons we have societies. While [the Institutional stage] achieved the awareness of a social system [a post-Institutional stage] proceeds to ask, 'What is the moral validity of that system?' At this higher stage the response is in terms of those features which every human being desires to maximize: physical life and liberty. Liberty, the ability to make one's own decisions and to pursue one's inclinations, necessarily includes the freedoms of speech, assembly, and action. From the moral viewpoint such rights are basic to human beings and exist prior to societies. As a procedural matter these rights must be adjusted when they conflict with the equally valid assertion of such rights by another. However, any action which purports to support a law or maintain a system at the expense of individual rights would be logically and thus morally incorrect, since the very legitimacy of the system is the maximization of such rights."

Candee says he is unable to find any post-Institutional reasoning among the Watergate participants. "However," he says, pointing to this statement by former Special Prosecutor Archibald Cox, "it lay at the very crux of their most sophisticated critics:

'If man is by nature a social being—if we are destined to live and work together—if our goal is the freedom of each to choose the best he can discern—if we seek to do what we can to move toward the realization of these beliefs, then the rights of speech, privacy, dignity and other fundamental liberties of other men such as the Bill of Rights declares, must be respected *by both government and private persons.*'[23]

Post-Institutional meaning-making at the level of political life amounts to a capacity to transcend an exclusive loyalty to one's particular faction in confirmation of an ultimate loyalty to the whole. In the Haggadah, a collection of Hebrew stories and prayers that commemorate the Jews' exodus from Egypt, much of the material is flagrantly ideological. The borders of humanity often get drawn where the Chosen People stop and their oppressors begin. God is urged to punish those who are not on the side of the Jews and He is often seen as the private possession of one group. But there are at least two moments of a different nature in this story. When it comes time to recount the ten plagues which were visited upon the Pharaoh's people for refusing to "let my people go," it is traditional to spill a few drops of wine from one's cup at the mention of each terrible plague. And why? The gesture expresses a different sentiment. Jews are instructed, in response to a recitation of the plagues, to diminish their own lot, to reduce their own pleasure, in recognition that the suffering of *any* person, even one's enemy, is most of all a suffering shared by all; that however divided the Jews and the Egyptians might be, it is a preliminary division in the face of their truer commonality in the human community. A similar moment comes after the Egyptian soldiers are drowned by the closing of the Red Sea. The Jews are joyous, but the angels in heaven weep. "Are not these who have drowned also God's children?"

For a more local example of the contrast between the Institutional and post-Institutional constructions of political leadership, we can turn to the controversies around forced busing for school desegregation in Northern cities. We would not suggest that one could conclude anything about a person's moral meaning-making on the basis of whether he or she was for or against busing; as always, the issue is *how* one constructs the situation. But one of the confrontations in the Boston crisis that we found most interesting was between the white, Irish judge who ordered the busing and a white, Irish school committeewoman who opposed it. The committeewoman seemed to speak at the time for a large portion of a heavily Irish neighborhood which was against the disruption forced busing would cause in its community. The judge had carefully studied the school situation and concluded both that black children in largely black schools were not being afforded an equal opportunity to quality education and that the school committee was unable or unwilling to rectify the situation on its own. In her testimony in one of many suits arising out of the controversy, the committeewoman made a fascinating statement: she said, "Integration is being forced upon us by a man who is Irish and doesn't want to be." The statement fails to understand the possibility of taking action against one's special-interest group on behalf, not of some other group, but of the bigger community of persons to which *all* special-interest groups are relativized.

A last example returns us to the Mideast, where the tensions between groups continues three thousand years after the Exodus. Steinberg and Kegan did a study on Israeli soldiers' attitudes toward their Arab enemies.[24] Steinberg gave Israeli soldiers Kohlberg moral-judgment interviews and open-ended interviews about their attitudes. Most of the soldiers were Interpersonal or Institutional, and most drew the lines of the human community as firmly as their predecessors in the Hagaddah; the Arabs were simply not considered as human as the Israelis. A few of the soldiers took a remarkably different view toward their real-life situation. While they were fighting with no less a sense of having their backs to the sea, they maintained a sense of being only part of a bigger collective to which even the Arabs had also to be admitted, however begrudgingly. This was a matter not merely of speculation and concept but also of actual behavior. Soldier-medics were asked about their treatment of enemy wounded. Most would take little or no measures to care for them and one even suggested it was preferable to murder them to eliminate the chance of their killing more Israelis. One man, Asher, dealt quite differently with the situation:

"In the last war and also in this war I took care of the enemy's wounded. Now if you understand from that that I took care of them in the exact same manner as I took care of Israelis—well, if you're talking about the medical part it's correct. If you're referring to the spiritual part it's incorrect. If he has to receive some kind of treatment he'll receive it, just as every Israeli and every other soldier, without any problem. But with an Israeli I always have a desire, some kind of empathy with him, some kind of will to work and do everything, in order that he'll be saved. Regarding the Arab I'll do the same actions, but I'll do it not out of love—well, out of—I don't know, not out of love for the man, but out of some kind of a duty I feel I have toward him."

We found this a moving and authentic statement. It seems he is speaking the very language of a differentiation *and* an integration greater than the group-bound, Institutional morality. Of course it does not feel exactly the same, he says, treating one's enemy and treating one's own; there is a special affection for a member of one's own group, nation, or ideology. But he is also saying that, in a way which may even seem a bit strange to him, this group affection is not finally ultimate; it is never forgotten, but it is not controlling, either. Somehow there is a supervening affection toward something else, toward something that looks more like the human community, the community of all persons, to which this man feels even more strongly compelled. In the face of the recent massacre of the Lebanese, it appears that modern Israel's fate as a nation of justice again depends on whether its leaders take an Institutional or post-Institutional perspective on its mission in history.

And this is no less true for our own country. In its protections of the individual whose rights are not subordinated to the state, in its creation of a state governed by each citizen, in its demand that even the most powerful can be called to account and the lowest among us be able to bring the full force of the law to his cause, the American Constitution is a post-Institutional statement of principles. We are taught that the Constitution is a living document; it can be changed and corrected. This is true and is a feature of its post-Institutional logic; it is self-reflective, self-correcting. But what is living is also perishable. The fragility of the American democratic experiment can be found in considering that it is guided by a post-Institutional set of principles and only a minority of its *adult* citizens have themselves reached a post-Institutional level of development (Kohlberg's studies suggest perhaps 20 percent[25]). It is dangerous enough to democracy to have a followership that is not post-Institutional. It can be life-threatening when our leadership is not. However, our country's founders were not utopianists; they knew they were not building heaven on earth, that our leaders and our followers would be lower than the angels. They rejected the Interpersonal logic that one could put one's trust in princes, and the Institutional logic that would allow power to preserve and defend itself against those who might be dissatisfied with the way it was being exercised. When Richard Nixon candidly admitted in a reflective moment of a national television interview that he felt "legal is whatever the Chief Executive says is legal; if he does it, it cannot be against the law,"[26] he confirmed Harry Truman's assessment that "Nixon never understood the Constitution."[27] But, as Kohlberg has said, "Fortunately for us, the Constitution understood him."

Perhaps the final implication of developmental psychology for the study and practice of leadership is that the story of successive ways of organizing reality does not only speak to the *means* to understanding leadership but to the hoped-for *ends* of leadership itself. Any form of leadership is expressive of some way of knowing, and—as Kohlberg's work especially would suggest—every form of knowing is intrinsically related to a form of valuing. *All* leadership is expressive of a morality, and some moralities are more inclusive, fairer, more impartial, and more protective than others. The crudest way for a leader to make use of developmental theory is to insure that he or she appeals to the needs and yearnings of each of the different realities as they are represented in his or her constituency; in other words, becoming better able to co-opt people to his or her own purposes. But people do not *grow* by having their realities only confirmed. They grow by having them challenged, as well, and being supported to listen to, rather than defend against, that challenge. We defined *leadership* as the exercise of authority. But a person whose way of being in the world— in a family, at work, or as a citizen—amounts to the exercise of authority *on behalf of facilitating the development* of those around him or her, is the person who can truly be called a leader.

APPENDIX: MAPPING ADULT DEVELOPMENT

	20-30 LEAVING HOME AND ENTERING ADULT WORLD	30-40 ROOTING AND EXTENDING	40-50 MID-LIFE
CAREER L THAT IS THOUGHT, FELT, AND ONE IN RELATION TO WORK	- Exterior - -Job exploration, training/education, and trial entry -Establishing career orientation and initial goals -Commitment to specific work area —or— re-evaluation and change —or— continued job transcience - Interior - -Establishing specific work identity (importance of models) -Commitment to generativity or productivity with push upward/ahead (importance of formulating a "Dream", i.e., some vision of what one is building toward)	- Exterior - -Committing to set career pattern and striving for vertical movement —or— readjusting, undergoing training modification -Women entering/re-entering career arena -Women leaving career arena to bear children - Interior - -Readjusting career goals to realign with changing expectations both of self and of significant others (compromising the "Dream") -Seeking mastery, promotion, recognition, credentials, and confidence ("Making It") -Crystalizing work identity	- Exterior - -Entering period of peak work commitment, achievement, and recognition -Taking on supervising, mentoring, and managing functions -Possible mid-life career change: **To meet changing personal values and priorities, or **To develop own business, or **Forced change due to age-related organizational displacement - Interior - -Redefining work role/goals in light of changing values/priorities/possibilities
FAMILY ATIONS WITH NUCLEAR AND TENDED FAMILY INCLUDING EVELOPING INTERACTION ERNS OF THE FAMILY SYSTEM; S RULES, ORGANIZATION, GOALS, VALUES HOME MANAGEMENT	- Exterior - -Separating from family of origin -Couples involved in: **Locating/developing/managing a home **Negotiating relationships with in-laws **Negotiating/delineating a plan for a family **Beginning/delaying child-bearing **Adapting relationship to entrance of first child - Interior - -Developing an identity and establishing social supports that are separate from the family of origin -Couple balancing bonds to each other with allegiance to their families of origin	- Exterior - -Balancing multiple roles/responsibilities to work/mate/family/community -Childbearing/child rearing -Instituting "family plan" and adjusting this vision to demands of reality —or— dissolution of nuclear family -Negotiating relationships to in-laws and extended family - Interior - -Parenting/generativity (fostering growth of new generation) -Committing to "family plan" and investing in the growth, development, and social integration of family members -Coming to view parents as fellow adults	- Exterior - -Stabilization of family resources (economic/physical/emotional) and peak of community extension/involvement -Parenting adolescents — adapting family system to growing intensity and independence of adolescent children -Beginning to assume increased responsibility for aging parents - Interior - -Mother renegotiating relationships to husband and children -Responding to need for increased differentiation in family structure -Reassessing marriage — breaking or recommitting
INTIMACY THE ENTIRE RANGE OF ERPERSONAL RELATIONSHIPS OM THE MOST IMPERSONAL TO THE MOST PRIMARY INTIMATE RELATIONSHIP IS ARACTERIZED BY SIMILARITY, CIPROCITY, COMPATIBILITY, INTERDEPENDENCY, AND MUTUAL CONCERN	- Exterior - -Establishing social support system and exploring various forms of intimacy -Exploring dynamics of primary relationships — trial coupling with commitment or re-evaluation -Couple learning to function together (shared commitments, mutual support, compromising, motivating, planning, and delineating expectations for one another) - Interior - -Stabilizing sexual identity -Bonding — investing trust and life energy toward goals and concerns shared with another	- Exterior - -In maximizing investments to career and family, couple suffers some loss of intimacy — support system narrows, consolidates — couple becomes counter-dependent and isolated -Single individual begins to feel isolated — feels increasing social and internal pressure to form primary bond -Second marriages peaking (age 35) - Interior - -Redefining primary relationship to reflect familial changes and shifting lifestyle demands (birth of children, job transfers, etc.) -Developing a system of familial intimacy -Breaking of primary relationship if couple cannot resolve growth differences and adapt to changing personal needs	- Exterior - -Re-evaluating/reconsolidating social network and familial relations - Interior - -Adjusting primary relationship to impending "launching" of children -Increased acknowledgement and acceptance of individual differences within primary relationship — increased differentiation -Deepening of primary and other intimate relations as experience and mutual investment strengthens commitment and competence in mutual accommodation -Breaking of primary relationship if shifting values, needs, priorities arise and cannot be resolved
INNER LIFE INS TO SELF DEVELOPMENT ND SELF DIFFERENTIATION: LECTIONS OF THE SELF ON SELF AND ITS RELATIONS TO OTHERS ELOPMENT OF MIND, SOUL, AND BODY EVELOPMENT OF VALUES, LIEFS, AND ORGANIZING PERCEPTIONS OF LIFE	-Establishing oneself as an adult: **Developing personal autonomy and competence **Committing/extending oneself to others — establishing primary relationships **Gaining self-knowledge — differentiating self-concept and role identifications **Establishing personal world view — envisioning possibilities and generating productive energy (i.e., future-goal orientation based on a "Dream"), organizing perceptions of how the world works, and developing personal values, beliefs, priorities, and goals **Detaching primary allegiance from parents and family of origin **Developing a sufficient sense of personal worth and identity to permit bonding with another	-Committing to generativity (investment in the next generation and striving for productivity) -Integrating/prioritizing multiple commitments/responsibilities to work, family, mate, friends, and community -Compromising and adjusting goals, values, assumptions, "dreams", and priorities to demands of reality -Beginning to feel concern about physical aging of oneself and one's parents	-Beginning mid-life review-reappraisal/stock-taking — facing contradictions within self and world — adjusting goals, values, priorities, and commitments -Adjusting to metamorphosis of nuclear family -Feeling the mid-life shift in time perspective **Beginning to personalize death **Accepting increasing dependency of aging parents **Accepting one's own aging **Beginning to project life structure for second half of lifespan -Male/female orientation reversals — women becoming more concerned with work/achievement/social orientation, while men generally begin moving inward and giving more attention to individual needs/introspection/primary relationships

Vertical column labels (between 20-30 and 30-40): RECOMMITMENT/SETTLING OR BREAKING/RE-ESTABLISHING — CATCH 30 — RE-EVALUATION OF 20's CHOICES

Vertical column labels (between 30-40 and 40-50): MAJOR RE-EVALUATION AND REVIEW

Adapted from "Mapping Adult Life Changes," David Wortley and Ellen Amatea, *Personnel and Guidance Journal* (April 1982), p. 480.

- Exterior - -Career culminating, acting as mentor/advisor, "putting in time" -Ensuring retirement security -Unskilled may face increasing age-related employment problems or forced termination - Interior - -Beginning to disengage from work role —or— postponing and ignoring upcoming retirement -Evaluating and reviewing work accomplishments resulting in feelings of satisfaction/integrity or disappointment	- Exterior - -Preparing for and realizing retirement -Detaching from formal work role with related changes in status, income, and life structure -Exploring part-time or volunteer work -Cultivating avocations and leisure orientation — doing what one "always wanted to do, but didn't" -Fulfilling honorific positions and sage roles - Interior - -Redirecting physical and emotional energy into other activities —or— settling into satisfied or dissatisfied inactivity	-Cultivating leisure activities and avocations -Establishing new outlets for skills and personal resources -Fulfilling honorific positions and sage roles (formal/informal)	CAREER Brim, 1966 Havinghurst, 1972 Levinson, 1977a, 1977c Lowenthal, et al., 1975 Neugarten, 1968 Super, 1969 Vaillant, 1977
- Exterior - -Launching/letting go of children and adapting to dissolution of nuclear family -Grandparenting and establishing renewed connection to adult children -Continuing dependency reversal with aging parents — "placement" of aged parents -Reconciling extended-family differences — "pulling together" of older generation - Interior - -"Empty nest" issues -Adapting to grandparent role and coming to view children as fellow adults — relinquishing authority -Opening to entrance of new family members (in-laws/grandchildren) through marriages of children	-Adjusting to numerous lifestyle changes resulting from retirement — possible relocation or restructuring of living situation -Establishing increased connections with adult children —or— resolution to greater isolation -Expansion of grandparenting and family mentoring roles -Family attrition — dealing with the loss of the older generation -Dealing with loss of spouse	-Negotiating final (often mutual) caretaking arrangements with adult children -Securing satisfactory living arrangements and settling into new surroundings -Dealing with loss of spouse	FAMILY Carter and McGoldrick, 1980 Duval, 1971 Gould, 1978 Minuchin, 1974 Sheehey, 1976 Solomon, 1973 Troll, 1971
- Exterior - -Continuing to adapt and consolidate social network as family system empties -Adjusting primary relationship to the various changes brought on by retirement (e.g., more free time together) -Entering into extended family relationships (grandchildren and in-laws) as children marry and bear children - Interior - -Final stabilization and reconciliation of primary relationship -Couple dealing with their changing sexual expectations	-Couple settling into increasing interdependence -Couple compromising on how to spend remaining time -Loss of spouse — bereavement and adjustment to survivorship (Note: this represents one of the most traumatic adaptation demands of lifespan, and fundamentally affects rest of survivor's life) -Rebonding with a companion (compatibility/similarity) or support group —or— choosing isolation -Securing or re-establishing close relationships with friends or family	-Survivorship — adjusting to loss of spouse -Finding companionship —or— accepting isolation -Accepting increasing dependence on adult children	INTIMACY Gould, 1977, 1978 Luthman, 1972 Rollins and Feldman, 1970 Sheehey, 1976 Spanier, Lewis, and Cole, 1971
-Consolidating (physical and emotional) resources in response to recognition of increasing vulnerability -Restabilizing support systems and preparation for reinvestment of physical and emotional energies upon retirement -Moving toward peak dependency reversals with aging parents -Burying parents -Increasing personalization of death and consciousness of physical vulnerability	-Detaching personal identity from work role -Developing avocational/leisure orientation and striving for life enrichment -Adapting to increased distance from mainstream — accepting "subculture" status -Reversing trend toward generativity/productivity — beginning to conserve one's life energies -Adapting to decreasing physical vigor -Burying parents	-Beginning a comprehensive life review and reminiscence (as a means of getting closure and preparing oneself for death) -Beginning final consolidation of symbolic belief system or teleological world view — achieving "ego integrity",(i.e., the feeling that one's life had meaning and was well spent) -Accepting some loss of personal autonomy and competence and accepting aid from adult children -Facing increasing social separation and multiple losses — burying friends and family -Dealing with physical frailty — transcending physical preoccupation —or— surrendering to decline -Dealing with alone-ness —or— dealing with loss of privacy	INNER LIFE Butler, 1968 Erikson, 1963 Gould, 1975, 1978 Jacques, 1965 June, 1933 Levinson, 1977a, 1977b Sheehey, 1976 Vaillant, 1977 GENERAL REFERENCES ON ADULT DEVELOPMENT Bockneck, 1977 Brim, 1966 Bromley, 1974 Buhler, 1972 Erikson, 1963 Gould, 1972, 1975, 1977 Levinson, 1977c Lowenthal, et al., 1975 Neugarten, 1968, 1976

NOTES

1. Erik H. Erikson, *Childhood and Society*, 2nd ed. (New York: W.W. Norton & Co., 1963) and *Identity: Youth and Crisis* (New York: W.W. Norton & Co., 1968). *See also* Daniel Levinson and others, *The Seasons of a Man's Life* (New York: Knopf, 1978).
2. Lawrence Kohlberg, "Stage and Sequence: The Cognitive Developmental Approach to Education," In David Goslin, ed., *Handbook of Socialization: Theory and Research* (New York: Rand McNally, 1969), and *Collected Papers on Moral Development and Moral Education* (Cambridge, Mass.: Center for Moral Education, 1976).
3. *See* Jane Loevinger, *Ego Development* (San Francisco: Jossey-Bass, 1976) and Robert Kegan, *The Evolving Self: Problem and Process in Human Development* (Cambridge: Harvard University Press, 1982).
4. David Wortley and Ellen Amutea, "Mapping Adult Life Changes," in *Personnel and Guidance Journal* (April 1982), pp. 478–81.
5. William G. Perry, Jr., *Forms of Intellectual and Ethical Development in the College Years* (New York: Holt, Rinehart & Winston, 1970).
6. Kegan, *The Evolving Self: Problem and Process in Human Development*.
7. *See* Charles Sarnoff, *Latency* (New York: Jason Aronson, 1976) and Kegan, Ibid.
8. Our vignettes in this section are basically fictionalized amalgams from written and spoken remarks of teachers. We are especially indebted to the work of Sarah LeVine ("Relationships between the School as an Organizational Context and the Potentials for Adult Development," unpublished Doctoral Dissertation, Harvard University, 1980), whose ground-breaking study of adult developments in an elementary school inspired this section. While our "teachers" are invented for purposes of making specific points, readers will find in LeVine's dissertation real teachers carefully listened to, and their underlying epistemologies thoughtfully described. Where we occasionally insert quotes in these vignettes we are drawing directly from LeVine's study. Robert Putnam's ("A Constructive-Developmental View of Group Dynamics," Unpublished Paper, Harvard University, 1980) analysis of group dynamics in a work environment was especially helpful to our thinking about employees' experiences of alienation.
9. The reader is reminded that a self-system can operate on behalf of all kinds of purposes, including relationships. "What" the system is about is not the province of constructive analysis.
10. William Torbert, *Creating a Community of Inquiry: Conflict, Collaboration, Transformation* (New York: John Wiley, 1976).
11. Chris Argyris and Donald Schon, *Organizational Learning: A Theory of Action Perspective* (Reading, Mass.: Addison-Wesley, 1978).
12. Stanley Milgram, *Obedience to Authority* (New York: Harper & Row, Pub., 1974).
13. Daniel Yankelovich, *Generations Apart* (New York: Columbia Broadcasting System 1969).
14. Lawrence Kohlberg, "Stage and Sequence: The Cognitive Developmental Approach to Education," and *The Philosophy of Moral Development*, (New York: Harper & Row, Pub., 1981).
15. Kohlberg, *Collected Papers on Moral Development and Moral Education*.
16. Solomon Asch, "Effects of Group Pressure Upon the Modification and Distortion of Judgment," in Harold Guetzkow, ed., *Groups, Leadership and Men* (Pittsburgh: The Carnegie Press, 1951).

17. David Liberman, "Differential Response Patterns Across Developmental Levels to Perceptual and Logical Tasks Under Conditions of Group Pressure to Conform," Unpublished Doctoral Dissertation, Harvard University, 1976.
18. Daniel Candee, "The Moral Psychology of Watergate," *Journal of Social Issues*, Vol. 31, No. 2 (1975).
19. All Candee's quotes in this section are from Ibid., pp. 184–87.
20. Quoted in Ibid., p. 185.
21. Quoted in Ibid., p. 186.
22. Quoted in Ibid., p. 186.
23. Quoted in Ibid., p. 187.
24. Roberta Steinberg and Robert Kegan, "Israeli Soldiers' Attitudes Toward Arab Enemies: Moral Judgment and Moral Action," Unpublished Manuscript, Harvard University, 1978.
25. Kohlberg, *Collected Papers on Moral Development and Moral Education.*
26. David Frost, *I Gave Them a Sword: Behind the Scenes of the Nixon Interviews* (New York: Ballantine, 1978), p. 127.
27. Merle Miller, *Plain Speaking: An Oral Biography of Harry S. Truman* (New York: Putnam, 1974), p. 135.

11

ASSESSING POLITICAL LEADERS
The Criterion
of "Mental Health"*

Stanley A. Renshon

It is a standard principle of democratic theory that leaders should be freely chosen, and assessed periodically thereafter. These two tenets, coupled with the expectation of responsiveness, underlie political accountability. Thus, those countries that take democratic procedure seriously place a large burden on their citizens, both at the point of selection and afterwards, in evaluating leadership performance.

Citizens do not bear this responsibility alone. There are a number of institutions and individuals who specialize in providing perspectives on those who would fill political roles. Still, it is a curious feature of contemporary democracy that while the norm of leadership assessment is firmly established, the criteria by which it would best be accomplished are not.

However, the absence of such criteria has proved no deterrent to judgments about political leaders before and especially after they assume political roles. As the vicissitudes of presidential incumbency over the last decade suggest, citizens have become increasingly less reluctant to judge leaders by the criteria of immediate effects. But short-term effectiveness in specific policy areas represents only one and not necessarily the most

*This chapter and the research that underlies it were supported in part by a grant to the author from the Earhart Foundation, and also by a Faculty Award Grant from the Research Foundation of the City University of New York. I would like to express my appreciation to each of these agencies for their encouragement and facilitation.

important measure of leadership capacity and performance. Moreover, many evaluations both during candidacy and incumbency are based on narrow, inappropriate, and in some cases, irrelevant criteria. It is already clear, for example, that the skills and capacities necessary to obtain political office are not necessarily the same as those which facilitate governing wisely and effectively once in political office.

The difficulties in assessing leadership are compounded by the fact that certain of our political traditions have become increasingly problematic. A good illustration of this may be found in the relationship between political ideology and political parties. In the past, American political leaders arrayed themselves along a continuum of general policy positions associated with particular party labels. Political parties in turn stood for certain broad approaches to public problems. Candidates of these parties would then refine these broad orientations, sometimes in the form of specific programs, in order to capture an electoral majority. In this way, certain progammatic thrusts typically become associated with one of the major political parties, even though the particular solutions, and even the problems themselves on occasion, might change. Party labels, therefore, became a good general guide to a candidate's views on a wide range of political issues.

Over the past decade, however, the meanings of such traditional terms as *liberal* or *conservative,* in relation to political parties, their candidates, and even specific policy orientations or programs have become blurred. This blurring has not resulted, as in the past, from the movement along policy lines by both parties but rather reflects a tendency of recent candidates for high office to borrow broad orientations and specific positions from both major parties. Thus Richard Nixon, always considered to the right ideologically, and a staunch anti-Communist, surprised many by initiating his "opening to China." Nixon himself eschews traditional party labels, and one observer, after trying unsuccessfully to pinpoint Mr. Nixon's political ideology, concluded that, "he rejects the extreme wings of both parties and within these bounds it is hard to place Nixon as a liberal-leaning or conservative-leaning Republican."[1] Along similar lines, 1976 Democratic presidential nominee Jimmy Carter ran as a fiscal conservative who wanted a strong defense, programs to help the disadvantaged, *and* a reduction in government spending. Small wonder that a preelection poll found that "the bulk of his liberal supporters think him liberal, the bulk of his conservative supporters think him conservative, [and] the bulk of his moderate supporters think him moderate."[2]

Of course all this assumes that party programs have a direct relationship to public problems. In a world unencumbered by uncertainty and complexity, assessment of political leaders would simply involve selecting the best policy programs and evaluating subsequent adherence to them. In this situation, which characterized American politics for many decades, candidates for leadership were not so much of interest in and of themselves as they were as purveyors of policies designed to meet specific public problems. Over the last several decades, however, a subtle but important change has taken place. Rather than ask where candidates stand, citizens are much more likely to ask what they are like. In place of programs, we are now offered personas. It is not that public problems have become less pressing; obviously they have become more so. Rather it is ironic that at the same time that the range and complexity of social problems have made "the issues" more important than ever, the failures to find solutions have made the elaboration of policy programs, and assumptions about their efficacy, increasingly suspect. In the absence of confidence in any policy, the American public has increasingly turned toward a search for "leadership," which, it is hoped, will somehow prevail where specific programs have not. Aspiring leaders, in turn, have not offered concrete programs or indications of how they will proceed, but rather they have emphasized their capacity to cope. In some cases, the mere assertion of capacity has taken precedence over its actual existence, as numerous advisers (programmatic and political) strain to project images of control, competence, and above all, success.

In many ways concern with character and other aspects of personality is a reasonable response to a world where many important problems cannot be anticipated, let alone solved. It also reflects an increasingly sophisticated understanding on the part of the public, gained at the cost of harsh experience over the past two decades, of the role that personal skills and capacities play in shaping numerous aspects of incumbency and performance. One recent by-product of this understanding is that judgments about the integrity, competence, and knowledge of aspiring leaders are now routinely made by the electorate.[3]

In response to this, however, aspiring leaders have been quick to sense the public's concern with character and personal characteristics and to integrate that concern into their election strategies. The discussion of the "new Nixon" in 1968 was clearly designed to counter public uneasiness about the old one. In 1976, running against the excesses of former President Nixon, candidate Jimmy Carter reminded the American public that "character was an issue" and directly contrasted his with that of his predecessor. In 1980, feeling that he was unable to campaign on a record of sufficiently solid accomplishment, then President Carter again tried to make character the major issue, but not with the same results. In a revealing postmortem, President Carter's media adviser, Pat Caddell, acknowledged that there had been widespread unhappiness with Carter all along and went on to add that, "our campaign fought hard to keep these feelings out—to keep real events out. We knew we had to win on narrower grounds, on which man had the best character to handle the job."[4]

It seems clear that developing useful criteria for evaluating political leaders and leadership performance will require going well beyond simply considering political ideology, or even evaluating programs, as important as these will continue to be. An important aspect of this task will be to increase our understanding of the tasks of political leadership in democracies, and from that knowledge to develop criteria regarding the personal characteristics and skills necessary to accomplish them.

But there is yet another aspect to this. Having developed sufficiently rich theory on the relationship between personal capacities and political performance, we might want to consider individual or structural interventions designed to enhance these capacities and neutralize or minimize any adverse tendencies. Examining such appraisal and intervention questions will involve addressing a complex set of interrelated issues. These will include the nature of character and psychological functioning, their relationship to the work of political leadership in a democracy, technical questions of psychological assessment, including issues of validity and reliability, and a host of political, legal, and ethical considerations.[5] The formulation of criteria in these areas, and the development of the theory and understanding necessary to support them, will be a complex and difficult task, and one which, as Alexander George has pointed out, will have to be addressed by diverse groups of specialists working together (or in tandem) over many years.[6]

One obvious and important place to begin is with that area of theory, research, and practice which addresses itself to effective and impaired psychological functioning, namely clinical psychology and psychiatry. We are, of course, ultimately interested in whether the models developed by psychology and psychiatry over the past six decades are relevant to the assessment of psychological functioning in political roles, and if so, in what ways. There is already a body of work in political science dating back to the thirties that has argued that such models do have relevance for understanding the functioning of individuals in political roles, but the models themselves have rarely been subject to close analysis.[7] Instead the emphasis has been on their application. But if clinical psychology and psychiatry are to make any real contribution to the assessment of political leaders and the evaluation of their performance, the models they put forth must finally be addressed. Indeed, this essay will do just that by focusing on those aspects of clinical theory that are relevant to the tasks at hand.

But before examining the work that has been put forward as relevant to the problem of leadership assessment, it is worth noting that such work forms the foundation of a variety of proposals aimed at improving both the selection and performance of political leaders. These range from the suggestion for a formal psychiatric screening board to evaluate candidates before they take office with regard to their "mental health," to various proposals for psychiatric intervention as an adjunct to executive decision making. Such proposals have come from many quarters, among them a distinguished past president of the American Political Science Association,[8] and the Committee on Governmental Agencies, a task force of the Group for the Advancement of Psychiatry.[9] What gives some of these proposals[10] growing plausibility and cogency is the development of an increasingly sophisticated framework within which the necessary psychological and political observations can be made and assessed.

It is now almost a century since Sigmund Freud's classic work on *The Interpretation of Dreams (1900)* marked the beginning of a systematic and scientific treatment of general psychological structure and functioning. Since that time, clinical theory has developed a diverse and comprehensive body of theory and data on individual, interpersonal, and group functioning. Equally important, there have been several decades of social application of clinical theory in diverse arenas such as education, law, and community intervention. Such applications have, of necessity, departed from the strict intrapsychic emphasis of Freud. They have been heavily influenced by, among others, the interpersonal theories of Sullivan, the developmental theories of Erikson, and the cultural perspectives of Horney.

Indeed, Freud's original formulations of intrapsychic structure and process have themselves been modified and enlarged. These modifications, added to an already powerful model of psychological functioning, serve as a comprehensive framework within which applications to social contexts may be carried out. The advancement of knowledge in this area, coupled with an increasingly strong sense that such a framework can and should be applied to the political process, form the basis of what might well be termed *political psychiatry*. Simply stated, political psychiatry involves the belief that clinical psychoanalytic theory, as developed by Freud and modified by his successors, can be applied to the institutions, processes, and problems of democratic government. With regard to leadership, the application of such a perspective must of necessity be concerned with more than intrapsychic phenomena, since leadership involves functioning effectively in multiple, complex, and frequently ambiguous political environments which are themselves bounded by norms, expectations, constraints, and opportunities.

The purpose of this chapter, then, is to explore some key issues with regard to the relationship between political psychiatry and the assessment of psychological suitability for political roles. To that end I will first present some general perspectives on the psychological functioning of political leaders, a prerequisite for specifying any criteria for psychological suitability. I will then examine some of the basic tenets of the medical model and its attendant conceptualizations (mental health and mental illness), as criteria for evaluating political performance. Finally, I will examine the concept of impairment and make some suggestions for its extention to the political arena, as a step in the direction of developing useful criteria for establishing psychological suitability for public office.

THE PSYCHOLOGICAL
FUNCTIONING OF POLITICAL
LEADERS: SOME
PERSPECTIVES ON A PROBLEM

Of the many important questions raised by political psychiatry, none is more central, or controversial, than those having to do with the criteria for evaluating the psychological functioning of political leaders. Attempts to formulate and apply such criteria are crucial to political psychiatry, which rests on the premise that in politics, as in the consulting room, every diagnosis carries with it remedial implications. This being the case, knowledge of such processes is a crucial precondition for intervention.

Yet, it is clear that procedural or other interventions can only be evaluated with reference to the specific problems they purport to mitigate. This, in turn, requires a comprehensive specification of exactly what is at issue. More is of course required if we are to move from theory to intervention, but little will be accomplished in the absence of this first step.

Regrettably, in view of the seriousness of the issues which are raised by the attempt to assess and improve the quality of psychological functioning of political leaders, much discussion in this area has been superficial, sensational, and sometimes beside the point. The loose use of terms such as *irrational, abnormal, mental illness,* and *insanity,* not to mention *normality* and *health* permeate such discussions even by some who ought to know better. The problem, as all who are familiar with these terms know, is that they frequently mask more than they uncover. When these terms represent at once both a start and a conclusion, they become an exercise in labeling rather than understanding. It adds little to our knowledge of these important and complex issues to write about "The Mental Health of Our Leaders,"[11] or to ominously forewarn of times "When Insanity Holds the Scepter."[12]

Perhaps the first question to be asked at the outset of a discussion such as this one is whether, in fact, there is a problem. That is, taking as a starting point even a general understanding of what is conveyed by the terms of discourse in political psychiatry, is there sufficient evidence of a problem to warrant the search for a solution? How we answer this question will depend not only on the data we adduce but also on the way in which the question is phrased.

The most persistent and dramatic formulation of the problem is the "psychotic leader case." In informal discussion this takes the form of worrying about leaders who must be chased around with nets;[13] in more intelligent lay understanding, a concern with leaders who have or might experience "mental breakdowns;" and in professional discourse, a concern with public officials exhibiting clear psychotic symptoms. A parallel and only somewhat less dramatic formulation of the problem focuses on the extreme behaviors or traits of political leaders, with the implicit (sometimes explicit) corollary that such behavior is on its face evidence of severe psychological impairment. Here the emphasis in not on a general and pervasive decomposition of the personality system but rather on a severe disturbance in limited areas of it. Examples might inlude the cruelness of Ivan the Terrible, the suspiciousness of Joseph Stalin, and the politics of extermination pursued by Adolph Hitler.

While these three represent the worst case presentations of the problem they are not the only ones that can be made. Nor, paradoxically, are they necessarily the strongest formulations of the problem that can be made in support of the concerns of political psychiatry. But before going on to consider other perspectives, let us pause here to consider what evidence is available to support "worst case" formulations and the concerns and suggestions which follow from it.

To begin with the obvious, it is evident that clear, reliable evidence on this (and related questions) is extremely difficult to obtain. From the few well-documented cases of political leaders who have suffered from severe psychological impairments while in office, it is clear that even dramatic symptoms per se are no guarantee that the impairment will be recognized for what it is. Arnold Rogow's carefully documented account[14] of former Secretary of Defense James Forrestal's clinical depression, auditory hallucinations, persecutory beliefs, and subsequent suicide makes very clear that the first response to the increasingly evident signs that something was wrong, was to misunderstand the problem. As Rogow writes, "Most of those among his friends and associates who were aware that Forrestal was suffering from extreme physical and nervous exhaustion, that he had lost a good deal of weight during the preceding months, and that he more and more frequently was experiencing moods of deep depression, were convinced that he required nothing more than a long period of rest and relaxation."[15]

Several reasons could be advanced for such lapses. One is that psychological impairments of less than dramatic, psychotic proportions are frequently unrecognized for what they are, or else "misdiagnosed." Discrete symptoms may not be recognized as the precursors or reflections of impairment syndromes.

Sometimes, however, the failure to see is less a result of technical ignorance than a conscious disregard of the obvious. Those with the most consistent and direct access to the leader are usually those with the most emotional and political investment in continuing current arrangements. There need not be anything sinister implied by this, only that individual loyalty, a lengthy or intense history of association, and enjoyment of one's position may lead those in a position to know, to underplay or otherwise distort such information. So, too, it may very well be that politics is one arena where the unusual or the excessive may be more acceptable. Many personal eccentricities may be tolerated by those close to the leader, and seen as nothing more than a reflection of the unusual constellation of talents that brought the leader into power.[16]

A final related barrier to the recognition of psychological impairment is the assumption that such problems simply do not exist. This Rogow characterizes as the "mental health mythology of official Washington,"[17] namely, that while ordinary people suffer from psychological impairments, VIPs do not. One does not usually notice what one believes will not be there.

But even when these barriers to recognition are surmounted, it does not necessarily lead to public knowledge. Indeed, from the detailed case materials available in the area, it is clear that once a leader is diagnosed as having a severe impairment (either physical or psychological, but especially the latter), strenuous efforts are made to keep such information from the public.

One can see this pattern at work in the 1972 presidential campaign. After his nomination, but before the election, vice-presidential candidate Thomas Eagleton disclosed at a press conference that he had been hospitalized three times for what he termed "nervous exhaustion."[18] These hospitalizations had been for four weeks, four days, and three weeks respectively, and, according to Senator Eagleton's account, were the direct result of his hard driving, intense character, and his disposition to push himself too hard.[19] That same day, *The New York Times* carried a story entitled, "Eagleton Illness Known to Associates," confirming that Senator Eagleton's hospitalizations were, "well known in political circles in his home state and among some associates on Capitol Hill, but had never been used against him in a campaign."[20]

In the case of Forrestal, the decision to admit him to Bethesda Naval Hospital rather than the Menninger Foundation in Topeka, Kansas was based in part on the desire to keep the nature of Forrestal's condition secret from the general public.[21] It was felt that since Bethesda was a general hospital, this would be easier to accomplish than with the Menninger Foundation, which was solely concerned with "mental illness." While there were other, persuasive reasons for treating Forrestal at Bethesda, it is clear from this and other cases that concern over public reaction plays an important role in considerations of what should be done, as well as what is disclosed.

For sitting officials the reason for such concern is obvious. Questions of psychological functioning are bound to raise public anxiety about the direction and management of public affairs. Even, as in the case of Forrestal, when the impairment becomes obvious after the official has left office, this still raises questions about the conduct of affairs while the person had responsibility. Rogow writes that official Washington was very sensitive to the implications of Forrestal's illness for fear that the Russians would use it for propaganda purposes, which they did.[22]

Finally, there are important considerations of individual and family privacy in cases involving psychological impairment. Especially in cases of severe impairment, there is reluctance on the part of family members and friends to elaborate details of what is surely a painful and disruptive experience for all concerned. Although there are legitimate questions regarding the weight that should be accorded this consideration in the case of public officials, it is understandable that those involved would wish to deal with such difficulties privately, without the increased tension brought about by public scrutiny.

The net result of all of these factors, however, is to deprive us of knowledge which would help to inform and clarify what is surely an important and complex public issue. In place of detailed, reliable information, we are left with discrete anecdotes, professional speculations, and partial case histories. Worse, the area has attracted its own group of "exploitation artists" more concerned with sensationalism than understanding. Given these factors, it is small wonder that the simple question raised at the beginning of this section is far from easy to answer.

One way to approach the question of whether severe impairment of political leaders is a problem is by studies of incidence. In typical epidemiological studies, a syndrome or set of specific symptoms are specified, operational indicators of their existence generated, and a representative sample selected and examined regarding the problem at hand. Leaving aside the question of specifying syndromes, symptoms (even for those consensually validated), and their indicators, we simply do not have available to us the kind of comprehensive epidemiological data that would give us some sense of how prevalent the problem is. Nor are we likely to have it.

Another approach would be to survey historical records to see to what extent severe impairment among political leaders has been a problem. The eccentricities and excesses of political leaders have always been fertile ground for both the merely curious and the concerned, and there are several works which survey the politically influential from this perspective. Frequently, however, the titles betray a bias, as for example T. F. Thiselton's *Royalty in All Ages: The Amusements, Eccentricities, Accomplishments, Superstitions and Frolics of Kings and Queens of Europe*, published in 1903,[23] or Dr. Angelo S. Rappoport's *Mad Majesties: or Raving Rulers and Submissive Subjects*, published in 1910.[24] While containing potentially useful information, such "histories" suffer from a preoccupation with the bizarre, and an ultimately fatal lack of theory.

At least the latter problem was alleviated by the pioneering work of Freud, after which a number of more sophisticated investigations of historical incidents of severe impairment among leaders were undertaken. One result of these efforts is that we now have available several excellent detailed case studies of such events.[25] While such studies are an invaluable addition to our understanding of this area, they still do not constitute by themselves a comprehensive historical survey undertaken by researchers versed in psychological theory.

In the early 1960s, however, just such a survey was undertaken by the late Dr. Robert L. Noland, a professor of psychology at the University of Dayton. Using a wide variety of primary and secondary sources, covering non-Western as well as Western nations, and going back at least four centuries, he found that, "at least 75 chiefs of state have led their countries, actually or symbolically, for a total of several centuries, while suffering from severe mental disturbances."[26] Dr. Noland concluded that, "there is little reason to assume that we could never be faced with a similar problem in the United States."[27]

In examining this conclusion and the data which give rise to it,[28] several points deserve to be mentioned. First, the "severe mental disturbances" which Professor Noland records from his historical sources consist of several different kinds of maladies. Grouped together are rulers who were congenital inbeciles or feebleminded, along with those judged mentally unstable or "insane." The latter is by far the most frequent category but still leaves unanswered exactly what is meant by the term. Some of the historical accounts are clearer in their characterizations than in their descriptions of the behavior which gave rise to them.

Moreover, there are several reasons to believe that Professor Noland's data underrepresent the problem. Perhaps most importantly, the data was collected only for chiefs of state, not for the wide range of other public officials, both major and minor, who form part of the potenial sampling universe of political leadership. Second, it is clear that major categories of severe impairment, such as borderline conditions or manic-depressive psychosis, are only hinted at in the historical records. It seems likely that given the traditional lack of formal institutional restraints on political leaders, and the tendency toward authoritarian rule, leadership excesses were more the rule than the exception. Such behaviors might well be viewed differently today from a clinical perspective.[29] A further problem is the assumption that severe impairments must take the form of extreme or bizarre behavior. Performance mistakes, miscalculations, and lapses can arise from disturbances of psychological functioning which are neither extreme or bizarre, but which have nonetheless widespread consequences. Finally, Professor Noland's published data were preliminary, and in going over his notes and references for the basic data, I found other instances, not included in his published count, of rulers characterized by their contemporaries as suffering from insanity.

The question remains, however, what implications, if any, may be drawn from such a study for the problem we raised at the outset of this section. Even considering the qualifications raised, at least two significant points emerge from these data. First, on their face, they suggest that historically, by any reasonable measure, the severe impairment problem is not a unique event. Second, the amount of time that such rulers were in power both individually and collectively is striking, as are the numbers of people whose lives they affected. Given this historical experience and more recent illustrations of it in our own century, we have no reason to be complacent about the worst case argument adduced by some proponents of political psychiatry.

It could be reasonably argued, however, that concern with incidence is really beside the point, since such an approach equates importance with frequency. This is clearly a dubious assumption in cases where even one occurrence is cause for alarm. Cataclysmic events such as nuclear wars, holocausts, and reigns of terror may be historically infrequent but are no less important or transformational for that. To be sure, many discussions in political psychiatry have been haunted by the specter of a presidential "Dr. Strangelove" following a tortured private vision to nuclear annihilation. Unfortunately, such Hollywood inspirations promote the luxury of believing that such behavior exhausts the problem. What is not sufficiently realized is that psychological impairment, even when severe, comes in many forms, not all of them overtly dramatic.

But the issue of importance, defined as other than frequency, goes beyond the possibility of nuclear annihilation, although this is undoubtedly its single most important illustrative event. Leaving aside nuclear weaponry, modern technology and social complexity have transformed the power of political leaders. Instantaneous communication, access and control of vast human and material resources, coupled with the interdependency (and thus vulnerability) of contemporary social structure and the individuals who inhabit it, tend to magnify the already formidable institutionally based power of those who determine and carry out public policy. The general growth of government involvement at every level of society shows no signs of abatement, regardless of temporary or episodic regressions. Part of the reason for this is said to be the increasing transformation of private wants into public needs. But such formulations fail to consider that the size and complexity of the social forces which individuals confront in modern, complex societies increasingly do not lend themselves to individual, private solutions.

Simply put, then, contemporary social structure and political process tends to amplify the consequences of leadership decisions and behavior. It does so in three ways. First, it does so because the arenas covered by political decisions have expanded and continue to do so; second, because the scope of important personal values affected by such decisions has also increased as a consequence of the first; and third, because the number of people who are affected by such decisions have increased. It follows from this that arguments in favor of examining the psychological functioning of political leaders and the quality of the decisions they make need not rest solely either on incidence or on the possibility for catastrophe, as important as we might agree these are. Rather, this more general approach begins with the "potential for effect" inherent in the exercise of policymaking in contemporary societies, and draws its formulations of importance from these calculations.

THE MENTAL HEALTH
OF POLITICAL LEADERS:
SOME PRELIMINARY
CONSIDERATIONS

Essential to any discussion of the psychological functioning of political leaders, and crucial to any proposals for intervention, is, as suggested above, the formulation of evaluative criteria. Yet, it is hard to think of a more difficult, complex, and controversial subject area. It is in this context that terms such as *mental health, mental illness, normal, irrational,* and the like enter into discussions, frequently to the disadvantage of the problem being considered.

The concepts and models employed by political psychiatry in the public arena are no less controversial in the privacy of the consulting room. Is there really such a thing as "mental illness," and if so, of what does it consist? What is "normal" behavior, and is that the same as "mental health"? Aren't all great men "different," and if so, how can we evaluate our political leaders by everyday standards? These are only a sampling of the questions that must be asked, given a concern with the psychological functioning of those who make and carry out public policy. They are, as noted, difficult questions, but they cannot be avoided if the concerns of political psychiatry are to be taken seriously.

A major concern of political psychiatry has been with actual or potential psychological impairment of political leaders; or, to put it another way, that leaders may be or become "mentally ill" while in office. From a technical standpoint, and as I will argue more fully at a later point, this formulation is too narrow and limited. But it does require us to face some basic conceptual problems, the most immediate of which is, what exactly is "mental illness"?[30]

One approach to this question begins with what is called "the medical model."[31] As its name implies, this model assumes tht mental health and illness are analogous to their physical counterparts. This in turn involves at least three distinct propositions. First, and I think most importantly, the medical model assumes that physical and mental (psychological) concepts of disease are analogous. It follows from this that we understand mental illness in much the same way as we understand physical illness. Second, the medical model assumes that certain bodies of information do exist regarding the nature of mental illness, and that mastery of this body of knowledge is essential to correct diagnosis, understanding, and treatment. It follows from this that such technical and specialized knowledge should and can be used only by properly trained and recognized "experts." Third, the medical model assumes that once someone is diagnosed as ill by a properly certified expert, the person so designated enters into a "sick role," which alters his network of social obligations, responsibilities, and privileges.

All of these assumptions are controversial, but none more so than the first. Perhaps the most radical critique of the model has come from Thomas Szasz, whose well-known position is that "mental illness" is a myth.[32] Szasz bases his objections on two fundamental points. First, he argues that the medical model requires that mental illness, like physical illness, be ultimately traceable to some physiological deficiency. According to this line of argument, mental illness must ultimately be found to be a disease of the brain (significantly, and I think erroneously, not of the mind[33]) in the same way that physical symptoms reflect disturbances of interior organic systems. His second, and stronger point, is that evaluations of mental health symptoms involve some judgment on the part of those making the diagnosis, which is radically different from the judgments made regarding physical symptoms.

According to Szasz, and it is worth quoting his remarks here:

> . . . the concept of illness, whether bodily or mental, *implies deviation from some clearly defined norm*. In the case of physical illness, the norm is the structural and functional integrity of the human body. Thus, although the desirability of physical health as such is an ethical value, what health *is* can be stated in anatomical or physiological terms. What is the norm deviation from which is regarded as mental illness? This question cannot be easily answered. But whatever this norm might be, we can be certain of only one thing: namely that it is a norm which must be stated in terms of *psycho-social, ethical,* or *legal* concepts.[34]

Szasz goes on to argue that the discipline of psychiatry is more closely tied to ethics than to medicine. The reason for this is that mental illness refers in practice to "problems in living," not of physiology, and that such problems can only be analyzed within a social and ethical framework. The consequence of this requirement is that such judgments are inevitably biased by the personal values of the individual making them as well as the shared social values of the society to which the evaluator belongs.

This position also has implications for advocates of psychiatric interventions in politics. If, as Szasz argues, clinical judgments are based in essence on personal values, then inviting psychiatrists (or psychologists) to perform a preelection screening function is to assign greater importance and political weight to their values than to those of the electorate, without any scientific grounds for doing so. There may well be reasons other than this why we might not wish to institute such a system, but even if there were not, this criticism, if accurate, would represent a convincing argument against the proposal. It is therefore of some importance to examine Szasz's argument more closely.

The first set of Szasz's arguments refers to the ultimate referents or sources of the phenomenon characterized as *mental illless*. Szasz would accept the term if it could ultimately be shown to refer to some physical lesion in the brain, a position which denies ontological status to anything incapable of ostensive reference. The problem is that on these restricted grounds, any discussion of physical disease would be ruled out as well since, "although diseases might be *caused* by the presence in the body of some such entity (as a cold may be caused by a virus), and although they might be associated with *symptoms* that are concrete entities (e.g., the fluid present in the sinuses), a physical illness is not identical with its causes or its symptoms."[35] In short, as L. S. King has pointed out, "Diseases are not things in the same sense of rocks or trees, or rivers, diseases . . . are not material."[36] Of course, many concepts in science are given ontological status in spite of the difficulty of specifying their concrete referents (examples include forces, electrons, and so forth); and, as Moore points out, we are not reticent in science or in everyday speech and understanding to confer "thinghood" on abstract qualities such as, "squareness shape, zoological species, or more to the point perhaps, psychological states."[37]

The real question here is not whether mental illness has some specific, concrete physiological location (which it may ultimately be found to have, but which is, in any case, beside the point of this argument), but whether it is legitimate and useful to extend the term to cover impairments for which there is no known physiological cause or site.[38] Of course, if the construct cannot be legitimately extended to cover psychological impairments, it makes no sense to build a specific psychological theory of political-role impairment, or to apply the relevant clinical theory to individual political leaders. There is, however, substantial reason to believe that such extensions are legitimate, and that the political application thereof is possible.

Margolis points out that the line between physical and mental illness is not as sharp as Szasz would like to have us believe.[39] He mentions psychosomatic and hysterical conversions as two illustrations of a class of impairments of functioning which present concrete physical symptoms but which do not have "concrete" organic or neurological causes. Moreover, it is not necessarily the capacity to locate specific causes which permits us to refer to something as an illness, but rather its effects. The history of medical science is replete with illustrations of "diseases" which were recognized as such (for example, polio) well before any particular physiological origin was uncovered. According to this argument it is the *pattern of illness*, not the cause, which supports the concept of disease being applied. A similar point is made by Moore in discussing the appropriateness of terming hysteria an "illness":

> The activities for which one is incapacitated by a paralyzed arm differ not a wit, no matter if the paralysis is anatomical or hysterical. In either case, one cannot, for example, play baseball or tend after one's father effectively, etc. . . . Being in a state properly called "ill" then does not depend on one's knowing, or even . . . of there being any particular physiological condition. It depends on one being in a state characterized (roughly) by pain, incapacitation, and the prospect of a hastened death. There is nothing mythical about such states, whether they are due to a broken leg or a broken home.[40]

Any theory of political-role impairment could not easily use the criteria advanced by Moore. The third, hastened death, is neither suitable nor practical, and the other two would have to be modified. Incapacity, for example, would have to be modified to include degrees of inability, and even this would have to be specifically derived from an understanding of the requirements of particular political roles. It may well be, for example, that the functional requirements for some political roles, such as the presidency, require such an extensive range of skills and capacities that any definition of impairment would have to distinguish between what is really necessary and what is only useful. The other criterion, pain, could in fact easily be transposed to political contexts via such manifestations as substantial stress, emotional discomfort, or other reflections of intrapsychic, interpersonal, or role conflict, but would need to be supplemented. However, even if the extension of the terms *mental health* and *illness,* (and theory and data which underlie them) are not in principle an insurmountable criticism, there are further difficulties that must be addressed.

Szasz writes that one difference between physical and mental illness is that in the former the disturbance is referenced by signs (for example, fever) or symptoms (pain), but that in the latter we refer "to a person's communications about himself, others and the world around him."[41] Szasz argues that the former is more "public" than the latter, which he terms "private," surely a curious understanding of the two terms. More importantly, there is no a priori reason to confer any less status to "communications about himself" than for any other signs or symptoms.

It is true that persons other than professionals enter into evaluations of "mental health" symptoms (or communications), but this by itself is neither a necessary nor sufficient reason to call for abandonment of diagnosis. Indeed, Szasz is perfectly willing to continue such characterizations so long as they are termed *problems in living* rather than mental illness, but if the former refer to the same set of "symptoms" as the latter, it is hard to see just what is accomplished by the change. In fact, it is perfectly plausible and logically consistent to say that someone has been having "problems in living," and to also characterize that as an illness.

Of course, from the standpoint of assessing political leaders, especially before entering office, we might well wish to know whether there are "problems in living," and if so what kind. Modern clinical theory still rests on the well-founded observational perspective that every manifestation of the individual is part of a related whole. So, for example, while there is substantial and legitimate debate over the demarcation of "private" and "public" information about political leaders, from a clinical perspective it cannot be seriously argued that the former has no relevance for the latter.

Beyond this, however, lie questions of whether there are particular "problems in politics," which are analogous to Szasz's concept of "problems of living." Here again, any formulations would have to be tied explicitly to a theory of functions in leadership roles. This in turn underscores the need for any comprehensive theory of political-role impairment to link clinical theory directly with political theory.

MENTAL HEALTH AND THE PROBLEM OF NORMALITY IN POLITICAL PSYCHIATRY

It is Szasz's second set of contentions rather than his first that is in fact the more troublesome. There is general agreement that concepts of illness, whether physical or mental, imply deviation from some norm; but the crucial question is which one. Szasz argues that beyond the problem of linguistic designation there is the even more basic problem, namely, that clinical judgments ultimately rest on departures from psychosocial, ethical, or legal norms. Moreover, "the judgment entails . . . a covert matching of the patient's ideas, concepts and beliefs with those of the observer and the society in which they live."[42] If such matching can be shown to be ill-conceived, inappropriate, or unreflective of the phenomenon they purportedly clarify, then any judgments based on these matchings will clearly be called into question. Given these circumstances there can be little value either in political psychiatry or the interventions it proposes.

There are several ways in which the concept of *normal* is used within the context of discussions of *mental health*. The first and most frequent use of the term refers back to a form of statistical norm. Here the idea is that normality is defined in part by occurrence, but such a formulation quickly runs into well-known problems, the most immediate of which spring from the inclination to equate statistical frequency with "health." Tooth decay, for example, is widely prevalent in our society, and in that statistical sense might be considered normal, but one would hardly wish to argue that it is healthy. Nor must infrequency imply pathology. Moore[43] asks us to imagine a person with a cubical stomach, which, while abnormal in its physical structure, performs efficiently in digesting food and allows its owner an equally long life compared to someone with a "normal" stomach. As these illustrations indicate, normality in the limited sense of frequency may be quite irrelevant to the questions posed by concepts of health and illness.

Similar problems arise when we consider psychological conditions or behaviors from the standpoint of statistical frequency. Narcissism, use of defensive mechanisms that distort reality, and unconscious conflicts are just some examples of psychological conditions which are assumed by many psychiatrists to be well nigh universal, but they (and we) would not necessarily conclude that these conditions represent "healthy" lines of development simply by virtue of their widespread presence. Moreover, if these conditions are to some degree considered pathological in the sense that they impede "optimal functioning," then we are left with the position that everyone is a little "sick," and "health" becomes a matter of degree.

There is nothing inherently suspect about such a position, and it is the one which I will adopt here. But it does impose the as yet too stringent requirement of being able to distinguish between the more subtle degrees of impairment. As in many other areas of human functioning, it is only the extremes that are easy to recognize. This dilemma poses special difficulties for the interventions suggested by political psychiatry, which have typically rested on "worst case analyses," because the most potentially dangerous and widespread political problems arise from the milder gradients of impairment, rather than the worst case scenario of psychosis. But if this is the case, then any proposed interventions must be realistically bound by our ability to distinguish among the degrees of impairment.

This is one reason that suggestions for formal psychiatric assessment of candidates for high office, while well intentioned, are, at present, not even theoretically feasible. The fact of the matter is that neither clinical theory nor clinical judgment has advanced to the point where this task could successfully be carried out. Although psychiatric assessment might well be considered a worthy and important undertaking, the tools to accomplish it are not yet in hand.

But even if they were, many legal, political, and even practical concerns would remain. Among them is the issue of whether constellations of traits and capacities which one might not want in one context might be acceptable and even sought after in another. Or, put another way, should the criteria by which we evaluate political leaders be different from those we use for other occupational roles? In turn, this point raises the question of cross-contextual aspects of normality, and the dilemma of cultural relativity.

The problems raised by statistical concepts of normality become even more pronounced when we consider the variations that occur cross-culturally in "normal behavior." As Karen Horney pointed out many years ago, "The conception of what is normal varies not only with the culture but also within the same culture, in the course of time."[44] Visions, communications with deceased ancestors, and trance states are only some of the behaviors that are treated routinely in some cultures, but which would be considered evidence of gross disturbance in ours. One implication of this is that we cannot assume that the same behavior reflects the same underlying etiology, or as Jahoda puts it, "Similarities in symptoms must not be mistaken for identical disturbances in functions."[45] Such considerations certainly mitigate against the development, at present at least, of an agreed-upon set of criteria to make cross-cultural judgments of mental health or illness.

It must be emphasized, however, that this does not necessarily invalidate the notion of political psychiatry in *one* culture. It may very well be that we don't yet understand the ways in which specific disturbances manifest themselves in different behaviors across cultures, or even within one culture, for that matter, but attempting to understand and intervene in the second case is not dependent on our ability to do so in the first.

Yet a special problem may arise in the examination of one culture: the existence of socially patterned impairments. In some cultures, particular impairments may be so widespread that their pathology is not recognized, much less acknowledged. The anthropologist Ruth Benedict found that the Kaakiutl Indians of British Columbia engage in behavior that is,

> by our standards, paranoid and megalomaniacal. Their world view is similar to a delusion of grandeur in our culture.[46]

Such findings do not necessarily negate the possibility that members of a particular culture may make useful and valid analyses, but they do however, suggest, caution.

Nor must particular characteristics necessarily be widespread in order to pose a problem. Take the case of the enormous ambition that is typically necessary to reach the upper levels of political leadership. In contemporary politics such enormous ambition is fused, for both strategic and psychological reasons, with other drives, and so is rarely seen publicly in pristine form. One result of this is that the great drive necessary to gain high public office is now routinely assumed. But the implications of this extreme ambition for political performance remain unclear. The unusual, not the commonplace, is where investigation usually begins.

We have no trouble recognizing the way in which cultural ideals may facilitate or even glorify extremes in other circumstances. As Jahoda has argued, the failure to distinguish between the normative and statistical aspects of normality, "leads back into an extreme cultural relativism according to which the storm trooper . . . must be considered as the prototype of integrative adjustment in Nazi culture."[47] My point here is not to argue that enormous ambition (for example) is equivalent to the pathology of the storm trooper, but to underscore the difficulty of making the necessary distinctions when it is *our* ideals and assumptions about normality which are at issue. The task, although admittedly difficult, is nonetheless necessary as one begins to ask specific questions regarding psychological functioning of particular groups (for example, political leaders) in particular (decision-making) contexts.

It is clear, for example, that judgments regarding the appropriateness of certain political behaviors must be viewed against the background of the requirements for obtaining and maintaining political roles in contemporary politics. The example of ambition is only one of the ways in which the nature of the contemporary political process acts as both a barrier and an impetus for certain kinds of persons in the recruitment process. Another illustration, brought about by the increasing importance of television and the decline of more conventional sources of information about candidates, is the capacity to skillfully portray oneself in a way which is congruent with public moods and concerns. The capacity to project reassurance, competence, or whatever else is called for may well be an important component of leadership in mass societies, but it raises delicate issues of integrity, authenticity, and, not incidentally, questions of informed consent and accountability. It will be difficult and perhaps ultimately useless to deal solely with personal aspects of leadership recruitment and performance without identifying those aspects of role structure and political process which are related to them and which would also benefit from or facilitate change.

Problems with statistical concepts of normality, and their equation by some with "health," make clear that Szasz's criticisms of clinical judgments are not without some foundation. He is certainly correct in stating that such judgments are related to the social system in which they take place, but I think he errs in the implications he draws from this association. Szasz argues that a crucial matching which takes place occurs between the patient's behaviors and psychosocial, ethical, and legal norms. He maintains that the personal values of the psychiatrist enter into the analysis at this step, implying that psychiatrists take societal norms as their criterion for health. An alternative position is that a knowledge of social norms and process are important not because the psychiatrist necessarily assumes that they are correct or embody wisdom or health but because the way an individual deals with the ongoing set of opportunities and losses which are part of every culture provides important insights into a person's psychological functioning. Thus, knowledge and understanding of social process, far from being an impediment to accurate assessment, may be a precondition for it.

Of course, to say that a psychiatrist's personal values enter into the diagnostic process is to immediately invite a resort to the value relativity argument according to which values reflect mere preferences, and should certainly not be the basis of anything as serious as diagnosis. No one would deny that personal values can and do enter into clinical judgments, but it would be a mistake to assume that the latter can be reduced to the former. When we say that someone has personal values, we refer to preferences which have no other ultimate rationale aside from their selection by the individual concerned. I can value truth above beauty, and rest content in the fact that my personal preference is both a necessary and sufficient justification. Clinical judgments, on the other hand, rest on theories of psychological functioning which are subject to public and professional scrutiny, and which become modified in the light of theoretical developments and clinical experience. Above all, they involve a respect for functional relationships and the potential for multiple causes and outcomes, both of which may take place within a fairly wide range of behavior.

However, while it is certainly true that clinical theory and personal values are not synonymous, it would be a mistake not to recognize the potential role of the latter in the interventions proposed by proponents of political psychiatry. Proposals for formal (and even informal) psychiatric assessment of political candidates, as well as those calling for psychiatric intervention as an aid to decision makers, will place those involved into a highly charged political context and public role. There is reason to be concerned that the evaluation of political leaders, especially those involved in controversial or unpopular policies, would severely test the capacities of those involved to separate political preferences from clinical theory. There is no reason to believe that clinicians are immune from the effects of highly charged political debate; indeed, on the basis of their education, occupational status, and income we would expect them to be more attuned and involved. These kinds of issues do not ordinarily arise in the consulting room, but it is clear that involvement with persons of significant prestige, power, and resources will call for special characteristics on the part of those involved in any such interventions.

Ultimately, of course, diagnosis must reflect a comparison between a present state and some criterion state. Szasz repeatedly argues that such states are ultimately psychosocial, ethical, or legal, as if this statement by itself constituted an irremedial indictment. Yet, aside from the involvement of forensic psychiatrists in the legal system, it is not clear why Szasz includes legal norms as part of the general criteria for psychiatric assessment. Certainly clinical training and theory does not rest on legal distinctions regarding capacity; if anything the relationship is the reverse.

A somewhat more compelling case can be made for the use of ethical norms as part of clinical judgments. Generally stated, ethical norms refer to the web of obligations and responsibilities that arise in human relationships. But again, clinical judgment rests not so much on whether the person is right or wrong but whether the patient is able to see, weigh, and act on this set of responsibilities and obligations. The consistent failure to do so, or the clear inability to ever "take the role of other," may reflect developmental and interpersonal difficulties as well as unethical behavior according to some personal or public standard. Characterizing behavior in terms of the latter does not negate the existence of the former.

However, it is the first norm, the psychosocial, which is clearly the most relevant of the three for clinical assessment. By grouping all three together Szasz leaves one with the impression that they are all equally relevant (and suspect). Yet, of the three, it is only the first which is clearly and unequivocally related to general psychiatric assessment through clinical theory and training. This theory rests on more than personal values.

But agreeing that psychosocial norms are important in the clinical assessment of psychological functioning provides only a framework, not a ready-made set of answers. It is still necessary to establish just what norms are being referenced, on what basis, and with what consequences. This task is decidedly more advanced in the case of physical health than it is for psychological health. When physicians address the concept of the *normal* in physical health they do so in accordance with a well-grounded functional perspective. As C. Daly King pointed out many years ago in the *Yale Journal of Biology and Medicine,* "The normal . . . is objectively, and properly, to be defined as that which functions in accordance with its design,"[48] and most medical authorities have followed this perspective. Psychiatrists and psychologists, too, have attempted to adapt this approach to escape the difficulties with such concepts as *health* and *normality* discussed at length above. Redlich and Freedman, for example, in one of the standard psychiatric texts, adapt what they term the *clinical approach,* which, they say, "defines as abnormal anything that does not function according to its design."[49] The problem, however, as the authors are quick to point out, is that frequently in behavior disorders, "we do not know what design or function a certain behavior pattern serves."[50] Behaviors serve many purposes, not all of them evident to the observer, or even to the person engaging in them. Still, this framework provides a way of asking questions, collecting data, and interpreting results which grounds such an inquiry in the empirical rather than the ethereal.

THE CONCEPT OF IMPAIRMENT: PSYCHOLOGICAL AND POLITICAL

The concept of impairment lies closer to the functionalist perspective outlined in the last section and appears to be less burdened by connotations of excess than a term such as *mental illness.* In its most general sense, an impairment refers either to a lack or a diminishing of some capacity. In both cases, there is a contemporaneous deficit, although in the first instance this is being compared to some typical or "ideal" state which never was present, while in the second, it is being compared only to a previous level of functioning. There is, in either case, the attendant implication that outcomes which could reasonably or ordinarily be expected, or which are considered preferable, do not occur on a regular basis.

Impairments are frequently accompanied by some level of psychological distress (for example, disappointment, regret, anxiety, depression). Clinical judgments regarding impairments, then, may be made according to any of the following four criteria: 1) emotional distress to self (or others); 2) failure to perform at "average expectable levels"[51] of functioning; 3) failure to develop capacities which are routinely observable at least to some degree in others; or 4) the frequent occurrence of outcomes which are clearly not desired. The presence of any, some, or all of these criteria suggests to a clinician the existence of an impairment, and there are other criteria that may be added to this list.

The theories underlying these four are, of course, not derived from specific occupational contexts, but it is not difficult to envision how they might be applied to our concerns. The presence of the first, emotional distress, brought about by a difficult decision or some other form of role conflict, might well be reflected in increased speech tempo, changes in voice tone or quality, irritability, increased eye blinking, and so forth, all of which are readily accessible public indicators.[52] Manifestations of emotional distress might also be reflected in difficulties in staff or peer relationships.

The second criterion, a decline in performance, would require some baseline data with which to compare present behavior. Underperformance may reflect (among other possibilities) an inadequate sense of personal control. The third criterion covers a wide range of behaviors and would have to be linked to a greater understanding of the requirements of political roles. If, for example, we accept that a fundamental part of the leadership role is decision making, then we will be interested in assessing the leader's approach to this task. Leaders who are highly "rational" decision makers may lack an affective perspective on policy issues. On the other hand, leaders with a highly developed sense of the public mood may find this capacity makes a disproportionate claim on their assessments of public problems. In both cases the leaders would not have developed the *composite* skill sets necessary to carry out critical decision-making tasks.

Another illustration involves the leader whose skills at manipulating relevant aspects of the political process, even while they result in "success," reveal a failure to develop a capacity for empathetic identifications. The point in any case is not that such problems should necessarily disqualify persons from leadership roles. Rather it is that the functionalist perspective on impairment, by addressing political-role requirements, might well look to any deficiencies with an eye toward amelioration as well as theory development.

The last criterion, that of unwanted effects, points to the discrepancy between leadership aspirations and accomplishments. Political history is replete with the ironies (not to mention tragedies) of discontinuities between intentions and achievement. Too often leaders fail to consider how to make the transition from wish to realization.

Critics of this position might well point to the constraining effects of external factors on leadership performance. There is no doubt that leaders are limited by the realities of context, but constraint does not eradicate altogether the discretion to make certain choices. Rather it serves to erect boundaries within which opportunities are seen and, sometimes, grasped. It is precisely within these limits that we must evaluate the discrepancies between aspirations and accomplishments.

This is not intended as an exhaustive survey of how certain criteria might be applied to political contexts, nor even, as I said, of the criteria themselves. But what is clear even from this brief review is that the development of contextually specific criteria, functionally related to the tasks of political leadership, will have a salutary effect on both political theory and public practice. Of course, the applications of these criteria (or any others) involve judgments, and one is certainly justified in inquiring about their basis.

It will be recalled that Szasz argues that such judgments ultimately rest in part on psychosocial norms. If this is understood to include a person's experience of himself and others, and is not merely a reference to societal norms of appropriateness, then Szasz is surely correct. But if the implication of this statement is that such judgments rest solely on personal values, divorced from clinical theory and experience, then the point is debatable.

Clinical judgments grow out of a complex interplay between theory and experience. Adapting the functionalist perspective, however, requires some formulation of the relationship of performance to design. This, as we noted in the last section, is easier to discern for biological than psychological systems. Still the present state of knowledge does allow for more than a preliminary understanding of what is necessary in human relations and experience (although questions regarding teleology remain unclear).

Clinical formulation of what is required for a sense of well-being and a capacity for effectiveness comes not only from clinicians' theories (for example, that relatedness with others and a sense of autonomy are related to effective functioning, and a sense of well-being) but also from their observations of the consequences of deficits in these (or other) areas during the course of "treatment." Equally important, they can observe the effects of interventions based on their frameworks or hypotheses on actual (in the consulting room) and reported (outside the consulting room) behaviors, as well as the affect and understandings that accompany them. No claim is made here that such information is definitive, only that it goes well beyond the clinician's mere personal preferences. A clinician may come to value and thus prefer, for example, greater autonomy as opposed to dependence, but such a preference is based on theory and experience, not whim.

The same is true for all criteria of impairment—those I listed, and those to be added. As a person trained and experienced in examining human behavior from a systematic perspective, the clinician makes use of large bodies of data[53] concerning the existence and frequency of certain capacities. It is from this perspective that, for example, judgments can be made regarding failures to perform at "average expectable levels" of functioning, or to develop capacities which theory and observation suggest are a part of the potential of every person.

But clinical judgments involve more than reference to general theory, since human capacities and the behaviors that reflect them do not appear in isolation. Clinicians must make judgments which encompass a number of attributes whose range and relations vary and which are deeply embedded in particular social contexts. Frequently, therefore, such judgments involve an assessment of the relative "weight" of several factors, as well as an appreciation of their combined effects when applied to a particular situation. At this point, too, clinical theory and, more importantly, experience, play a crucial role. Attributes which underlie human functioning are best understood as lying along continuums and indeed, it is precisely this point which creates so much trouble for the application of clinical theory to politics. As suggested earlier, the extremes of impairment are always easier to discern than the more subtle manifestations. Harold Lasswell pointed out many years ago that the demarcation between "health" and "illness" is a gradient, not an abyss.[54]

So, too, personal capacities are embedded in a context of role demands. These are themselves contained within a larger social and institutional structure. It is sometimes overlooked that one aspect of the knowledge that clinicians draw upon in making their assessments and interventions is general understanding of the recurring external contexts which are brought into the consulting room in the form of the patient's experience. Yet despite these understandings, there has been little theoretical work with regard to functional or occupational specificity.[55] The failure of clinical psychiatry to develop theory along these lines must be viewed with regret by those who would apply such efforts to political contexts.

Indeed, the failure to advance in this area has had a direct effect on the problem at hand, namely, our ability to develop a concept of impairment that might usefully be applied to the political arena. While the notion of impairment allows us to bypass some of the problems associated with the use of terms such as *mental illness*, it is still encumbered by its connotations, and it in no way alleviates the problem of operationalizing the concept. What we need is a knowledge of political structures and processes as they relate to the expectations and demands associated with particular political roles. Such knowledge is still in its infancy, if it can be said to exist at all.

Another problem with the application of the term impairment to politics is the difficulty of assessing the political consequences of a personal deficit. In the consulting room, judgments regarding consequences come from two sources: the patient and the therapist.[56] In cases of voluntary treatment, the effects of personal dysfunctions on immediate others are relevant but they are not the primary focus. Concern with the impact of dysfunctions on larger social and interpersonal contexts is even less frequently a consideration. The chief concern of the clinician, under most circumstances, is "the patient," and not the larger social units to which the patient may belong.

Quite the opposite is true when we consider the application of the concept of impairment to public life. While we may certainly be concerned with the leader who is impaired, our primary concern is with the effects produced. This perspective implies the willingless to apply the framework of political psychiatry, regardless of the leader's understanding or even acknowledgment of any difficulties. But the willingness to do this does not by itself solve the problem of how we are to determine when an impairment is present. In the consulting room, one very important indicator is the experience of personal distress, but this is clearly too narrow a criterion for use in the political arena. It seems clear that what we need to develop are indicators of the specifically political manifestations of impairment which are analogous to those currently in clinical use for interpersonal and other social contexts.

A further problem for those attempting to apply the concept of impairment to political leadership is the lack of theory, or data for that matter, regarding the specific ways in which impairment might manifest itself in particular leadership roles.[57] Unless we are willing to subscribe to the dubious assumption that psychological and political impairment are synonymous, it is incumbent on those who propose such extensions to suggest the precise ways in which political impairment can be determined. Just how difficult this will be is suggested by trying to apply to the political arena the four clinical criteria we have already discussed. But if we cannot at this point say with any certainty just what form such indicators must take, we can at least outline some general possibilities.

One of the major difficulties in applying psychological concepts to politics is the lack of comparative guidelines. When we say that an impairment implies a failure to develop that which routinely exists, and which increases effectiveness and the sense of well-being, we imply a knowledge of the former and its relationship to the latter. So, too, when we say that impairment implies a diminishing of capacity and effectiveness, we imply knowledge of the level of past performance against which the impairment is measured. This much is obvious, but the point is that such comparative statements are not yet easily made in relation to political leadership. The reason for this is that we lack comprehensive theory in several crucial areas, namely, what it is that political leaders actually do, and what capacities are necessary for them in order to be able to do it.

Of course, we all know intuitively what political leaders do: they provide leadership. Unfortunately this does little more than label a process which is as yet only poorly understood. And, in the absence of this knowledge, it is not possible to say what constitutes adequate performance, let alone impairment.

Political scientists have identified numerous leadership roles in politics. Some, like Lasswell, have favored functional demarcations (for example, agitators, theorists, administrators),[58] while others have stayed more closely tied to formal political roles (executive, legislative, judicial). The latter approach would seem to provide more opportunities to describe leadership functions, since legally designated positions usually carry with them formally enumerated responsibilities. This is exactly the direction that arguments about the meaning of *disability* under the guidelines of the Twenty-fifth Amendment dealing with presidential incapacity have taken.

The difficulty here is that formal functions do not exhaust the scope of political leadership and thus the range to which the concept of impairment may be applied. Such formulations do not cover the various "informal," "implied," and "attendent" responsibilities that may be crucial to leadership performance and evaluation. Moreover, this approach neglects the frequent finding that formal role demands give only a poor indication of performance *opportunities*. Performance varies widely within the same political role because of inherent ambiguities in the nature of the role, and because of the differences in the personal dispositions of those who fill the role. Again, a comprehensive understanding of impairment (or adequacy) in political roles must await a more systematic understanding of just what it is that leaders do, and what personal capacities they need to accomplish this.

One other point deserves our attention here, and that is the relationship between concepts of psychological impairment in leadership roles and the nature of the system in which these evaluations are made. Each political system places certain demands and responsibilities on those who occupy leadership roles. We judge leaders in part by the extent to which their behaviors reflect acceptance and protection of these responsibilities. So, for example, when a president is voted out of office, we do not expect him to make a plea to the armed forces to return him to power. Nor do we expect legislators to take bribes, or judges to sell decisions. It is not a far step from these observations to suggest that every form of political arrangement carries with it an implicit set of boundaries regarding the personal characteristics of those who would best "fit in with" its particular forms of political institutions and processes. To take an extreme example, political systems which have not routinized the transfer of power will make suspiciousness a functional "virtue" for aspiring political leaders. When this is accompanied by a history of violence to obtain and maintain power, suspicion may not only be sustained but also encouraged by the "reality" of the political system.

Other kinds of political systems carry with them different prerequisites for effective institutional and procedural functioning. Democracies, for example, require that their chief executive weigh and balance the conflicting public demands and then persuade others of the virtues of the positions that were finally taken. The personal capacities necessary to do these things effectively are very different from those necessary to successfully lead a revolution, or, for that matter, to rule once it has succeeded.[59] Even within a particular system there is wide variation in the personal requisites for different political roles. It is for these reasons that no general set of personal characteristics is likely to be helpful for all types of political roles. But there is, in principle, no reason that knowledge of specific role demands and expectations cannot be combined with an understanding of the more general requirements of a particular system to generate progress on the problem of personal impairment, and on the more important but still neglected criteria of adequate and superior performance. It is this task which deserves our most careful attention in the years ahead.

NOTES

1. James David Barber, *The Presidential Character* (Englewood Cliffs, N.J.: Prentice-Hall, 1972), p. 360.
2. *New York Times*, February 13, 1976, p. 30.
3. *See* for example, Gregory B. Markus, "Political Attitudes during an Election Year: A Report on the 1980 NES Panel Study," *American Political Science Review*, 76 (1982), pp. 539–42.
4. *New York Times*, November 9, 1980, p. 36.
5. This essay can only treat a small number of these issues in any detail. A fuller consideration of these issues can be found in Stanley A. Renshon, *The Psychiatric Assessment of Public Officials* (forthcoming).
6. Alexander L. George, "Assessing Presidential Character," *World Politics*, 26 (January 1974), p. 280. Students of these issues are indebted to Professor George for his careful and thoughtful analysis.
7. The pathbreaking work in this area is Harold D. Lasswell, *Psychopathology and Politics* (Chicago: University of Chicago, 1930, revised 1960). Lasswell himself, in an afterward published thirty years later, distinguished between the theoretical system and the observational standpoint (for example, the specific procedures by which theory is linked to a field of observation of psychoanalytic theory). Lasswell opted to emphasize the latter, noting that, "I was more impressed by the observational procedures innovated by Freud than by the theory or its then available results."
8. Harold D. Lasswell, "The Interconnections of Political Power, Psychotherapy, and World Community," *Political Communication and Persuasion*, I (1981), pp. 116–18.
9. Group for the Advancement of Psychiatry, *The VIP with Psychiatric Impairment* (New York: Scribner's, 1973).
10. *See also* Ernest Jones, M.D., "Can Civilization be Saved?", a paper read at the symposium held by the Federation of Progressive Societies, November 27, 1938, and reprinted in Ernest Jones, M.D., *Psycho-Myth, Psycho-History: Essays in Applied*

Psychoanalysis (New York: Hillstone, 1974). *See also* Harold D. Lasswell, "What Psychiatrists and Political Scientists Can Learn From Each Other," *Psychiatry*, 1 (1983), pp. 33–39, and more recently, Fred I. Greenstein, "Private Disorder and the Public Order: A Proposal for Collaboration between Psychoanalysts and Political Scientists," *Psychoanalytic Quarterly*, 37 (1968), pp. 261–81.

11. Arnold A. Hutschnecker, M.D., "The Mental Health of Our Leaders," *Look Magazine*, 33 (July 1969), pp. 51–54.

12. Russell V. Lee, M.D., "When Insanity Holds the Scepter," *New York Times*, April 12, 1974, p. 30.

13. For example, in July of 1979, former President Jimmy Carter left Washington for his Camp David retreat. While there he suddenly and unexpectedly canceled what had been billed as a major policy address to the nation. Thereafter, in quick succession numerous advisers, academic theorists, labor leaders, and others were seen shuttling in and out of the camp, all under the watchful eye of the press. After many days of public and private soul-searching, Carter moved quickly and dramatically. Three members of his cabinet were fired, and several others offered their resignations and had them accepted.

    Reaction to these events was also dramatic, with several senators wondering aloud whether President Carter "might be having some sort of mental problem." When Majority Leader Robert F. Byrd criticized his colleague Senator Ted Stevens for making these comments on the Senate floor, Stevens retreated, but just a little. "I don't think anyone's saying he's crazy," Stevens explained, "but the pressures on him are so great, we are wondering if he's having some sort of breakdown." Senator Lowell Weiker of Connecticut, in discussing President Carter's response to his political problems, was moved to point out that, "we have no way of removing a president who lacks capacity for the job unless he's at the point where he has to be chased down with a net."

    Senator Stevens's remarks were reported in the *New York Times*, July 21, 1979, p. 1; while Senator Weiker's remarks were reported in *The Miami Herald*, August 10, 1979, p. 1E.

14. Arnold A. Rogow, *James Forrestal: A Study of Personality, Politics and Policy* (New York: Macmillan, 1963).

15. Ibid., p. 2.

16. There are four separate issues raised by this comment. The first is the extent to which specific psychological impairments and their importance can be considered apart from specific political or leadership roles. Phrased in another way, the question is whether "impairment" of judges, presidents, cabinet officers, legislators, and so forth take the same forms and should be considered and treated (in terms of any intervention) in the same way. A second question is the relationship between leadership recruitment and any form of psychological "impairment." That is, to what extent does the process of selection to leadership roles foster or inhibit characteristics or performance which would be considered psychologically "impaired." Third, and a related question, is the extent to which actual performance upon reaching leadership positions fosters or inhibits the same characteristics. A fourth and final question concerns the extent to which cultural expectations and historical circumstance influence the preceding factors.

17. Rogow, *James Forrestal, A Study of Personality, Politics and Policy*, p. 344.

18. *New York Times*, July 26, 1972, p. 1.

19. Excerpts from the Eagleton News Conference, *New York Times*, July 26, 1972, p. 20.

20. James M. Naughton, "Eagleton Illness Known to Associates," *New York Times*, July 26, 1972, p. 20.
21. Rogow, *James Forrestal: A Study of Personality, Politics and Policy*, p. 8.
22. Ibid., p. 345.
23. T.F. Thiselton, *Royalty in All Ages: The Amusements, Eccentricities, Accomplishments, Superstitions and Frolics of Kings and Queens of Europe* (London: John C. Nimno, Ltd., 1903).
24. Dr. Angelo S. Rappoport, *Mad Majesties: or Raving Rulers and Submissive Subjects* (New York: Brentano's 1910). On the flyleaf Dr. Rapoport is also listed as the author of *Royal Lovers and Mistresses* and *The Curse of the Romanoffs*.
25. *See*, for example, D.H. Henry, "The Psychiatric Illness of Lord Castlereagh," *The Practitioner*, 204 (1970), pp. 318–23; Leo Alexander, M.D., "The Commitment and Suicide of King Ludwig II of Bavaria," *American Journal of Psychiatry*, 111 (1954), pp. 100–107; I Macalpine and R. Hunter, *King George and the Mad-Business* (New York: Pantheon, 1969). This list is illustrative, not exhaustive. A number of different literatures provide parts of problems which this work examines.
26. Robert L. Noland, "Presidential Disability and the Proposed Constitutional Amendment," *American Psychologist*, 21 (1966), p. 232.
27. Ibid., p. 232–33.
28. Mrs. Robert F. Noland generously made available to me a portion of her late husband's notes and data concerning this issue.
29. Some have argued, quite plausibly, that social structure and process and the experiences encountered therein do give rise to the specific syndromes we encounter. It follows that if social structure and process change significantly, so, too, will the psychological experience and distortions they generate. For an application of this perspective to some contemporary clinical entities, *see* Alice Miller, *Prisoners of Childhood* (New York: Basic Books, 1980). This argument might alter the point with regard to narcissistic and borderline disorders, and somewhat less so for other character disorders (for example, obsessive-compulsive types). It should also be noted that many of the royal blood lines which formed the basis of recruitment into major political roles suffered from genetically-based impairments, resulting from too frequent and too close intermarriages. This is clearly less the cause of severe impairment among political leaders today. On the other hand, there is evidence that the borderline and major character disorders are on the increase, and are not unrelated to political recruitment.
30. The literature on conceptualizations of mental health/illness and the epistemological problems involved in such formulations is immense. Two extremely thoughtful and strong analyses of the conceptual difficulties involved may be found in Ruth Maklin, "Mental Health and Mental Illness: Some Problems of Definition and Concept Formulation," *Philosophy of Science*, 29 (1972), pp. 341–65; and Michael S. Moore, "Some Myths about 'Mental Illness,' " *Archives of General Psychiatry*, 32 (1975), pp. 1483–97. Some of the discussion which follows draws upon their analyses.
31. Actually, there are several different uses of the "medical model" concept, but I will confine my discussion to those aspects relevant to diagnosis and understanding of disease entities. For a fuller discussion of the various ways the model has been employed, *see* M. Siegler and H. Osmond, *Models of Madness, Models of Medicine* (New York: Macmillan, 1974).
32. Thomas S. Szasz, "The Myth of Mental Illness," *American Psychologist*, 15 (1960), pp. 113–18.

33. As Moore, "Some Myths about 'Mental Illness,' " p. 1489 points out, "Since the concept of mind is intimately connected with our concept of what it is to be a person, predicating mental experiences, actions, and intentions to another human being is not only necessary before we will say that he has a mind, but also before we think of that being as a person."
34. Szasz, "The Myth of Mental Illness," p. 114.
35. Moore, "Some Myths about 'Mental Illness,' " p. 1484.
36. L.S. King, "What Is Disease?" *Philosophy of Science,* 21 (1954), pp. 193–203.
37. Moore, "Some Myths about 'Mental Illness,' " p. 1484.
38. Maklin argues that the question as to whether it is *ever* legitimate to extend or enlarge a concept, as admitting to an uncontroversial affirmative answer; *see* Maklin, "Mental Health and Mental Illness: Some Problems of Definition and Concept Formulation," p. 361. She then goes on to quote Joseph Margolis, who makes the point that, "Szasz is absolutely right in holding that Freud reclassified types of suffering. But what he fails to see is that this is a perfectly legitimate (and even necessary) maneuver." *See* Joseph Margolis, *Psychoanalysis and Morality* (New York: Random House, 1966), p. 73.
39. Ibid., p. 73.
40. Moore, "Some Myths about 'Mental Illness,' " p. 1490. A similar point is made by Boorse, who distinguishes between disease and illness. He writes that: The point is that illness is merely a subclass of diseases, namely, those diseases that have certain normative features reflected in the institutions of medical practice. An illness must be, first, a reasonably *serious* disease with incapacitating effects that make it undesirable. A shaving cut or mild athlete's foot cannot be called an illness, nor could one call in sick on the basis of a single dental cavity, although all these conditions are diseases. This quote is taken from Christopher Boorse, "On the Distinction Between Health and Illness," *Philosophy and Public Affairs,* 5 (1975), p. 56.

    Two questions arise here, though: First, by what means will we determine whether a disease is serious *enough* to be termed an illness, and second, is it the individual or some other person or group which will make the characterization of the illness as undesirable? Boorse does not deal with the first question, and regarding the second he writes, "I do not actually have serious doubts that disorders such as neurosis and psychoses diminish human happiness" (p. 63), and thus are presumably undesirable to the individual who experiences them. But of course, this supposes that happiness is a preferred state.
41. Szasz, "The Myth of Mental Illness," p. 114.
42. Ibid.
43. Moore, "Some Myths about 'Mental Illness,' " p. 149.
44. Karen Horney, M.D., *The Neurotic Personality of Our Times* (New York: W.W. Norton, 1937), p. 15.
45. Marie Jahoda, *Current Concepts of Positive Mental Health* (New York: Basic Books, 1958), p. 12.
46. Ruth Benedict, *Patterns of Culture* (New York: Houghton Mifflin, 1934), quoted in Jahoda, *Current Concepts of Positive Mental Health,* p. 12.
47. Ibid., pp. 15–16.
48. C. Daly King, "The Meaning of Normal," *Yale Journal of Biology and Medicine,* 17 (1945), pp. 493–94.
49. Frederick C. Redlich and Daniel X. Freedman, *The Theory and Practice of Psychiatry* (New York: Basic Books, 1966), p. 113.
50. Ibid.

51. The concept of "average expectable levels of functioning" refers to the expectations of any temporal cross section of successively refined subjectve and objective estimates of performance, based on theory and experience.
52. An excellent review and analysis of stress indicators in political contexts may be found in Margaret G. Hermann, "Indicators of Stress in Policymakers During Foreign Policy Crises," *Political Psychology*, 1 (1979), pp. 27–46.
53. Most clinicians gather information from large ranges of diverse literatures and experience during the course of their training and subsequent careers. These include materials from general, social, psychoanalytic, and developmental psychology, to name but a few.
54. Lasswell, *Psychopathology and Politics*, p. 27. Students of the issues discussed in this essay are deeply indebted to the late Professor Lasswell for his pathbreaking uncovering and discussion of these issues.
55. There are some exceptions to this statement, but in general psychology and especially the psychoanalytic branch of treatment have not moved towrd specialized, clinically based services for particular groups which are occupationally oriented. The reasons for this arise from the theory of psychoanalytically oriented psychotherapy, which need not concern us here. It should be noted that such considerations are relevant to proposals to provide some form of psychiatric or psychological aid to political decision makers in the hope of improving the quality of public decisions and policies. This and other related issues are taken up in Stanley A. Renshon, "Psychiatry and Beyond: Improving Presidential Decision Making," paper presented to the Southern Political Science Association Meetings, October 28–30, 1982.
56. The patient, of course, brings into the consulting room his version of external events which serves as one source, but the more important source is the experience of the therapist (and the patient) of the relationship unfolding between them.
57. Solitary exceptions to this statement are to be found in Barber, *The Presidential Character*, which examines the problem from an ego psychology perspective; Irving L. Janis, *Groupthink: Psychological Studies of Policy Decisions and Fiascoes* (Boston: Houghton Mifflin, 1982), which examines the problem from a small-group psychology perspective; and Alexander L. George, *Presidential Decision-making in Foreign Policy: The Effective Use of Information and Advise* (Boulder, Co.: Westview, 1980), which examines the problem from a cognitive psychology and structural (staff) perspective.
58. Lasswell, *Psychopathology and Politics*, chapter IV.
59. Or, in other words, the capacities needed to obtain power are not necessarily the same as those needed to exercise it effectively.

LEADERSHIP **12**
The Socratic Model

Leonard Grob

Western philosophers have never been silent on the question of leadership. From Plato's philosopher-king to Machiavelli's prince, from Hobbes's sovereign to Nietzsche's *Übermensch,* philosophy has said its piece on the nature of the ideal leader. But it is not my purpose in this chapter to merely survey the range of philosophical opinions on leadership—opinions, it may be noted, which largely address questions of *political* leadership. To do so would be to depict a history of ideas at the expense of inquiring into the nature of the unique disciplinary perspective on leadership offered by the philosopher qua philosopher. The issue to be addressed in these pages is the determination of that peculiar reflection on leadership which, I will argue, is demanded by the philosopher's vocation as such.

Where must such a quest begin? The endeavor to locate a truly philosophical perspective on leadership in any historical consensus on the essence of leadership is certain to fail. It is clear to even the beginning student of philosophy that the great thinkers of the West—and here we will address only a few representative thinkers in this tradition—are far from agreement with regard to a depiction of the nature of the ideal leader. For Plato, writing in the fourth century B.C., Athens, the authority by virtue of which the philosopher-king rules the state, is an authority derived from his knowl-

edge of the one Truth. What distinguishes the ideal leader from his followers, in other words, is the possession by the former of "wisdom,"of an
"intellectual vision" informing the principles of government, as it informs
the principles of human conduct in general. "*Until . . . political greatness and
wisdom meet in one,*" Plato exclaims in his *Republic*, "*and those commoner natures
who pursue either to the exclusion of the other are compelled to stand aside, cities
will never have rest from their evils—no, nor the human race, as I believe. . . .*"[1]
Although the presence of the philosopher-king does not in itself guarantee
the realization of the state as the embodiment of absolute justice, it is
nonetheless true that without the guidance of *one who knows the essence of
justice,* the state is doomed to be ruled in an arbitrary, ultimately capricious
fashion.

It is the inevitably arbitrary character of the rule of popular leaders
which prompts Plato's utter scorn for all so-called democratic principles of
government. Those alleged leaders chosen either by lot or by virtue of the
persuasiveness of their oratory are, for Plato, no leaders at all. Like those
mutineers—described in Book VI of the *Republic*—who take charge of a
ship without knowledge of the pilot's art, the practitioners of democracy
necessarily bar the way to a realization of the genuine "ship of state." Just
as the mutineers forget "that the true pilot must pay attention to the year
and seasons and sky and stars and winds, and whatever else belongs to his
art . . . and that he must and will be the steerer, whether other people like
or not . . . ,"[2] so the populace, the demos, forgets that only the philosopher
is equipped to direct the course of the state, that only by a knowledge of
the form of the ideal state can the leader rightfully exercise his leadership.

Whereas Plato's political philosophy is based on a distinction between
a real and an ideal world, the analyses of the Renaissance philosopher
Niccolo Machiavelli, and the seventeenth-century thinker Thomas Hobbes,
are securely rooted in a view of how human beings do, in fact, behave.
Thus, for Machiavelli, political philosophy finds its proper ground in conclusions to be drawn from the comparative analyses of past modes of government: "But my intention being to write something of use to those who
understand, it appears to me more proper to go to the real truth of the
matter than to its imagination . . . for how we live is so far removed from
how we ought to live, that he who abandons what is done for what ought
to be done, will rather learn to bring about his own ruin than his preservation."[3] What the study of history teaches Machiavelli is that if political
anarchy is to be avoided, moral considerations must be subordinated to the
mechanics of a struggle for power. Thus neither moral nor immoral conduct is to be cultivated for its own sake. Given the dictates of the circumstances at hand, the leader must be prepared to employ any and all means
in the service of his sole end: the establishment, maintenance, and continued welfare of the state in his charge.

The necessity of establishing a "prince," a strong ruler, as head of state is determined not only by the lessons learned from political history but by an analysis of human nature as well. For Machiavelli all human beings are motivated by the desire for power. In the midst of inevitable conflict among individuals so motivated, the leader is one who succeeds best at the game of power in which all are involved. The Machiavellian prince is thus moved by the same passions as his subjects; his leadership consists in his superior ability to wield instruments of physical and psychological force in the process of establishing order among those who would otherwise destroy themselves as a political entity. "The only way to establish any kind of order," Machiavelli concludes in his *Discourses,* "is to establish some superior power which, with a royal hand, and with full and absolute powers, may put a curb upon the excessive ambition and corruption of the power."[4]

The theme of the leader as guarantor of the integrity of the state is taken up and given a new turn by Hobbes in his *Leviathan,* published in 1654. Here the sovereign emerges by the consent of followers who wish to establish their places in a political order but who, by virtue of their bellicose, appropriative natures, cannot succeed on their own in so doing. Hence the erection of a "common power" to whom authority is granted so that the people may be compelled to behave according to what is ultimately their true self-interest: "For by this authority, given him by every particular man in the commonwealth, he hath the use of so much power and strength . . . that by terror thereof, he is enabled to form the wills of them all. . . ."[5]

Unlike Machiavelli, Hobbes does not base his philosophy of leadership in any fundamental sense on the observable data to be gleaned from a history of governments. When he speaks of a "natural state of war" preceding the establishment of a political order, Hobbes proceeds according to a deductively determined sequence of philosophical assumptions: if humans are ruled by their passions for self-preservation and self-aggrandizement, and if the play of these passions leads to the "war of all against all," then such self-interest—coupled with a natural ability to reason—leads inevitably to the erection of a sovereign power, the sole center around which a political body can take form. In Hobbes's words, the transfer of power takes place by means of a ". . . covenant of every man with every man, in such manner, as if every man should say to every man, *I authorize and give up my right of governing myself, to this man, or to this assembly of men, on this condition, that thou give up thy right to him, and authorize all his actions in like manner.*"[6] The fact that such a covenant establishes the very concept of sovereignty in the name of all present and future subjects ensures the preservation of the sovereign as the locus of a power which is nothing short of absolute.

With the thought of Friedrich Nietzsche in the late nineteenth century, the philosophy of leadership again turns toward prescriptive rather than descriptive analysis. The Nietzschean *Übermensch,* the "superman," is a leader by dint of his unique ability to transcend what had been thought to be a given human nature: "I teach you the superman. Man is something that should be overcome. . . . What is great in man is that he is a bridge and not a goal. . . ."[7] As the embodiment of this awareness, the *Übermensch* leads by creating ever-new values to replace the ones destroyed in his "overcoming" of the previous ethical, religious, and political order. The leader, in Nietzschean terms, heralds nothing short of an ongoing, radical transformation of society in all of its dimensions.

The Nietzschean superman, therefore, is not to be characterized by the possession of any determinate set of leadership attributes. The *Übermensch,* rather, is the embodiment of an ever-renewed desire to move beyond all fixed attributes in an eternally creative act of transcendence. As the guide urging us to "dance beyond ourselves," the superman is not ultimately to be identified with any one person in the history of humankind:

> There has never yet been a Superman. I have seen them both naked, the greatest and the smallest man.
> They are still all-too-similar to one another. Truly, I have found even the greatest man—all-too-human![8]

In thus provoking us to surpass the "merely human" in any and all epochs— and particularly the "merely human" representative of Christian morality who dominates our present age—the *Übermensch* serves ultimately as the image of the ideal leader.

What are we—given over to the task of discovering a fundamentally philosophical perspective on leadership—to make of the wide divergence of ideas on leadership to be found even in our very brief excursus into the history of Western thought? To which philosophers, to which set of theoretical overviews should our inquiry turn if it is to discover that fundamental disciplinary perspective on leadership of which it is in search? If, as Alfred North Whitehead contends, "European philosophy is founded upon Plato's dialogues,"[9] and if, as Martin Heidegger proclaims, Socrates is "the purest thinker in the west,"[10] then it is to the Socratic dialogues of Plato that we might well turn to begin to address the issue at hand. Indeed, students of Western thought find themselves in rare agreement with one another with regard to the claim that Socrates is the prototype of the philosopher, literally, the lover of wisdom. As the creator of a tradition which has for twenty-four hundred years helped to determine the unique quality of our intellectual existence, Socrates beckons to us as the sole point of departure for a philosophic inquiry into the nature of leadership. No search for a philosophical perspective on leadership can fail to take as its starting point those Socratic teachings in which philosophy itself is born into Western culture.

SOCRATES: THE PHILOSOPHER
AS LEADER

Socrates himself wrote nothing; the vast majority of our knowledge of the
Socratic teachings comes from a reading of the dialogues written by his
student, Plato, dialogues in which Socrates functions—in the main—as central personage. At the outset of our inquiry we must distinguish in these
dialogues between the image of Socrates as philosopher-in-action and that
of Socrates as mere spokesperson for the beliefs peculiar to Plato and to
the Platonism of the Academy founded in the fourth century B.C., Athens.
If Whitehead's contention, cited above, is to be understood as anything
more than mere hyperbole, it is to the *person* of Socrates himself, rather
than to the Platonic doctrines for which, it is argued, he served as central
mouthpiece, that we must look for an understanding of philosophic enterprise in general and a genuinely philosophic view of leadership in particular.[11] The teachings of Socrates, in other words, must assume for us,
as Nietzsche exclaims, their "supra-Greek" import.[12] This is not to deny
the importance of the Platonic vision of leadership, the vision of the philosopher-king articulated in Book V of the *Republic* and summarized briefly
above. Rather this depiction of the leader, along with all other such depictions in the history of philosophy, must be situated within a more fundamental understanding of the phenomenon of leadership offered in the
dialogues by the image of Socrates himself *as philosopher.*

It is not to any one truth enunciated by Socrates that we can look for
a sense of the essence of leadership. Indeed, Socrates goes to great lengths
to recall to his fellow Athenians the fact that he has no hold on this or any
other truth. In the *Apology*, his defense against the charges of impiety and
corruption of the youth of Athens at his trial in 399 B.C., Socrates devotes
himself to detailing the origins of his humility. In response to his puzzle-
ment at the declaration of the Delphic oracle that no one is wiser than he,
Socrates exclaims:

> I know very well that I am not wise, even in the smallest degree. Then what
> can [the Oracle] mean by saying that I am the wisest of men? It cannot be
> that he is speaking falsely, for he is a god and cannot lie. For a long time I
> was at a loss to investigate his meaning. Then, very reluctantly, I turned to
> investigate it in this manner: I went to a man who was reputed to be wisest,
> thinking that there, if anywhere, I should prove the answer wrong. . . . When
> I conversed with him I came to see that, though a great many persons, and
> most of all himself, thought he was wise, yet he was not wise. Then I tried
> to prove to him that he was not wise. By doing so I made him indignant. . . . So
> when I went away, I thought to myself: I am wiser than this man: neither of
> us knows anything that is really worth knowing, but he thinks that he has
> knowledge when he has not, while I, having no knowledge, do not think that
> I have.[13]

This paradox of Socratic "ignorance" serves as the basis for an understanding of philosophy as the love of wisdom: philosophy is not itself a body of wisdom but rather the striving or aspiring toward that end. In this conception, philosophy is a *way* of living one's life, an activity, a verb rather than a noun. Thus, prior to the attempt to define leadership, prior to *all* forms of human inquiry, must come the acknowledgment of an ultimately infinite interval separating the seeker from the wisdom sought. In Socrates' own words, in a summary of his encounter with the oracle:

> . . . I believe that the god is really wise, and that by this oracle he meant that human wisdom is worth little or nothing. I do not think he meant that Socrates was wise. He only made use of my name and took me as an example, as though he could say to me, "He among you is the wisest who, like Socrates, knows that his wisdom is really worth nothing at all."[14]

That this commitment to the *love of wisdom* is no mere posturing, no mere exercise of the intellect, is evidenced by Socrates' behavior as the trial progresses. With his life "on the line," Socrates continually reaffirms by his actions the mission of the philosopher of which he so eloquently speaks. Reflecting on the possibility that his accusers will exonerate him on condition that he renounce the life of the philosopher, Socrates exclaims:

> I say, if you offered to let me go on these terms, I should reply . . . "As long as I have breath and strength, I will not give up philosophy and exhorting you . . . saying, as I am accustomed, 'my good friend . . . are you not ashamed of caring so much for the making of money and for fame and prestige when you neither think nor care about wisdom and truth and the improvement of your soul?'"[15]

Indeed, Socrates' openness to a life of critique cannot be separated from the conclusion of the tale told in this and the accompanying "death dialogues." The reader must see Socrates in action in the final days of his life: Socrates faced with the opportunity to abandon the philosopher's life in order to obtain a verdict of innocence at his trial; Socrates given the choice to escape the death penalty by admitting guilt and posing banishment as his punishment; and, finally, Socrates granted the opportunity to escape his prison cell before the moment of the drinking of the hemlock. Socrates must embody (body forth) the infinite aspiration toward wisdom of which he speaks.

What Socrates advances in these words—and what he offers in particular to the student of the philosophy of leadership—is his embrace of what I shall term the *critical spirit* as the moral ground of all human endeavor. If, as Socrates claims later in the *Apology*, "an unexamined life is not worth living,"[16] then it is incumbent on the philosopher to subject him or herself to the practice of an endless humility: the practice of opening oneself to the limitedness of one's perspective and thus, in effect, to the finitude of one's being. It is his lived affirmation of the centrality of the "examined life" for the conduct of a moral existence which, I will contend throughout this paper, makes Socrates the prototype of the philosopher-as-leader.

LEADERSHIP
AS A MORAL ACTIVITY

If, as Socrates teaches, the willingness to examine the conduct of one's life in all of its aspects serves as the moral ground of all human endeavor, then leadership, *more than any other kind of human activity,* must demand of its practitioners a willingness to open themselves to critique. As that process by virtue of which human beings are moved to realize aims and fulfill purposes, leadership must be born—and perpetually sustained—in the movement to turn back upon itself and establish its own credentials. If, at a minimum, to lead is to assume the initiative in a relationship with others (followers) toward the pursuit of some goal,[17] then insofar as this initiative is something other than the brute exercise of power—insofar as leadership is the work of humans who are moral agents—it must root itself in that exercise of humility which is the mark of the philosopher. Indeed, I will argue below that the superior resource which leaders, by definition, bring to the leader-follower relationship is their very openness to the conduct of an examined life in the particular arena—family, small group, school, state, to name just a few—in which the relationship is realized: subtending *all* forms of leadership is that philosophic "ignorance" which makes possible, indeed, demands an initiative of the leader which is moral and thus human in the fullest sense of that word.

Two observations pertaining to the terms *moral* and *philosophic* in which my contention is offered must be made at this juncture. First, it should be noted that in identifying the "fully human" initiative of the leader with "moral" initiative, I am in no sense subscribing to any understanding of morality arbitrarily derived from a history of ideas. Rather, the link that I would establish between being human and being moral is grounded in the contemporary philosophic claim that to be authentically human is to see our conduct as problematic. As twentieth-century existentialist analysis and literature have so vigorously sought to call to our attention, *how we act is for us always an issue.* Unlike the plant that bends with the wind—unlike the representative of any alleged "human nature" with fixed attributes which are automatically manifested—the human qua human is one the shape of whose existence is always in question for itself.[18] Indeed, to refuse this status as a problematic being is, ontologically speaking, an impossibility, since this refusal must itself be adopted as a response to a perceived problematic and thus affirm the very self-questioning it would deny. In the very endeavor to refuse our freedom as moral agents—in the endeavor to liken ourselves to things, to entities which fall on a causal continuum—we betray ourselves as "choosing not to choose"! In attempting to cover over our moral nature, in refusing to participate in the endeavor to justify our conduct *before ourselves,* we fail to acknowledge our role as beings who *act* in the fullest sense of that word; in refusing to justify our conduct *before others,* we fail to acknowledge our roles as beings who *communicate* in the fullest sense of that word as well. I will return below to these two failures and their relationship to a philosophical understanding of the leader's vocation.

Second, it should be evident to the reader that in speaking of the leader's vocation as at root *philosophic,* I am using the term in a sense which extends beyond its ordinary usage in pointing to a given academic discipline. If the leader is to be identified with the philosopher, it is with the practitioner of that discipline which at its primordial moment has no specific content. Thus (professional) philosopher-leaders stand under the same obligation as their fellow leaders in all human arenas to turn back upon themselves in a perpetual movement to acquire what T. S. Eliot calls "the wisdom of humility."[19] Indeed, it might be argued that to the extent that the (professional) philosopher's "business" is to inquire into the nature of all that is, he or she must be unusually zealous in the attempt to guard against substituting the rhetoric of the sophist (literally, one who knows) for the dialogue of the philosopher (one who loves and aspires toward wisdom). Thus, for example, Socrates' reply to Critias, who has accused him of intellectual bullying in place of an earnest search for truth:

> How can you think that I have any other motive in refuting you but what I should have in examining into myself? This motive would be just a fear of my unconsciously fancying that I knew something of which I was ignorant.[20]

Socrates as the prototype of the philosopher-leader is at home not in the schools, but in the marketplace in which his unique commitment to the perpetual calling into question of his own presumption to know can be more fully realized. At the core of this ideal of leadership is that questioning of all resources which is the ultimate resource of the leader as moral agent.

LEADERSHIP AND POWER

In pointing to the critical spirit as the ground of all leadership, my intent has been to argue that without that willingness to examine one's life, alleged leaders in any and all areas of human endeavor must, of necessity, become identified with their purposes, purposes which inevitably congeal into fixed doctrines or dogma. In short, potential leaders *without this ground* find themselves in the service of fixed ideas or causes, and thus agents of the use of power in their behalf. *No longer nourished by a wellspring of critical process at its center, leadership "dries up" and becomes, finally, the mere wielding of power on behalf of static ideals.* Human discourse becomes, at best, the attempt on the part of the mightier of body and/or mind to impress their views on the weaker by means of exhortation, harangue, sermon. At worst, such an imposition of ideas is accomplished by means of that threat of the exercise of brute force which is the work of the tyrant.

Once again the image of Socrates serves to exemplify the work of the leader as opposed to that of the mere wielder of power. Perhaps nowhere in the Platonic corpus is the distinction between power and critical process more fully celebrated than in the dialogue—named after a famed sophist or rhetorician of the period—*Gorgias.* Centered around a discussion of the difference between the vocation of the rhetorician and that of the philosopher, the dialogue derives its force by virtue of its essentially self-illustrative nature: Socrates and his three interlocutors are the practitioners of the vocations which, respectively, they defend. By the time Socrates encounters Callicles, the third representative of the rhetorician's art, the crucial distinction between rhetoric and philosophy—between the exercise of naked power and that of the spirit of critique—has become clear. In an extended monologue Callicles sings the praises of the rhetorician's art of persuasion through use of verbal might: "This," he proclaims, "is . . . how justice is determined: the stronger shall rule and have the advantage over his inferior."[21] Philosophy, on the other hand, avails its practitioners nothing at all in the struggle for dominance over others:

> Of course, Socrates, philosophy does have a certain charm if one engages with it in one's youth and in moderation; but if one dallies over long, it's the ruin of a fellow. . . . A boy who doesn't play with philosophy I regard as illiberal. . . . Whereas when I see an older man still at his philosophy and showing no signs of giving it up, that one seems to me, Socrates, to be asking for some hard knocks. . . . For as the situation is now, if anyone were to arrest you . . . declaring that you'd broken the law though you hadn't done a thing, you know perfectly well that you wouldn't be able to help yourself.[22]

Philosophy, Callicles asserts, is ineffective in that game of power which constitutes the essense of human existence in general and leadership activity in particular.

Socrates' immediate reply to Callicles' speech calls attention to the crucial nature of the conversation to follow. Indeed, he is overjoyed to have encountered Callicles, that ultimate "touchstone" who, whenever he agrees with him about any matter whatsoever, gives Socrates the assurance that "it must be the whole truth."[23] The dialogue that follows starkly contrasts not only two opinions rooted in two seemingly diametrically opposed Weltanschauungen but also two ways of being-in-the-world, two fundamental stances of the human being qua human. What Plato teaches is that insofar as Callicles attempts to enter into dialogue with Socrates, and thus insofar as he implicitly appeals to a standard of rationality which lies beyond his personal resources, he is tacitly abandoning his claim to the primacy of might in the conduct of leadership. Thus it is the case that Callicles' alleged position or world view is no view, no philosophy at all. To engage in discourse—as opposed to the brute exercise of rhetorical persuasion—is already to have acknowledged the primacy of the philosopher's critical thrust, his or her search for wisdom. In order for Callicles to win the day, in other words, he must resort to the exercise of verbal or physical blows: the rhetorician, indeed any practitioner of power, is barred by definition from dialogue, from presenting his or her case before the forum of reason. Power wielders can thrive only in the superior presentation of arms against arms; philosophers, on the other hand, can lead, can "lead out" another, only by refusing the presentation of arms, only by disarming themselves and their interlocutors in a work of peace.

No wonder, then, that those of Socrates' interlocutors who refuse philosophy as a way of life are depicted as either hurling abuse at the philosopher[24] or as fleeing from that setting in which their participation in dialogue is required.[25] Callicles, representative of the rhetorician as wielder of verbal power, cannot peacefully coexist with his interlocutor in a universe which is common to both:

> Tell me, Socrates, are we to take you seriously at this point or are you only jesting? For if you're serious and what you say is really true, won't human life have to be turned completely upside down? Everything we do, it seems, is the exact opposite of what we ought to do.[26]

And Callicles is certainly correct: the implications of Socrates' embodiment of the critical spirit are so radical, so "root," as to be dizzying! Nor is this revolution in human affairs the simple reversal of truth and falsehood that Callicles proclaims: it is not the case that all opinions or acts must be "turned completely upside down," but rather that all so-called truths of human knowledge and conduct must take on an ultimately provisional cast. Truth is now seen to reside not in a given doctrine or set of behaviors but rather in the give-and-take of critical process in which ever new perspectives on the issue in question are progressively disclosed. For the fixed absolutes of the truth and falsehood of philosophical views is to be substituted the *living* absolute of the exercise of a critical spirit animating human conduct in general and the work of the leader—initiator of the conduct of others—most particularly.

Nor is the above to be construed as a mere quibble among those inclined to metaphysical or epistemological speculation. If leadership is to be other than mere power wielding, it must be rooted in what I, following the teaching of the *Gorgias*—indeed, the teaching of the entire Socratic tradition—have termed throughout this chapter a *moral* initiative. For Socrates morality is not merely a derivative of metaphysics, that branch of philosophy which deals with such concepts as good and evil. Contrary to the main body of Western thought extending from Aristotle in the fourth century B.C. to Hegel in the nineteenth century A.D.—a body of thought which with few exceptions has viewed metaphysics as its central concern— Socratic tradition is firmly rooted in morality as "first philosophy." Socrates' interlocutors in the dialogues go away empty-handed not because of any intellectual deficiency on their parts. They fail in their discourse with Socrates for lack of a concern with the "care of their soul," which, I have argued, is precisely that which distinguishes true leaders from mere practitioners of power. The Socratic leader teaches no doctrine, no fixed body of knowledge: what he or she teaches is the desire to be taught.

LEADERSHIP AS DIALOGUE

The Socratic image—prototype of the ideal leader—is an image which Plato frequently identifies with the "gadfly." Socrates is morally justified in "prodding" others to act, however, only insofar as he has subjected his own actions to critical scrutiny. The work of the gadfly-leader is to be clearly distinguished from that, for example, of the teacher-leader who knows an "answer" in advance, but who, for the sake of promoting some ideal of learning, wishes to elicit that answer from the student-follower himself or herself. ". . . Critias," Socrates exclaims on this subject in the dialogue entitled *Charmides*, "but you come to me as though I professed to know about the questions which I ask, and as though I could, if only I would, agree with you. Whereas the fact is that I am inquiring with you . . . just because I do not know. . . ."[27] Nor does Socrates play the role of a devil's advocate. Although interlocutors are contested on each and every point advanced, and although irony is present throughout the dialogues, all discourse is entered into by Socrates with a seriousness of purpose which must be distinguished from the more superficial notion of search implied in devil's advocacy. In the words of the contemporary French philosopher Maurice Merleau-Ponty:

> The irony of Socrates is not to say less in order to win an advantage in showing great mental power, or in suggesting some esoteric knowledge. "Whenever I convince anyone of his ignorance," the *Apology* says with melancholy, "my listeners imagine that I know everything that he does not know." Socrates does not know any more than they know. He knows, only that there is no absolute knowledge and that it is by this absence that we are open to the truth.[28]

What is at stake here is nothing short of the "healing" of that fatal illness of the presumption-to-know which leads at best to complacency and the interruption of meaningful discourse, and at worst to the employment of power in the service of unquestioned ideas, of dogma.

With this image of the gadfly-leader in mind, it now becomes evident that the use of the dialogue form in the Socratic dialogues of Plato is no accident, no gratuitous choice of format. Just as the declamation, the harangue, the propaganda piece, is the work of the wielder of power, the adherent of a static truth, so must dialogue serve as the medium for the philosopher-leader whose image we are exploring in this chapter. Given over to the realization at one and the same time of the finite nature of his or her perspective and the infinite nature of the quest for truth, the leader in the Socratic sense must of necessity embark on that give-and-take of critique which is the process of dialogue itself: the leader's medium is, indeed, the message. Nor is this to argue that any concrete expression of dialogical form guarantees the exercise of the critical spirit which has here been advanced as the essence of all leadership. In the words of Martin Buber, ". . . there is monologue disguised as dialogue, in which two or more men meeting in space speak each with himself in strangely tortuous or circuitous ways. . . ."[29] Rather than look to any external format as sufficient evidence for the presence of dialogical thrust in human interaction, we must look to an underlying commitment to critical process for proof of the existence of dialogical activity in the full range of settings in which we speak of leaders and their followers.

In dialogical interactions, moreover, what distinguishes leaders from followers is the possession by the former of a degree of critical perspective lacking in the latter. The teacher-leader, for example, can educate (literally, *e-ducere*, lead out) only insofar as he or she knows better than the apprentice-follower the infinite nature of the task of imparting truth. ("The teacher," exclaims Martin Heidegger, "is capable of being more teachable than the apprentices.")[30] Followers, however, are followers only insofar as this ability to perceive the ever-widening series of perspectives in which the issue at hand must be situated is, *at a given juncture*, less developed than that of the leader. Followers are not locked into their followership. The very essence of dialogue consists in that mutual offering of perspectives which allows for—indeed, promotes—the movement of followers into leadership roles both in relation to others less aware than they of the need to acknowledge their (Socratic) ignorance and, also, in relation to those (former) leaders whose horizons of meaning may now be more limited than those of their (former) followers! In this sense leadership is a dialogical movement in which both participants engage in that process of critique—the love of wisdom—in which their very identities as the leader and the led are continually in question.

Leadership understood as a dialogical activity manifests itself in a wide variety of human settings. The child-follower in the parent-child relationship, for example, is one who at this stage in his or her life lacks knowledge of the complexities surrounding a given issue that is possessed by the parent-leader. In the endeavor to articulate a truly philosophic notion of leadership, however, it must be recalled that the mere acquisition of knowledge on the part of the parent-leader is in and of itself no guarantee that it will be used on behalf of genuine leadership activity. To be a leader in the situation described above, the parent must preserve an openness not only to possible inadequacies with regard to quantities of information but, more importantly, to the possibilities of prejudgment or presupposition which lie at the root of *all* inadequacy of knowing. Such an awareness of this all-too-human presumption to know is the prerequisite for that dialogical interchange with the child-follower which is the setting for true leadership activity.

The presence of dialogue, moreover, implies no given *style* of interaction. The "mechanics" of the process may be different in each and every leadership situation. At one juncture a tenor which is inspirational may prevail; at another, one which is closer to what is termed *managerial*. In one instance leadership may be expressed in a mode which more closely resembles the activist's "call to action"; in another, an (allegedly) passive "leadership by example" may be operative. Underlying all expressions of leadership, however, must be that willingness on the part of leaders to subject themselves to critique which prohibits coercion or force in any or all of its many guises.

POLITICAL LEADERSHIP

Leadership in the political sphere is to be understood in the same manner as leadership in the school or home. Indeed, the implications of our conception of leadership for an understanding of the essence of participatory democracy are nothing short of profound. Although the concrete external forms in which such democracies manifest themselves may vary, the core of democratic process is embodied in our notion of leadership as a dialogical activity. If it is the case that leaders qua leaders open themselves to dialogical interchange with their followers, then all questions surrounding the basis for the consent of the governed to those who govern, all queries concerning the ratification of the decisions of leaders by the led, are rendered superfluous. The justification for consent, in other words, is to be looked for neither in the needs or abilities of leaders and/or their followers nor in the demands of historical circumstance, but rather in the nature of leadership itself. Moral leadership as a dialogical activity is itself the realization of the essence of participatory democracy.

The statesperson-leader, in our depiction of Socratic leadership, is thus one who steadfastly acknowledges his or her ignorance of a static truth in the affairs of the polis, one who refuses to be identified with any credo, any unquestioned set of beliefs which might acquire the status of an absolute. Nor is this to advocate or even suggest a lack of coherent policy in the conduct of the affairs of state. The policymaker-leader is one who, paradoxically, takes a stand and, at one and the same moment, is prepared to call that very stand into question! The provisional nature of such a stand in no sense serves to remove it from a ground, a rootedness in human resolve. On the contrary, the moral status of such resolve, and thus its fully human ground, is assured—indeed, made possible—by the critical spirit in which it originates and in which it is perpetually maintained. As that living "stand" which is both formulated and continually offered in dialogue with others, the leader's policy is *ultimately provisional,* but in no ordinary sense *merely tentative.* Rather, as that living truth which has been reached between interlocutors in the process of dialogue, it represents the sole sense of "truth" which can pertain to human beings qua human and thus falls outside any "tentative-fixed" continuum on which we might be tempted to place it.

Leadership in the Socratic sense, then, in no way is to be equated with a hindering or postponement of political action. Not only does the exercise of political leadership in dialogue not hinder or inhibit effective action but a sense of "empowering" here manifests itself, an empowering which, in sharp contrast to the "power" employed in verbal or physical coercion, accounts for the deep gratitude we extend to the true leaders of our past and the yearning we express for the birth of those who will so lead us in the future. It is the very presence of what I have called the critical spirit in the work of the leader which opens up the necessary "interval" within which choice can be exercised and activity undertaken which is creative in nature. Indeed, for participants in dialogue to be challenged and perhaps disabused of assumptions concerning the nature of a given human context is already for these individuals to move toward an understanding of truth-as-a-process in which they come to see their responsibility for the shaping of human affairs and thus the possibility for genuinely new and effective political action. As long as one is in the service of fixed notions and static ideals, creative expression is, by definition, rendered impossible. The leader-follower relation which I am endeavoring to articulate here is one which *empowers* the follower—indeed, *both* members of the relationship—to that creative activity in which the horizons of meaning surrounding the issues at hand are perpetually stretched.

This generative or empowering act of leadership, moreover, is one not lightly chosen. In eschewing all certainties of knowledge, all fixed truths, political leaders in the Socratic sense open themselves up to what Jean-Paul Sartre and has fellow existentialists in twentieth-century continental philosophy have termed the *anguish* accompanying authentic choice. Anguish, in the Sartrean sense, is to be distinguished from *fear*, with which it is often confused. Anguish is always experienced *before myself*; fear is fear of beings in the world. More precisely, I am fearful of *things* and their possible harmful effects on me; I am anguished, on the other hand, at the realization that *no thing* can determine for me which of my possible futures I will choose, which meaning I will attribute to the me-who-is-about-to-be. Such anguish, however, poses no barrier to decisive political action. "All leaders know that anguish," Sartre exclaims. "It does not prevent their acting, on the contrary it is the very condition of their action, for the action presupposes that there is a plurality of possibilities. . . ."[31] Without situating oneself in that interval opened up by the acknowledgment of the primacy of critical process, the so-called political leader will act in the name of an ideal itself unexamined and thus fail to act—in the full sense of the word— at all!

THE LEADER AS MIDWIFE

Where, then, have we come in our endeavor to articulate a genuinely philosophic view of leadership? In looking to Socrates as prototype of the ideal leader, we have been guided less by a consideration of the crucial role which Plato's philosophy has played in the history of ideas in the West, and more by a consideration of the Socratic *image* as fundamental in the articulation of the moral ground of human activity. As initiators of change in the human arena—and thus as primary movers of human learning—leaders, more than any other figures in the human landscape, must fulfill their roles by dint of their embrace of the critical spirit embodied by Socrates. The absolute primacy of this image for an articulation of the nature of leadership, moreover, is a primacy which resists the corroding forces of a judgment which would locate it in a history of philosophical notions and thereby challenge its very claim to the status of an absolute. Because it exhausts itself in its will to submit itself to judgment, the Socratic teaching— at root—has no content which would limit it to the expression of one idea among many in the progression of Western thought. As a *living* absolute, the Socratic "message" is *nothing but* the continual movement of a "freeing of itself from a presumption to know."

The acknowledgment of this absolute which, I have argued, must subtend all forms of leadership activity yields no immediate fruit in the endeavor to resolve the major issues which beset the student of leadership. The substantial issues of historical causation, of the relative weight of the "great person" as opposed to that of historical circumstance, for example, admit of no easy resolution as a result of the deliberations in this chapter. Nor is any immediate light shed either on the question of what specific properties a so-called great person must possess or on the question of what specific characteristics a given sociopolitical context must manifest for it to play a role in the causal process issuing in leadership activity. To say that the leader must be the bearer of a so-called critical spirit is, in one sense, to leave everything "as it is." And yet, paradoxically, a characterization of the ground of leadership as the exercise of Socratic humility leaves nothing untouched. No given set of characteristics accruing to a leader nor any determinate list of circumstances out of which a leader-follower relationship is allegedly born can, in themselves, give rise to the phenomenon of leadership without the presence of that willingness to aspire to wisdom, that openness to truth-as-a-process, which is the Socratic teaching itself. Thus, as a result of these reflections none of those traditional characterizations of the leader as, let us say, intelligent, knowledgeable, or aggressive comes to be seen to play any less—or more—of a role in the determination of authentic leadership than had previously been thought to be the case. The acknowledgment of the Socratic teaching, however, points to that moral ground in which all of these alleged traits of a leader must be situated in order for them to be considered as leadership traits in a fully human sense. The same may be said for responses to those sociopolitical circumstances, such as poverty or civil strife, which allegedly call forth leadership activity. Without a "home" in the infinite endeavor to question one's own presumption to know, any response to these "givens" fails to root itself in a conduct of leadership which is truly moral.

Perhaps the most powerful metaphor for the Socratic image of which we have been speaking is to be found in the Platonic dialogue *Theaetetus*. Here Socrates refers to himself not "merely" as the gadfly who awakens a "sluggish" people from their slumber but also as the "midwife" who knows that such an awakening is precisely the birth of all learning:

> I am so far like the midwife that I cannot myself give birth to wisdom; and the common reproach is true, that though I question others, I can myself bring nothing to light because there is no wisdom in me. The reason is this: heaven constrains me to serve as a midwife, but has debarred me from giving birth.[32]

This creating or empowering aspect of Socratic leadership of which we have spoken receives its fullest expression in the development of this metaphor:

> . . . those who seek my company have the same experience as a woman with child; they suffer the pains of labor and, by night and day, are full of distress far greater than a woman's; and my art has power to bring on these pains or to allay them.[33]

The midwife-leader, then, is the epitome of the leader as one who, having acknowledged his or her own need to examine the course of a life, enables the other—in a dialogical setting—to move toward a similar openness to truth-as-a-process. Kierkegaard is certainly addressing Socrates-as-leader when he exclaims, some twenty-three hundred years later, "[Socrates] entered into the role of midwife and sustained it throughout; not because his thought 'had no positive content,' but because he perceived that this relation is the highest that one human being can sustain to another."³⁴ If we are to acknowledge the import of Kierkegaard's encomium—as well as the Nietzschean injunction to "overcome" our present selves—it is the Socratic image of leadership which may well serve as our guide.

NOTES

1. Plato, *Republic*, trans. Benjamin Jowett, in Erwin Edman, ed., *The Works of Plato* (New York: Random House, 1956), p. 431. Books V and VI of this work contain the fullest expression of the concept of the philosopher-king.
2. Ibid., p. 447.
3. Niccolò Machiavelli, *The Prince*, trans. Luigi Ricci, *The Prince and The Discourses* (New York: Random House, 1950), p. 56. The primary works of Machiavelli to be consulted for an understanding of his views on leadership are *The Prince* and *The Discourses on the First Ten Books of Titus Livius*.
4. Machiavelli, *The Discourses*, trans. Christian Detmold, *The Prince* and *The Discourses*, p. 255.
5. Thomas Hobbes, *Leviathan* (Oxford, Basil Blackwell, 1946), p. 112. Parts I and II of this work contain the essence of Hobbes's philosophy of leadership.
6. Ibid.
7. Friedrich Nietzsche, *Thus Spake Zarathustra*, trans. R.J. Hollingdale (Baltimore: Penguin Books, 1969), pp. 41–44. For other articulations of Nietzsche's concept of the *Übermensch*, see for example, *The Anti-Christ* and *Ecce Homo*.
8. Ibid., p. 117.
9. Alfred North Whitehead, *Adventures of Ideas* (New York: New American Library, Mentor Books, 1964), p. 229.
10. Martin Heidegger, *What Is Called Thinking?* trans. Fred Wieck and J. Glenn Gray (New York: Harper & Row, Pub., 1972), p. 26.
11. The discussion continues among classical scholars as to the degree of faithfulness-to-life of the Platonic portrait of Socrates. *See* in this regard: A.E. Taylor, *Socrates* (Garden City, N.Y.: Doubleday, Anchor Book, 1953), and A.R. Lacey, "Our Knowledge of Socrates," in Gregory Vlastos, ed., *The Philosophy of Socrates* (Garden City, N.Y.: Doubleday, Anchor Book, 1971). The debate between scholars who argue for the accuracy of historical portrait and those who claim that Socrates is a literary invention of Plato and others fails to address directly the question of a fundamental Socratic teaching, which is my concern in this paper.
12. Quoted in Walter Kaufmann, *Nietzsche: Philosopher, Psychologist, Antichrist* (Princeton: Princeton University Press, 1968), p. 406.
13. Plato, *Apology*, trans. F.J. Church (Indianapolis: Bobbs-Merrill, 1956), p. 26.
14. Ibid., pp. 27–28.
15. Ibid., pp. 35–36.
16. Ibid., p. 45.

17. This preliminary formulation emerges from a reading of James MacGregor Burns, *Leadership* (New York: Harper & Row, Pub., 1978), especially chapter I.
18. See in this regard Martin Heidegger's definition of *human reality* as a being who "in its very Being, that Being is an issue for it." In *Being and Time*, trans. John Macquarrie and Edward Robinson (New York: Harper & Row, Pub., 1962), p. 32.
19. T.S. Eliot, *Four Quartets* (New York: Harcourt, Brace, & World, 1943), p. 27.
20. Plato, *Charmides*, trans. Benjamin Jowett, in Edith Hamilton and Huntington Cairns, eds., *The Collected Dialogues of Plato* (New York: Random House, Pantheon Books, 1961), p. 112.
21. Plato, *Gorgias*, trans W.C. Helmbold (Indianapolis: Bobbs-Merrill, 1952), p. 52.
22. Ibid., pp. 52–54.
23. Ibid., p. 55.
24. Plato's depiction of the character of Polus in *Gorgias* is a fine example of this.
25. *See*, for example, Plato's *Euthyphro*.
26. Plato, *Gorgias*, p. 49.
27. Plato, *Charmides*, p. 111.
28. Maurice Merleau-Ponty, *In Praise of Philosophy*, trans. John Wild and James Edie (Evanston: Northwestern University Press, 1963), p. 39.
29. Martin Buber, "Dialogue," trans. Ronald Gregor Smith, in *Between Man and Man* (New York: Macmillan, 1965), p. 19.
30. Heidegger, *What Is Called Thinking?* p. 15.
31. Jean-Paul Sartre, "Existentialism is a Humanism," trans. Philip Mairet, in Walter Kaufmann, ed., *Existentialism From Dostoevsky to Sartre* (New York: New American Library, Meridian Book, 1975), p. 552.
32. Plato, *Theaetetus*, in *Plato's Theory of Knowledge: The Theaetetus and the Sophist of Plato*, trans. Francis M. Cornford (New York: Bobbs, Merrill, 1957), p. 26.
33. Ibid., pp. 26–27.
34. Soren Kierkegaard, *Philosophical Fragments*, trans. David Swenson (Princeton: Princeton University Press, 1962), p. 12. Kierkegaard includes an explanatory footnote following the phrase "had no positive content," elaborating on this nineteenth century critique of Socratic philosophy.

INDEX

Abrahamsen, David, 16
Abzug, Bella, 149
Achievement, 41–42, 101
Acton, J. E. E., 2
Adams, Pres. John, 7
Adler, Alfred, 8, 11, 12, 16, 18
Administrative competence
(Mann), 123
Administrators (Lasswell), 75,
256
Adolescence, 200, 203–4, 207
Adult psychology. *See* ch. 10;
Parent-child relationships
Age groups, 45, 49–50
Age-related tasks. *See* ch. 10
Agitators (Lasswell), 75, 256
Agricultural societies, 50–51
Alpert, Jane, 142
Alpha leadership, 151
Amatea, Ellen, 201, 227–28
Ambition (Renshon), 248–49
Anthropology, x, xii. *See also* ch.
3
Apollinaire, Guillaume, 190
Archipenko, Alexander, 191,
192
Arendt, Hannah, 38 *n*.18, 175
Argyris, Chris, 218
Aristotle, 149, 273
Arp, Hans, 189, 190, 196 *n*.60
Artistic leaders. *See* ch. 9
Art patrons, 181
Asch, Solomon, 220
Ascriptive criteria, 41–42, 47*t*,
49
Ataturk (Mustafa Kemal
Ataturk), 5
Attribution theory, 101–2,
132–33, 169–73
Australian aborigines, 47
Authoritarian leadership, 64,
67*t*, 55–58, 104; followers,
101; styles, 94, 96, 97, 98,
105, 106
Authoritarian societies, 41,
56–57, 77–78, 107
Authority (*see also* Power): in
family relationships, 26–30,
37 *n*.10, 206; followers' need
for, 81, 82; Freud's theories,
31–36; and pluralism, 33–36;
of political leaders, 71; and
power wielding, 43; in the
psychoanalytic process, 25;
and the socialization process,

23–24, 30–31; Simmel's
theories, 158–60, 167; U.S.
attitudes toward, 65–66, 85;
Weber's types, 24, 160–63
Autocratic leaders. *See*
Authoritarian leaders
Autonomy, 204, 212
Avant-garde leaders. *See* ch. 9
Ayman, Roya, 102–3, 104–5,
106
Aztec civilization, 55

Baetz, Mary, 118
Bailyn, Bernard, 6, 7
Balint, Michael, 9
Ball, Hugo, 194
Banton, Michael, 39–40
Barber, James David, 18;
typology, 76–77; *Presidential
Character*, 8, 16, 17, 76–77
Barrett, Gerald, 104
Barzun, Jacques, 14
Bass, Bernard M., vii, 99, 104,
132–33
Bauhaus, 192
Behavioral theories, 94–95, 99,
114, 115 *fig.*
Benedict, Ruth, 248
Berg, Alban, 189
Berger, Peter, 157, 168
Bergler, Edmund, 37 *n*.11, 38
n.17
Berry, John W., 103–4
Beta leadership, 151
Big Men (New Guinea), 50–51
Bismarck, Otto von, 4
Blair, Diane Kincaid, 149
Blaue Reiter group (Munich),
183, 186, 187, 188, 190–92;
Almanac, 187, 189, 194
Bohemianism, 181, 183
Boorse, Christopher, 260 *n*.40
Borderline personality, 9, 240,
259 *n*.29
Boundary management, 206–8
Braque, Georges, 180
Brod, Max, 185
Broder, David, 68–69
Brodie, Fawn, 7, 16–17
Brogan, Hugh, 14
Brücke group (Dresden), 183,
186
Buber, Martin, 274
Bullitt, William, 10–11
Bunch, Charlotte, 142, 151

Bureaucracy: in authoritarian
regimes, 56–57, 77–78; and
social evil, 175; Torbert's
theories, 216–17; Weber's
theories, 162. *See also*
Organizational leadership
Burke, Edmund, 72
Burliuk, David and Vladimir,
180
Burns, James McGregor, xv, 18,
140; on antifeminism,
144–45; on leadership types,
79–81; *Leadership*, ix, 15, 19,
64, 79, 133, 144–45; *Roosevelt*,
15–16
Burrows, Edwin G., 7
Byrd, Sen. Robert F., 258 *n*.13

Caddell, Pat, 233
Calder, Billy J., 102
Clader, Bobby, 172
Campendonk (Dutch artist),
190, 191
Candee, Daniel, 220–23
Canopy of legitimations
(Berger), 168–69, 171
Capitalism, 55, 56, 58–60;
power, concepts of, 43,
58–59, 60, 140, 152 *n*.9
Carrol, Susan J., xv
Carter, Pres. Jimmy, 17, 67, 68,
147; Camp David retreat, 258
n.13; 1980 campaign, 233;
political ideology, 232
Cassirer, Paul, 191, 193
Categorical leadership (Rosen),
49–50
Causal inferences, 170–73. *See
also* Attribution theory
Center for American Women
and Politics, 147
Central persons (Redl), 82–83
Cézanne, Paul, 182, 189
Chagall, Marc, 191
Character disorders, 259 *n*.29.
See also chs. 1, 2, 11
Charisma of office, 162
Charismatic bands, 161, 162
Charismatic leadership, vii, 3,
57, 83, 133; in contingency
theories, 132–34; in
managerial hierarchies, 122;
Weber's theories, 161–64
Chemers, Martin M., xv, 102–3,
104–5, 106, 113
Chesen, E. S., 16

281